Charming hotels and cou
in ITAL

We invite you to explore the heartland of Italy, a land of multiple faces and home to an incredibly rich legacy of historic and artistic treasures that have inspired artists and travellers since time immemorial. While each region has its own particular charm, ancestral recipes and regional produce, you can be certain of a warm, family welcome in each of our picturesque and historic establishments.

We have travelled the length and breadth of Italy, through towns and countryside, mountains and seaside resorts, to provide you with a selection of characteristic restaurants, inns, guesthouses, hotels and bed & breakfast establishments offering the best possible value for money. Finally we have also prepared a brief history and introduction to each region, as well as a collection of culinary specialities to help you make the most of each place you visit.

Every page of this guide is full of the colours and flavours of the enchanting and exciting Bel Paese.

While every effort is made to ensure that all information printed in this guide is correct and up-to-date, Michelin Travel Publications (a trading division of Michelin Tyre PLC) accepts no liability for any direct, indirect or consequential losses howsoever caused so far as such can be excluded by law.

Contents

Abruzzo – Molise 9

Basilicata 21

Calabria 33

Campania 47

Emilia Romagna 75

Friuli Venezia Giulia 109

Lazio 121

Liguria 145

Lombardia 161

Marche 195

Piemonte 223

Puglia	279
Sardegna	301
Sicilia	313
Toscana	341
Trentino Alto Adige	437
Umbria	481
Valle d'Aosta	523
Veneto	535

Activity breaks	570
Local produce breaks	576
Index of Hotels and B&Bs	580
Index of Country Guesthouses	590
Establishments with dining facilities	595

Regional maps

Symbols used in the guide

 Hotel or Bed & Breakfast

 Country Guesthouse

 Price for two people in low and high season

Establishments with a restaurant

 The little extra that makes the hotel or country guesthouse different

 Hotel on the regional map

Country guesthouse on the regional map

Breakfast included in the price of the room

Credit cards not accepted

Restaurant on the regional map

How to use this guide

This new edition of Michelin's Hotels and Guesthouses in Italy features a selection of 450 places to stay and over 50 restaurants throughout Italy. Our incognito inspectors selected establishments on the basis of price, location and the quality of facilities and service. Our familiar *We most liked* aims to highlight the little extra that we particularly liked and want to share with you, whether it be "The beautiful pool in the shade of olive trees", "Your hosts' friendly welcome" or simply a few words to set the scene.

▶ Finding your way round the guide ▶

The guide is divided into the 19 administrative regions of Italy, organised in alphabetical order, with the exception of the "Abruzzo & Molise" chapter, which brings these two regions together. The establishments are listed by place, again in alphabetical order, within each region. The name of each place is followed by the two letters which correspond to the regional capital, for example, RM for Rome. The number at the top of the establishment's description corresponds to its location on the map at the beginning of each chapter. At the beginning of each region, you will find:
- a general introduction to the region
- a tourist itinerary indicating the sites not to be missed
- a section devoted to regional gastronomy: typical recipes, regional wines and anecdotes
- a selection of three picturesque restaurants that serve regional specialities at reasonable prices.

▶ Maps ▶

A map at the beginning of the guide shows the different regions of Italy. In addition, at the beginning of each chapter is a regional map showing our selection of establishments with their number in a small square box (hotels are marked in blue and country guesthouses in green). A round box in red indicates a restaurant. The maps and directions in this guide use the metric system for reasons of practicality; as a reminder 1km = 0.6miles.

▶ Hotel ▶

Our selection of hotels has been chosen for their location, atmosphere and hospitality. Some offer dining facilities and half board accommodation.
We definitely recommend booking ahead; you should also call if you think you may arrive late in the evening.

▶ Country Guesthouses (Agriturismi) ▶

Country guesthouses were originally conceived as an opportunity to combine accommodation and the chance to taste the products made on the farm (among them olive oil, wine, honey, vegetables and meat). Often converted mills, country houses or farmsteads, they are also the private homes of the people who will welcome you and endeavour to make your stay as pleasant as possible. They are ideal for those looking for peace and quiet in the countryside. Because of their ever-increasing popularity it is important to book well in advance, particularly during the summer or for long weekends, and to reconfirm your booking if you expect to arrive late.

▶ Meals ▶

The 🍴 indicates whether the establishment has dining facilities.

▶ Rates ▶

Prices are per double room in high season. For example:

👥 €60-150: the price of a double room depending on the season and type of room.

We suggest you enquire about possible low season promotions.

Note that many establishments offer several rooms for under €100. However, certain establishments do also offer rooms or suites at higher rates. Please ensure, therefore, that you check the room rate at the time of reservation.

Breakfast

The ☕ symbol indicates that breakfast is included in the price of the room. Whenever this is not the case, we have indicated the price of breakfast per person.

Credit cards

Where credit cards are not accepted, the 🚫 symbol indicates this.

Reservations

A credit card number or deposit is often required to confirm the reservation of a room.

Telephoning

To call Italy, dial 00 + 39 + the telephone number, including the first 0.

▶ Directions and facilities ▶

For each establishment, we provide:
_ a list of the facilities available (swimming pool, tennis courts, fitness facilities, etc.) and whether dogs are welcome or not,
_ directions from the nearest town.

▶ Indexes ▶

At the end of the guide, all the establishments are listed, by region and place, in several indexes:

Activity breaks: establishments that offer at least one sporting activity (gym, riding, tennis, golf, etc.).
Local produce: establishments that offer tasting sessions and sell local produce.
Hotels.
Country Guesthouses.
Establishments with dining facilities.

▶ Exploring Italy with Michelin ▶

To find out more about the area of Italy you intend to visit, you might also want to delve into the Michelin Green Guide Italy for further historical and cultural information. Michelin map 735 Italia is a practical map on a scale of 1:1 000 000 which shows the whole Italian road network. Michelin maps 561-566 give detailed information on the area you wish to tour.

Internet users can access personalised route plans,
Michelin maps and town plans through the website at
www.ViaMichelin.com

▶ Your viewpoint ▶

We have endeavoured to make this guide practical and readable and trust that it will accompany you on family holidays and romantic weekends. Please do not hesitate to let us know should you find any mistake or omission in the information provided. We have included a questionnaire at the back of the guide: all your comments and suggestions for new addresses are not only most welcome but indispensable.

Abruzzo – Molise

Prior to being absorbed by the Kingdom of Naples in the 12C, Abruzzo and Molise were fought over by a succession of kings, emperors and dynasties. This wild and rugged region of empty plains, rocky massifs and forests was prized not for its riches, but as a strategic gateway to neighbouring areas.

Today, it has three national parks within its boundaries, making it one of Italy's most unspoilt regions and a haven for flora and fauna.

Beach lovers will be pleased to know that the coastline has in recent years greatly improved its facilities; the seaside resorts of Abruzzo and Molise are an increasingly popular family holiday destination, not least because of the excellent value for money which they represent.

The region's cities and towns are rich in artistic heritage, and make for a pleasant alternative to the packed streets of Italy's most famous tourist centres.

In bygone times, poets celebrated the local countryside and its fecundity; today that same natural abundance is evident from the ubiquitous lamb dishes, always appetising whatever the recipe and to be found in every restaurant.

7 establishments

Recommended sites and circuits Abruzzo & Molise

> The pleasure of being on the open road for miles on end in a magnificent setting, going through small villages, finding that every town is worth visiting, and discovering the legends and treasures hidden within the ancient palazzi and narrow streets that have survived the centuries.

The city of Aquila harbours many mysteries: churches built according to the constellations of stars and edifices concealing pagan, Masonic or esoteric symbols. Little wonder that Frederick II of Hohenstaufen, founder of the city, wanted to make it the "New Jerusalem" when one considers Aquila's points in common with the holy city. First, the two cities are located on top of a hill with a river running through. The Fontana delle 99 Cannelle is reminiscent of the Siloe pool mentioned in the Bible, and some researchers think that it was not only used as a public washing place, but that it may have been a temple dedicated to the initiation of Cistercian knights (of which the Templars were the armed branch). The **Basilica di Collemaggio** constitutes an additional phase of this mystic circuit: its façade is decorated with the Rose-Cross, symbol of the Templars, and within its walls lie the seals of King David and King Solomon. The position of the three rose windows is also remarkable. Each summer solstice, at sunset, its rays indicate a specific point on the floor, the Labyrinth...

In many other places in Abruzzo, history and religion cohabit. **Campli** is home to the Scala Santa staircase, a masterpiece of sacred architecture built in the late 18C and attributed the power of absolving the sins of anyone who climbed it on their knees. At the top of the stairs the altar is richly embellished with symbols and decorations, and exhibits two small pieces of wood from the cross of Christ.

Continuing southward, you will arrive in **Molise**, where the pace of life is dictated by nature. This is an ideal place to stroll in luxuriant woods and thickets, inhaling the heady aroma of oregano.

Termoli, one of the region's main towns, is dominated by an imposing castle dating from the time of Frederick II. Its old town is well worth the detour for its little white fishermen's houses and narrow streets leading to a large square from where one can admire the sea. From the port, it is also possible to set sail for the Tremiti Islands.

Bojano, meanwhile, will always be associated with its churches. A staircase in the cathedral crypt with seven steps, at the foot of which lies a spring, symbolises the way to the redemption of Baptism (the seven steps representing the deadly sins). Water also greets you at the entrance of the town, whose spring, known as the "Sorgente di Pietre Cadute" is a delightful oasis.

A recipe to try, wines and... a nugget of information

🍷 Abruzzo wines

_Montepulciano d'Abruzzo
_Trebbiano d'Abruzzo

🍷 Molise wines

_Molise Tintilia riserve D.O.C.
_Pentro di Isernia red D.O.C
_Biferno white D.O.C
_Molise Greco white

Ingredients

▸ 12 slices of farmhouse bread
▸ a few pork meat or pork liver saucages

Local specialities

Abruzzo - Cheese: *pecorino*, sheep's ricotta, *giuncata*, *caprino*, *caciotta* (sometimes spicy), *scamorze* (eaten raw, or cooked over embers or in the oven), *caciocavallo*. Meat and cooked cold meats: *Annoje* (spicy tripe sausages), spicy liver sausages, black pudding, *matte* sausages (made with rind and scraps of meat), *coppa*. Alcohols: *Centerba* (liqueur), *nocino*, *ratafia* (alcohol made by distilling black cherries). Santo Stefano di Sassanio black lentils, vetch, Paganica chick peas and beans, saffron.

Molise - Polenta (served as a main dish with meat sauces), lentils, broad beans, chick peas, beans, vetch, spelt, *pamparella* (pork belly dried with chilli peppers), *ventricina* and *soppressate* (cooked meats), liver sausages, *scripelle* (crêpes served with or without broth).

BRUSCHETTA ALLA SALSICCIA

Method

Cut the slices of bread in half lengthways and toast them. When they are golden, cover them with slices of sausage and serve immediately.

Food for thought

The rite of *panarda* is a Pantagruelian banquet, at times consisting of up to 50 courses. Historically a sort of compensation for the long periods of deprivation suffered by the inhabitants of the region, today the rite still exists but only as part of folkloric events. Needless to say, guests had to sample every single dish!

Our favourite places to eat

HOSTARIA L'ARCA
Viale Mazzini 109 – Alba Adriatica (TE) – Tel. 0861 714647
Closed Sat lunchtime and Tue.
A la carte menu €21-43
 The carefully selected ingredients: a mark of quality.
This restaurant's menu is like a gastronomic Noah's Ark. The owners are clearly eager to transcend regional and even national borders in order to select the finest products. L'Arca offers an extremely diverse choice of specialities, ranging from cold meats to cheese, fresh pasta to meat (all of the meat is certified with the exception of the fresh fish). You can find most of the products, almost all of which are certified organic, in the shop next door.

TAVERNA DE LI CALDORA
Piazza Umberto I 13 – Pacentro (AQ) – Tel. 0864 41139
Closed Sun eve and Tue.
A la carte menu €23-41
 The atmosphere of pure pleasure, from the beautiful artwork to the tasty dishes.
Enjoy the sights as you wander through the little streets of this medieval market town, on your way to one of the best restaurants in the Abruzzi region, located in an imposing 16C palace in the heart of the village. To reach the taverna, head down the stairs leading to what was once the cellar. Inside, a whole range of local specialities awaits you, starting with the antipasti: ricotta made with sheep's milk, green bean soup, mushrooms, lamb, omelette, marinated mushrooms and grilled vegetables.

TAVERNA 58
Corso Manthoné 46 – Pescara (PE) – Tel. 085 690724
Closed 24 Dec-1 Jan, Aug and public hols, Sat lunchtime and Sun.

A la carte menu €30-39
 The place to go when you long for the simple things of bygone days.
Until quite recently Pescara was still a village, known as Castellamare. Despite its rapid and somewhat chaotic growth, the town has managed to retain the feel of a small village. The taverna is located in the Corso Manthone quarter, between the D'Annunzio and Flaiano residences. One of the two rooms is an 18C extension. Access to the cellar, covered by Roman-era flagstones, is via a small stairwell, where the decor transports you back in time as you walk down. The menu proposes an original overview of the specialities of Abruzzi: simple provincial dishes, cold meats, pasta, meat, cod and freshwater fish.

ABRUZZO & MOLISE

AGNONE (IS)

SELVAGGI

Sig.ra Lucarino
Strada provinciale Montesangrina km 1
86061 Agnone (IS)
Tel. 086 57 77 85 - Fax 086 57 71 77
staffoli@staffoli.it - www.staffoli.it

 52-93€

Closed 10-23 Nov • 15 double rm • Half board €47 • Parking • Riding, guided tours

 Menu €17/27

 The harmonious setting in the surrounding landscape.

A country track leads to this fortified farmhouse dating from 1720, tucked away among woods and fields which provide the ideal backdrop for riding, walking and fishing. The genuine and sincere hospitality here manifests itself in the friendly service and the rustic simplicity of the interior; in the vaulted dining room guests can savour locally-produced cheese, and cured and cooked meats. The perfect spot for a holiday of complete relaxation, or for those fond of walking and riding.

Access: 15km from the centre towards Carovilli

ABRUZZO & MOLISE

ALBA ADRIATICA (TE)

LA PERGOLA

Sig.ra Ischi
Via Emilia, 19
64011 Alba Adriatica (TE)
Tel. 08 61 71 10 68 – Fax 08 61 71 10 68
info@hotelpergola.it – www.hotelpergola.it

60-90€

Open 15 Mar to 31 Oct • 1 single rm, 9 double rm • No dogs; parking

 The cheery atmosphere created by the management.

A little slice of Switzerland on the Adriatic Riviera, this seemingly paradoxical establishment is an utter delight. The management are of Swiss descent, and an alpine theme is very much to the fore, most notably in the decorative scheme employed in the bedrooms. Breakfast hours are flexible, and there is a pleasant seafront restaurant.

Access: Centrally located, two minutes from the beach

ABRUZZO & MOLISE

CELANO (AQ)

LE GOLE

Sig. Paris
Via Sardellino
67041 Aielli (AQ)
Tel. 08 63 71 10 09 - Fax 08 63 71 11 01
info@hotellegole.it - www.hotellegole.it

90-110€

Open all year • 40 double rm • Half board €107-127 • Parking, garden, dogs not admitted

 **Menu €16/33**

 The imposing beams supporting the roof.

Carefully used, the simplest building materials such as brick, stone and wood, can create a work of art. After several years' work, the result here is striking, giving the feel of a Tuscan fortified farmhouse. Inside, a courtyard with well gives onto the rooms, all of which are decorated in period style with plenty of dark wood and exposed beams in evidence. Despite the ambience of days gone by, levels of comfort and technology are up to the minute.

Access: 1.5km from the centre towards the motorway tollbooth

ABRUZZO & MOLISE

LORETO APRUTINO (PE)

4

LE MAGNOLIE

Sig. Tortella
Contrada Fiorano, 83
65014 Loreto Aprutino (PE)
Tel. 08 58 28 98 04 - Fax 08 58 28 95 34
lemagnolie@tin.it - www.lemagnolie.com

70-120€

Closed 1-28 Feb • 2 single rm, 9 suites • Half board €60 • Parking, garden, swimming pool, small dogs welcome • Bicycles available, guided tours, sale of oil

 Set Menu €25 for residents only

 The hearty agricultural feel of the place.

A truly rural location. This 17C farmhouse, which has been completely restored, is set in 26 hectares of olive groves, orchards and market gardens. There is a minimum two night stay, but this is no imposition; the rooms have antique furniture coupled with comfortable modern beds, and guests who enjoy outdoor cooking can use the barbecue facilities near the pool. Those in quest of the rustic idyll can gather fruit and vegetables from the surrounding farmland, and eggs from the hens which roam freely in the courtyard.

Access: 5km from the centre in the countryside

ABRUZZO & MOLISE

MOSCIANO SANT'ANGELO (TE)

5

CASALE DELLE ARTI

Sig. Di Domenico
Strada Selva Alta
64023 Mosciano Sant'Angelo (TE)
Tel. 08 58 07 20 43 – Fax 08 58 07 27 76
casalearti@tin.it – www.casaledellearti.it

65-70€

Open all year • 2 single rm, 12 double rm, 2 suites • Half board € 53-65 • Parking

 Set Menu €30 and 40 for residents only

 The contrast between the verdant countryside and the hues of the house.

As the name implies, the emphasis here is on art; in the garden is a fountain incorporating an unusual modern sculpture, while inside the well restored building there is a fine collection of contemporary works, some by better known artists than others. The rooms have a simple elegance, with period furnishings and wrought iron beds. The restaurant is a hive of activity; popular with the locals, it also hosts functions and receptions. Located in a panoramic spot and well placed for both the sea and the Gran Sasso mountain range.

Access: 4km from the centre, near the motorway tollbooth in Selva Alta

ABRUZZO & MOLISE

PESCASSEROLI (AQ)

6

VILLA LA RUOTA

Sig.ra Gentile
Colle Massarello, 3
67032 Pescasseroli (AQ)
Tel. 08 15 44 61 09 – Fax 08 15 64 49 11
bnb@villalaruota.it – www.villalaruota.it

👤👤 **90-100€**

Open all year • 7 double rm • Parking, garden, no dogs

 The bathrooms with fine ceramics and co-ordinated accessories.

Situated out of town, this delightful B&B retains the charm of a private house. In the public areas the ambience of hospitality is elegantly conveyed by features such as the open fireplace and small bar area. Although not large, the rooms are enhanced by many personal touches. At any time of the year, this is an ideal spot from which to explore the natural beauties of the Abruzzo region, much of which is protected parkland.

Access: In the residential neighbourhood

ABRUZZO & MOLISE

TERMOLI (CB)

7

RESIDENZA SVEVA

Sig. Vincitorio
Piazza Duomo, 11
86039 Termoli (CB)
Tel. 08 75 70 68 03 - Fax 08 75 70 68 03
info@residenzasveva.com
www.residenzasveva.com

👤👤 **79-119€** ☕

Open all year • 12 double rm

 Discovering the history of this picturesque medieval town.

As you stroll around the maze of picturesque streets and lanes, it is difficult not to let your imagination run away with you. In the heart of the town's historic district, this establishment is the incarnation of the albergo diffuso, a concept that seeks to respect the traditions of catering and heritage. The spacious and comfortable rooms, all different, are located in several buildings. Lovely ceramic tiles enhance the sophisticated and unusual decoration. From June to September, you can also enjoy the Cala Sveva spa establishment.

Access: In the historic town

Basilicata

Bordering both the Tyrrhenian and Ionian seas, Basilicata manages to unite disparate shorelines, traditions and communities, but it is its hinterland rather than its coasts which defines the region's character. Matera, the second city after Potenza, is renowned for its rock dwellings, where for centuries its inhabitants have found shelter deep in the ground.

The local economy remains primarily agrarian, which means that Basilicata's landscape remains beautiful and unspoilt.

These days Basilicata is renowned for its proud and united people but is popular with tourists looking to get off the beaten track in unspoilt surroundings. Its countryside is virtually untarnished by industrialisation and is rich in natural beauty sought out by the film and advertising businesses.

Visitors heading home would be well advised to return with the odd bottle of Aglianico del Vulture in addition to their holiday snaps.

7 establishments

Recommended sites and circuits
Basilicata

> A magical land of clay and light, forests and mountains, contrasts and legends, where magical pagan rites, closely linked to Christianity, have generated an intense and richly symbolic mysticism.

As soon as you see it, the town of **Matera** will have you under its spell: its Sassi, troglodyte habitations classified by UNESCO as a world heritage site, are a truly historic miracle of urban development. Constructed in the shelter of two limestone valleys, these maze-like concentrations of narrow streets, squares, caves and churches in the rock never fail to amaze visitors. Often the roofs of the constructions serve as the floors of those above. The lower, whiter part, called the *Sasso Barisano*, with its constructions that cling to the hillside, progressively gives way to the *Sasso Caveoso*, habitations that are actually hollowed out from the rock. Evacuated in the 1950s due to safety concerns, the Sassi have since been restored and today look better than ever. Don't miss the Parco delle Chiese Rupestri, a park which is as fascinating for its incredible history as for its natural beauty. This rocky land, almost devoid of vegetation and punctuated with crevices, which seems to lead directly down to the Underworld, is actually home to 150 small churches and numerous archaeological sites which go back to the Paleolithic period (like the **Grotta dei Pipistrelli**) and to the Neolithic period.

Once closer to the coast, however, this hostile landscape progressively takes on a more Mediterranean feel, alternating craggy promontories and isolated rocky inlets. The coastline is made up of tiny beaches and limestone grottoes that used to serve as landmarks for Saracen pirates. The town of **Maratea**, nicknamed "the pearl of the Tyrrhenian Sea", is located in a maritime region that is rich in archaeological history and particularly beloved of divers. Some even maintain that the name of the town comes from the latin *Thea Maris*, which means "Goddess of the Sea". In the old town centre there are impressive historical and archaeological buildings as well as a large number of churches, which earned it the nickname "town of 44 churches".

Yet the region's artistic marvels, crystal-clear waters and enchanting landscape are not its only assets: the thermal springs of **Latronico** (Polino national park) and Rapolla (Mount Vulture) offer an unforgettably relaxing stay.

A recipe to try, wines and... a nugget of information

 Wines
_Aglianico del Vulture
_Asprino
_Malvasia bianca di Basilicata
_Lambrusco del Basento

Local specialities
Pane cotto (bread soup), *ciaudedda* (vegetable ragoût), *taralli salati* (salty biscuits made with herbs and spices). Cold meats: *soppressata, capocollo, pezzente* and local sausages. Cheeses: *burrino, caciocavallo, cacioricotta* and *ricotta forte*

PASTA AL FORNO

Ingredients
- 500g fresh lasagne-type pasta
- 800g peeled tomatoes
- 150g minced pork
- 150g minced veal
- 4 eggs
- 2 cloves garlic
- 1 tablespoon oregano
- 10cl extra virgin olive oil
- oil to fry
- grated pecorino cheese
- salt

Method
In a large bowl, mix together the minced meat, oregano, garlic, one egg and salt. Make between 60 and 70 little balls. Heat the oil in a frying pan and fry the meatballs. Blend the tomatoes, put them in a pan, add oil and salt and cook over a low heat for 20min. The sauce should be fairly liquid. Pour half of it into a frying pan, add the meatballs and simmer over a low heat, allowing the meatballs to absorb some of the sauce. Cook the pasta then dress it with the rest of the sauce (saving a glassful) and scatter over some of the pecorino. Boil the eggs for 8min, leave them to cool, then peel them and cut them into thin rounds. Spread a layer of pasta in the bottom of an oven dish, add the meatballs, and finally the slices of egg. Finish with another layer of pasta and cover with the rest of the sauce and the pecorino. Cook in the oven at 180°C for 40min, until the top looks crispy. Leave to cool for 30min before serving.

Food for thought
The sausage was invented in Basilicata; in certain regions, people continue to call it lucanica or luganega (from "Lucania", the old name for the region). This tasty regional product can be eaten fresh, dried or preserved in oil.

Our favourite places to eat

AL BECCO DELLA CIVETTA
Vico I Maglietta 7 – Castelmezzano (PZ) – Tel. 0971 986249
Closed Tue.

A la carte menu €21-33
 The spectacular winter snowfall and long walks in the market town.

Castelmezzano is a medieval market town with narrow little streets that you reach via a winding coastal road affording unparalleled panoramic views over the Lucanian Dolomites. The Santoro family will welcome you into their simple restaurant that offers a vast array of regional specialities, including tasty antipastis: *capocollo* (a spicy cold meat), *caciocavallo* (a traditional pouch-shaped cheese), marinated mushrooms and seasonal vegetables, as well as *cavatelli* (a regional pasta), lamb, and traditional Lucanian pastries.

NOVECENTO
Contrada Incoronata – Melfi (PZ) – Tel. 0972 237470
Closed 15-31 Jul, Sun eve and Mon.

A la carte menu €23-31
 The creativity and subtlety combined with the flavours of traditional dishes.

A stone's throw from the town of Melfi, this elegant restaurant is made up of two rooms, one of which has a panoramic veranda. The whole family will greet you with a warm welcome and delicious regional fare, served in spacious and comfortably furnished rooms. Generous portions of ham, cheese and vegetable antipasti and bruschetta are almost enough to fill you up. An excellent wine list complements the impressive dishes on offer.

LUNA ROSSA
Via Marconi 18 – Terranova del Pollino (PZ) – Tel. 0973 93254
Closed 1-7 Oct and Wed. Booking advisable.

A la carte menu €22-30
 The opportunity to sample the region's flavours and recipes dating from another era.

To get to this restaurant we recommend you leave your car outside the town centre and go on foot through the little streets that lead to a superb outdoor terrace (in summer) offering a panoramic view over the valley. The real attraction, though, is the food: the owner is passionate about it, collecting recipes of yesteryear and drawing inspiration from Roman-era recipe books and concoctions that were in fashion during the Renaissance period. That's not to say he neglects Lucanian tradition; try his pasta dishes with unusual sauces to get a good idea of the cuisine from the Basilicata region.

BARILE (PZ)

LA LOCANDA DEL PALAZZO
Fam. Botte
Piazza Caracciolo, 7
85022 Barile (PZ)
Tel. 09 72 77 10 51 – Fax 09 72 77 10 51
info@locandadelpalazzo.com – www.locandadelpalazzo.com

👤👤 98€

Closed 15-30 July • 2 single rm, 9 double rm • Breakfast €5 • Garden

Menu €43/53

The tasteful use of colour and materials, here elevated to an art form.

Once overlooked, the borderlands between Puglia and Basilicata are now very popular, and deservedly so on account of the colourful local landscape and people. Formerly used for wine making, this well presented establishment has an elegant lobby and spacious, luxuriously restored accommodation with splendid bathrooms. The restaurant offers sophisticated cuisine to satisfy even the most exacting of palates.

Access: In the heart of the village

BASILICATA

BERNALDA (MT)

RELAIS MASSERIA CARDILLO

Sig.ra Dei Rocco
Strada Statale 407 Basentana al Km. 98
75012 Bernalda (MT)
Tel. 08 35 74 89 92 – Fax 08 35 74 89 94
info@masseriacardillo.it
www.masseriacardillo.it

  120-156€

Open from 1 Apr to 31 Oct • 10 double rm • Half-board €78-96 • Garden, parking, tennis court, swimming pool, dogs not admitted • Sale of oil and wine

 Set Menu €25 and 30

 An immense farming estate two minutes from the main tourist sites.

In the heart of Metapontino, renowned for its rich agricultural traditions, archaeological treasures and landscape, this establishment stands on three adjacent hillsides. It makes a splendid base camp from which to explore the region. The masterfully renovated barns of the 18C farm are now home to a welcoming guesthouse that pays homage to the traditional mansions of Lucane: comfortable spacious rooms and a small elegant sitting room with a brick vaulted ceiling. Farm produce on sale includes honey, oil, jam and fruit.

Access: On the Bastentana, 3km from the village towards the coast

BASILICATA

CHIAROMONTE (PZ)

3

COSTA CASALE

Sig.ra Cucinotta
Contrada Vito
85032 Chiaromonte (PZ)
Tel. 09 73 64 23 46 – Fax 09 73 64 23 46

Open all year • 4 double rm, 1 suite • Half board €45 • Parking, garden, no dogs • Riding, organised trips, cured meats, cheese and jam for sale

 Menu €18/28

 The presence of hares and fallow deer in the vicinity of the farmhouse.

Previously the farmstead of the De Salvo family, this establishment nestles among the olive groves and orchards of the Lucania countryside. Little has changed over the years; the natural lushness of the place has been further enhanced by the establishment of the Pollino National Park, while the old farmstead has become an agriturismo (after careful restoration) and the De Salvo family, who continue to farm the surrounding land, extend a warm welcome to visitors to the area. The restaurant offers dishes cooked with home grown ingredients.

Access: A few hundred metres from the town

BASILICATA

MATERA (MT)

LOCANDA DI SAN MARTINO

C.E.D.A.T.S.Srl
Via Fiorentini 71
75100 Matera (MT)
Tel. 08 35 25 66 00 – Fax 08 35 25 64 72
info@locandadisanmartino.it
www.locandadisanmartino.it

👤👦 **86-129€** ☕

Open all year • 1 singe rm, 21 double rm and 7 suites • Dogs not admitted

 Sleeping in a troglodyte room – a unique experience!

Matera is famed for its houses and caves carved out of the rock. This delightful inn, not far from the church of San Martino, gives onto the road of the same name. The atmosphere and architecture of the establishment echo the town's authentic character. A few yards from the centre, the inn offers discreetly elegant rooms, most with their own private terrace, originally located in natural caves. Fitted with all the modern comforts you could wish for, they are linked to the inn's public area by passages carved out of the rock.

Access: In the historic centre

BASILICATA

MATERA (MT)

5

SASSI HOTEL
Sig. Cristallo
Via San Giovanni Vecchio 89
75100 Matera (MT)
Tel. 08 35 33 10 09 - Fax 08 35 33 37 33
hotelsassi@virgilio.it - www.hotelsassi.it

87-99€

Open all year • 5 single rm, 20 double rm, 1 suite

 The primeval experience of sleeping in a rock dwelling.

This hotel defies standard terms of definition; a curious labyrinth of a structure incorporating 18C buildings and rock dwellings laid out over six storeys, with accommodation accessed by an external staircase. The rooms carved from the rock face are without doubt the most appealing, albeit the simplest. In addition, there are fine views over the Unesco World Heritage site of the town of Matera and its cathedral.

Access: In the historic centre of Matera

BASILICATA

TERRANOVA DI POLLINO (PZ)

6

PICCHIO NERO

Sig.ra Genovese
Via Mulino, 1
85030 Terranova di Pollino (PZ)
Tel. 097 39 31 70 – Fax 097 39 31 70
picchionero@picchionero.com - www.picchionero.com

♂♀ 67€ ☕

Closed 1 Nov to 31 Dec • 25 double rm • Half board €57 • Parking, garden, no dogs

 Menu €21/30

  The splendid position in the Pollino National Park.

Few places in Italy have managed to remain as unspoilt as the Pollino National Park, established a little over ten years ago to protect the fauna, flora and landscape of this area. Occupying two buildings situated within the park boundaries, this hotel is the ideal base from which to discover the beauties of the surrounding mountain scenery. After a hard day's exploring, guests can return to savour some delicious local cuisine, the area's other great natural resource.

Access: In the heart of the village

BASILICATA

TRIVIGNO (PZ)

LA FORESTERIA DI SAN LEO

Sig. Guarini
Contrada San Leo, 11
85018 Trivigno (PZ)
Tel. 09 71 98 11 57 – Fax 09 71 44 26 95
mariagiovanna.allegretti@tin.it

76-100€

Closed 1 Nov-31 Mar • 5 double rm, 2 apartments with kitchen • Half board €54-70 • Parking, garden, no dogs • Riding, bicycles lent out, cooking lessons, honey and cheese for sale

Menu €25/35 for residents only

The serenity of the hermitage setting up in the hills.

The well presented rooms are colourfully decorated in contrast to the plain stonework in the public areas, giving visitors a feel for the long history of this secluded place, previously a Benedictine monastery dedicated to Saint Leo. In addition to its interesting heritage, the hotel also has its own stables, giving guests a chance to explore the meadows and woods which stretch out over the surrounding hills towards the high mountains beyond.

Access: 5km from Trivigno, follow the signs to the Camastra dam

Calabria

Forming the toe of the Italian peninsula, this harsh and wild region is the home of the red pepper, and has some areas of unimaginable beauty.

Each season has its own appeal here: in winter the snowy slopes of the Sila, Pollino and Aspromonte draw skiers and visitors from all over southern Italy; in autumn and spring the woods and plains are a fragrant blaze of colour, while in summer the long coastline attracts sun worshippers in their droves.

Against this backdrop, certain places stand out: Maratea, Tropea, Stilo, Pentadattilo, Scilla and Palmi, to name but a few.

The red pepper features large in Calabrian cuisine, while other important ingredients include ricotta and pecorino cheese, Tropea onions, liquorice and citrus fruits. Wine buffs will be familiar with the region's famous Cirò label.

8 establishments

Recommended sites and circuits
Calabria

> This enchanting region promises countless delights, from the natural beauty of its breathtaking sunsets, lush forests, dream beaches and rolling green hills to its history, monuments and works of art, to be enjoyed time and again. This is a region where nature and ancient civilisations, ethnic groups, dialects and religious traditions compose a splendid mosaic.

Diamante is as precious a place as its name suggests. Thanks to its immense and immaculate beaches and stunning cliffs, this town nestled between the sea and the mountains is one of Calabria's major seaside resorts. The balmy fragrance of the Tyrrhenian Sea is almost intoxicating, captivating the senses of all who come to contemplate its crystalline waters and silvery beaches contrasting with the azur sky. In town, the murals that decorate the historical centre lend the narrow streets the feel of an open-air museum. The neighbouring island, **Cirella**, famous for its ruins and period lighthouse, offers divers an unforgettable underwater experience.

Opposite the Aeolian Islands and Stromboli lies **Tropea**, another of the treasures of the Tyrrhenian Sea. Perched on top of a rocky spur plunging down to the sea, between the inlets and craggy islets, the old Norman cathedral dominates the landscape. The names of the surrounding beaches reflect their original shape and their history A *linguata* (tongue), *U bacino* (basin), I *cancini*, formerly home to a garden whose railings were visible from the sea, and *I puzzi* (well), once used by fishermen. If you go along the coast, one of the most beautiful in the region, you will reach **Capo Vaticano**, whose sheer cliffs constitute a sort of natural reserve, ideal for nesting birds. At the top, don't miss the little path bordered by prickly pear trees that leads you around the lighthouse to breathtaking viewpoints and, weather permitting, offers views as far as the Aeolian Islands.

Further on, the mythical **Scilla** rock juts out over the sea, standing out from the steep and abrupt slopes of Aspromonte and the Costa Viola coast (so called because of the violet colour of the corals and turtles that grace its waters). Here, Ruffo Castle dominates the cliffs, which seem to look into the distance towards the Sicilian shores, while the sea still whispers of the legendary feats of Ulysees.

A recipe to try, wines and… a nugget of information

 Wines
- Cirò
- Greco di Bianco
- Arghillà
- Locride
- Verbicaro

Local specialities

Chili peppers, *caviale dei poveri* (spicy anchovy caviar), *pecorino* (ewe's milk cheese, often with black pepper or chili pepper), *giuncata*, *butirro* (cheese stuffed with butter), *caciocavallo silano*, *nduja* (a type of spicy smoked sausage similar in shape to salami), *capocollo* and *soppressata* (cooked meats), Tropea red onions, cedars, bergamot oranges, figs, liquorice.

CUZZUPE

Ingredients
- 1kg flour
- 4 eggs (2 or 3 more for decoration)
- 250ml milk
- 250g sugar
- 2 packets baking powder
- 150g vegetable oil
- Zest of 1 lemon
- Coloured sugar lumps

Method
Beat the 4 eggs with the sugar until the mixture turns white; mix in the flour gradually (to avoid lumps) then add the milk, baking powder, oil and lemon zest. Keep stirring until you obtain a smooth, compact dough; shape as desired (crown, plait, etc), keeping some aside for later. Place a few eggs (after washing the shells) on the cake and fix them using the strips of spare dough. Bake in the oven at 190°C for approximately 30min, brush the cake with beaten egg, add the sugar cubes and put back in the oven for a further 5min.

Food for thought
Despite its close links to religion, Calabrian cuisine has retained certain traditions of pagan origin. According to tradition, Calabrians are meant to eat macaroni at Carnival time, lamb with a special kind of bread at Easter, and should prepare exactly thirteen dishes at Christmas and Epiphany.

Our favourite places to eat

FRAMMICHÈ
Contrada Ceraso – Filandari, Mesiano (VV) – Tel. 338 8707476
Closed lunchtime, Sun in Aug and Sep, mon Oct-Jul
Menu €20

 The old-style Calabrian charm and cuisine.

It is advisable to ask for directions when making a reservation at this restaurant, located in the open countryside off a dirt track. Its peaceful setting and rural feel, and the shady terrace, perfect in summer, make it well worth the detour. The intriguing interior of this small former farmhouse boasts a colossal fireplace hung with cooked meats and old photos. The menu, recited aloud by the waiter, offers a superb assortment of Calabrian antipastis and specialities.

BAYLIK
Vico Leone 1 – Reggio Calabria (RC) – Tel. 0965 48624
Closed Mon and Jul.
A la carte menu €29-43

 The surprisingly well-balanced fusion of Calabria and Sicily, Italy and Turkey.

The name of this restaurant, meaning "fish" in Turkish, gives a good idea of the specialities you can look forward to sampling here. The aluminium chairs and paintings on the walls make for an original and distinctly modern decor. The menu offers creatively presented seafood dishes with a hint of Sicilian style: the grilled calamari are served stuffed and the sea urchins have an accompaniment of aubergines. This skillful demonstration of originality brings surprises from starter to dessert.

LA VECCHIA HOSTARIA
Via Matteotti 5 – Siderno (RC) – Tel. 0964 388880
Closed Wed, except Jul and Aug. Booking advisable.
A la carte menu €27-40

 The warmth of the wooden decor rivalled by that of the service.

This spacious restaurant located in an old city-centre building has a typical groin-vaulted ceiling and stone and brick walls. Classic service, and the owner personally extends a warm welcome to diners. Seafood is the predominant culinary theme, and the fish on the menu vary according to the season and the chef's mood; the waiter recites the menu aloud. For those wishing to sample the traditional regional dishes, Calabrian specialities also grace the menu.

CIRELLA (CS)

DUCALE VILLA RUGGERI

Sig.ra Ruggeri
Via Vittorio Veneto, 254
87020 Cirella (CS)
Tel. 098 58 60 51 – Fax 098 58 60 51
info@ducalehotel.net – www.ducalehotel.net

👫 65-100€

Open all year • 22 double rm • Half board €46-90 • Parking, private beach, no dogs in the restaurant

 Set Menu €20

 The well-kept lawned gardens.

The rocks, pebbled beaches, turquoise waters and islets of the Calabrian coast form the backdrop of the Villa Ducale, built by descendants of the Gonzaga family in the 18C and subsequently owned by the Ruggeri, who today continue to run the establishment. The ambience is genteel and refined, and there are delightful well planted gardens. Inside, the furnishings vary in origin; some are unusual antiques, while others are more everyday. The spacious restaurant offers Calabrian and other Italian dishes. Meals are also served in the gardens.

Access: In the centre, two minutes from the sea

CALABRIA

GERACE (RC)

LA CASA DI GIANNA

Sig.ra Terranova
Via Paolo Frascà 4
89040 Gerace (RC)
Tel. 09 64 35 50 24 - Fax 09 64 35 50 81
info@lacasadigianna.it
www.lacasadigianna.it

 120-130€

Closed from 1 to 30 Nov • 1 single rm, 9 double rm • Half-board €83-88 • Small dogs welcome

 Menu €17/30

> The family atmosphere that reigns in this elegant abode of a bygone era.

Poised between the sea and the mountains, this aristocratic residence stands on a green hilltop that was a military camp in Imperial times, but also the religious and administrative capital of the region. Today it has become a hotel of quite unique charm. Decorated in a low-key, welcoming and functional style, it is ideal for a few days' rest: reading a good book in front of the fire, daydreaming as you listen to music or cat napping in the sophisticated rooms, whose bed linen is made out of hand-embroidered linen. The former cellar adorned with stone arches is now a restaurant where you can enjoy the delicious local cuisine.

Access: In the historic centre

CALABRIA

MORANO CALABRO (CS)

3

LA LOCANDA DEL PARCO

Sig.ra Tamburi
Contrada Mazzicanino, 12
87016 Morano Calabro (CS)
Tel. 098 13 13 04 – Fax 098 13 13 04
info@lalocandadelparco.it
www.lalocandadelparco.it

🧍🧒 **60-70€**

Open all year • 2 single rm, 6 double rm and 1 suite • Half board €45-50 • Parking, garden, swimming pool, no dogs • Guided tours, cooking lessons, sale of jam, cured meat and oil

 Set Menu €20 and 25

 The rocky setting of the extraordinary spa pool.

Conveniently close to the motorway but set in open country, this hotel is dominated by Mount Pollino and its national park. Inside, guests will find a welcoming lounge area with a family ambience, while the dining room is more rustic in feel with communal tables. The rooms take their names from musical notes and have many personal touches including period style furnishings. A second building close to the pool has two further rooms. Horses may also be hired from the stables.

Access: 500 metres from the motorway exit

CALABRIA

MORANO CALABRO (CS)

VILLA SAN DOMENICO

Sig. Vacca
Via Paglierina 13
87016 Morano Calabro (CS)
Tel. 09 81 39 98 81 – Fax 098 13 05 88
villa-sandomenico@tin.it
www.albergovillasandomenico.it

 103€

Open all year • 1 single rm, 7 double rm and 3 suites • Half-board €65 • Parking, garden

 Set Menu €25 and 30

 Charm and old-fashioned nobility in a haven of peace and quiet.

Located in the heart of the historic centre, in the shade of century-old elm trees and close to the old monastery of San Bernardino, this handsome opulent 16C house still has its original, beautifully restored, façade. Guests are welcomed by staff who are as pleasant as they are efficient. Inside the elegant atmosphere is enhanced by fine antique furniture. Admire the view of the Pollino mountain range from the terrace of your room. Under the sloping ceiling of the dining room, you will be invited to taste authentic and sophisticated dishes which exalt the flavours and savours of a bygone era.

Access: Two minutes from the historic centre

CALABRIA

NOCERA TERINESE (CZ)

5

VOTA
Fam. Mauri
Contrada Vota, 3
88047 Nocera Terinese (CZ)
Tel. 096 8915 17 – Fax 096 89 15 17
info@agrivota.it – www.agrivota.it

♈♈ 66€

Open all year • 8 double rm • Breakfast €3; half board €46-55 • Parking, garden, swimming pool, no dogs • Sale of oil and wine

 Set Menu €18 and 25

 The panoramic view towards the sea.

Situated high up in a panoramic spot halfway between Nocera and Falerna, this agriturismo is a truly original holiday destination offering something for everyone. From the poolside terrace, beach lovers can see the beach, 5km away and easily reached by car. Those in quest of unspoilt countryside can explore the 35 hectares of olive groves and citrus orchards. However guests choose to spend their days, come evening they will welcome the traditional Calabrian cuisine incorporating genuine local products.

Access: 5km towards Falerna and the sea

CALABRIA

PIANOPOLI (CZ)

LE CAROLEE

Sig. Gaetano
Contrada Gabella, 1
88040 Pianopoli (CZ)
Tel. 096 83 5076 – Fax 096 83 50 76
lecarolee@lecarolee.it – www.lecarolee.it

 91-100€

Open all year • 7 double rm • Half board €65-74 • Parking, garden, swimming pool, dogs not admitted • Bicycle hire, tasting and sale of cured meat and oil

 Menu €35/45

 The rugged Calabrian scenery, impervious to the passage of time.

The Calabrian hinterland is one of Italy's wildest landscapes; over the centuries it has been the domain of those seeking isolation, be they saints or brigands. Such a history explains why this 19C residence was originally fortified. The building encloses a small inner courtyard, while a swimming pool is set in its garden. On the whole, this hotel represents Calabria updating itself by drawing upon its past and presenting it with modern enhancements.

Access: 3km from the village

CALABRIA

ROSSANO STAZIONE (CS)

7

TRAPESIMI

Sig. Pace
Contrada Amica
87068 Rossano Stazione (CS)
Tel. 098 36 43 92 – Fax 09 83 29 08 48
info@agriturismotrapesimi.it
www.agriturismotrapesimi.it

68€

Open all year • 7 double rm • Half board €52-60 • Parking, no dogs in the restaurant • Organised trips, lessons on regional history, archaeology and regional cooking

 Set Menu €15 and 20

 Views of the sea to the front, flanked by the olive groves of the Sila.

Situated several hundred metres down a narrow track, this isolated building is of recent construction but is in the style of the farmhouse which preceded it on this site. From the terrace there are views over the timeless landscape of the plain with its ancient olive groves, and the gulf of Sibari, a crossroads of society since the days when the Greeks founded colonies here. This agriturismo also hosts conventions on various subject from ecological issues to history; the ideal place for combining a relaxing holiday with a little culture.

Access: 4km from the village in the countryside

CALABRIA

TORRE DI RUGGIERO (CZ)

I BASILIANI

Sig.ra Martelli
Strada Statale 182 - Contrada San Basile
88060 Torre di Ruggiero (CZ)
Tel. 09 67 93 80 00 – Fax 09 67 93 80 00
info@ibasiliani.com – www.ibasiliani.com

  64-80€

Open from 7 Apr to 31 Oct • 8 double rm, 6 apartments with kitchen • Half board €57-65 • Parking, garden, swimming pool, no dogs in the restaurant • Cookery courses, pétanque, sale of jam, honey and cured meats

 Set Menu €25 and 35

 The remains of the monastery, redolent of timeless contemplation.

Once dedicated to prayer, this place became a farmhouse before its latest transformation into a country guesthouse. The path through the woods remains, winding towards the village of Torre di Ruggiero; travelling along it on foot or on horseback it is easy to imagine how pilgrims would have come this way, crossing the land which divides the Ionian and Tyrrenhian seas, perhaps heading for the Cattolica church in Stilo, a thousand year old masterpiece of Byzantine art.

Access: On the main road 2km from the centre

Campania

Those in quest of an authentic flavour to their travels will not be disappointed by Campania, its rich cuisine – pastries made with ricotta cheese and candied fruit, seafood dishes, homemade pasta with a rich Neapolitan sauce, not to mention its trademark pizzas with buffalo mozzarella topping – reflecting the warmth of the local people.

Visitors more interested in sightseeing cannot fail to be impressed by Vesuvius, Capri and Ischia; the Sorrento peninsula reaching out into the Tyrrhenian sea, its steep scrubby slopes interspersed with the rocky outcrops of the Lattari hills. Inland, the wild Appenine landscape is softened by farmland plains irrigated by the Volturno, Calore and Sele rivers. Those still not convinced by Campania's charms should be swayed by its history, both Ancient, as represented by Pompeii and Herculaneum, and more recent, namely the golden age of the Kingdom of Naples. Its sumptuous court occupied some of Italy's most impressive palaces, most notably at Caserta, symbol of the Bourbon apogee and Naples at its height.

23 establishments

Recommended sites and circuits Campania

> The enchanting colours of the Amalfi coast have always exerted a hold over travellers. The green of the seafront and the intense blue of the clear waters, coupled with the beauty of the artistic and architectural wonders of its villages, make it one of the most cherished places in the world.

Occasionally wild but always romantic, the Amalfi coast is a real treasure. With its vertiginous cliffs and jutting rocks, the force of nature reigns here. Here, after all, are the **Oasi di Valle di Porto**, the **Grotta dello Smeraldo**, the **Conca dei Marini** and the **Furore** fjord. **Positano** sparkles like a jewel in the mountain with its multicoloured little houses that seem to hurtle down the slope, and its steep little streets, lined with boutiques, which descend to the beautiful turquoise waters of Marina Grande. The church St. Maria Assunta dominates the main square and indeed the surrounding countryside, thanks to its dome, which is covered with multicoloured ceramic. Further along the coastline is **Amalfi**. Here the majesty of the mountains blends in with the picturesque entanglement of little streets and stairways that lead to the square on which you find the amazing multicoloured façade of the Duomo. Not far from here you find **Atrani**, which at the time of the Amalfi Republic was inhabited by the most well-off families. The ceramics on the dome and steeple of the church of the Maddalena, with their bright colours, stand out against a background of little streets, arches, squares and courtyards. Take the motorway to **Grotta dei Santi**, from where you can see the ruins of the Benedictine monastery of Saints Quirico and Giulitta.

Located high in the mountains amongst vineyards and olive trees, the village of **Furore** owes its name to the sound of the wind during storms and to that of the sea breaking upon the steep banks of the fjord which traces a sheer descent from the high plains of Agerola. This coastline has an irresistible charm. The façades of its houses are decorated with paintings illustrating ancient legends made up of devils and saints, various animals, warrior invasions and miraculous fishing trips.

The smell of the lemon and orange trees will direct you to Cilento. This coastline, although a little less well-known, reveals just as many delights. It's a fusion of myth, history and landscape that gives rise to countless legends and traditions. The jutting rocks and imposing cliffs, such as **Punta Tresino, Punta Licosa, Capo Palinuro**, and the **Baia degli Infreschi**, are perfect places to go swimming, as are the little rocky islands of **Cala dei Monti della Luna**, which are however only accessible by sea.

A recipe to try, wines and... a nugget of information

 Wines

_Taurasi
_Lacryma Christi
_Vesuvio
_Greco di Tufo
_Fiano di Avellino
_Coda di Volpe Bianca
_Aglianico del Taburno
_Vesuvio
_Capri

Ingredients
- 8 slices of bread
- 1 large mozzarella
- 2 eggs
- flour
- oil to fry
- salt

Local specialities

San Marzano tomatoes, buffalo mozzarella, *caciocavallo*, *cacioricotta*, *pecorino di Laticauda*, Sorrente lemons, *pisto* (a mix of spices including cloves, nutmeg, cinnamon and pepper), Cilento white figs, *nocillo* (hazelnut and aromatic herb liqueur), annurca apples, Vesuvius apricots, Sorrente hazelnuts, *pastiera* (Easter cake), *sfogliatelle* (layered pastries), *strufoli* (biscuits), Paestum artichokes.

MOZZARELLA IN CARROZZA

Method
Remove the bread crusts and on each slice place a small round of mozzarella and cover with another slice of bread. Fasten into a cross shape with kitchen thread. Beat the eggs and pour them over the bread, making sure that the liquid is well absorbed. Heat the oil in a frying pan and cook two or three little sandwiches until they are golden on both sides. Put them on a warm plate, add salt and garnish with parsley if you wish. Serve hot.

Food for thought
Both Naples and China claim to have invented spaghetti (even though Chinese spaghetti is really rather different). A few centuries ago spaghetti was cooked in large pans in the street and, like pizza and other dishes, was sold from stands lining the streets and eaten with ones hands at any time of the day.

Our favourite places to eat

LA PIGNATA
Viale Dei Tigli 7 – Ariano Irpino (AV) – Tel. 0825 872355
Closed 15-30 Sep and Tue.
A la carte menu €21-35
The charisma, the decor and the dishes on offer.
This restaurant just outside the historical centre is set in a spacious room with columns and a vaulted ceiling. In keeping with the food, the atmosphere is pleasantly rustic. The menu proposes a small selection of Campanian products. To whet your appetite you can sample the soups made from bread (*pancotto*) or green beans, before moving on to the different varieties of pasta, such as paccheri, or orechiette. You can also try delicious tripe-, rabbit- or cod-based dishes.

PASCALUCCI
Via Dannassi – San Nicola Manfredi (Benevento) (BN) – Tel. 0824 778400
Open all year round.
A la carte menu €19-36
The appetising dishes served in the shade of a large summer veranda.
This restaurant is without doubt one of the most renowned in the province and many customers regularly make the seven-kilometre journey from Benevento. This devotion is due in part to the Pascalucci family's commitment to improving the premises, which they are continuously developing. The selection of fish dishes, which manages to combine Campanian tradition with more sophisticated culinary ideas, is served either in the large rooms with exposed beams or under the veranda.

IL PAPAVERO
Corso Garibaldi 112/113 – Eboli (SA) – Tel. 0828 330689
Closed for ten days in Jul, ten days in Nov, Sun eve and Mon.
A la carte menu €24-31
The creative dishes served in a design-oriented atmosphere.
A discreet contemporary atmosphere reigns in this restaurant, located just next to the town hall in the historical city centre, and its two small white-walled rooms decorated with paintings. At once refined and informal, the decor seems to reflect the restaurant's youthful and dynamic cuisine. Whether cooking meat or fish, traditional dishes or innnovations, the chef's imagination knows no bounds. On offer are *pancotto, fusilli campani, gelatine* (gelled broth), as well as a range of velouté soups. A genuine gastronomical journey that blends culinary tradition with a touch of originality.

CAMPANIA

AGROPOLI (SA)

1

LA COLOMBAIA
Sig. Botti
Via La Vecchia 12, Piano delle Pere
84043 Agropoli (SA)
Tel. 09 74 82 18 00 – Fax 09 74 82 18 00
colombaia@tin.it – www.lacolombaiahotel.it

👤🧒 80-100€

Closed 1 Jan-28 Feb • 10 double rm • Half board €68-72 • Parking, garden, swimming pool, no dogs

 Set Menu €18 and 22 for residents only

 The pool situated among olive trees.

An imaginative development project has transformed an imposing country residence into a little fairytale castle; the results are extraordinary and undoubtedly very original. The distant sea is framed by the hills, and the surrounding grounds planted with olive groves create an air of calm and relaxation for the hotel's privileged clients. Inside, there is an air of gentility, both in the public areas and in the well-equipped rooms. The terrace is another attractive feature, with seating, umbrellas and a fine pool.

Access: From piazza Moio, follow the signs for around 2km

CAMPANIA

BACOLI (NA)

VILLA OTERI

Sig. Faga
Via Lungolago, 174
80070 Bacoli (NA)
Tel. 08 15 23 49 85 - Fax 08 15 23 39 44
reception@villaoteri.it - www.villaoteri.it

 85-110€

Open all year • 9 double rm • Parking, small dogs welcome

 Menu €22/39

 The breakfast of freshly squeezed orange juice, cappuccino and croissants...and the view.

Delightful setting, breathtaking views, conveniently located for exploring the delights of Campagna far from the madding crowd. Villa Oteri meets all these criteria, a patrician residence in a splendid location, now transformed into a hotel which is a happy union of the convenient and the stylish. The well-equipped rooms are kitted out in up to the minute style but retain a period feel, while the service is first class. The restaurant serves a wide variety of dishes, though the emphasis is on fish.

Access: Near the lake, on the panoramic road towards monte di Procida

CAMPANIA

CASTELLABATE (SA)

LA MOLA

Sig.ra Favilla
Via A. Cilento 2
84048 Castellabate (SA)
Tel. 09 74 96 70 53 - Fax 09 74 96 77 14
lamola@lamola-it.com - www.lamola-it.com   👥 114-124€

Open from 1 Mar to 31 Oct • 6 double rm • Half-board €90 • Dogs not admitted

 Set Menu €40 and 60

 The stone arch in the sitting room, in homage to the house's ancient architecture.

The medieval historic centre of the town of Castellabate is home to an old family house that owes its name to the discovery of the remains of an old press within its walls. Superbly located, it enjoys a panoramic view of the sea and coastline and its warm family atmosphere is perfect to make the most of the seaside, countryside and local culture and gastronomy. Adorned with old furniture and splendid bed linen, most of the rooms command a panoramic view of the gulf of Salerno. Whenever the weather permits, meals of local inspiration are served on the terrace.

Access: In the heart of the village

CAMPANIA

CASTELNUOVO CILENTO (SA)

4

LA PALAZZINA

Sig. Vacchiano
Via Contrada Coppola 41
84040 Castelnuovo Cilento (SA)
Tel. 097 46 28 80 – Fax 097 46 21 09
info@hotellapalazzina.com
www.hotellapalazzina.com

80-120€

Open all year • 2 single rm, 10 double rm, 4 suites • Half-board €50-80 • Parking, park

 Menu €21/29

 The luxurious setting and generous proportions are an invitation to relax and wind down.

In the heart of the Nature Park of Cilento a few kilometres from the coast, the 18C Palazzina with its typical pink façade has been enlarged and restored to its former glory. Nestling in an immense garden planted with century-old trees and lush green Mediterranean plants, the rooms are rustic in style and some have oak or poplar beams. They are all decorated with a few simple elegant pieces of furniture or local craft work. The courtyard has been turned into a pleasant room that is ideal for receptions.

Access: At Casal Velino Scalo for 8km, near the small artificial lake

CAMPANIA

CERASO (SA)

LA PETROSA
Sig. Soffritti
Via Fabbrica, 25
84052 Ceraso (SA)
Tel. 097 46 13 70 – Fax 097 47 97 14
staff@lapetrosa.it – www.lapetrosa.it

50-90€

Closed 1 Nov-28 Feb • 6 double rm • Half board €40-60 • Parking, garden, swimming pool, dogs not admitted in restaurant • Organised trips, archery, pétanque, sale of oil and jam

 Menu €19/27

 The rooms in the castle and the marvellous surrounding countryside.

Also known as Vigna della Corte, La Petrosa is part of the district of Ceraso in the Palistro valley (within the Cilento national park) around 10km from the sea and also close to Monte Sacro (1700m). The surrounding landscape is a lush mix of olive groves, orchards and fields. Visitors may opt for camping, apartments or rooms. This last category occupies the finest building, the old main house (a castle-like edifice) and a farmhouse near the pool.

Access: 7km from the village. At Petrosa, follow the signs

CAMPANIA

DRAGONI (CE)

6

VILLA DE PERTIS

Sig. De Pertis
Via Ponti, 30
81010 Dragoni (CE)
Tel. 08 23 86 66 19 – Fax 08 23 86 66 19
info@villadepertis.it – www.villadepertis.it

75€

Open all year • 7 double rm • Half board €51 • Garden, no dogs in the restaurant

 Menu €21/28

 The staircase with stone steps and unusual arches.

Dragoni is a small village around 30km from Caserta on the Volturno coast, a peaceful setting for the Villa De Pertis, a country residence of 17C origin. The rooms are unusually decorated and an inexpressible charm seems to pervade the entire establishment: sitting room and fireplace and a panoramic garden terrace. Nothing is too much trouble for the dynamic staff, all of which in a spirit of informal hospitality. In the restaurant you will sample homemade starters, grilled vegetables, fresh pasta and regional cured meats.

Access: In the historic centre

CAMPANIA

DUGENTA (BN)

TORRE GAIA WINE RESORT

Torrenova Srl
Via Boscocupo 11
82030 Benevento (BN)
Tel. 08 24 97 83 74 - Fax 08 24 97 83 37
info@torre-gaia.com - www.torre-gaia.com

150€

Open all year • 1 single rm, 11 double rm, 1 suite • Half-board €100 • Parking, swimming pool, garden, small dogs welcome

 Menu €33/41

 A restful landscape and an outstanding atmosphere: ideal to find out more about ancient traditions.

At the gateway to the Telesina Valley, a winegrowing region of ancient traditions, stands this farm, a majestic early 20C building, tastefully restored in a rustic style. This historic establishment features sophisticated interior fittings, well-suited for individual holidays and for conferences, meetings or large receptions. The elegant rooms sport antique furniture. The cuisine, a successful blend between regional tradition and the creative talents of a maestro chef, also attracts many visitors.

Access: On the outskirts of the village, towards Caserta

CAMPANIA

FISCIANO (SA)

8

BARONE ANTONIO NEGRI

Sig.ra Negri
Via Teggiano, 8
84084 Fisciano (SA)
Tel. 089 95 85 61 – Fax 089 89 11 80
info@agrinegri.it – www.agrinegri.it

80-110€

Open all year • 6 double rm • Half board €60-75 • Parking, garden, swimming pool • Tasting and sale of hazelnut products

 Set Menu €25 and 30

 The cakeshop, where guests can savour fresh hazelnut biscuits.

In a panoramic and peaceful position among the hills that separate the Salerno coastline from Avellino, this historic establishment, the grandest of the estates in the Fisciano district, is run in dedicated fashion by the last of the line of the Negri family. Hospitality and comfort go hand in hand with history and tradition here, making this relaxing place the ideal spot from which to explore the Sorrento peninsula and Naples.

Access: 2km from the motorway exit at Lancusi

CAMPANIA

FURORE (SA)

SANT'ALFONSO

Sig.ra Cuomo
Via Sant'Alfonso, 6
84010 Furore (SA)
Tel. 089 83 05 15 – Fax 089 83 05 15
info@agriturismosantalfonso.it
www.agriturismosantalfonso.it

 80-90€

Closed Nov • 10 double rm • Half board €60-65 • Garden, parking, dogs not admitted • Hiking, sale of jam, wine and preserves

 Menu €22/31

 The terrace, offering fine views of the sea.

A steep climb up 500m of stone steps leads to this haven of peace and quiet tucked away in the terraced hillside between the coastline and the Monti Lattari. The building's origins are lost in the mists of time, but it is thought to date from the 16C and was definitely in use as a convent in the 19C. Today it is the ideal place for a relaxing break in peaceful surroundings; named after aromatic herbs, the rooms are simply furnished, in keeping with the architectural style of the house. The house wine is made on the premises and fresh water is drawn from a working well.

Access: Near the village, go up the panoramic steps for about 500m

CAMPANIA

GIFFONI SEI CASALI (SA)

10

PALAZZO PENNASILICO

Sig. Pennasilico
Via Le Piazze, 27
84090 SIETI (SA)
Tel. 089 88 18 22 - Fax 089 88 18 22
info@palazzopennasilico.it
www.palazzopennasilico.it

👤👤 **120€**

Closed Jan, Feb • 2 double rm, 2 suites • Parking, garden, no dogs

 The terrace overlooking the village of Sieti.

The property of the Pennasilico family since the 16C, this delightful palazzo is located in Sieti, a small textile village deep in the Monti Picentini Park. The palazzo has only recently opened its doors to guests, who will delight in the magnificent frescoes and decor of the drawing rooms, corridors and private chapel. The bedrooms, also furnished in a very individual style, are grouped into two categories; the Alcova suite is particularly stunning. Also worthy of note is the courtyard where the bread oven, oil press and stables were once situated. Friendly, hospitable owners.

Access: In the heart of the historic centre

ISCHIA (ISOLA D') (NA)

11

CASA SOFIA
Sig. Katz
Via Sant'Angelo, 29/B - Loc. Sant'Angelo
80070 Ischia (NA)
Tel. 081 99 93 10 – Fax 081 90 49 28
info@hotelcasasofia.com – www.hotelcasasofia.com

👫 100€

Closed 11 Nov-14 Mar • 2 single rm, 9 double rm • No dogs

The stunning views and the many personal touches.

It is difficult to decide which view is best here; there are so many from which to choose. The hotel is tastefully furnished, with each piece seeming to have been selected individually, thus giving every room a unique feel. With books and magazines the lounge area is very welcoming, while the restaurant serves diners on a fine terrace in summer, or indoors (yet equally panoramic) in poor weather.

Access: In the village, near the lake

CAMPANIA

ISCHIA (ISOLA D') (NA)

12

IL VITIGNO

Sig.ra Turrisi
Via Bocca, 31 - Loc. Forio
80075 Ischia (NA)
Tel. 081 99 83 07 - Fax 081 99 83 07
info@agriturismoilvitigno.it
www.agriturismoilvitigno.it

 80-100€

Closed Dec, Jan, Feb • 1 single rm, 16 double rm • Half-board €50-60 • Parking, heated swimming pool, garden, no dogs • Sale of jam

 Set Menu €15 and 20

 The attractive wrought iron tables and chairs.

Panoramically situated among olive groves and vineyards in a hilly part of the island, this verdant oasis has stunning views over the sea. There are around ten rooms, all of which are attractively furnished in simple, tasteful style. Although the sea is close by, those wishing to stay put can enjoy the small but charming swimming pool. The restaurant offers Ischian and Campanian specialities using locally grown produce.

Access: Outside the centre, before reaching the village

CAMPANIA

MASSA LUBRENSE (NA)

13

PICCOLO PARADISO

Sig. Cacace
Piazza Madonna della Lobra, 5
80061 Massa Lubrense (NA)
Tel. 08 18 78 92 40 - Fax 08 180 8 90 56
info@piccolo-paradiso.com
www.piccolo-paradiso.com

97-114€

Open from 15 Mar to 15 Nov • 4 single rm, 50 double rm • Half board €73-81 • Swimming pool, no dogs in the restaurant

 Menu €30/44

 The Vietri-style ceramics.

Far from the noise and sophistication of the famous hot-spots of the Bay of Naples and the Amalfi Coast, Massa Lubrense is a typical fishing village built from tufa stone. The Piccolo Paradiso is a more modern construction, regularly renovated by the enterprising Cacace family who have managed the hotel for years. The bedrooms here are light and the bathrooms furnished with colourful ceramics. One of the highlights of the hotel is the attractive swimming pool located on the spacious, panoramic terrace. The restaurant, which serves a selection of fresh Mediterranean dishes, is situated in a large dining room.

Access: 2km from the centre of Marina Lobra, near the sanctuary

CAMPANIA

MELIZZANO (BN)

14

MESOGHEO

Sig. Carola
Contrada Valle Corrado, 4
82030 Melizzano (BN)
Tel. 08 24 94 43 56 – Fax 08 24 94 41 30
info@mesogheo.com – www.mesogheo.com

 100€

Open all year • 10 double rm • Half board €75 • Parking, garden, swimming pool, no dogs in the restaurant • Guided tours, sale of oil and jam

 For residents only

 The open fireplaces in every room, perfect for cooler evenings.

A little dedication is required to find this establishment, tucked away as it is up a poorly signposted track, but the visitor will find the extra effort worthwhile. The main building is a typical local farmhouse, with the restaurant on the ground floor and the owner's apartment upstairs. Guests will find their accommodation in one of two smaller buildings closer to the pool; there are around ten rooms, with many personal touches in evidence and a pleasant feel. All in all, a great place to stay.

Access: Near the centre, take the dirt track

CAMPANIA

NAPOLI (NA)

15

B&B L'ALLOGGIO DEI VASSALLI

Sig. Antonelli
Via Donnalbina, 56
80134 Napoli (NA)
Tel. 08 15 51 51 18 - Fax 08 14 20 27 52
info@bandbnapoli.it - www.bandbnapoli.it

👤👤 93-99€

Open all year • 5 double rm

 Dvd player and free drinks in every room.

Centrally located close to the city's artistic and cultural highlights, this gem of a place stands out among the many hotels which have sprung up in recent years to cater for the ever increasing number of tourists. Occupying an 18C palazzo, the well presented rooms have a historic charm which, along with frescoed ceilings, preserve the original atmosphere of the place.

Access: Near the post office

CAMPANIA

NAPOLI (NA)

16

BELLE ARTI RESORT

Sig.ra Arena
Via Santa Maria di Costantinopoli 27
80138 Napoli (NA)
Tel. 08 15 57 10 62 – Fax 081 44 78 60
info@belleartiresort.com
www.belleartiresort.com

👤👤 **80-100€**

Open all year • 6 double rm

 The heart of old Naples, renowned for its art and shops.

A perfect balance between past and present, this hotel will delight the traveller in search of old-fashioned elegance, but without having to forgo the convenience of modern life. It is located in the heart of the town's historic centre on a street packed with edifices of artistic interest, dating back to the 16C when the walls were built. This establishment lies in the Palazzo dei Baroni Sgueglia della Marra, an elegant late-17C building, now treated to a stylish modern interior. The spacious well-equipped rooms are adorned with frescoes and other unusual decorative features.

Access: Very close to the National Archaeological Museum

NAPOLI (NA)

IL CONVENTO

Confort Hotels s.a.s.
Via Speranzella 137/a
80132 Napoli (NA)
Tel. 081 40 39 77 – Fax 08140 03 32
info@hotelilconvento.com
www.hotelilconvento.com

100-150€

Open all year • 4 single rm and 10 double rm

 The Spanish district, where culture and business rub shoulders in a relaxed spirit.

Right in the heart of the historic centre, a few minutes walk from the Via Caracciolo seaside promenade, the Palazzo Real and San Carlo Theatre, this hotel is next door to the Convent of Santa Maria Francesca dalle cinque piaghe. The establishment offers comfortable «cells» adorned with tasteful period furniture, in addition to junior suites under the eaves or with a small flower-decked roof terrace. This 18C palace, whose restoration aimed at enhancing the unusual structural quality of the building without forgoing modern comforts, is an ideal choice for tourists and business travellers alike.

Access: Near the Umberto 1st Gallery

CAMPANIA

PAESTUM (SA)

SELIANO

Sig.ra Baratta
Capaccio
84063 Paestum (SA)
Tel. 08 28 72 36 34 – Fax 08 28 72 45 44
seliano@agriturismoseliano.it
www.agriturismoseliano.it

 70-120€

Open from 15 Mar to 31 Oct • 2 single rm, 13 double rm • Half-board €55-75 • Garden, swimming pool, parking, dogs not admitted in restaurant • Cookery lessons, sale of jam and oil

 Set Menu €25 and 30 for residents only

 Buffalo and horses have been reared in the region for over three centuries.

Located near an ancient city in Magna Grecia, this hamlet has been restored and is now home to this elegant inn, whose rich heritage mingles with the flavours of family recipes. In the heart of an immense garden, this farm extends a warm welcome to guests in search of a few days of rest, and peace and quiet. In keeping with the original architectural style, the comfortable rooms are rustic in inspiration and furnished with antiques. The breakfast table is laden high with homemade pastries, plum cakes and marmalade. In spring and autumn, you can take a cooking lesson and learn how mozzarella is made in the cheese factory.

Access: In the historic town of Capaccio Scalo

CAMPANIA

PERDIFUMO (SA)

LA MIMOSA

Sig.ra Chiariello
Contrada Difesa
84060 Perdifumo (SA)
Tel. 09 74 85 19 98 – Fax 09 74 82 40 22
lamimosa@agriturismo.com
www.agriturismolamimosa.it

92-112€

Closed from 1 to 15 Nov • 1 single rm, 12 double rm • Half-board €56-60 • Parking, swimming pool • Sale of oil, cured meats, jam and preserved vegetables

 Set Menu €20 and 30

 The excursions, and homemade preserves, on a hilltop surrounded by olive groves and fruit trees.

This rural guesthouse lies in the heart of the Nature Park of Cilento, two minutes from the historic centre of Castellabate. A welcoming well-cared for establishment down to the tiniest details, it is ideal for a well-earned break in the beautiful countryside. Indoors, the light airy rooms are graced with modern furniture; in the pleasant dining room you will be invited to sample the "Cilentana" cuisine prepared with farm-grown produce. A swimming pool surrounded by the green hillsides awaits you in the garden. Ideal for lovers of regional folklore and sports enthusiasts.

Access: Towards Castellabate, at Contrada Difesa, 7km from the village

CAMPANIA

POZZUOLI (NA)

20

VILLA GIULIA

Sig.ra Carunchio
Via Cuma Licola 178
80078 Pozzuoli (NA)
Tel. 08 18 54 01 63 – Fax 08 18 04 43 56
info@villagiulia.info – www.villagiulia.info

  95-130€

Open all year • 6 double rm • Garden, swimming pool, parking

 Set Menu €20 and 30 for residents only

 Near the Roman ruins: the intimate sophisticated atmosphere of the 18C.

In the heart of the green countryside in the vicinity of Lake Averno, very close to the archaeological remains of Campi Flegrei, this late 18C country house built out of soft white limestone is ideal for both culture and relaxation. The building, fully restored from top to toe, is comprised of six apartments with fireplaces, each of which is personalised and decorated with attractive works of art and opulent fabrics. Outside, the sweetly scented flower gardens are home to a large swimming pool, two barbecues and a bread oven. From May to October, the establishment organises one-week stays comprising a mixture of excursions and cooking lessons to discover the secrets of Neapolitan cuisine.

Access: In Cuma near the archaeological area

CAMPANIA

RUVIANO (CE)

LE OLIVE DI NEDDA

Sig.ra De Majo
Via Crucelle Superiore, 14
81010 Ruviano (CE)
Tel. 08 23 86 30 52 - Fax 08 23 86 30 52
info@olinedda.it - www.olinedda.it

 80€

Open all year • 8 double rm • Half board €65 • Parking, garden, no dogs • Horse riding, angling, sale of cured meat, oil, wine and preserves

 Set Menu €30

 Enjoying the evening breeze from the pergola.

The Telesina valley derives its name from Telesia, an ancient Samnite and subsequently Roman settlement, the ruins of which still exist. This rustic establishment sits in a plain, with views of olive groves along the valley which extends between hills. Nearby flow the waters of the river Volturno, and all around the farmhouse are fields, woods and a garden with pergola offering a cool retreat from the heat of the day. Out of season, guests can enjoy views over the landscape from the comfort of the fireside.

Access: Drive for 4km on the main road to Alvignanello, then follow the signs

CAMPANIA

SANT'AGATA DE' GOTI (BN)

22

MUSTILLI

Sig.ra Mustilli
Piazza Trento 4
82019 Sant'Agata de' Goti
Tel. 08 23 71 81 42 – Fax 08 23 71 76 19
info@mustilli.com – www.mustilli.it

👤👤 80€ ☕

Open all year • 6 double rm, 1 apartment • Half-board €65 • Parking, dogs not admitted

 Set Menu €25 and 30

 Sleeping in rooms steeped in history and waking up to the smell of baking.

The Mustilli family moved to this town of countless paved lanes and ancient courtyards in the 16C. In five centuries the vines have little by little become indistinguishable from the stucco ornaments of this abode steeped in history. This farmstead is ideal for travellers eager to explore Italy's top cultural sites, but who also appreciate a warm family welcome and the taste of tradition. A rich heritage that you can discover and savour amidst the home's many works of art and unusual frescoes. Not to be missed: the visit to the passages, made out of soft white limestone, which lead to the former cellars.

Access: In the heart of the village

CAMPANIA

VICO EQUENSE (NA)

LA GINESTRA
Sig.ra Belforte
Moiano - Località Santa Maria del Castello
80060 Moiano (NA)
Tel. 08 18 02 32 11 – Fax 08 18 02 32 11
info@laginestra.org – www.laginestra.org

👫 **90€** ☕

Open all year • 1 single rm, 7 double rm • Half board €90 • Parking, garden • Bicycles lent out, organised trips, sale of honey, oil, cured meat and jam

 Set Menu €16 and 20

 The elegance of this patrician villa between the scrubby hinterland and the sea.

It is no accident that the original builders decided on this spot for their patrician villa; 600m above the gulf of Salerno and flanked by the scrub covered slopes of Monte Faito, this is a stunning location which time has left untouched. The restored property has well equipped accommodation, a terrace where meals are served in summer, and a games area. Nuts, honey, oil and fruit are on sale in the large lounge area converted from the old stables. The proprietors will arrange guided tours of the area on request.

Access: *On Mont Faito, go past Moiano and continue for 2.5km towards Santa Maria del Castello*

Emilia Romagna

In order to understand this region, it is worth following the course of the Po, the great river which emerges from the hills of Piedmont before making its way across the plain and forming the boundary with Lombardy. Dykes separate it from the surrounding flat farmland which extends to the Apennine foothills. Parallel to its course runs the via Emilia, forming a cultural route which takes in the marble of Parma's Romanesque baptistery, the terracotta of Bologna's university, the gold of Ravenna's mosaics, and the ducal splendours of Ferrara, bearing witness to the historical legacy of Romans, Byzantines, the medieval communes and the warring states of the Renaissance period. The landscape is on a human scale, with town and country remaining distinct, and a network of roads which invite travel by bicycle or on foot. The region's cultural richness is matched by its gastronomy; the birthplace of Verdi boasts cuisine which is a veritable symphony of flavours, accompanied by wines such as Sangiovese and Lambrusco.

27 establishments

Recommended sites and circuits
Emilia Romagna

> With its historic old cities, market towns and farms, Emilia Romagna seems to be suspended in time; here, the traditions, culture and quality of life help you forget the negative aspects of modern life.

Located on the Via Emilia, between the land and the sea, **Faenza** (renowned for its ceramics), has managed to retain all of its former charm. 15C elegance and Neoclassicism coexist in visions of rare beauty, the elegant palaces with frescoes in the historical centre alternating with a multitude of art studios, refined boutiques, wine-tasting salons and extremely inviting osterias.

Brisighella, a medieval market town, dominated by the Rocca Manfredina (its fortress), the clock tower and the Monticino sanctuary, also flaunts its ancient origins. The old Via del Borgo, a covered street dating from the 12C, stands out in a maze of typical little streets with sculpted stucco staircases and ancient segments of city ramparts. Famous for its highly original architecture, this street is also known as "Donkey Street" as it offered shelter to the donkeys that belonged to carters who lived here in the market town. The calm that reigns here, as well as the thermal springs, will help you to unwind. Just a few kilometres away you can enjoy visiting the **Parco Carnè**, the **Grotta Tanacia** and walking along the various footpaths of the **Vena del Gesso**.

This region is also the ideal destination for those who like their tourism "green". For a start there is **Casa Valsenio**, from where you can take different footpaths including the "Lavender Path" and the "Path of Forgotten Fruits". The first one goes from Brisighella to the Santerno Valley and takes you through enchanting countryside resplendent with lily blossoms; the second leads you to the **Rocca di Monte Battaglia**, and owes some of its reputation to the rare and ancient varieties of fruit trees that border it.

It would be a shame not to visit **Comacchio**, one of the most original and fascinating historical centres in the Po delta. This little town has ancient origins which go back to medieval times. Built upon thirteen small islands, the town founded its economic and urban development upon the water surrounding it. Fishing, and with it the culture of its salt marshes, was at once the basis for its wealth and for its periodic declines due to the conflicts that often pitted it against Venice. Comacchio, a town which depends upon its canals, offers visitors a glimpse of a unique style of architecture.

A recipe to try, wines and... a nugget of information

Wines

_ Sangiovese di Romagna
_ Barbera dei Colli Bolognesi
_ Albana
_ Trebbiano
_ Pagadebit

Local specialities

Tortellini, *tagliatelle*, *lasagne*, Parma ham, *mortadella*, Felino sausage, *zamponi* (stuffed pigs' trotters), *cotechini* (sausages), *salama da sugo ferrarese* (cooking sausage), Parmigiano Reggiano (parmesan), *borlengo di Modena* (pancakes), *gnocco fritto bolognese* (fried gnocchi), Brisighella shallots, extra virgin olive oil, balsamic vinegar.

PIADINA

Ingredients

- 500g plain flour
- 50g lard (or 5 tablespoons extra virgin olive oil)
- salt
- pinch of bicarbonate
- warm water

Method

Tip the flour onto your work surface, making it into a mound. Add the lard (or oil) then the salt and bicarbonate. Knead it all together with a little warm water until you have a firm ball of dough. Divide the dough into eight and leave it to rest under a tea-towel for about 30min. Roll out the balls of dough with a rolling pin to form rounds that are 25cm in diameter and 3mm thick. Cook for a few minutes on each side in a pre-heated frying pan. Serve them just as they are, with roast meats, or stuffed with cold meats, fromage frais, chicory or fresh onion, or even (in winter) with cabbage and herbs.

Food for thought

The origins of the *piadina* go back to the 13 BC. The recipe was in fashion in the Middle Ages and during the Renaissance, particularly among peasants who couldn't afford leavened bread. The poet G. Pascoli called it "the bread of the Romagnols". Enriched since then with lard, it can be stuffed with all kinds of fillings.

Our favourite places to eat

TASSI
Viale Repubblica 23 – Bondeno (FE) – Tel. 0532 893030
Closed 1-4 Jan, 23 July-13 Aug, Sun eve and Mon.
Set menu €18-22 – A la carte menu €32-40

Discovering the traditions of the Ferrara region in the Pô valley.
In spite of its modern appearance, Tassi has already celebrated its centenary. It was originally a hostel, with no restaurant. However, after the Second World War the establishment's food began to gain a reputation. To this day, to the immense satisfaction of those with large appetites, "Papa Enzo", uncompromising when it comes to quality produce, continues to propose a wide range of local specialities, from *passatelli* (filled pasta) to risotto, from *slama da sugo* (spicy sausage) to *bolliti* (a kind of stew).

MONTE DONATO
Via Siepelunga 118, Monte Donato Sud: 4 km from Bologna (BO)
Tel. 051 472901
Closed Sun in Jul and Aug and Mon the rest of the year.
A la carte menu €27-42
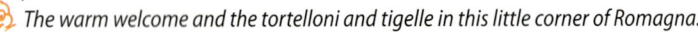
The warm welcome and the tortelloni and tigelle in this little corner of Romagna.
Monte Donato is the ideal destination for a walk in the countryside. The hilltop location affords a splendid view and gives you the impression of being a million miles away from the town. If it's an authentic traditional trattoria you're after, then you won't be disappointed by this convivial restaurant, with its simple check tablecloths and basic place settings. The menu proposes regional specialities which vary according to the season: copious servings of tagliatelles with Bolognese sauce, spinach and ricotta *tortelloni*, shank of pork, tigelle served with *squaquerone* (pancakes with soft white cheese).

PACINI
Via Castello di Montebello 5/6 – Torriana, near Montebello (RN) – Tel. 0541 675410
Closed Jan and Wed (except Jul and Aug).
A la carte menu €21-32
The medieval market town, a mix of local tradition and Apennine influence.
This restaurant has an unbeatable view over the valley of the Marecchia river, and is located in a charming little market town dating from the Renaissance. The atmosphere and service are that of a quintessential regional trattoria, a charming family welcome. The menu includes local cuisine enriched by the influence of the Apennine region: *piadina* (regional pancakes), fresh homemade pasta, a selection of braised meats, and, in season, truffles and *porcini* mushrooms.

EMILIA-ROMAGNA

ALBINEA (RE)

GARDEN VIGANÒ

Sig.ra Spicuglia
Via Garibaldi, 17
42020 Albinea (RE)
Tel. 05 22 34 72 92 - Fax 05 22 34 72 93
info@hotelgardenvigano.it - www.hotelgardenvigano.it

👤👤 77€

Open all year • 5 single rm, 13 double rm, 4 suites • Breakfast €10 • Parking, park, no dogs

 The delightful dining room where breakfast is served.

The winding roads heading up from the plain lead to this haven of tranquillity located within the Fola park. The ancient cypress preceding the entrance heralds the visitor's arrival. Of 18C origin, the building is typical of the local area, an elegant construction in austere brickwork. There are just under 20 rooms of various sizes, all furnished in rustic style and spotlessly clean.

Access: On the outskirts of the village on the road to the hills

EMILIA-ROMAGNA

BESENZONE (PC)

LE COLOMBAIE

Sig.ra Merli
Via Bersano, 29
29010 Besenzone (PC)
Tel. 05 23 83 04 43 – Fax 05 23 83 04 43
lecolombaie@colombaie.it – www.colombaie.it 90-100€

Closed 20 Nov-28 Feb • 2 single rm, 2 double rm, 2 suites • Parking, garden • Bicycles available

 The childlike pleasures of cycling through the countryside.

Imagine an unspoilt village at the heart of the Po plain, in the area between Piacenza and Parma known as Verdi country. From here a dirt track leads through open country to this hotel. Beyond its rose garden, the recently restored building appears, its colourful interior tastefully furnished with contemporary design objects which blend well with the rustic Lombard backdrop. Once a humble stable block with hay barn, it is difficult to believe that such a transformation has taken place here.

Access: On the road to Bersano

EMILIA-ROMAGNA

BUSSETO (PR)

3

I DUE FOSCARI

Sigg. Bergonzi e Morsia
Piazza Carlo Rossi, 15
43011 Busseto (PR)
Tel. 05 24 93 00 31 – Fax 052 49 16 25
info@iduefoscari.it – www.iduefoscari.it

87€

Open all year • 20 double rm • Breakfast €8; half board €77.50 • Parking, garden, no dogs

Menu €33/49

The uniquely majestic dining room.

The ideal place to stay for those looking for something a little different. From the exterior, this unusual establishment looks like a castle, an imposing edifice with stone gateways. On entering the lobby, the overall style becomes clearer: gothic without being dark, making for a curious theatrical effect. Spacious rooms, antique furniture and carefully-sourced fixtures all make this a place well worth a visit.

Access: In the centre of the village

EMILIA-ROMAGNA

CARPINETI (RE)

LE SCUDERIE

Le Scuderie Srl
Via Regigno, 77
42033 Carpineti (RE)
Tel. 05 22 61 83 97 – Fax 05 22 71 80 66

👤👤 **52-55€** ☕

Open all year • 7 double rm • Half board €45 • Parking, garden • Sale of local produce

 Menu €18/25

 The relaxing atmosphere in which to bask after exploring the surrounding area on horseback.

'Paradise lost among the Reggiano Alps' announces the brochure; perhaps an exaggeration but only a slight one. Occupying a fine stone built country house, this establishment is surrounded by unspoilt woodland and fields. There are some fine local landmarks, most notably the castle where in 1077 Matilda of Canossa sheltered Pope Gregory VII during his flight from the wrath of Emperor Henry IV. The restaurant offers classic Emilian cuisine. Those yet to be convinced of the merits of the place may be interested to know that there is also the opportunity to discover the area on horseback.

Access: 2km from the village in San Domino

EMILIA-ROMAGNA

CASTEL D'AIANO (BO)

5

LA FENICE

F.lli Giarandoni
Via Santa Lucia, 29
40040 Castel d'Aiano (BO)
Tel. 051 91 92 72 – Fax 051 91 90 24
lafenice@lafeniceagritur.it – www.lafeniceagritur.it

👤👤80€ ☕

Closed 7 Jan-7 Feb • 14 double rm, 1 suite • Half board €60-80 • Parking, garden, swimming pool, no dogs admitted in restaurant • Guided tours, sale of cured meat and wild fruit

 Menu €23/36

 The stone and woodwork, the open fireplaces and the hidden passageways.

The Giarandoni brothers were pioneers of the agriturismo sector, having opened their doors to guests in the late 1980s. Their experience built up over the years means that this establishment is today one of the best run in the area. It is charmingly situated in a small village of wood and stone construction, surrounded by delightful countryside. The many open fireplaces and hidden passageways linking the different parts of the building give it great character, also evident in the restaurant which specialises in traditional Emilian cuisine.

Access: On the main road to Santa Lucia

EMILIA-ROMAGNA

CASTELFRANCO EMILIA (MO)

6

VILLA GAIDELLO

Sig.ra Bini
Via Gaidello, 18/22
41013 Castelfranco Emilia (MO)
Tel. 059 92 68 06 – Fax 059 92 66 20
info@gaidello.com – www.gaidello.com

👤👤 93€ ☕

Closed Aug • 2 double rm and 7 suites • Parking, garden, no dogs • Bicycles available

 Set Menu €40 and 50

 Life on the plains... at its most authentic.

The open landscape is typical of the local area. Tomato fields surround the historic range of buildings, their interiors providing a welcoming atmosphere for visitors. Accommodation is available in the main house and a second building a little distance away, both of which are well proportioned with period fixtures, wood beamed ceilings and a rustic ambience. The restaurant, serving traditional Emilian cuisine and excellent home made pasta, occupies another building.

Access: On the outskirts of the village

EMILIA-ROMAGNA

CASTENASO (BO)

7

IL LOGHETTO

Sig.ra Mazza
Via Zenzalino Sud, 3/4
40055 Castenaso (BO)
Tel. 05 16 05 22 18 – Fax 05 16 05 22 54
www.illoghetto.it

 95€

Closed Jan, Aug • 3 single rm, 7 double rm • Parking, dogs not admitted • Bicycles available, fishing, sale of jams

 Menu €33/42

 A game of billiards after dinner in the lounge area.

The entrance to this hotel is easily missed, being tucked away in a narrow and busy street. After overcoming this initial hurdle, the visitor can begin to enjoy the charming particularities of this large establishment. The recent extensive renovation has greatly enhanced levels of comfort without detracting from the typically rustic structure. A friendly and helpful family management team, well-proportioned rooms and great attention to detail all serve to make this an attractive place to stay.

Access: Outside the village towards Budrio

EMILIA-ROMAGNA

FERRARA (FE)

B&B CORTE DEI GIOGHI

Sig.ra Tagliavini
Via Pellegrina, 8
44100 Ferrara (FE)
Tel. 05 32 74 50 49 - Fax 05 32 74 50 50
info@cortedeigioghi.com - www.cortedeigioghi.com

👤👤 75-85€

Open all year • 6 double rm, 1 suite • Parking, swimming pool

We most liked: The magnificent wooden beds which give such character to the rooms.

At the entrance to the city, close to the cathedral in the old San Giorgio district, this hotel is reminiscent of a picturesque country residence, with imposing brick walls, dark wooden shutters and an attractive portico which provides welcome shade in the hot summer months. The charming rooms are well proportioned, with beamed ceilings and period furnishings. Breakfast is served in a welcoming, rustic-style dining room, or outside in summer. Ample parking available to guests.

Access: Near the historic village of San Giorgio

EMILIA-ROMAGNA

FERRARA (FE)

9

ALLA CEDRARA
Sig. Marzetti
Via Aranova, 104 località Porotto
44044 Porotto (FE)
Tel. 05 32 59 30 33 – Fax 05 32 77 22 93
info@allacedrara.it – www.allacedrara.it

👤👤 **62-72€**

Open all year • 1 single rm, 3 double rm, 4 suites • Parking, garden, no dogs • Organised trips

 The large open fireplace in the lounge area.

This establishment is approached down a long dirt track, with visitors leaving a trail of dust and the stresses of urban life behind them. Situated only 10km from Ferrara, yet already in the heart of the countryside, this hay barn conversion is surrounded by gardens and parkland with a wide variety of recently planted trees. Bicycles may be borrowed (no charge) to explore the area, and the comfortable rooms guarantee a restful stay.

Access: *In Porotto, 7km from Castello Estense*

EMILIA-ROMAGNA

FERRARA (FE)

LOCANDA CORTE ARCANGELI

Fam. Arcangeli
Via Pontegradella, 503
44030 Ferrara (FE)
Tel. 05 32 70 50 52 – Fax 05 32 75 26 06
info@cortearcangeli.it – www.cortearcangeli.it

 73-85€

Open all year • 5 double rm, 1 suite • Half board €55-65 • Parking, no dogs • Bicycles available, guided tours

 Menu €27/57

 Excursions on the bicycles available to guests.

The Arcangeli family, the owners of this charming farmhouse in the countryside outside Ferrara, have prudently reinvented themselves; these days they provide welcoming hospitality to visitors, offering a cheerful, restful ambience in which to stay. The charming surroundings boast brick vaulted and wood beamed ceilings, and rustic furnishings typical of country residences. The excellent breakfasts are robust, varied and generous.

Access: On the main road from Pontegradela

EMILIA-ROMAGNA

FERRARA (FE)

LOCANDA DELLA LUNA

Sig.ra Anteghini
Via Ravenna 571/5
44100 Ferrara (FE)
Tel. 05 32 71 90 65 – Fax 05 32 71 71 19
info@locandadellaluna.it – www.locandadellaluna.it

82-98€

Open all year • 4 double rm, 2 suites • Parking, swimming pool and garden

 Owl, tree, pond: nature is even present in the names of the rooms.

This establishment is located in a late 19C house, nestling in an immense park planted with oak, magnolia, Lebanese cedar, lime trees and other species, ideal for walking and relaxing. Restored from top to toe according to organic architectural principles, the ground floor of what was originally the main house is now home to four rooms which overlook the garden. Two suites, more modern and functional, have been fitted out by the owner, an architect by trade, with furniture created specially by a cabinetmaker.

Access: At Gaibanella drive for 8km on the main road towards Ravenna

EMILIA-ROMAGNA

FINALE EMILIA (MO)

12

CASA MAGAGNOLI

Sig.ra Magagnoli
Piazza Garibaldi 10
41034 Finale Emilia (MO)
Tel. 05 35 76 00 46 – Fax 053 59 11 35
info@casamagagnoli.com
www.casamagagnoli.com

70-90€

Open all year • 5 single rm, 7 double rm, 1 suite • Parking

 The colour of the bedrooms is perfect for gentle morning awakenings.

Located on the main square of the town, this historic edifice was for a long time the workshop of a famous avant-garde photographer. Today it is home to a suite with a roof terrace that commands a panoramic view, and to rooms and apartments, all of which are pleasant and modern in style and named after doctors, politicians, artists and writers who were among the prominent citizens of Finale Emilia. Organic and fair trade produce takes pride of place on the breakfast table.

Access: In the heart of the village

EMILIA-ROMAGNA

GAZZOLA (PC)

CROARA VECCHIA

Croara Vecchia Società agricola
Località Rivalta Trebbia
29010 Gazzola (PC)
Tel. 33 32 19 38 45 – Fax 05 23 95 76 28
gmilanopc@tin.it – www.croaravecchia.it

 90€

Closed Nov, Dec, Jan, Feb • 1 single rm, 4 double rm • Parking, garden, swimming pool • Horse riding, bicycles available

 The covered riding school, available in all weathers.

It is difficult to imagine how the friars who lived here in the 16C would have felt about this place becoming a rural guesthouse, and plenty of changes have taken place since then. Situated on the banks of the Trebbia and surrounded by gardens, the hotel also has an equestrian centre for horse lovers. The accommodation is furnished with tastefully simple pieces, as is the pleasant breakfast room. The perfect spot for a weekend away from it all.

Access: Around 2km from Rivalta Trebbia at Corara Vecchia on the river bank

EMILIA-ROMAGNA

MALABERGO (BO)

IL CUCCO

Sig.ra Tosatti
Via Nazionale, 83
40051 Altedo (BO)
Tel. 05 16 60 11 24 – Fax 05 16 60 11 24
info@ilcucco.it – www.ilcucco.it

 72-105€

Closed Aug • 3 single rm, 8 double rm • Half board €72 • Parking, garden, no dogs in the restaurant • Bicycles available

 Menu €20/24

 The home-made specialities, available for tasting and purchase.

Heading north from Bologna, this country guesthouse is to be found on the outskirts of Altedo near Malalbergo; visitors must leave the main road and follow a dirt track for several hundred metres prior to reaching their destination, a classic farmhouse surrounded by gardens, vegetable plots and chicken runs. Behind the brick façade is spacious and characterful accommodation with exposed beams, and well equipped bathrooms. The owners prepare the excellent cuisine themselves; the local speciality bread (tigella) is not to be missed.

Access: On the main road through the village

EMILIA-ROMAGNA

MISANO ADRIATICO (RN)

15

LOCANDA I GIRASOLI
Sig. Leardini
Via Cà Rastelli 13, Misano Monte
47843 Misano Adriatico (RN)
Tel. 05 41 61 07 24 – Fax 05 41 61 25 77
info@locandagirasoli.it – www.locandagirasoli.it

👤👤 150€

Open from 1 Mar to 31 Oct • 6 double rm • Parking, swimming pool, tennis court and garden

 Menu €39/50

 The most difficult choice is what to eat!

Fields of cereal crops, vegetables and sunflowers, a garden with century-old pine trees, tennis courts, a swimming pool and a children's play area set the scene for this haven of peace and quiet a few minutes from Ravenna. A country house built in the late 19C, it was transformed in the 1990s into an elegant, rustic-style restaurant whose tables are laid with Romagna and Flemish table linen, where theme tasting evenings are organised. Wood prevails in the attractive bedrooms, in addition to earthenware tiles and bare beams. In summer, treat yourself to a candlelit dinner or a business lunch around the pool.

Access: 5km from the sea, on a hill

EMILIA-ROMAGNA

MONGHIDORO (BO)

16

LA CARTIERA DEI BENANDANTI

Sig.ra Cevemini
Via Idice, 13
40063 Monghidoro (BO)
Tel. 05 16 55 14 98 - Fax 05 1 55 14 98
lacartiera@tin.it – www.lacartiera.it

74-84€

Open all year • 2 single rm, 3 double rm, 2 suites • Half board €58 • Parking, garden • Bicycles available, archery, guided tours, sale of cured meat and cheese

 Set Menu €15 and 23

 A day's mountain biking followed by a hearty meal.

This old mill has been completely rebuilt in stone and its charming appearance belies the newness of its construction. Its light interior has an elegant ambience and high standards of comfort. The cuisine relies heavily on home grown products and the menu focuses on Romagna specialities. Approached by a steep track which winds through much of the establishment's surrounding farmland.

Access: On the banks of the River Idice

EMILIA-ROMAGNA

OSTELLATO (FE)

17

VILLA BELFIORE

Sig.ra Schincaglia
Via Pioppa, 27
44020 Ostellato (FE)
Tel. 05 33 68 11 64 – Fax 05 33 68 11 72
info@villabelfiore.com – www.villabelfiore.com

👤👤 100€

Open all year • 18 double rm • Half board €70-75 • Parking, swimming pool, garden, no dogs

 Set Menu €23 and 28

 The many rugs which provide warmth and decoration throughout.

The tranquillity of the countryside has an ever more elusive quality so in demand from city dwellers, namely silence. Villa Belfiore also offers efficient service, impeccable cleanliness and an orderly ambience. The rustic yet elegant furnishings are stylish, enhancing the public areas and rooms alike. The restaurant serves genuine Romagna cuisine and home made pasta, while the swimming pool is a welcome feature during the summer months.

Access: Outside the village towards the marshy coves

EMILIA-ROMAGNA

PAVULLO NEL FRIGNANO (MO)

VANDELLI

Sig. Vandelli
Via Giardini Sud, 7
41026 Pavullo nel Frignano (MO)
Tel. 053 62 02 88 – Fax 053 62 36 08
info@hotelvandelli.it – www.hotelvandelli.it   65-78€

Open all year • 18 single rm, 18 double rm, 3 suites • Half board €55-68 • Parking, no dogs in the restaurant

 Menu €25/49

 The surprising value for money.

Roughly equidistant from Reggio Emilia, Modena and Bologna, Pavullo is around 700m up among the woods and valleys of the Frignano district, the ideal backdrop for a holiday away from the hustle and bustle of contemporary life. Owned by Signor Vandelli, this hotel is on the town's main street and is distinctive for the quality of its furnishings. The lobby has fine wood panelling, the public areas are spacious and well laid out, and the tastefully decorated rooms have many personal touches.

Access: On the main road through the village

EMILIA-ROMAGNA

PORTICO DI ROMAGNA (FC)

AL VECCHIO CONVENTO

Sig.ra Raffi
Via Roma, 7
47010 Portico di Romagna (FC)
Tel. 05 43 96 70 14 – Fax 05 43 96 71 57
info@vecchioconvento.it – www.vecchioconvento.it   👤👤 73€

Closed 12 Jan-12 Feb • 3 single rm, 12 double rm • Breakfast €8.50; half board €74 • No dogs in the restaurant

 Menu €26/38

 Savouring Romagna specialities beneath the restaurant's imposing stone arches.

The old convent from which this establishment derives its name is barely apparent, having been superseded by a 19C stone palazzo with a well preserved facade and interior with wood and terracotta detail. The impression is one of rustic solidity which is also apparent in the rooms, furnished with late 19C pieces. During the summer months guests can bask in the cool shade of the garden's trees, while in winter the open fireplaces provide warmth and ambience.

Access: In the historic centre

EMILIA-ROMAGNA

REGGIO NELL'EMILIA (RE)

20

DEL VESCOVADO

Sig.ra Bergomi
Stradone Vescovado, 1
42100 Reggio nell'Emilia (RE)
Tel. 05 22 43 01 57 – Fax 05 22 43 01 43
frabergomi@yahoo.com

  85€

Closed Aug • 6 double rm • No dogs

 The sense of being guests rather than clients.

'A home away from home' states the brochure for this B&B, and everything seems presented with this slogan in mind. The rooms are simple, spacious and bright, furnished with period pieces which make for a comfortable family ambience. Breakfast, including home made pastries, can be served in the room or downstairs, and the kitchen is always available for the peckish to fix themselves a snack. Well situated in the city centre, not far from the cathedral which stands out as a masterpiece of Romagna architecture.

Access: In the heart of the village

EMILIA-ROMAGNA

REGGIOLO (RE)

21

VILLA MONTANARINI

Sig. Ferrando
Via Mandelli 29, località Villa Rotta
42046 Reggiolo (RE)
Tel. 05 22 82 00 01 - Fax 05 22 82 03 38
villamontanarini@virgilio.it
www.villamontanarini.com

👤👤 **150€**

Closed from 24 Dec-3 Jan and 5-26 Aug • 7 single rm and 9 double rm • Park, parking, dogs not admitted

 Menu €41/57

 Ancient kiosks and wrought-iron and ceramic tables set the scene for candlelit dining.

This historic nobleman's villa nestles in an immense wood-lined park in the countryside of Reggio Emilia. In the 17C it was sold to the religious community of Guastalla Cathedral and used to accommodate pilgrims who wanted to stop over night. It was then bought by the Montanarini brothers, in exchange for the payment of income tax, and restored. The current comfortable interior is adorned with sumptuous tapestries, Persian carpets and old sofas, and the immense rooms are luxurious. In the pretty dining room you can taste dishes inspired by the region, and also experiment with new aromas and savours.

Access: On the outskirts of the village towards Guastalla

EMILIA-ROMAGNA

SALSOMAGGIORE (PR)

22

ANTICA TORRE

Fam. Pavesi
Cangelasio Case Bussandri, 197
43039 Salsomaggiore Terme (PR)
Tel. 05 24 57 54 25 – Fax 05 24 57 54 25
info@anticatorre.it – www.anticatorre.it

👤👤 80-100€

Closed Dec-Feb • 2 double rm • Half board €60-70 • Parking, garden, swimming pool, no dogs in the restaurant • Bicycles available, archery

Set Menu €20 and 25 for residents only

The ivy clad stonework of the old farmhouse.

Once the hard labour of convicted criminals was employed in this area to turn milling machinery used to grind salt excavated from locally occurring natural deposits. Times have changed and Salsomaggiore is now a quiet town, best known for the curative properties of its thermal springs. The low hills of the surrounding district, given over to farmland and woods populated by hares, pheasants and squirrels, are another good reason to visit, especially if choosing to stay here, a restored stone tower from where the view takes in fields, with distant mountains in one direction, and the rivers of the great plain in the other.

Access: Outside the village, towards the hills

SANTARCANGELO DI ROMAGNA (RN)

LOCANDA ANTICHE MACINE

F.lli Marconi
Via Provinciale Sogliano 1540
47822 Santarcangelo di Romagna (RN)
Tel. 05 41 62 71 61 – Fax 05 41 68 65 62
macine.montalbano@tin.it
www.antichemacine.it

👫 90-110€ ☕

Closed from 7-31 Jan • 2 single rm, 4 double rm, 3 suites • Parking, swimming pool • Bicycles available, sale of oil, wine and jam

 Menu €26/40

 Elegant interior decoration and homemade pastries: tradition meets sophistication.

In the hamlet of Montalbano, where monks in poor health used to come to regain their strength, this delightful country inn is located in an old mansion with a press dating from the 17C, the millstones of which are still visible and explain the establishment's name. Immersed in a pleasant family atmosphere, you can relax and enjoy the elegant well-cared for rooms, decorated with antiques and painted or wrought-iron bedsteads. A creative cuisine which enhances the savours of the land is served in a delightful dining room adorned with bare beams and bricks.

Access: 6km from the village in Montalbano

EMILIA-ROMAGNA

SANTARCANGELO DI ROMAGNA (RN)

24

IL VILLINO
Sig. Bombardieri
Via Ruggeri 48
47822 Santarcangelo di Romagna (RN)
Tel. 05 41 68 59 59 - Fax 05 41 32 62 23
info@hotelilvillino.it - www.hotelilvillino.it

👤👤 100-140€

Open all year • 1 single rm, 11 double rm • Garden, small dogs welcome

 The fountain of Francesca da Rimini: a tribute by Tonino Guerra to the famous lovers.

Surrounded by an immense garden planted with century-old trees and rare plants, this carefully restored 18C mansion is on the edge of the medieval town of Santarcangelo, very close to the exhibition halls of Rimini. The small hotel's atmosphere is full of history: bare bricks and beams, vaulted ceilings, period doors and windows, wrought-iron balconies and a small sitting room, simple yet elegant, perfect for a read or quiet chat. The twelve personalised rooms are graced with furniture from various periods with some elegant suites under the eaves. The owners have even restored the tuff rock caves.

Access: In the village near the medieval centre

EMILIA-ROMAGNA

TERENZO (PR)

25

SELVA SMERALDA

Sig. Raimondi
Località Selva Smeralda
43050 Sivizzano (PR)
Tel. 05 25 52 00 09 – Fax 05 25 52 00 09
www.selvasmeralda.it

👤👤 **70€**

Closed 1 Oct-31 Jan • 5 double rm • Half board €50 • Parking, garden, dogs not admitted in restaurant

 Set Menu €30

 The crenellated tower which dominates the establishment.

In Emilia, it is not unusual to be able to stay in a 14C castle, since the region's turbulent history saw the construction of many fortresses. What distinguishes this one from the rest, however, is its striking watchtower which, after seven centuries, continues to stand guard, impervious to the passage of time. Delightful surrounding scenery and imposing old walls complete the picture. There are also stables for those who wish to follow in the hoofprints of the feudal knights who were once here.

Access: Outside the village of Sivizzano, in Selva Smeralda

EMILIA-ROMAGNA

TORRIANA (RN)

26

IL POVERO DIAVOLO

Sig. Fratti
Via Roma 30
47825 Torriana (RN)
Tel. 05 41 67 50 60 – Fax 05 41 67 56 80
povero.diavolo@libero.it
www.ristorantepoverodiavolo.com

 90€

Closed from 28 May-15 Jun and 15-25 Sep • 4 double rm

 Menu €45/60

 Simple yet sophisticated: food and poetry reign over the well room.

At the foot of the impressive Scorticata rock, this handsome early 20C building is home to kitchens which do full justice to the flavours and scents of Montefeltro. A pleasant atmosphere pervades the attractive dining room adorned with a large fireplace, where you will be served dishes that respect the seasons and the land: stone ground flour in the last remaining watermill of Val Pareccchia and locally produced honey. What's more, the five welcoming but low-key rooms are ideal for quiet meditation or reading and a gentle awakening in this sleepy town.

Access: Near the castle

EMILIA-ROMAGNA

VERUCCHIO (RN)

27

LE CASE ROSSE

Sig.ra Savazzi
Via Tenuta Amalia, 141
47826 Verucchio (RN)
Tel. 05 41 67 8133 – Fax 05 41 67 88 76
info@tenutaamalia.com – www.tenutaamalia.com

 80€

Open all year • 1 single rm, 6 double rm • Parking, garden, golf • Wine for sale

 A residence fit for a queen in the heart of the Romagna countryside.

According to legend, this red walled farmhouse set among open fields was visited in the 18C by Caroline of Brunswick, wife of the future British king George IV. Restored in the 19C by the opera singer wife of a politician, this charming residence has subsequently become a pleasant country guesthouse. The ample breakfast of home grown products served here is very much in the rural tradition. Activities include exploring the local area on horseback or excursions to the nearby jewels of artistic heritage, Ravenna and Urbino.

Access: In the vicinity of Villa Verucchio hamlet

Friuli Venezia Giulia

Friuli Venezia Giulia is a frontier region which defies easy categorising. Once the via Postimia passed through here on its way to the eastern provinces of the Roman Empire. Traces from this era remain, like the mosaics at Aquileia and the early Christian churches at Grado, alongside evidence of later epochs and waves of invasion; the great Lombard works of art at Cividale, Venice's domination during the Renaissance period as evidenced by the fortifications of Palmanova, and the central European cosmopolitan feel of Trieste, the great port of the Austro-Hungarian empire. This quality of variety is not specific to the art and architecture; the geography is also disparate, ranging from the snow capped peaks of the Carniche Alps, through gradually softening hills and down into the farmlands of the plain, irrigated by rivers winding towards the Adriatic. The region's excellent cuisine includes fish, filled pasta shapes *(agnolotti)*, San Daniele ham and mountain cheeses, best enjoyed with a glass of Tocai or Picolit.

7 establishments

Recommended sites and circuits
Friuli Venezia Giulia

> The magic of this region can be felt in the elegant and reserved atmosphere, in the nostalgia and melancholy of its towns. The sharp contrasts of landscape are constantly surprising and the Adriatic Sea, which laps against the coastline of the region, seems to flow right to the heart of Europe and there draw on Latin, Germanic and Slavic influences. This is where East meets West.

Trieste is a surprising city, with a unique atmosphere made up of different kinds of art, impressions and flavours that change depending on where you are in the city. The city's atmosphere and poetry, which recall Central Europe (and memories of bygone eras), mingle with expectations of a future that seems to hesitate at the threshold. Trieste is a city unlike any other in Europe, with its superb Neo-classical palaces that are understated yet somewhat austere. It is only by walking through its streets, or by lingering in its alleyways and squares, that you can really get to know it and begin to understand that strange quality, omnipresent and "tormented", as the poet Umberto Saba put it, that makes it so alive.

Udine is well worth visiting. There is much to admire in the squares, the Loggia del Lionello, the clock tower and the Tiepolo frescoes (at the Palazzo Archivescovile). From the panoramic viewpoint at the top of the castle you can look out over the roofs of the city, the surrounding mountains, and the whole of Friuli. In this city built on a very human scale, art isn't made to be looked at; it lives. Let your imagination run free while walking through its little streets, as at each corner you encounter a magnificent palace, an old house or another romantic view. Be sure to make the most of the renowned historical cafés and of course the many osterias where you can order a *tajut*, the traditional Tocai drink.

Another stop not to be missed is the village of **Bordano**, also known as "butterfly village" because of the hundreds of painted wall murals depicting these magnificent insects.

In **Gorizia**, you can immerse yourself in history – from the majestic Castello dei Conti to the Baroque churches, the Museum of the Great War and the rather retro restaurants. This is the ideal place to forget all about the passage of time and enjoy the moment. Gorizia, once known as the "Austrian Nice" due to its temperate climate in all seasons, also boasts some splendid parks.

A recipe to try, wines and... a nugget of information

Wines

_Tocai
_Ribolla gialla
_Malvasia istriana
_Picolit
_Verduzzo friulano
_Refosco dal peduncolo rosso
_Schiopettino
_Terrano
_Pignolo
_Tazzelenghe

Ingredients
- 500g cornflour
- 80g butter
- grated cheese (mature *montasio* or *carnico*)
- milk
- salt

Local specialities

Rice, barley, sauerkraut, turnips, (very dense) polenta, San Daniele ham, *tabor* (cheese), smoked ham from Sauris, *pitina del pordenonese* (flavoured cold meats), Carnia green beans, raw ham from Karst, *montasio* (cheese), *grappa*, *gubana* (a cake filled with dried and candied fruits which have been marinated in liqueur), fried and sweetened polenta, *castagnole* (small doughnuts).

POLENTA CONCIA

Method
Bring about two litres of salted water to boil. As soon as it starts to boil, pour in the flour and mix well, getting rid of any lumps. Cook the mixture for about an hour, stirring all the while. Once it is cooked, spread a layer of the polenta in the bottom of a dish, then scatter grated cheese over it, add a little milk and melted butter and repeat the layering until the ingredients run out. Allow to stand for a few minutes before serving.

Food for thought
Frico, a kind of flat bread roll enriched with potato and other ingredients, was prepared by women before going out to the fields; they would leave a small frying pan with cheese rinds on the embers of the fire.

Our favourite places to eat

AL CASTELLO
Via San Bartolomeo 18 – Fagagna (UD) – Tel. 0432 800185
Closed 12-31 Jan and Mon.
À la carte menu €27-36
 The large interior courtyard with its decorative plants.

Adjoining the imposing castle that gives it its name, this restaurant has retained some elements of the former 18C farmhouse in which it is housed. Three small rooms with exposed beams provide an elegant decor. On the first floor, in a more rustic room initially used for wine-tasting, you can delight your taste buds by choosing from a range of traditional specialities and more innovative options, such as the famous local raw ham, the regional gnocchi carnici, melon in aspic and pasta stuffed with pigeon.

LOCANDA MARIO
Draga Sant'Elia 22 – Pesek, (Draga Sant'Elia) – (TS) – Tel. 040 228193
Closed Tue.
À la carte menu €27-42
 Discovering the spirit and cuisine of the Carso region.

It's no easy task to find this isolated restaurant situated right next to the Slovenian border. Fortunately, the owners are at your service before you even get there and will provide invaluable instructions. Beyond the bar area are the restaurant's bright and spacious rooms, which exude a pleasantly rustic and old-fashioned atmosphere. The menu is equally loyal to the Carso region's traditions: cold meats, barley soup, frogs' legs, snails, mushrooms and game are just some of the excellent reasons for making a stop here.

VECCHIA OSTERIA CIMENTI
Via Cesare Battisti 1 – Villa Santina (UD) – Tel. 0433 750491
Closed Mon.
À la carte menu €29-44
 The typical regional atmosphere: a chance to get acquainted with the Carnia dialect.

The warm welcome and convivial atmosphere provide the ideal setting in which to sample gastronomic delights that pay homage to the traditions and produce of the Carnia region. This love for the region is apparent in the menu, and some grounding in the local dialect would help you in deciphering it; but the owners will willingly help you out. No need for translation when it comes to enjoying the dishes, however: smoked trout, *tortelli di patate* (pasta filled with potato), the famous *cjarsons* (large ravioli with sweet or savoury fillings), roast meats, and, for those with a sweet tooth, mousses, bavarois and tarts.

FRIULI VENEZIA GIULIA

DOLEGNA DEL COLLIO (GO)

VENICA E VENICA - CASA VINO E VACANZE

Sig. Venica
Località Cerò, 8
34070 Dolegna del Collio (GO)
Tel. 048 16 01 77 - Fax 04 81 63 99 06
venica@venica.it - www.venica.it

85-95€

Closed 1 Nov-31 Mar • 6 double rm • Breakfast €14 • Parking, garden, swimming pool, tennis, no dogs • Wine for sale

The huge beam supporting the ceiling in the lounge area.

Since 1929, the Venica family has been involved in winemaking. Their property covers the slopes of four hillsides, and walking, cycling, tennis and swimming are all available. Authentic hospitality enhance the simple, rustic-style farm accommodation comprising plain yet welcoming rooms, plus a pleasant lounge area with tiled floors, rugs, plenty of woodwork in evidence, and a fine open fireplace.

Access: Near the church, follow the signs for Mernicco

FRIULI VENEZIA GIULIA

MEDEA (GO)

2

KOGOJ

Fam. Kogoj
Via Zorutti, 10
34076 Medea (GO)
Tel. 048 16 74 40 – Fax 048 16 74 40
kogoj@kogoj.it – www.kogoj.it

👤👤80€

Closed 7-30 Sep • 1 single rm, 4 double rm • Parking, swimming pool, small dogs welcome

 The warmth and hospitality of the owners.

This long established winemaking operation only opened its doors as a country guesthouse at the end of the last decade. Since then, the sensitively restored hay barn has provided accommodation in the shape of five comfortable, elegant and welcoming rooms. The property is surrounded by a pleasant garden, beyond which are the attractive vineyards which merit a closer look. The excellent breakfast includes many home made products.

Access: On the outskirts

FRIULI VENEZIA GIULIA

MUGGIA (TS)

TAVERNA FAMIGLIA CIGUI

Sig. Cigui
Via Colarich 92/D
34015 Muggia (TS)
Tel. 040 27 33 63 – Fax 04 09 27 92 24
pcigui@tiscali.it – www.tavernacigui.it

80-90€

Closed 1-15 Jan • 3 single rm, 3 double rm • Parking, garden

 Menu €30/40

 Homemade oil and wine, on the hillsides reflected in the gulf.

Deep in the green hillsides of Santa Barbara beyond Muggia, this taverna is surrounded by the vineyards of Malvasia. The generously proportioned premises are run by the enthusiastic Cigui family, who make it a point of honour to mix land and sea produce in their carefully prepared cuisine. The small hotel next door has six equally attractive and comfortable rooms. The vast menu based on carefully selected homemade produce is, however, what guests probably remember most. Fish, gnocchi and an impressive choice of desserts; whatever you do, don't miss the apple or nut strudel!

Access: 3km from Santa Barbara, in the hills

FRIULI VENEZIA GIULIA

SANTA MARIA LA LONGA (UD)

VILLA DI TISSANO

 Sig. Christoph
Piazza Caimo 4
33050 Santa Maria La Longa (UD)
Tel. 04 32 99 03 99 - Fax 04 32 99 04 35
info@villaditissano.it

👤👤 80-160€

Closed 16 Nov-14 Dec and 6 Jan-14 Mar • 1 single rm, 22 double rm • Parking, garden, swimming pool

 Menu €25/31

 The tower, barn, greenhouses and attendant's house set the scene for this splendid abode.

This former aristocratic residence, whose immaculate façade and interior have been restored and expanded countless times, comes complete with stucco ornamentation inside, small courtyards and superb gardens. Part of the villa is now a hotel-restaurant that invites guests to relax and savour the charm of country life from a former era. The modern functional rooms are located in authentic settings and furnished rustically. The former main kitchen, the inn hall, the attendant's kitchen and the baroque dining room offer guests the chance to enjoy an intimate romantic dinner and to taste local culinary traditions.

Access: After 4km at Tissano, head towards Udine

FRIULI VENEZIA GIULIA

SAURIS (UD)

SCHNEIDER

Futura & C. Sas
Via Sauris di Sotto, 92
33020 Sauris (UD)
Tel. 043 38 62 20 – Fax 04 33 86 63 10
futurasauris@libero.it

65-70€

Closed 7-28 Jun, 8-22 Nov • 1 single rm, 7 double rm • Half board €52 • Parking, small dogs welcome

Set Menu €23 and 36 for residents only

The view of the village; traditional buildings surrounded by meadows.

The mountains here have always been a border country between two cultures, and this is evident in Sauris, located in the Carnia district, where the local dialect is of German derivation. For two centuries, the Schneider family have run the Alla Pace inn, next to which a new building has been erected providing eight comfortable and spacious rooms. This is an ideal base from which to explore the local mountain scenery, including Lake Sauris.

Access: Outside the village in the direction of Tolmezzo

FRIULI VENEZIA GIULIA

TARVISIO (UD)

6

EDELHOF
De Meis Enrico Sas
Via Diaz, 13
33018 Tarvisio (UD)
Tel. 04 28 64 40 25 – Fax 04 28 64 47 35
info@hoteledelhof.it – www.hoteledelhof.it

🧍🧒 90€ ☕

Open all year • 15 double rm, 1 suite • Half board €65 • Parking, garden

Menu €27/43

 The warm ambience of the traditional stube.

Having been completely restored in keeping with the alpine gothic style once prevalent in the region, this hotel has an unusual quality. Particular care has been taken with the rooms, each of which has its own individual feel and decor. A splendid tiled open fireplace in the bar and the stube style dining room add to the mountain ambience.

Access: On the way into the village

FRIULI VENEZIA GIULIA

VIVARO (PN)

7

GELINDO DEI MAGREDI

Sig. Trevisanutto
Via Roma, 16
33099 Vivaro (PN)
Tel. 33 57 17 08 05 – Fax 042 79 75 15
info@gelindo.it – www.gelindo.it

70-85€

Open all year • 1 single rm, 9 double rm • Half board €60-70 • Parking, garden, no dogs • Horse riding, organised trips, archery, apple juice and wine for sale

 Menu €24/35

 The Magredi plateau; beautiful riding country in the shadow of the Dolomites.

Riders of all levels of proficiency should make for this rural guesthouse which combines equestrian facilities with a delightful location. Lying at the foot of the Friuli Dolomites, the Magredi is a rich alluvial plateau furrowed by numerous rivers. This establishment offers simple yet well presented accommodation and a family atmosphere. The polenta cutter appearing on the restaurant sign indicates that the emphasis here is on local cuisine. Also worth a visit is the small museum of rural and farm life, perhaps in the company of the friendly proprietor.

Access: Outside the village, head towards Spilimbergo

Lazio

"Est! Est! Est!", not the battle cry of the emperor Trajan setting forth to conquer new oriental provinces for Rome, but the name of a traditional local wine. 'Traditional' applies across the board in these parts and the visitor is met with the sight of important architectural remains at every turn; ancient monuments, Etruscan necropolises such as those at Tarquinia and Cerveteri, Roman roads impervious to the passage of time which continue to lead to the heart of the Empire. Situated on its famous hills between the Apennines and the sea, Rome stands as custodian of the history and spirit of the western world. Imperial splendour, medieval decadence, the Renaissance and Baroque periods; all have left their mark in the open-air museum that is the city of Rome. Richly decorated patrician palaces, ruined baths, temples and mausoleums come together to create a unique ambience of cultural heritage. A visit to the capital should not be missed, but neither should the other delights of Lazio; its peaceful countryside, the Tyrrhenian coast, the Roman castles by the volcanic lakes, all perfect settings in which to seek tranquillity against a historical backdrop.

18 establishments

Recommended sites and circuits
Lazio

> A rich and varied landscape of mountains and beaches, pine forests and hillsides, where the silence gives way to the echo of a legendary past. The renown of the place has dominated the history of humanity for centuries. Rome, the "Eternal City", is not only the capital of Italy, but the symbol of a powerful and glorious past.

Frascati, a town renowned for its wine and good food, is one of the favourite getaways for Romans. The historical and cultural wealth of this magnificent town overlooking the Roman countryside leaves visitors enchanted. In the past, the region's most eminent families used to holiday here, building sumptuous villas, some of which are veritable architectural masterpieces. Villa Aldobrandini, also known as Belvedere because of its panorama, is one of the most beautiful and important, graced by numerous works by the best Renaissance and Baroque artists and architects (frescoes, paintings, sculptures, gardens, caves, terraces and fountains with wonderful water games).

Tivoli, also steeped in mystery, has a timeless appeal intensified by the splendour of the setting overlooking the Roman countryside. The fascinating Villa d'Este, famous for its Italian garden, was built in the mid 16C for the rich and powerful Cardinal Ippolito d'Este. It was constructed on the remains of a Roman villa and its grounds boast hundreds of fountains, including the famous Fontana dell'Organa that plays music when its mechanism is activated by the pressure of the water.

Villa Adriana is another residence laden with history. Legend has it that the Emperor wanted all palaces, theatres and thermal baths to remind him, thanks to their shapes and names, of the places he had admired during his travels in Greece and the Orient, "the marble equivalent of the tents of Oriental princes". Each stone represents a particular wish, a memory, each atmosphere is a dream materialised. Let your imagination transport you back to the ancient splendour of those bygone days.

Ostia Antica is another site that seems to be suspended in time. To visit it is to be projected into the daily life of ancient Romans, immersed in the relaxing atmosphere, far from the frenzy of city life. Known as Rome's "Little Pompei", it was at the time the region's most important port. Today, beneath the Mediterranean pines, lie the vestiges of the roads, houses, taverns and temples that made this city one of the most important in the Empire.

A recipe to try, wines and... a nugget of information

Wines

_Frascati
_Marino
_Colli Albani
_Colli Lanuvini
_Cerveteri
_Velletri
_Aleatico di Gradoli
(liqueur)

Ingredients

- 8 veal escalopes
- 8 sage leaves
- 4 slices of raw prosciutto ham (not too thin)
- 50g butter
- ½ glass dry white wine
- salt

Local specialities

Guanciale (pig cheeks, the main ingredient of *pasta all'amatriciana*), *mortadella di Amatrice*, Roman mortadella, *pajata* (made from ox, lamb or veal calf intestines), *abbacchio* (baby lamb), *mezzancolle* (king prawns), Roman-style artichokes, wild asparagus and cheeses: pecorino, ricotta romana and caciotta.

SALTIMBOCCA ALLA ROMANA

Method

Flatten out the meat with a utensil to make it more tender; place half a slice of ham and a sage leaf in the centre of each escalope and fix them with a cocktail stick. In a large frying pan, melt the butter and fry the *saltimboccas*, ensuring that they become golden on both sides. Season as required, drizzle with wine and continue cooking for 5min.

Food for thought

Pasta alla matriciana or pasta all'amatriciana? The difference is not a question of grammar, but a veritable secular diatribe that divides Roman cooking. Of the two versions, the first is the original Roman recipe, while the second comes from Abruzzo.
The recipe that contains tomato sauce and onion is the real Roman "matriciana", the word deriving from the words *matari*, the goatskins in which tomatoes were kept in the past and *matriciale*, a typical aromatic plant. As for the Abruzzo recipe, it contains neither tomatoes nor onions.

Our favourite places to eat

LA VECCHIA MOLA
Via Vicinale Piè del Monte Fumone, 3 km south of Fumone (FR)
Tel. 0775 49771
Closed Sun eve, Mon, and Tue-Sat lunchtime.
A la carte menu €28-43

 The discreet sophistication and attentive service.

A winding road near the mountains brings you to "La Vecchia Mola", one of the best fish restaurants in the area. A warm atmosphere reigns in the small but pleasant dining area, which, with its beamed ceiling, is reminiscent of a chalet. Guests are treated to exceptionally attentive service and innovative cuisine consisting of imaginative seafood dishes painstakingly prepared with top-quality produce.

BISTROT
Piazza San Rufo 25 – Rieti (RI) – Tel. 0746 498798
Closed 20 Oct-15 Nov, Sun and Mon lunchtime.
A la carte menu €31-40

 The intriguing decor: the passion for fashion and the memory of bygone encounters.

This restaurant located on a small square on the edge of the pedestrian street known as the "struscio" utilises every nook and cranny of its two rooms. The rows of tables go right up to the entrance and decorative objects abound: wines, certificates, books and paintings, to name but a few. The sociable and charismatic owner has a friendly word for regulars and first-timers alike. This same creative and attentive sparkle is present in the food, a mix of local specialities and inventive dishes.

GIUDA BALLERINO
Via Marco Valerio Corvo 135 – Rome, SE urban area (RM)
Tel. 06 71584807
Closed Aug, Wed, and Mon-Thurs. lunchtime.
A la carte menu €44-55

 The opportunity to meet comic strip enthusiasts, artists and writers.

This restaurant near Cinecittà (which may prove hard to find for the uninitiated) has an unelaborate interior, with tightly packed tables and a decor revealing a penchant for comic strips. The food is the undisputed star here. The carefully prepared dishes show great creativity and ingenuity. The chef uses select products and such innovative combinations as celery jelly, coffee sauce, and goose bologna with juniper-flavoured potatoes. At the end of the meal you can choose from a selection of cigars and liqueurs.

LAZIO

BAGNOREGIO (VT)

ROMANTICA PUCCI

Sig.ra Perno
Piazza Cavour, 1
01022 Bagnoregio (VT)
Tel. 07 61 79 21 21
hotelromanticapucci@libero.it
www.hotelromanticapucci.it

👫 80€ ☕

Open all year • 8 double rm • Parking

Menu €20/38

The tasteful choice of furnishings throughout.

Located in the historic heart of Bagnoregio, this small hotel was opened a few years ago by a couple previously in the fashion business. The care with which its five rooms have been decorated is apparent, each one having its own distinctive style. Antique furniture and wrought iron or wooden four poster beds set the tone. Equally attractive are the formal dining room and the breakfast room in an internal covered courtyard. Pets welcome and catered for.

Access: In the heart of the village

LAZIO

CANINO (VT)

CERROSUGHERO

Sig. Tarantino
Località Cerro Sughero
01011 Canino (VT)
Tel. 07 61 43 72 42 – Fax 07 61 43 81 55
info@cerrosughero.com – www.cerrosughero.com

👤👥 65-75€

Open all year • 12 double rm • Half board €50-58 • Parking, garden, swimming pool, dogs not admitted • Bicycles available, guided tours and sale of honey and oil

 Menu €21/34

 The home-produced olive oil, the ideal culinary souvenir for friends and family.

Three hundred metres up in the Maremma district on the Tuscany Lazio border, this 210 hectare estate of woodland, pasture and olive groves provides agriturismo facilities in the shape of four farmhouses. The main property has a large, attractive lounge area and a restaurant with characteristic sloping roof. Accommodation takes up the other three buildings; the rooms are spacious and the suites have charming open fireplaces. Families and groups can stay in apartments with kitchen facilities. Guests are free to explore the 10km of footpaths around the property, or they might prefer to lounge by the swimming pool.

Access: Outside the centre, near the main road

LAZIO

CASPERIA (RI)

LA TORRETTA

Sig. Scheda
Via Mazzini, 7
02041 Casperia (RI)
Tel. 076 56 32 02 – Fax 076 56 32 02
latorretta@tiscalinet.it – www.latorrettabandb.com

👤👤 **75-85€**

Open all year • 1 single rm, 6 double rm • Small dogs welcome

 The beauty of the place, which takes the visitor by surprise on arrival.

A winning combination of an English wife, bringing with her the knack of creating a welcoming family atmosphere, and an Italian husband, whose training as an engineer has ensured a very successful restoration (during which original frescoes were uncovered) of this 15C aristocratic residence. Located at the top end of the village, there are fine views from the terrace and from the rooms, which are tastefully decorated in a manner which, if not luxurious, certainly marks them out as being somewhat special.

Access: In the historic centre in a pedestrian zone

LAZIO

CIVITA CASTELLANA (VT)

RELAIS FALISCO

 Finceram S.r.l./Sogear Srl
Via Don Minzoni 19
01033 Viterbo (VT)
Tel. 07 61 54 98 – Fax 07 61 59 84 32
relaisfalisco@relaisfalisco.it –
www.relaisfalisco.it

140-150€

Open all year • 7 single rm, 29 double rm, 6 suites • Parking, dogs not admitted

 Menu €39/47

 The refreshing flower-decked garden and 18C fountain.

The town of Civita Castellana rises out of a steeply sloped plain of tuff rock. This elegant 17C palace, in the heart of the historic town, a few metres from the Duomo dei Cosmati and the Forte Sangallo, has perfected the art of hospitality. Guests cannot fail to be won over by its rich historic legacy and distinctive atmosphere. The simply decorated rooms are furnished in attractive dark wooden pieces. The former storerooms on the first floor of the palace have been turned into three conference rooms. The cellars are now a fitness room, while the sauna and hydromassage pool are located in the Etruscan cave.

Access: In the centre of the village

LAZIO

GROTTE DI CASTRO (VT)

5

CASTELLO DI SANTA CRISTINA

Sig. Mancini Caterini
Località Santa Cristina
01025 Grotte di Castro (VT)
Tel. 076 37 80 11 – Fax 076 37 80 11
info@santacristina.it – www.santacristina.it

130€

Closed 15 Jan-28 Feb • 14 double rm • Breakfast €5 • Parking, swimming pool, tennis court, dogs not admitted • Horse riding, guided tours, bicycles available

 A relaxing stay in a former cardinal's residence.

The medieval castle of Santa Cristina, home to a series of famous religious figures such as Cardinal Prospero Caterini, advisor to Pope Pius IX, rises between Monte Amiata and Lake Bolsena in the heart of the Alta Tuscia plateau near the Grotte di Castro. A few yards from the fortress are the 17C outbuildings that are now home to comfortable apartments and welcoming bedrooms decorated with antique furniture. On the ground floor guests have the run of a spacious taverna where they can play billiards or table tennis. Tennis courts, bicycles, horseriding and a swimming pool are some of the outdoor activities available in the lush green estate.

Access: On the road to Pitigliano and the castle of the same name

LAZIO

MONTEFIASCONE (VT)

6

URBANO V

Sig. Cappannella
Corso Cavour, 107
01027 Montefiascone (VT)
Tel. 07 61 83 10 94 – Fax 07 61 83 41 52
info@hotelurbano-v.it – www.hotelurbano-v.it

👫 **80-100€**

Open all year • 4 single rm, 17 double rm, 1 suite • No dogs

 We most liked The imposing stone vaulting over the entrance.

Laid out around a charming inner courtyard, this restored 17C palazzo is conveniently located in the centre of town. Beyond the impressive doorway there is an interesting old well, bearing witness to the building's rich history, but the real joy of this place is its terrace, providing all round views over the city and out towards the hills and lake Bolsena; the ideal spot to enjoy a bottle of Est! Est!! Est!!!, the well known local wine. The elegant rooms are classically decorated with period furniture and matching fabrics.

Access: In the centre of the village

LAZIO

ORTE (VT)

LA LOCANDA DELLA CHIOCCIOLA

Sig. De Fonseca
Località Seripola
01028 Orte (VT)
Tel. 07 6140 27 34 – Fax 07 6149 02 54
info@lachiocciola.net – www.lachiocciola.net

110-130€

Closed from 15 Nov-28 Feb • 8 double rm • Parking, garden, swimming pool, dogs not admitted

 Set Menu €27 and 32

We most liked: The buffets in the shade of the old oak tree and the modern wellness facilities.

Guests are welcomed to a 15C farmhouse made out of stone and tuff and the old peasant's house next door, both of which are set in an immense garden in the heart of Umbria. The eight personalised rooms are graced with period furniture made by craftsmen, and some boast wrought-iron four-poster beds. The dining room does full justice to its enormous 17C fireplace, which creates a warm, welcoming atmosphere for meals featuring good plain cooking in keeping with local traditions. Breakfasts, composed of cakes, homemade desserts, cheese, cured meat and dried fruits, are served in the veranda which commands a panoramic view of the hillsides.

Access: Outside the village towards Amelia

LAZIO

PICINISCO (FR)

8

VILLA IL NOCE

Sig.ra Ponzi
Via Antica, 1
03040 Picinisco (FR)
Tel. 077 66 62 59 – Fax 077 66 62 59
villailnoce@email.it – www.villailnoce.com

👤👤 80€

Open all year • 4 double rm • Parking, garden, swimming pool, tennis, no dogs

We most liked — The friendly and welcoming ambience prevailing throughout.

Uniquely situated at the head of a valley composed of wooded hillsides and picturesque farmland, this flower bedecked little villa has four rooms ideal for those in quest of the authentic B&B experience. Inside, care has been taken with the decor and the emphasis is on comfort, while outdoors guests can enjoy the garden and swimming pool. The surrounding countryside is the perfect backdrop for gentle strolls, vigorous walks, cycling and fishing.

Access: Outside the village on the road to Borgo Costellone

RIETI (RI)

PARK HOTEL VILLA POTENZIANI

Edolo Srl
Via San Mauro 6
02100 Rieti (RI)
Tel. 07 46 20 27 65 – Fax 07 46 25 79 24
info@villapotenziani.it – www.villapotenziani.it   **130€**

Open all year • 26 double rm, 1 suite • Half-board €90 • Parking, park, swimming pool, tennis court

Menu €35/53

The impressive steps that lead to the woods full of natural beauty.

Villa Potenziani, built on the summit of the hill of San Maura in the 18C, was the hunting lodge of the family of the same name in the early 20C. Surrounded by an immense garden, frescoes, ornamentation, decorative features and stucco work grace the interior of the opulent abode, also home to cosy bedrooms enhanced with carefully chosen period or antique furniture and equipped with handsome marble bathrooms. Regional cuisine takes pride of place in the restaurant which is located in the largest room of the edifice, a richly decorated "reception hall" with an intricately carved wooden ceiling and immense fireplace.

Access: On a hill near the city ramparts

LAZIO

ROMA (RM)

10

ANNE & MARY

Sig.ra Moroni
Via Cavour 325
00184 Roma
Tel. 06 69 94 11 87 – Fax 066 78 06 29
info@anne-mary.com – www.anne-mary.com

👤👤 **120-130€**

Open all year • 6 double rm • Small dogs welcome

 A warm welcome and graceful hospitality in a setting worthy of the Roman Empire.

The "Anne and Mary" guesthouse is located on the first floor of an elegant 19C palace, two minutes from the Coliseum and in the vicinity of countless historic and artistic sites, without forgetting the shops of some of Italy's top fashion designers. This establishment features welcoming functional rooms fitted out with taste and graced with warm wooden furniture, to ensure that you make the most of your stay in the capital. The management organises excursions around the town, and throughout Italy, as well as guided tours of the museums and main cultural and leisure activities sites.

Access: In the historic centre of Foro Romano - Colosseo

LAZIO

ROMA (RM)

A CASA DI SERENA

Sig.ra Mencarelli
Circonvallazione Trionfale, 1 - Int. 4
00195 Roma (RM)
Tel. 06 39 73 55 70 – Fax 06 68 80 55 86
serena@ilbedandbreakfastaroma.com
www.ilbedandbreakfastaroma.com

 80-120€

Open all year • 3 double rm • Dogs not admitted

 The nocturnal peace and quiet for sweet slumbers.

Within easy reach of San Pietro Basilica, the third floor of this edifice is home to a simple, elegant guesthouse that offers three peaceful rooms overlooking inner courtyards. All have a roomy balcony and are well looked after and decorated with "arte povera" furniture, matching fabrics and lithographies on the walls. Unlike other establishments of the same ilk, Casa di Serena also boasts a lovely spacious beautifully decorated sitting room.

Access: Near the Vatican Museum, at the beginning of viale Medaglie d'Oro

LAZIO

ROMA (RM)

12

58 LE REAL DE LUXE

Sig.ra Cortellesia
Via Cavour, 58
00184 Roma (RM)
Tel. 064 82 35 66 – Fax 064 82 35 66
info@58viacavour.it
www.bed-and-breakfast-rome.com

👤👤 70-125€

Open all year • 7 double rm • No dogs

 The convenient location coupled with the quality of the accommodation.

Via Cavour is one of central Rome's main thoroughfares, linking Via dei Fori to Termini station and passing close to the Colosseum and Santa Maria Maggiore, one of the city's four basilicas. On a nearby street corner stands a typical late 19C patrician residence; occupying its fourth floor, this establishment offers well presented, spacious and comfortable accommodation which is more akin to a hotel than a B&B. The ideal spot for those in quest of a simple and welcoming place to stay in the heart of Rome.

Access: Near Termini railway station

SAN DONATO VAL DI COMINO (FR)

13

VILLA GRANCASSA

Sig.ra Di Fazio
Via Roma 8
03046 San Donato Val di Comino (FR)
Tel. 07 76 50 89 15 – Fax 07 76 50 89 14
info@villagrancassa.it – www.villagrancassa.it

👤👤 **100€**

Open all year • 3 single rm, 23 double rm • Half-board €75 • Parking, park, tennis court

 **Menu €18/31**

 The impressive stone staircase that leads upstairs.

Built in the 17C according to the instructions of the priest Francesco Nardone and artistocrat Felice Grancassa, the villa is an historic edifice with richly decorated rooms. To enter, guests pass under a beautifully carved gateway, the work of San Donato artists. Some ten years ago, the villa was turned into a luxury hotel with splendid rooms, some of which command views over the garden and valley. Guests have the run of an attractive sitting room where they can leaf through one of the library's books or take a seat and play board games. In the refined dining room, you will be treated to a selection of typical dishes, historic menus and unusual flavours.

Access: In the heart of the village

LAZIO

SERMONETA (LT)

14

PRINCIPE SERRONE

Sig. Cacciotti
Via del Serrone, 1
04010 Sermoneta (LT)
Tel. 077 33 03 42 - Fax 077 33 03 36
principeserrone@virgilio.it
www.hotelprincipeserrone.it

👤👤 75-90€

Open all year • 6 single rm, 11 double rm • No dogs

 The timeless quality of the old buildings.

In the oldest quarter of the medieval village of Sermoneta, close to the imposing Caetani castle, an alley opens up between two houses, a connecting passageway running above it. This heralds the entrance to the Principe Serrone, as if from the pages of a historical novel. Built entirely of stone, with a decorative frieze embellishing the first floor, it has been carefully refurbished inside without detracting from its authenticity. Its rooms and corridors, with wood panelled or cross vaulted ceilings, give the visitor the impression of having travelled back in time.

Access: In the heart of the medieval town

TARQUINIA (VT)

15

PEGASO PALACE HOTEL

Sig.. Franci
Viale Martano a Marina Velca
01016 Tarquinia (VT)
Tel. 07 66 81 00 27 - Fax 07 66 81 07 49
info@hpegaso.it - www.hpegaso.it

80-100€

Open all year • 24 single rm, 24 double rm • Half board €80 • Parking, swimming pool, garden, beach, no dogs

 Menu €24/35

 The peaceful setting by the sea.

Not far from Tarquinia and the motorway, this modern establishment is strongly Mediterranean in style. The luminous colours employed on the exterior are also used in the spacious rooms, many of which provide sea views. Meat and fish dishes feature on the menu, which draws heavily on the traditional cuisine of the region. The delightful location close to the water's edge is ideal for beach lovers, while those in quest of culture can explore the area's rich Etruscan heritage.

Access: 9km from Marina Velca at the seaside

LAZIO

TUSCANIA (VT)

16

LOCANDA DI MIRANDOLINA

Sig.ra Lubowski
Via del Pozzo Bianco, 40/42
01017 Tuscania (VT)
Tel. 07 61 43 65 95 – Fax 07 61 43 65 95
info@mirandolina.it – www.mirandolina.it

👤👤 **60-70€**

Closed 10 Jan-15 Feb • 2 single rm, 6 double rm • Half board €55-60

 Menu €24/48

We most liked The loquat tree, cascading ivy and jasmine.

From here there are fine views over the surrounding countryside, yet this little inn is situated in the historic heart of Tuscania and makes for a pleasant alternative to staying in a hotel. The façade has been colonised by ivy and jasmine, giving off a heady scent when in bloom. A large loquat tree stands in the outdoor area where typical local cuisine is served to guests. The rooms are very simple, yet not without an intimate charm.

Access: In the heart of the village

LAZIO

VELLETRI (RM)

DA BENITO AL BOSCO

Sig. Morelli
Via Morice, 96
00049 Velletri (RM)
Tel. 069 63 39 91 – Fax 069 64 14 14
benitoalbosco@virgilio.it – www.benitoalbosco.com

 80€

Open all year • 20 single rm, 30 double rm • Half board €65 • Parking, garden, swimming pool, no dogs

 **Menu €28/39**

 The verdant chestnut and pine woods surrounding the swimming pool.

Originally just a restaurant, this establishment now also offers accommodation. It is tucked away among pines and chestnuts growing in a parkland setting which makes for an attractive backdrop, particularly in the evening when the poolside lighting illuminates the scene. The modern rooms are spacious, with wood furnishings and floors. Traditional regional cuisine with plenty of seafood, bought direct from Anzio fish market.

Access: Outside the village, drive for 2.5km along Via Carlo Angeloni

LAZIO

VEROLI (FR)

18

ANTICO PALAZZO FILONARDI

Sig.ra Ferriello
Piazza dei Franconi, 1
03029 Veroli (FR)
Tel. 07 75 23 52 96 – Fax 07 75 23 50 79
info@palazzofilonardi.it
www.palazzofilonardi.it

👤👤 85-110€

Closed 8-31 Jan • 2 single rm, 29 double rm • Half board €65-75 • Parking, no dogs in the restaurant

 Menu €33/41

 The hilly landscape of the Ciociaria viewed from the rooms.

The medieval hill settlement of Veroli is located in the heart of the Ciociaria district; constructed in the 19C, this establishment was in use as a convent until 1996. A closed order of nuns still occupies the building next door, and figures in habits may occasionally be glimpsed in the garden. The hotel's previous incarnation as a religious house is evident from its chapel, which remains consecrated. In addition to stunning views, the rooms are delightfully tranquil, a reminder to guests that this was once a place of prayer.

Access: In the heart of the medieval town

Liguria

Imagine a winding road hugging the coastline, above which extend slopes planted with olive groves running up to the tree line, punctuated by little stone built hamlets clinging to hilltops. Such is the landscape of Liguria, a narrow and ancient region separating mountains from the sea. Once one of Europe's great mercantile powers, Genova remains a dynamic commercial powerhouse. Although a major industrial centre, it retains its medieval centre of imposing patrician palaces and criss-crossed by *carugi*, the narrow alleys so characteristic of Liguria. Although most of the coastline is quite developed, some unspoilt strips remain, notably the Portofino promontory between Camogli and Santa Margherita with its paths winding through scrubland, emerging occasionally to provide stunning views. This wild backdrop has influenced the character of the local population, an understated and determined people, the region's cuisine, best exemplified in its fish dishes and its famous pesto sauce, and its wines, most notably Vermentino and Pigato.

10 establishments

Recommended sites and circuits
Liguria

> In Liguria, parallel valleys and undulating countryside alternate in an endless succession of dips and rises. Many poets have lauded the beauty of this region that boasts to its east one of the most suggestive landscapes in Italy, the Cinque Terre, and to its west the picturesque market towns of the Riviera di Potente.

Monterosso, Vernazza, Corniglia, Manarola and Riomaggiore are the five market towns that make up the Cinque Terre. Located right on the seafront, they are connected by a network of paths and stairways in a sumptuous setting of vineyards and olive trees. The Road of Love, which runs between Manarola and Riomaggiore, is a narrow sheer path over the sea, which offers a uniquely romantic atmosphere and enchanting landscapes. The Sentiero Azzurro, the path that connects the five towns, is rather flatter but the views are equally spectacular.

On the Riviera di Ponente, the small market town of **Bussana Vecchia** has a singular history. Destroyed by an earthquake over a century ago, then abandoned, it was later reconstructed lower down. In the 1960s a group of artists breathed life into it again by building up an autonomous community there. Since then, the "magic" of Bussana has lived on in the ruins, amongst which laboratories and handicrafts boutiques have sprung up.

Dolceacqua, another jewel of the Riviera di Ponente, is a little market town located in the shadow of a castle, which you reach after negotiating a maze of little streets. Arches, arcades and old houses are dotted here and there with handicraft shops.

The little streets of **Triora**, "land of witches", are home to many a legend. The town is famous for its witchcraft trial of 1588, which ended with the condemnation of women accused of causing the food shortages that had been the bane of the village. This episode is remembered in the Museum of Ethnography and Witchcraft, to the delight of local boutiques, which have strange witch dolls in the windows and sell "witch liqueurs" and "slug milk" (grappa with aromatic herbs). The medieval market town is an artistic delight whose defences, composed of gates, archways, narrow streets and forts, have remained intact. All that is left of the castle is a few ruins of the tower.

Taggia is a port of call not to be missed. With its flowers, olive and citrus trees, it is one of the oldest towns on the Riviera dei Fiori. Here you can visit the ramparts and medieval towers, and admire the works of art in the Dominican convent. The town's fame is due in part to the olive tree, introduced in the 12C by Benedictine monks, one variety of which, *taggiasca*, produces an oil of particular repute.

A recipe to try, wines and... a nugget of information

Wines

_Cinque Terre
_Vermentino
_Pigato
_Sciacchetrà
(limited production)
_Bianchetto
_Rossese di Dolceacqua

Ingredients

- about 40 basil leaves (as freshly picked as possible)
- 2 cloves garlic
- 1 handful pine kernels
- 4 tablespoons grated Pecorino Sardo cheese
- 4 tablespoons grated Parmigiano Reggiano (Parmesan)
- $^1/_2$ teaspoon rocl salt
- 1 glass extra virgin olive oil
- marble mortar and wooden pestle (or a blender)

Local specialities

Sardenaira (a pizza typical of the west of Liguria), olives, Triora bread, *agliata* (garlic sauce), *lagaccio* biscuits, *brusso* (soft cheese with an intense flavour), *farinata* (galette made with chick-pea flour), *panissa fritta* (polenta made with chick-pea flour).

TROFIE AL PESTO

Method

If you want to adopt the traditional method, crush the garlic and salt in the mortar, then add the basil and continue to crush the mixture with a revolving motion. When the basil turns dark green (a sign that it has released its essential oils) add the pine kernels until you have a creamy mixture. Add the pecorino, the parmesan and half of the oil (a spoon at a time). Keep working the mixture until it has a creamy consistency. If you do use a blender, you won't get quite the same result as the chopped basil releases fewer essential oils. Put the garlic, pine kernels, salt and half of the oil in the blender and mix until you have a creamy paste. Put it in the fridge for 10 mins, then add the basil, pecorino, parmesan and the other half of the oil. Mix until the basil is broken up. Cook the pasta and drain it, making sure to save a little of the cooking water, put it in a dish, add the pesto and stir until the sauce is evenly spread. Serve.

Food for thought

The name "basil" may come from Latin: *basiliscus* (the mythological monster who could kill you just by looking at you and against whom the plant was an antidote); or from the Greek *basilikòs*, which means "royal".

Our favourite places to eat

DA CASETTA
Piazza San Pietro 12 – Borgio Verezzi (SV) – Tel. 019 610166
Closed Tue and lunchtime (except Sat, Sun and public hols Oct-Jun).

A la carte menu €29-47

The pesto alla genovese made according to the traditional recipe.
Nestled in the *carruggi*, steep streets typical of the historic centre, Da Casetta is located in a building which used to be a post office, and, prior to that, cellars. This delightful restaurant has a raised terrace outside and two rooms with exposed brick barrel-vaulted ceilings. You can sample typical Ligurian cuisine, from regional specialities based on meat and fish to *picagge* (a sort of pasta) and *gnocchi al pesto*. It's no coincidence that the owner is a member of the Order of the Knights of the Brotherhood of Pesto.

MAGIARGÈ VINI E CUCINA
Piazza Giacomo Viale – Bordighera (IM) – Tel. 0184 262946
Closed Tue lunchtime and Mon, open evenings only in Jul and Aug.

A la carte menu €28-37

The sign which evokes ancient traditions, historical and culinary.
The name of the restaurant, meaning "fallen woman" in local dialect, is taken from a legend going back to the time when Bordighera was taken by pirates, according to which a young girl they had kidnapped sought refuge here. Beyond the entrance, you will find a rustic, yet distinguished looking restaurant, where you can sample the wholesome homemade fare, presented on a blackboard. And how better to start than with the *Brandecujun*, a typical Liguran cod-based speciality.

ANTICA TRATTORIA DEI MOSTO
Piazza dei Mosto 15/1, Conscenti – Ne (GE) – Tel. 0185 337502
Closed 10 days in Jun, 4 weeks in Jan and Feb, Wed, and lunchtime Jul and Aug.

A la carte menu €28-31
The rabbit alla genovese and the mushrooms with lettuce – seasonal specialities
Originally an inn frequented by travellers and merchants passing through, the Antica Trattoria is now a pleasant restaurant on the first floor of a building overlooking the village square. In the comfort of the wooden interior decorated with period photos, you will be won over by the regional cuisine: a platter of antipasti samples including Genoan-style vegetable pie and *focaccine* (small pizzas without sauce) served hot with local cold cooked meats and homemade and seasonal main dishes.

CAMOGLI (GE)

LA CAMOGLIESE
Sig.ra Rocchetti
Via Garibaldi, 55
16032 Camogli (GE)
Tel. 01 85 77 14 02 – Fax 01 85 77 40 24
info@lacamogliese.it – www.lacamogliese.it

👤👤 **75-100€**

Open all year • 6 single rm, 15 double rm • No dogs

 The view over Golfo Paradiso together with the smell of the sea.

This little jewel is located in one of the pearls of the Ligurian riviera; a small, family run hotel which makes for the ideal destination either for a weekend break or a longer stay on the coast. After a recent major refit, the rooms are well presented; the best are those overlooking the bay. Improvements are ongoing; among those anticipated is an expansion of the currently limited public areas.

Access: In the heart of the village on the coast

LIGURIA

CASTELNUOVO MAGRA (SP)

LA VALLE

Sig.ra Tendola
Via delle Colline, 24
19030 Castelnuovo Magra (SP)
Tel. 01 87 67 01 01 - Fax 01 87 67 40 75
agriturismolavalle@virgilio.it

👫 **70€** ☕

Closed 1-22 Jan • 6 double rm • Parking, garden, no dogs • Sale of wine and oil

 Set Menu €20 and 25

 The vineyards and olive groves surrounding the house.

This large yellow house, deep in the Ligurian hinterland, stands close to the border with Tuscany. La Valle is perfect for those looking for a peaceful and relaxing holiday, as well as visitors interested in exploring the area's artistic heritage and attractive coastline. The Lunigiana, an area which borders three different regions, has a rich history and strong local traditions, most of which focus on the land rather than the sea. The agriturismo, situated on the road leading to the village, has comfortable rooms decorated with hand-crafted wooden furniture. Authentic local cuisine (fixed-price menu) accompanied by regional wine makes the restaurant here a must.

Access: In the country, just 1km from the village

LIGURIA

CENOVA (IM)

NEGRO

Fam. Negro
Via Canada, 10
18020 Rezzo (IM)
Tel. 018 33 40 89 – Fax 01 83 32 48 00
hotelnegro@libero.it – www.hotelnegro.it

75-80€

Closed 8 Jan-8 Mar • 4 single rm, 8 double rm • Parking, swimming pool, no dogs

 Menu €25/45

 The swimming pool, from where there are panoramic views across the countryside.

Cenova is a typical mountain village of the Arroscia valley, deep in the Ligurian hinterland. Most of its houses are stone built, perched on the steep hillside among the cultivated terraces so characteristic of Liguria. The Negro family's hotel is located in a panoramic spot at the very top of the settlement. A wood and stone structure, the building has a natural warmth and friendliness to it. Although simply furnished, the accommodation provides high standards of comfort. The restaurant, also very popular with non-residents, focuses on creative local specialities.

Access: In the outskirts of the village on the hillside

LIGURIA

FINALE LIGURE (SV)

4

ROSITA

Sig. Monesiglio
Via Mànie, 67
12024 Finale Ligure (SV)
Tel. 019 60 24 37 – Fax 019 60 17 62
info@hotelrosita.it – www.hotelrosita.it

65-85€

Closed 7-30 Jan, Nov • 1 single rm, 8 double rm • Half board €45-55 • Parking, no dogs in the restaurant

 Menu €31/41

 Gazing at the sea from the bedroom balcony.

Panoramic views over Finale and Varigotti, the tranquillity of the countryside, the silence and coolness of the evening; this hotel is in an excellent location, reached by following the road away from the beach and up into the hills, where a warm welcome awaits from the family management team. All the simply furnished rooms have balconies with sea views, while the restaurant serves Ligurian specialities and fish dishes. For the energetic, mountain bikes are available.

Access: In the village – past Via Aurelia

LIGURIA

IMPERIA (IM)

5

RELAIS SAN DAMIAN
Fam. Kranz-Gardini
Strada Vasia 47
18100 Imperia (IM)
Tel. 01 83 28 03 09 – Fax 01 83 28 05 71
info@san-damian.com – www.san-damian.com

 120-140€

Closed 1-30 Nov • 9 double rm • Parking, garden, swimming pool, dogs not admitted • Virgin olive oil sold

 The scents, colours, peacefulness and the ancient oil-pressing techniques.

In the heart of the olive groves of the Ligurian countryside, you will be awoken by the sound of birdsong every morning while dancing fireflies illuminate your nights. The luxury San Damian establishment belongs to a family for whom hospitality is a way of life and who has set a few rooms aside in their private home for guests. The renovated premises have retained their former charm with arcades, earthenware fireplaces and logs of wood piled up in readiness. The authentic character of old country homes pervades the spacious airy rooms and apartments, equipped with modern fixtures and fittings. Breakfasts are very generous.

Access: In the countryside, 7km from the town towards Vasia

LIGURIA

LEVANTO (SP)

STELLA MARIS
Sig.ra Pagnini
Via Marconi 4
19015 Levanto (SP)
Tel. 01 87 80 82 58 – Fax 01 87 80 73 51
renza@hotelstellamaris.it – www.hotelstellamaris.it

Closed 1-28 Feb and 1-30 Nov • 1 single rm, 7 double rm • Half-board only €100-150 • Parking, garden, dogs not admitted in restaurant

 For residents only

 The immense garden full of palm trees and Mediterranean scents is an oasis of peace and quiet.

Two minutes from the sea, the first floor of this 19C palace in the heart of the historic centre is the setting for Hotel Stella del Mare in a baroque ambience of great elegance. The ceilings are adorned with frescoes and stucco, the furniture is antique and lavish lace curtains enhance the appeal of each room. The rooms are also equipped with water-heating facilities for tea and coffee. Regional specialities take pride of place in the buffet breakfasts, and in the evenings your tastebuds will be delighted by the regional cuisine.

Access: In the village

LIGURIA

LEVANTO (SP)

7

VILLANOVA

Sig. Massola
Località Villanova
19015 Levanto (SP)
Tel. 01 87 80 25 17 - Fax 01 87 80 35 19
Info@agriturismovillanova.it
www.agriturismovillanova.it

🧍🧍 **110-130€**

Closed 7 Jan to 8 Feb • 8 double rm, 2 suites • Breakfast €10 • Parking, garden, dogs not admitted • Guided tours, bicycles lent, sale of oil, wine and jam

The rooms are painted in a rainbow of lilac, yellow and pale pink.

Levanto, an old seafaring town, boasts a picturesque historic centre with colourful façades, pretty churches and tiny narrow lanes. It is also home to this splendid property made up of two distinct buildings: the 18C manor house and its farming outbuildings and the presbytery next door to the family chapel. The apartments and rooms of the Villanova are perfect down to the tiniest detail. Period furniture, family portraits and old engravings set the scene for this voyage back in time. Breakfast, served on blue tables in the delightful garden, is a feast of pastries, honey and homemade jams.

Access: Towards Cinque Terre near the fire station

LIGURIA

MONTEROSSO AL MARE (SP)

8

LOCANDA IL MAESTRALE

Sigg.Celsi e Grasso
Via Roma 37
19016 Monterosso al Mare (SP)
Tel. 01 87 81 70 13 – Fax 01 87 81 70 84
maestrale@monterossonet.com –
www.locandamaestrale.net

👤👤 **90-135€** ☕

Open all year • 1 single rm, 5 double rm • Dogs not admitted

 The elegant sobriety of the rooms lit up by the changing colours of the sun's rays.

Those who appreciate tasteful but not too formal settings will adore this retreat. Stefania and Giovanni have restored this 17C palace, equipping the well laid out rooms with modern comforts, whilst retaining as much of the original decoration as possible, such as the frescoes on some of the ceilings. The yellow and blue painted rooms and apartments are named after famous seaside resorts along the coast. The vast terrace where breakfast is served enjoys a panoramic view of the town and the arch of Via Roma, the main road through the historic centre.

Access: In the heart of the village

PORTOVENERE (SP)

LOCANDA LORENA

Sig. Basso
Via Cavour, 4 località Palmaria (Isola)
19025 Portovenere (SP)
Tel. 01 87 79 23 70 – Fax 01 87 76 60 77
locanda_lorena@virgilio.it

 90-100€

Closed 1 Jan to 15 Feb • 9 double rm • Landing stage to the island

 Menu €40/68

 The colourful bedrooms and creative fish dishes.

The charm of this small inn begins to take effect long before you arrive. Located on the island of Palmaria, opposite Portovenere, it can only be reached on board a private boat. The building was originally a post office and shop for sailors to stock up on supplies. Today its pleasant colourful rooms now overlook either the bay of Portovenere or an inner garden. The reputation of its cuisine is well established and features classical dishes inspired by regional traditions and local specialities, all of which served in a handsome room whose bay windows overlook the sea and can be slid open to transform the room into a terrace when the weather permits.

Access: On the island of Palmaria

LIGURIA

SANTA MARGHERITA LIGURE (GE)

10

ROBERTO GNOCCHI

Sig. Gnocchi
Via Romana, 53 località San Lorenzo
16038 Santa Margherita Ligure (GE)
Tel. 01 85 28 34 31 – Fax 01 85 28 34 31
roberto.gnocchi@tin.it

 100€

Closed 16 Oct-30 Apr • 12 double rm • Half board €70 • Parking, garden, no dogs in the restaurant • Jam and oil for sale

 Set Menu €20 for residents only

 The view of the gulf of Tigullio, where the coast seems to wrap itself around the sea.

A winding track heads off the main road and up the hill between Santa Margherita and San Lorenzo, leading to two buildings providing accommodation in the form of nine rooms which are simple, bright and furnished with imposing wood pieces. All around are the olive trees which for centuries have been synonymous with the Ligurian landscape, but the greatest attraction of this establishment is its view of the sea. From the terrace, where meals are also served, guests can enjoy the panoramic Tigullio coastline lapped by white crested waves.

Access: 3km from San Lorenzo

Lombardia

Apart from coastline, Lombardy has everything; mountains, hills, plains, rivers, lakes and cities rich In history. Named after the Lombard invaders who settled here, it was subsequently carved up between city states who for generations engaged in conflict, siding either with the pope or Holy Roman emperor. Eventually Milan emerged as the dominant power, becoming one of Europe's richest and most vibrant centres in the process, and the subject of bitter rivalry between the era's greatest kings and emperors. Today, the city is synonymous with business and industry, but in earlier times it was capital of the Roman Empire and one of the centres of the Renaissance, when Bramante and Leonardo worked here, leaving their legacies in the masterpieces that are Santa Maria delle Grazie and the Last Supper. But Lombardy is also an important agricultural region, its fields in the Po plain growing wheat and maize, and its vineyards producing Franciacorta and Oltrpo Pavese grapes. To the north rise the mountains, with alpine lakes reflecting their steep side shorelines in a spectacular play of dark and light.

29 establishments

Recommended sites and circuits
Lombardia

> The Lombardy region is the birthplace of many illustrious figures – Virgil, Monteverdi, Stradivari and Donizetti to name but a few – and promises visitors beautiful landscapes of lakes, valleys and mountains, as well as charming towns that are still of a manageable size.

Lake Maggiore with its romantic and slightly melancholic atmosphere provides a backdrop for the magnificent Borromeo Islands named after Cardinal C. Borromeo, the area's principle patron saint. On Isola Bella, you can visit the 18C Palazzo Borromeo, with its charming Italian gardens, fountains, caves, statues and peacocks, which combine to lend it a fairy-tale atmosphere. **Isola Madre** is home to the botanical garden, while **Isola di San Giovanni** still enjoys the honour of having been the refuge of A. Toscanini. To reach these marvellous little islands, you can take a boat at **Stresa**, a small town with an old-fashioned appeal, ideal for a quiet stroll taking in the view of magnificent villas and their reflection in the lake.

Pavia is another city that plunges visitors into the tranquil charm of the past. Only a few of the 100 towers for which it is famous are still standing, proudly dominating the landscape. Here the medieval influence remains very pronounced and the best way to see the town is to wander with no specific aim, taking in the reminders of the past to be found at almost every step of the way along its narrow streets, charming churches, towers and tranquil little squares. One of the loveliest monuments is the Certosa Monastery, built in 1396, which stands just a few kilometres from the town.

Pavia Cathedral, whose eminent architects include Leonardo da Vinci and Bramante, is also well worth visiting.

As you approach the heart of the Padana Plain, you will come to **Mantova**, a very special town boasting a rich cultural heritage, where your imagination can roam free. This small, well-designed town was the home of Virgil, a place of refuge for Shakespeare's Romeo and the setting of Verdi's Rigoletto. It offers visitors numerous artistic treasures produced by such brilliant artists and architects as Mantegna, Pisanello, G. Romano and Leon Battista Alberti, who contributed significantly to the town's undeniable cultural fame.

A recipe to try, wines and... a nugget of information

Wines

_Cortese
_Malvasia
_Terre di Franciacorta
_Lugana
_Barbera Oltrepo Pavese
_Botticino
_Cellatica
_Valtellina Superiore

Ingredients

- 300g rice
- 60g butter
- 40g grated Grana Padano cheese
- 40g onions
- 40g beef marrow
- saffron in pistils
- 1 litre meat stock
- salt

Local specialities

Cheeses: *crescenza, gorgonzola, bitto* (matured for up to 10 years!), *magro di piatta, pannerone lodigiano* (white gorgonzola), *quartirolo, salva* (produced in May from the excess milk), *silter, taleggio, cotechino di Cremona*, liver *mortadella, violino* (ham made from goats' or sheep's leg), Cremona and Mantova mustards (the latter made with apples only), Mantova pear liqueur.

RISOTTO ALLA MILANESE

Method

In a saucer, soak about 20 saffron pistils in a ladle of boiling stock. Peel an onion and chop it finely. Sweat it over low heat in a pan with half the butter and the beef marrow. Add the rice and stir gently for a few minutes. Add the stock a little at a time and leave to cook for around 15min. Add a pinch of salt, then the saffron and its water. After a few minutes remove the rice from the heat and add the rest of the butter and the grated cheese. Stir everything together thoroughly.

Food for thought

Legend has it that *risotto à la milanaise* was invented around the middle of the 16C when a craftsman who was working on the Duomo's stained glass window married the daughter of the master glazier. To impress the wedding guests, the man "painted" the rice with a little of the saffron that he used to paint the windows.

Our favourite places to eat

TIPAMASARO
Via Cavour 31 – Gavirate (VA) – Tel. 0332 743524
Closed 10-25 Jul and Mon.
A la carte menu €24-34
 The extensive appeal of the establishment, extending beyond the cuisine.
This restaurant a stone's throw from Lake Maggiore is perfectly located for you to treat your taste buds after a day by the lake. Here you can sample homemade food in an informal, family atmosphere, untouched by the passage of time. The dishes may not all be regional but they are all the handiwork of the talented cook. Particularly memorable are the quaint self-service antipasti buffet, the *raviolis della nonna*, and the meat and fish-based dishes. In summer you can eat outside, under the gazebo.

CAFFÈ LA CREPA
Piazza Matteotti 13 – Isola Dovarese (CR) – Tel. 0375 396161
Closed 10-23 Jan and 11-24 Sep, Mon and Tue.
A la carte menu €25-32
 The enamelled iron sign typical of late 18C osterias.
The splendid period sign indicates this restaurant located in the 15C Palazzo della Guardia. The atmosphere is reminiscent of a bistro or osteria. The dishes on the elegant menu show a resolutely regional bent. Starters include antipasti made with the best of Italian and Spanish cold meats. Main dishes range from fresh filled pastas to meat- and fish-based dishes, so many specialities drawn from the culinary traditions of Cremona and Mantova. Diners can also visit the cellars of the wine shop adjoining the restaurant.

OSTERIA DELLA VILLETTA
Via Marconi 104 – Palazzolo sull'Oglio (BS) – Tel. 030 7401899
Closed 25 Dec-3 Jan, 10-25 Aug, Sun and Mon.
A la carte menu €28-38
 Savour the silence and the atmosphere of a real osteria.
A typical atmosphere reigns in this authentic, rural trattoria housed in a small mansion near the train station. The restaurant, with its solid wood tables, paper tablecloths and daily specials board, has been in the same family for three generations and the owners take pride in still serving "old-style cuisine" after more than a century. Just like in olden times, your plate will be filled with the traditional specialities of Brescia: tripe, pork and cod-based dishes, or snails with mushrooms.

LOMBARDIA

ARGEGNO (CO)

LOCANDA SANT'ANNA

Fam. Peroni
Via Sant'Anna, 152
22010 Argegno (CO)
Tel. 031 82 17 38 – Fax 031 82 20 46
locandasantanna@libero.it
www.locandasantanna.it

88-98€

Open all year • 9 double rm • Half board €75-80 • Parking, garden

 Menu €31/41

 The greenery of the surrounding woods and fields, a prelude to the panoramic landscape beyond.

An establishment of less than ten rooms, but recently refurbished throughout. The restaurant provides the main focus and takes up most of the ground floor and, during the summer, part of the gardens too, around which are set a number of apartments. The property adjoins the Santuario di Sant'Anna; peace and quiet in abundance combined with panoramic views make this a pleasant place to stay and enjoy the nature, history and traditions of this borderland between Italy's Lake Como and Switzerland's Lake Lugano.

Access: 3km away in Sant'Anna Schignano, behind the church

LOMBARDIA

BALLABIO (LC)

SPORTING CLUB

F.lli Tagliaferri
Via Casimiro Ferrari, 3
23811 Ballabio (LC)
Tel. 03 41 53 01 85 – Fax 03 41 53 01 85
info@albergosportingclub.it – www.albergosportingclub.it

 75€

Open all year • 6 single rm, 8 double rm • Half-board €55-65

 Menu €26/35

 Outdoor sports facilities for enthusiastic climbers.

This peaceful and hospitable establishment, at the foot of the Grigne mountains and in the heart of the historic centre, is as popular with business travellers as it is with sporting enthusiasts. Greatly favoured by climbers on their way back from the Ballabio mountains, this modern family-run hotel, ensconced in a pretty garden, proposes sober, functional facilities. Terrace with sundeck and reading room. A diet menu and classic cuisine in the restaurant.

Access: 1km towards Ballabio Superiore

LOMBARDIA

BASCAPÉ (PV)

TENUTA CAMILLO

Sig. Nidasio
Località Trognano
27010 Bascapé (PV)
Tel. 038 26 65 09 – Fax 038 26 65 09
agrimillo@libero.it – www.agriturismo.com/tenutacamillo   ♂♀ **70€**

Open all year • 6 double rm • Breakfast €5 • Parking, garden, swimming pool • Rice for sale, angling

 Menu €20/30

> **The bygone atmosphere of this beautiful farmstead.**

In 1903, the antecedents of the proprietors Mariolina and Franco established a fine farm here in the classic Lombard tradition. Today its doors are open to guests who may stay in the spacious rooms furnished with original pieces from between the wars. During the summer months the courtyard pool is in operation, bicycles are available for the energetic and creative types can study decorative arts with Mariolina! The restaurant serves classic Lombard cuisine.

Access: Outside the village towards Riozzo

LOMBARDIA

BERGAMO (BG)

4

LA VALLETTA RELAIS

Sig. Reguzzi
Via Castagneta 19
24129 Bergamo (BG)
Tel. 035 24 27 46 – Fax 03 52 28 12 17
info@lavallettabergamo.it
www.lavallettabergamo.it

👤👤 90-100€

Closed Dec and Jan • 8 double rm • Parking

 Strategically located a few yards from the hiking trails.

In the heart of the Parco dei Colli, this large home just 800m from the historic centre is comprised of generously proportioned, refined and personalised rooms graced with period furniture. Guests can choose between five comfortable rooms, each in a different colour, equipped with wrought-iron beds. Delightful paths ideal for long walks. Whether on foot, mountain bike or horseback, the park is ideal for outings and excursions. The airy and welcoming dining room moves outdoors under the portico as soon as the sun's first rays begin to warm the air.

Access: Beyond the upper town, in Parco dei Colli. 1200m from the historic centre

LOMBARDIA

BRIOSCO (MI)

LEAR

Fam Rossini
Via Col de Frejus, 3
20040 Briosco (MI)
Tel. 03 62 96 69 20 – Fax 03 62 96 69 60
info@ristorante-lear.com – www.ristorante-lear.com

 95€

Closed Jan and Aug • 2 single rm, 7 double rm • Parking, dogs not admitted in restaurant

 Menu €46/64

 A succession of styles: antique, classical, modern and contemporary.

This Lombardy farmhouse, home to the same family of farmers since its construction in a small hamlet on the edge of the village, is now also home to nine spacious modern rooms on the first floor, decorated with taste. An ideal destination to get away from it all. The simple but refined cuisine features appetising and unusual dishes, served in a rustic room that has been treated to a contemporary-style makeover. Outdoors in the vast park is a fine collection of works of art by famous artists of the last century.

Access: Outside the village, some 2km away in the Fondazione Pietro Rossini Park

LOMBARDIA

CALOLZIOCORTE (LC)

6

LOCANDA DEL MEL

Sig. Panzeri
Piazza Vittorio Veneto, 2
23801 Calolziocorte (LC)
Tel. 03 41 64 12 96 – Fax 03 41 63 02 65
hotel@locandamel.com – www.locandamel.com

👤👤 **78-88€**

Closed 8-26 Aug • 2 single rm, 7 double rm • No dogs

The rooms: well presented, stylish and individual.

What distinguishes this hotel is the accommodation offered here. The individual touches, careful presentation and quirkiness of the top floor rooms provide an excellent solution to those here to enjoy the delights of Lake Como without spending a fortune. The public areas are a little cramped, though, with the exception of the bar, which is large, lively and popular with non-residents as well. Breakfast may be taken in the bedrooms, the bar or on the terrace, and is consistently generous and tasty.

Access: On the village square

LOMBARDIA

CANTELLO (VA)

MADONNINA

Sig. Limido
Largo Lanfranco 1, località Ligurno
21050 Cantello (VA)
Tel. 03 32 41 77 31 – Fax 03 32 41 84 03
info@madonnina.it – www.madonnina.it

👫 100€

Open all year • 1 single rm, 9 double rm, 1 suite • Breakfast €8, half-board €90 • Parking

Menu €37/47

The charm of a house of yesteryear surrounded by a vast park.

Formerly on the road for travellers arriving from Northern Europe, this establishment is still strategically located, both for those who wish to explore the region and for those who intend to pursue their journey further south. The impressive building, covered in sweet-smelling wisteria and ivy, offers unpretentious yet elegant rooms. The restaurant is equally sophisticated, as are the immaculately laid tables. The menu follows the seasons. Banquets possible.

Access: In the centre of the village

LOMBARDIA

CARNAGO (VA)

8

VILLA BREGANA

Sig. Garau
Viale dei Carpini
21040 Carnago (VA)
Tel. 03 31 98 76 00 – Fax 03 31 98 68 68
hotel@villabregana.it – www.villabregana.it

140€

Open all year • 7 single rm, 18 double rm • Half-board €85-105 • Parking, park, dogs not admitted

 Menu €32/56

 Star magnolia, mimosa and giant thuja.

This abode, which belonged to a local artistocrat, was built in 1722 for agricultural purposes. Today it is ideal for receptions, business lunches and cultural and sporting events, or just for anyone who fancies a break away from it all. The establishment offers simple but comfortable rooms, warm, attractively decorated communal areas, large conference rooms and smaller workshop rooms, in addition to elegant dining rooms in the west wing. The carefully prepared menu has a distinctly Mediterranean influence.

Access: Outside the village, on the road to Solbiate Arno

CERVESINA (PV)

IL CASTELLO DI SAN GAUDENZIO

Sig. Bergaglio
Via Mulino 1, località San Gaudenzio
27050 Cervesina (PV)
Tel. 03 83 33 31 – Fax 03 83 33 34 09
info@castellosangaudenzio.com
www.castellosangaudenzio.com

140€

Open all year • 7 single rm, 35 double rm, 3 suites • Breakfast €8 • Parking, park and indoor swimming pool

 Menu €28/37

 The stone well, weapons' room and ladies' parlour will take you back into the past.

Crenellated towers rise up at the four corners of this rectangular building, whose architecture is characteristic of medieval Lombardy castles. Inside the elegantly proportioned rooms feature a combination of local history and modern comforts. The picturesque bedrooms on the first floor are graced with period furniture, while those on the ground floor, recently renovated, open onto the Italian-style garden. Mediterranean-inspired cuisine is served in the equally attractive dining rooms with bare beams and two large fireplaces. A majestic baroque fountain and swimming pool with sundeck can be found in the peaceful park.

Access: In San Gaudenzio 3km away, near Pô

LOMBARDIA

COLOGNE (BS)

10

CAPPUCCINI

Sigg. Pellizzari e Tonelli
Via Cappuccini 54
25033 Brescia (BS)
Tel. 04 71 37 65 73 - Fax 04 71 37 66 61
info@cappuccini.it - www.cappuccini.it

160€

Open all year • 10 double rm, 4 suites • Breakfast €15, half-board €140 • Parking, garden, swimming pool, fitness facilities, dogs not admitted

 Menu €47/98

 The countless varieties of roses that nurture the mind and the palate.

This 16C abode, which stands in the heart of a green park planted with century-old trees, a rose garden of a thousand perfumes, a fruit orchard and medicinal plant garden, extends hospitality in keeping with traditions. Distinctive vaulted ceilings, convent-style corridors and spiral staircases lead up to the wood furnished rooms. In the restaurant you will be served authentic but creative dishes made with vegetables from the garden. Further on, a rustic house is now home to a wellness centre: treat yourself to a soak under the waterfall of the hydrotherapy pool carved out of the rock.

Access: On the slopes of Mont Orfano 2km away

LOMBARDIA

DRIZZONA (CR)

11

L'AIRONE

Sig. Dellavalle
Strada per Isola Dovarese, 2 Castelfranco d'Oglio
26034 Drizzona (CR)
Tel. 03 75 38 99 02 – Fax 03 75 38 10 21
info@laironeagriturismo.com
www.laironeagriturismo.com

 60€

Open all year • 1 single rm, 8 double rm, 1 suite • Half board €58 • Parking, no dogs in the restaurant • Bicycles available, fitness facilities

 Set Menu €25 and 35

 The farmland rolling out across the vast plain.

This 19C farmstead has been painstakingly restored with great attention to detail, taking care not to detract from the original architectural features. It is pleasantly situated a little out of town, within the parkland bordering the Oglio river, and its rooms are furnished with period style pieces and fabrics which make for an elegant ambience. The inner courtyard is enlivened by greenery, with plants chosen by the proprietors.

Access: On the outskirts of Castelfranco in the Parco Naturale Oglio Sud

LOMBARDIA

GAMBARA (BS)

12

GAMBARA

Sig. Ciccarello
Via Campo Fiera, 22
25020 Gambara (BS)
Tel. 03 09 95 62 60 – Fax 03 09 95 62 71
info@hotelgambara.it – www.hotelgambara.it

👤👤 **75€** ☕

Open all year • 1 single rm, 12 double rm • Parking

 The matching fabrics in the rooms.

Expect a cordial reception from the owners at this small country hotel which is a well managed and efficiently run operation. It has a dozen rooms, all lovingly decorated, with modern bathrooms, while its public areas are somewhat less dazzling. All in all, though, this establishment of early 20C vintage remains a good place to know for both tourists and business travellers, not least because it represents value for money.

Access: In the historic centre

GANNA (VA)

13

VILLA CESARINA

Sig. Ferraro
Via degli Alpini 7
21039 Ganna (VA)
Tel. 03 32 71 97 21 – Fax 03 32 71 90 07
villacesarina@libero.it – www.villacesarina.it

👫 **80-110€**

Open all year • 9 double rm • Half-board €60-75 • Parking, swimming pool, garden

 **Menu €35/51**

> The fireplace and piano in the main hall are ideal for lively evenings in good company.

A pure product of the 20C Liberty-style, this villa is tucked away within a vast park complete with swimming pool, sundeck, pavilions and a pétanque ground. From its peaceful, isolated site, the villa dominates the valley and Lake Ghirba, where you can swim in summertime. The establishment and park are also beautiful in winter when they are encased in ice. Inside the period furniture, tasteful decoration and original floors and frescoes create a romantic ambience. All the spacious airy rooms are personalised. Local specialities and produce take pride of place on the gastronomic menu.

Access: In the heart of the village

LOMBARDIA

LOMBARDIA

GARDONE RIVIERA (BS)

14

BELLEVUE

Sig. Pizzi
Corso Zanardelli 40
25083 Gardone Riviera
Tel. 03 65 29 00 88 – Fax 03 65 29 00 80
info@hotelbellevue-gardone.com
www.hotelbellevuegardone.com

106€

Closed from 11 Oct to 31 Mar • 30 double rm • Half-board €70 • Parking, swimming pool and park

 Set Menu €25

 An unforgettable stay thanks to the attentive professional staff.

Plain flower-decked railings and a garden lined with majestic trees lead the way to this splendid 18C manor house crowned with turrets. The elegant interior decoration reveals period furniture and spacious bedrooms in subtle tones, extended by sweet-scented balconies. In the luminous dining room with parquet floor, treat yourself to the flavours and odours of authentic Lombardy cooking. Behind the trees lies a lovely swimming pool. Whenever the weather permits, the breakfast buffet and evening meal are served on the terrace.

Access: On the main road through the village

GRAVEDONA (CO)

15

LA VILLA

Sig. Mallone
Via Regina Ponente, 21
22015 Gravedona (CO)
Tel. 034 48 90 17 – Fax 034 48 90 27
hotellavilla@tiscali.it – www.hotel-la-villa.com

👥 94€ ☕

Closed 20 Dec-10 Jan • 3 single rm, 11 double rm • Half board €67 • Parking, garden, swimming pool, no dogs

Menu €23/39

The spacious and pleasantly laid out terrace garden.

This austere yet elegant building is painted all in white with dark green shutters; down one side runs its large and airy veranda restaurant which opens out onto the garden with inviting pool. Above is a terrace from where guests can admire the fine views over the lake and surrounding mountains. The classically furnished rooms are well proportioned, the public areas thoughtfully laid out and the restaurant specialises in regional cuisine.

Access: 200m from Palazzo Gallio

LOMBARDIA

ISEO (BS)

16

RELAIS MIRABELLA

Sig. Anessi
Via Mirabella, 34 a Clusane al Lago
25049 Iseo (BS)
Tel. 03 09 89 80 51 – Fax 03 09 89 80 52
mirabella@relaismirabella.it – www.relaismirabella.it

👤👤 **140€**

Closed from 1 Jan to 28 Feb • 29 double rm • Breakfast €10, half-board €105 • Parking, garden, swimming pool, dogs not admitted

 Menu €40/52

We most liked — Taking the time for a quiet stroll through the peaceful Lombardy countryside.

This hotel, nestling in a park lined with ancient trees, enjoys a panoramic lakeside position in the hamlet of Iseo, in the heart of a little stone town. The tasteful interior decoration, modern spacious rooms with a view, large rooms ideal for meetings and a recently opened dining room, with a fireplace where traditional dishes are served, set the scene for the Mirabella. A splendid swimming pool awaits guests outdoors, and, a few metres away along a path through the woods, a pretty farmhouse home to the elegant "La Catilina" restaurant whose large windows overlook the lake.

Access: 1.5km from Clusane by the lake, on a small hill

LOMBARDIA

MONTORFANO (CO)

17

SANTANDREA GOLF HOTEL

Sig. Brendolini
Via Como 19
22030 Montorfano (CO)
Tel. 031 20 02 20 – Fax 031 20 02 20
info@santandreagolfhotel.it
www.santandreagolfhotel.it

120-160€

Closed from 23 Dec to 31 Jan • 3 single rm, 8 double rm • Half-board €95-120 • Parking, park, beach and golf

 Menu €51/73

 Sophistication, tranquillity, space and modernity in the heart of lush green countryside.

This stone farmstead with flowered balconies and an immense refreshing lakeside garden is ideal for banquets. The interior decoration is refined and modern, while the spacious rooms, some of which have a small sitting room, are adorned with inlaid furniture. The bay windows of the gracious dining room, decorated with period furniture, enjoy an attractive view of the countryside. In summertime, meals are served on the veranda.

Access: Outside the village on the banks of the lake

LOMBARDIA

POZZOLENGO (BS)

18

ANTICA LOCANDA DEL CONTRABBANDIERE

Sig.- Imerio
Località Martelosio di Sopra 1
25010 Pozzolengo (BS)
Tel. 030 91 81 51
info@locandadelcontrabbandiere.com
www.locandadelcontrabbandiere.com

 100€

Open all year • 3 double rm • Parking, garden, swimming pool, dogs not admitted

 Menu €27/54

 Admiring the magnificent sunset over a country dinner.

Courtesy, professionalism and elegance set the tone for this 14C farmstead, now a modern guesthouse surrounded by a lush green garden. Not far from Lake Garda, a distinctive relaxing atmosphere can be felt throughout the establishment, as much in the three guestrooms graced with period furniture and painted yellow, red and pink respectively, as in the small barrel-vaulted dining rooms, where they serve creative dishes made with fish from the lake and meat.

Access: Towards Castellaro Lagusello for 1.5km

LOMBARDIA

SALO' (BS)

FATTORIA IL BAGNOLO

Sig. Gnes
A Serniga, località Bagnolo
25087 Salò (BS)
Tel. 036 52 02 90 - Fax 036 52 18 77
info@ilbagnolo.it - www.ilbagnolo.it

👤👤 **90€**

Open all year • 9 double rm • Half-board €65 • Parking, garden

 Menu €25/32

 Sampling the farm produce by the fireside.

An ideal establishment for a family holiday. With fields as far as the eye can see, the kids will be delighted, and the peace and quiet of their elders guaranteed. The large stone house is totally in harmony with the landscape. Natural materials such as mountain pine and sunny, country colours in the welcoming bedrooms create a style that is both rustic and aristocratic. The warm welcome confirms the establishment's long tradition of hospitality. Nature is highlighted in the masterful cooking, which uses authentic old recipes made from meat, cheese, fruit and vegetables produced on the farm.

Access: Drive to Serniga 6km away, then continue as far as Bagnolo

LOMBARDIA

SAN BENEDETTO PO (MN)

20

CORTE MEDAGLIE D'ORO

Sig. Cobellini
Strada Argine Secchia, 63
46027 San Benedetto Po (MN)
Tel. 03 76 61 88 02 – Fax 03 76 61 88 02
cobellini.claudio@virgilio.it
www.cortemedagliedoro.it

 64€

Open all year • 2 single rm, 5 double rm • Half-board €60 • Parking, garden • Yoga lessons, fishing, archery, ceramics, gathering medicinal plants, sale of honey and jam

 The rooms in the old granary.

Once called the King of Rivers, the Po irrigates the vast fertile plain bordering it, which does indeed give it a majestic air. The richness of the local harvests is reflected in the name of this guesthouse; the gold medals referred to were won by the owner's grandfather for his exceptional fruit orchards. Located in the former granary, the pleasant rooms under wooden ceilings make for pleasant accommodation, from where guests can listen to the gentle sounds of living agriculture and the silence of the plain's hot summer afternoons.

Access: Near the bridge over the River Secchia

LOMBARDIA

SAN FELICE DEL BENACO (BS)

21

BELLA HOTEL E LEISURE

Sig. Mauro Biondo
Via Preone 6
25010 San Felice del Benaco
Tel. 03 65 62 60 90 – Fax 03 65 55 93 58
info@bellahotel.com – www.bellahotel.com

140€

Open all year • 5 single rm, 17 double rm • Half-board €90 • Parking, swimming pool, tennis court

 Menu €43/71

The tranquil site in the vicinity of the famous theme parks.

This hotel on the banks of Lake Garda, set in a vast garden with a swimming pool, has something for everyone: relaxation for some and leisure activities or cultural excursions for others. The simple and airy rooms are carefully decorated, and the large pleasant dining room commands a fine view. Take a seat on the lakeside terrace, protected by an unusual arbour, and feast on local and international cuisine.

Access: In the town of Porto di Portese 2km away

LOMBARDIA

SAN GIOVANNI IN CROCE (CR)

22

LOCANDA CA' ROSSA

F.lli Ceresini
Via Giuseppina, 20
26037 San Giovanni in Croce (CR)
Tel. 037 59 10 69 – Fax 03 75 31 20 90
locandacarossa@libero.it

 85€

Closed 23 Dec-5 Jan and 1-15 Aug • 6 single rm, 8 double rm • Parking, garden, fitness facilities no dogs

 Menu €35/52

 The spacious, well-kept grounds

This recently opened property comprises an 18C manor house with a large courtyard on one side and an attractive garden on the other. The complex is impressive, with its new interior decor of arte povera furnishings, matching fabrics and modern facilities. The elegant restaurant serves a range of regional and international cuisine. The gym and sauna are welcome additions to the property.

Access: In the village, behind the castle

LOMBARDIA

SESTO CALENDE (VA)

LOCANDA DEL SOLE

Sig. Milito
Via Ruga del Porto Vecchio, 1
21018 Sesto Calende (VA)
Tel. 03 31 91 42 73 – Fax 03 31 92 17 59
info@trattorialocandasole.it – www.trattorialocandasole.it

 80€

Closed 25 Dec-10 Jan • 1 single rm, 6 double rm • Breakfast €5 • No dogs

 Menu €29/43

 The genteel simplicity of the restaurant and the rustic charm of the accommodation.

Close to the point from where the waters of Lake Maggiore emerge to provide the source of the River Ticino is the old town of Sesto Calende where, at the junction of two streets in its historic centre, this establishment is located. Behind the rather municipal façade are seven charmingly rustic, well equipped rooms. The pleasant restaurant is elegantly decorated, and serves regional cuisine with particular emphasis on fish fresh from the lake.

Access: In the heart of the historic centre, near the River Ticino

LOMBARDIA

SIRMIONE (BS)

24

BOLERO

Sig. Bollero
Via Verona 254 località Lugana
25010 Colombare di Sirmione
Tel. 03 09 19 61 20 – Fax 03 09 90 42 13
info@hotelbolero.it – www.hotelbolero.it

👤👤 90-142€

Open all year • 8 double rm • Breakfast €14 • Parking, garden, swimming pool, dogs not admitted

 The fireplace and old objects that adorn the welcoming dining room.

800m from the new spa resort of Sirmione, this large farmstead of rustic elegance has been turned into a delightful family-run hotel. The interior has retained its original character, enhanced by the addition of modern comforts and splashes of colour. Surrounded by a park complete with swimming pool and sundeck, the hotel is decorated with 19C sideboards and cupboards, and attractive paintings adorn the walls. The spacious rooms are graced with murals above the beds. The breakfast buffet is served until late into the morning.

Access: 800m from the new Sirmione spa

LOMBARDIA

SIRMIONE (BS)

25

IDEAL

Sig. Fezzardi
Via Catullo 31
25019 Sirmione (BS)
Tel. 03 09 90 42 45 – Fax 03 09 90 42 76
info@hotelidealsirmione.it
www.hotelidealsirmione.it

👤👤 **130-160€**

Closed from 1 Nov to 31 Mar • 2 single rm, 28 double rm, 2 suites • Half-board €105 • Parking, beach, garden, dogs not admitted around the pool

 Set Menu €30 and 35

 Listening to the whisper of the wind and water as you awake.

Romanticism and relaxation are the key words to describe this evocative picturesque site, near the famous caves of Catullo, antique ruins and scented olive groves of the Sirmione headland. The hotel, surrounded by an immense garden ideal for a quiet read, sun bathing or a dip in the swimming pool, is spacious, modern and tastefully decorated. Most of the light functional rooms enjoy a view over Lake Garda. In the dining room with large bay windows, you will be treated to the authentic tastes and flavours of the region.

Access: Near the caves of Catullo

LOMBARDIA

TREMEZZO (CO)

26

VILLA MARIE

Sig.ra Canzani
Via Regina 30
22019 Tremezzo (CO)
Tel. 034 44 04 27 – Fax 034 44 04 27
info@hotelvillamarie.com
www.hotelvillamarie.com

80-150€

Closed 1 Nov to 31 Mar • 1 single rm, 12 double rm • Parking, swimming pool, garden dogs not admitted

 The Liberty-style interior whose sophistication goes hand in hand with the warm welcome.

This 19C villa, set in the midst of a large garden with a swimming pool and sundeck, has been converted into a small but comfortable family-run hotel. It is home to delightful sitting rooms adorned with period frescoes, light spacious guestrooms with every modern comfort and a pleasant terrace where the buffet breakfasts are served and where you can also enjoy a drink before dinner. Located on the superb golf course of Venere, this establishment is ideal for those who wish to take things easy, relax in the sun or go on a boat trip around Lake Como.

Access: On the banks of the lake, near Villa Carlotta

LOMBARDIA

TREMOSINE (BS)

27

VILLA SELENE

Siig.ra Ghidotti
Via Lò, località Pregasio
25010 Tremosine (BS)
Tel. 03 65 95 30 36 – Fax 03 65 91 80 78
info@hotelvillaselene.com
www.hotelvillaselene.com

87-133€

Closed 15 Nov to 18 Dec • 11 double rm • Parking, garden, dogs not admitted

 Breakfast is served on the lakeside terrace until midday.

This hotel, surrounded by hiking trails and interesting cultural walks, has been run by the same family since 1967 and enjoys an isolated position and panoramic views. The establishment offers comfortable elegant rooms with balconies, each of which is named after a flower whose colour sets the decorative theme of the room. There is a splendid garden from which you can admire the lake, a reading room and a terrace set aside for the breakfast buffet. Ideal for those in search of a quiet country retreat.

Access: On the high plateau overlooking the lake, in Alto Garda Bresciano Park

LOMBARDIA

VALDIDENTRO (SO)

28

RAETHIA

Sig.ra Giacomelli
Via Sant'Antonio, 1 Località Pedenosso
23038 Valdidentro (SO)
Tel. 03 42 98 61 34 – Fax 03 42 98 61 34
info@agriturismoraethia.it
www.agriturismoraethia.it

👤👤 **60-80€**

Closed 1-30 Nov • 8 double rm • Half board €40-53 • Parking, garden, no dogs • Sale of cured meat and cheese

 Set Menu €17 and 22

 The harmonious combination of wood and stone in a traditional atmosphere.

From this retreat built against a hillside at the rear of the Val Vezzola, it is still possible to see cheesemakers at work turning milk into cheese. Here you will be greeted by the Giacomelli family, whose passion for the mountains is communicative. In their rustic-style chalet you will find functional, tastefully decorated rooms from which you can admire the panorama of Valdidentro and the upper Valetellina. After a full day of leisure activities, you will be ready to sit down and do full justice to the generous dishes of tasty local cuisine: homecured meat, soups, sciatt (cheese and grappa pastries), pizzocheri (buckwheat flour noodles) and cheese and meat from the farm.

Access: Outside the village towards Cancano Lakes, near San Martino church

LOMBARDIA

VALMADRERA (LC)

29

VILLA GIULIA-AL TERRAZZO

Fam. Pagani
Via Parè 73
23868 Valmadrera (LC)
Tel. 03 41 58 31 06 – Fax 03 41 20 11 18
info@alterrazzo.com – www.alterrazzo.com   110-130€

Open all year • 2 single rm, 10 double rm • Parking, garden, small dogs welcome

 Menu €36/62

  Quenching your thirst in the shade of the superb magnolia tree.

An aristocratic late 19C abode dominating Lake Como, Villa Giulia is a luxury country hotel in which a peaceful romantic atmosphere reigns. The attractively decorated interior with frescoes on the ceilings and immense fireplaces also features four meeting rooms. However, the highlight of the establishment is undoubtedly its cuisine. International recipes, regional specialities and creative personal touches are the watchwords at "Al Terrazzo", the elegant restaurant that has welcomed countless figures from the worlds of politics and showbusiness over the years.

Access: On the banks of the lake

Marche

The blend of medieval and renaissance towns, rolling hills, varied coastline, hospitable inhabitants, traditional cuisine and pleasant wines all contribute to this region's unique charm.

The Marche represents central Italy at its best. Its history has left a ubiquitous legacy of art and culture, but the industrious nature of its inhabitants has also made it a manufacturing centre of excellence, most notably in the field of footwear.

In order to fully understand the region, visitors should divide their time between the coast with its seafaring traditions, and the undulating hinterland with its impressive artistic centres including Urbino, Macerata and Ascoli Piceno.

The region's capital is Ancona, a charming city and an important Adriatic port which in summer months is besieged by tourists from all over Europe boarding ferries for the Greek islands and Croatia.

23 establishments

Recommended sites and circuits Marche

> Art, nature and poetry are the principal attractions of this area, whose untamed beauty is captivating. Old towns are dotted about the landscape on the hilltops; noble palaces, narrow streets and ancient churches are so many marvels that inspired the imagination and the touched the artistic sensibilities of one of its most illustrious natives, the poet and philosopher Giacomo Leopardi.

In **Recanati**, Leopardi's birthplace, every step of the way is a reminder of him, from the famous square in his poem *Sabato del Villaggio* to the house of Teresa Fattorini, the real name behind his famous *Silvia*, and Palazzo Leopardi, a 18C noble palace whose library still houses the works of the young poet.

On the hillside opposite Recanati stands **Loreto**. Surrounded by 16C ramparts and bastions, this small town was built around the Sanctuary, which had been constructed to protect the house in which the Angel Gabriel came to the Virgin Mary. Legend has it that a line of angels transported the building to Loreto. According to historical studies, it is more likely that it was saved by the Crusaders when the Christians were forced out of the Holy Land.

Behind the Sanctuary stands the Ducal Palace of **Urbino**, a splendid example of Renaissance architecture. It was created by Federico da Montefeltro, who wanted a "city in the form of a palace" in which men and ideas could circulate freely.

Don't miss **Fano**, the so-called "city of fortune", named after the legendary temple *Fanum Fortunae*. In the historical centre, where the layout of the streets still reflects the Roman roads, medieval Fano meets its Renaissance counterpart. From here you can go to the **Rocca di Gradara** and **Rocca di San Leo**. The former owes its notoriety to Dante, who mentions the site in his *Divine Comedy*; according to legend, this is where the tragic story between Paolo and Francesca took place, and the atmosphere of this unlucky union still pervades the lovers' chamber inside the castle.

Rocca di San Leo was the last residence occupied by Giuseppe Balsamo, better known as the Count of Cagliostro. This alchemist, doctor and wizard is a figure who lies on the borderline between history and legend. Branded a con man, he was sentenced to death by the Pontifical Government, which decided to commute this sentence to life imprisonment in the isolated San Leo.

A recipe to try, wines and... a nugget of information

Wines

_ Rosso Conero
_ Verdicchio
_ Bianchello del Metauro
_ Vernaccia di Serrapetrona
_ Lacrima di Morro d'Alba

Local specialities

Caciotta di Urbino (cheese), *ciauscolo* (cold pork meat flavoured with garlic, fennel seeds, orange peel, salt, pepper and mulled wine), *mazzafegato* (smoked cold meat, made with pork liver and lungs ground up with meat and flavoured), truffles, *fossa* cheese, *pecorino*.

OLIVE ALL'ASCOLANA

Ingredients

- 20 green olives in brine (preferably large ones)
- 250g minced meat (beef, pork, chicken)
- 50g cured ham
- 50g mortadella
- 70g grated Grana Padano cheese
- 1 small onion
- 1 small carrot
- 1 celery stick
- 1 clump of parsley
- 20g bread without crusts
- 1 lemon
- 1 teaspoon tomato purée
- 3 eggs
- 6 tablespoons extra virgin olive oil
- flour
- bread crumbs
- nutmeg
- salt and pepper

Method

Remove the pits from the olives and cut the flesh in a spiral (in such as way as to be able to reconstitute the olive by rolling it around the stuffing). Cut the vegetables into big pieces and fry them in a pan with a little oil until golden; dilute the tomato purée with a little warm water and add it to the pan. Before the meat is cooked, season, then remove the vegetables and chop up the rest of the ham and mortadella. Mix in the spices, a pinch of lemon zest, an egg, the chopped parsley, the bread (run under the water and dried) and the grated cheese. Roll the olive spirals around the stuffing, dip them in the flour, beaten egg then the bread crumbs. Fry the olives then drain them on kitchen roll. Serve hot.

Food for thought

It was after the independence of the Kingdom of Italy (1861), and the end of the religious limitations on the consumption of meat, that the cooks of Ascoli's noble families started to stuff olives. In view of the cost and the lengthy preparation, at least during the first half of the 20C, this recipe was reserved for special occasions and illustrious guests.

Our favourite places to eat

VECCHIA FATTORIA
Via Manzoni 19 – Loreto (AN) – Tel. 071 978976
Closed Mon.
A la carte menu €28-44
 The ancient building housing the restaurant – a cross between a farm and a chalet.
The dome of Loreto's famous sanctuary can already be made out from the foot of the village. The restaurant is easy to get to and is housed in a charming building resembling a chalet perhaps more than a farm. The spacious interior has vaults, columns and paintings on the walls, and a bright, modern feel thanks to recent renovation. In summer, meals are served al fresco. The menu offers both fish- and meat-based regional specialities.

DEL TURISTA-DA MARCHESI
Località Cà Gianessi 7 – Novafeltria (PS) – Tel. 0541 920148
Closed Tue.
A la carte menu €18-30
 The welcoming atmosphere and the convergence of Marche and Romagna in the menu.
The ideal place for those torn between a typical Marche meal and a foretaste of Romagna? The restaurant, which attracts regulars from as far afield as Rimini, is located in Montefeltro, on the edge of Marche, and yet the food has distinctly Romagnan undertones. Ever faithful to its policy of serving copious portions at reasonable prices, this unpretentious restaurant decorated with rustic objects serves hams with toast, *tagliatelle* with a variety of sauces, *gnocchi* dishes and an extensive assortment of meats. In season, the menu features truffles and *porcini* mushrooms from the Apennines.

DAMIANI E ROSSI
Via della Misericordia 7 – Porto S.Giorgio (FM) – Tel. 0734 674401
Closed Jan, Mon, Tue and lunchtime, except Sun.
Set menu €35
 The unbeatable view: the Adriatic coast and the Sibillini mountains.
A steep road leads from the historical centre to the first foothills of Porto San Giorgio and on to the restaurant. Located in an isolated building overlooking the sea and the hillside, this former trattoria has been renovated and transformed into an elegant and refined dining space. The food is elaborate and beautifully presented. There is no menu – we recommend that you opt for the owner's "taster menu", consisting of a delicious spread of innovative samples.

MARCHE

CASTELRAIMONDO (MC)

1

IL GIARDINO DEGLI ULIVI

Sig. Cioccoloni
a Sant'Angelo, Via Crucianelli 54
62022 Castelraimondo (MC)
Tel. 07 37 64 21 21 - Fax 07 37 64 26 00
info@ilgiardinodegliulivi.com
www.ilgiardinodegliulivi.com

100-130€

Closed 9 Jan to 7 Mar • 5 double rm • Half-board €70-90 • Parking, dogs not admitted

Set Menu €25 and 35

The first floor view over silent green hillsides.

This farm, on the flanks of Mount Gemmo and within easy reach of the main historic and cultural sites, is ideally located for a country break in the Alta Valle del Potenza. Built on an isolated hillside spot, this small stone edifice dates back to the 13C. The interior is made up of a sitting room with library and five rooms, each decorated in a different colour and each with its own sitting room and fireplace, overlooking the village of Santa Maria. On the ground floor are an open-plan kitchen complete with well and three small dining rooms decorated with period objects where you will be served tasty traditional local dishes.

Access: Outside the village on the slopes of Monte Gemmo

MARCHE

FABRIANO (AN)

2

GOCCE DI CAMARZANO

Sig.ra Balducci
Località Camarzano, strada verso Moscano
60044 Fabriano (AN)
Tel. 336 64 90 28 – Fax 07 32 62 81 72
goccedicamarzano@libero.it
www.goccedicamarzano.com

70-85€

Open all year • 6 double rm • Breakfast €5 • Parking, garden, no dogs

 The frescoes which decorate parts of the first floor.

The versatile Signora Balducci runs not only her farm, but also this fine establishment occupying an aristocratic 17C villa, with the enthusiastic help of her family. The surrounding parkland provides tranquillity and panoramic views of the landscape as it changes with the seasons. The limited public areas are stylish, while the rooms have tasteful wood furnishings, wrought-iron beds and modern, spacious bathrooms. Happily, there are no televisions to interrupt the peace and quiet of the site.

Access: Outside the village, on the edge of Oasi ecologica di Vallemontagnana, in the heart of the Gola della Rossa Park

FABRIANO (AN)

VILLA MARCHESE DEL GRILLO

Fam. D'Alesio
Località Rocchetta Bassa
60044 Fabriano (AN)
Tel. 07 32 62 56 90 – Fax 07 32 62 79 58
info@marchesedelgrillo.com
www.marchesedelgrillo.com

👥 **105-160€**

Open all year • 15 double rm, 5 suites • Parking, garden, dogs not admitted

 Menu €37/60

 Discovering new scents and flavours in the Marche region.

A three-hectare park ideal for walking or jogging and an impressive abode, flanked by an elegantly rustic inn, set the scene for the 18C summer residence of the Marquess of Grillo. Two centuries later, the current owners have turned the abode into a luxury hotel. Two types of rooms are available: those in the villa, spacious and comfortably furnished in a Neoclassical style, and others, simpler and less formal in the inn. The former cellars are now dining rooms, specialising in country produce with typical, yet subtly updated, dishes.

Access: On the SS76 near the exit of Fabriano East, towards Rocchetta

MARCHE

MACERATA (MC)

LE CASE

Sig. Giosuè
Contrada Mozzavinci 16/17
62100 Macerata
Tel. 07 33 23 18 97 – Fax 07 33 26 89 11
ristorantelecase@tin.it – www.ristorantelecase.it

 125€

Closed 7-31 Jan and 9-23 Aug • 13 double rm, 1 suite • Parking, fitness facilities, swimming pool, garden, dogs not admitted

 Menu €23/44

 The sweet and savoury menu featuring country flavours and colours.

A healthy body and a healthy mind could be the motto of this warm and friendly establishment where you can commune with nature. The spacious and welcoming hotel, located on a 10C farm, is decorated with rare period furniture. The stylish rooms are modern and comfortable. The wellness centre has a swimming pool surrounded by columns and bay windows overlooking the garden, a Scandinavian sauna and fitness facilities. As for the food, you will have a choice between traditional dishes or a more creative, sophisticated cuisine in the Enoteca, all made with local produce.

Access: *On the road to Villa Potenza. Go past the bridge over River Potenza and continue towards the town centre, following the signs to "Le Case"*

MARCHE

MONTECOSARO (MC)

5

LA LUMA

Sig. Bartolini
Via Cavour, 1
62010 Montecosaro (MC)
Tel. 07 33 22 94 66 – Fax 07 33 22 94 57
info@laluma.it – www.laluma.it

77€

Open all year • 10 double rm, 1 suite • Half board €50 • Parking, garden, no dogs

 Menu €30/37

 The varied and original interior decor.

This delightful little hotel has been built into the ramparts of the town, using materials from the old wine cellars. The recently constructed accommodation is furnished in period style while the bathrooms are more contemporary in appearance. But the most attractive features of the place are the terrace offering spectacular views over the Marche hills along with the charming breakfast room. There is also a lovely restaurant with stone and brick walls and vaulting.

Access: In the historic centre, along the ramparts

MARCHE

MONTEFORTINO (AP)

6

ANTICO MULINO

Sig.ra Cesari
Località Tenna, 2
63047 Montefortino (AP)
Tel. 07 36 85 95 30 – Fax 07 36 85 95 30
anticomulino@virgilio.it – www.anticomulino.it

 55-70€

Closed 7 Jan-15 Apr, 6 Nov-23 Dec • 1 single rm, 14 double rm • Half board €42-50 • Parking, garden, no dogs • Bicycles available, angling, horse riding, sale of jam and cured meats

 Set Menu €15 and 20

 The history of the place, lost in the mists of time.

Deep in the Monti Sibillini natural park, the Antico Mulino sits by the river Tenna, which previously powered its milling machinery, but is today animated by no more than trout and other fish species. The originally fortified main building has an imposing air; accommodation is spread between this and adjacent structures. The rustic-style furnishings go perfectly with the tiled floors and beamed ceilings. Hearty local cuisine is a feature of the restaurant menu.

Access: 2km from the village on the minor road to Sossaso. On the edge of the Parco nazionale dei monti Sibillini

MARCHE

MONTELPARO (AP)

7

LA GINESTRA

Sig. Mostardi
Contrada Coste
63020 Montelparo (AP)
Tel. 07 34 78 04 49 – Fax 07 34 78 07 06
info@laginestra.it   www.laginestra.it

57-70€

Closed 10 Jan-20 Feb • 5 single rm, 38 double rm • Breakfast €6.50; half board €52-60 • Parking, garden, swimming pool, tennis, dogs not admitted in restaurant

 Menu €20/30

 The sporting activities against a verdant backdrop.

Perched on a panoramic hillside between the Sibillini mountains and the Adriatic, this hotel is the result of a recent project which has restored a number of stone buildings. In addition to the beautiful rural location, guests can enjoy a wide variety of sports facilities; there are six tennis courts, stables, crazy golf, mountain bikes and a swimming pool – great for health and fitness enthusiasts. The relaxing accommodation is simply decorated and furnished in dark wood, while the cuisine focuses on local fish and meat specialities

Access: 3km from the village towards S.ta Vittoria in Matenano

MARCHE

PESARO (PU)

LOCANDA DI VILLA TORRACCIA

Sig. Galeazzi
Strada Torraccia 3
61100 Pesaro
Tel. 072 12 18 52 - Fax 072 12 18 52
info@villatorraccia.it - www.villatorraccia.it

👤👤 100-130€

Open all year • 5 suites • Breakfast €8.50 • Parking, garden

 The ramparts that separate the terraces overlooking the Foglia Valley.

First a watchtower, it served as a lighthouse in the 13C to guide passersby on the way to Pesaro, then a manor house, the Torraccia has since become a welcoming guesthouse hidden in a lush green garden of century-old trees. Nowadays the villa is home to elegant suites, each of which is decorated with a different choice of furniture and colour scheme. The inn still boasts its original earthenware floors and attics with bare beams, characteristic of medieval architecture. An ideal destination for a holiday, or just a night for those seeking peace and quiet or who are keen to explore the region's cultural and gastronomic treasures in a totally delightful setting.

Access: 5km from the village, near the A14 motorway tollbooth

MARCHE

SAN BENEDETTO DEL TRONTO (AP)

LOCANDA DI PORTA ANTICA

Sig.ra Nulli
Piazza Dante 7
63039 San Benedetto del Tronto (AP)
Tel. 07 35 59 52 53 – Fax 07 35 57 66 31
info@locandadiportaantica.it
www.locandadiportaantica.it

👤👤 **104€** ☕

Open all year • 1 single rm, 4 double rm

 A taste of history in the heart of this tiny town of brick houses.

As soon as you cross the threshold of the old wooden door, you will be immersed in the friendly family atmosphere of this house, where everything evokes its thousand-year-old history. Not far from San Benedetto, in the maze of tiny lanes in the delightful historic centre, this small inn offers five comfortable rooms, attractively furnished with antiques, some of which have a fireplace and balcony. There is no breakfast room, but you can ask for breakfast to be served in your room. Pretty summer terrace.

Access: In the heart of the upper village near Corte dei Gualtieri

MARCHE

SAN COSTANZO (PU)

10

LOCANDA LA BRECCIA

Sig.ra Cattalani
a Cerasa, Via Caminate 43
61039 San Costanzo (PU)
Tel. 07 21 93 51 21 – Fax 07 21 93 51 21
info@locandalabreccia.com
www.locandabreccia.it

👦👧 **100-120€**

Closed Nov and Feb • 5 double rm • Parking, garden, swimming pool, dogs not admitted

 The pleasure of rediscovering the past without having to forgo modern comforts.

On the sleepy hillsides of the Marche, this old brick farmhouse has a bright, modern, comfortable interior. The five simple and comfortable rooms, minimalist in style, all overlook the green countryside. The sitting room and veranda, where breakfast and mouthwatering snacks are served, lead out onto a gravel terrace made from pebbles that are characteristic of the Marche region. In the garden, admire the elms, ancient mulberry trees and flowering climbing plants that grow round the small swimming pool overlooking the sea. The inn is ideally situated for excursions in the region to discover its art, history and gastronomy.

Access: Between San Costanzo and Solfanuccio, on Strada Cerasa

MARCHE

SAN LORENZO IN CAMPO (PU)

11

GIARDINO

Sig. Biagiali
Via Mattei, 4
61047 San Lorenzo in Campo (PU)
Tel. 07 21 77 68 03 – Fax 07 21 73 53 23
giardino@puntomedia.it – www.hotelgiardino.it

 74-85€

Closed 10 Jan-10 Feb • 16 double rm • Parking, swimming pool, no dogs

 **Menu €32/51**

 The blend of tradition and innovation delivered with courtesy and care.

Opened in 1971, this establishment began life as a trattoria with a few rooms, since when it has evolved considerably in terms of both its cuisine (the kitchen operates under the watchful eye of Mamma Efresina, the owner) and accommodation (now a well presented hotel with tasteful and stylish furnishings). The open fireplace in the lobby makes for a welcoming and elegant ambience.

Access: Outside the village towards Pergola, turn left onto the SS 424

MARCHE

SAN SEVERINO MARCHE (MC)

12

LOCANDA SALIMBENI

Fam. Traballoni
Strada statale 361
62027 San Severino Marche (MC)
Tel. 07 33 63 40 47 – Fax 07 33 63 39 01
info@locandasalimbeni.it – www.locandasalimbeni.it

 65€

Open all year • 9 double rm • Half board €52 • Parking, garden, swimming pool, no dogs

 Menu €22/36

 The Marche heritage evident in the cuisine and the decor.

Originally from San Severino, Lorenzo and Jacopo Salimbeni were artists active in the 14C and 15C. Many of their works remain in the city's churches and museums, and their legacy is celebrated in an art prize which bears their name. Another homage to their creativity is to be found in the restaurant of this establishment, where one of their works is reproduced alongside other landscape scenes. The rooms are furnished with antique pieces and four poster beds.

Access: On the SS 361 towards Castelraimondo

MARCHE

SENIGALLIA (AN)

ANTICA ARMONIA

 Sig. Colombaroni
Località Scapezzano - Via del Soccorso, 67
60010 Scapezzano (AN)
Tel. 071 66 02 27 – Fax 071 66 02 27
anticaarmonia@libero.it – www.anticaarmonia.it

80-90€

Closed 15-30 Oct • 8 double rm • Half board €65-70 • Parking, garden, swimming pool

 Menu €25/30

 The centuries-old olive groves surrounding the property.

This recently restored 19C farmhouse is set in its own parkland deep in the Marche hills – look out for the ancient mulberry tree peeping out above the olive groves. The tranquillity of the location is in stark contrast to the hustle and bustle of the coastal resorts. Inside, the atmosphere is relaxing, with open fireplaces, a billiards room and simply furnished accommodation which is ideal for guests seeking a peaceful stay.

Access: Outside the village, in the valley before Scapezzano

MARCHE

SENIGALLIA (AN)

14

L'ARCA DI NOÈ

Sig.ra Ceresi
Via del Cavallo 79
60019 Senigallia (AN)
Tel. 07 17 93 14 93 – Fax 07 17 91 57 00
rmorpu@tin.it
www.arcadinoecountryhouse.com

👫 96-135€

Open all year • 9 double rm • Half-board €68-87 • Parking, garden, swimming pool

 Menu €30/35

 We most liked The attentive service and good humuour of the staff is contagious, particularly when travelling with children.

This country house on the lower slopes of Senigallia, full of the scent of olive groves, makes children feel more than welcome. While they will not discover elephants, crocodiles or even unicorns, they may let their imagination run wild in the vast play area created specially for them near the swimming pool. After a day visiting cultural sites or lazing at the beach, you can relax in colourful modern rooms decorated with designer objects. The restaurant and veranda serves meals which vary with the seasons using market fresh produce.

Access: Outside the town, towards Ancône

MARCHE

SENIGALLIA (AN)

15

BEL SIT

F.lli Manfredi
Via dei Cappuccini, 15
60010 Scapezzano (AN)
Tel. 071 66 00 32 – Fax 07 16 60 83 35
info@belsit.net – www.belsit.net

👤👤 65-96€

Open all year • 38 double rm • Breakfast €7; half board €57-69 • Parking, garden, swimming pool, tennis court, sauna, no dogs in the restaurant

 Menu €20/40

 The tranquillity of this former convent.

In the Marche foothills and still within sight of the coast, this imposing 19C building sits in a verdant location. Once a convent and later a seminary, it is now a sensitively restored hotel. Its change of use from a house of God is evident from the swimming pool and tennis courts; spacious and peaceful accommodation allowing visitors to while away the days in total tranquillity, yet surprisingly close to civilisation.

Access: On arriving in the village from Senigallia, take the first turning on the left

MARCHE

SENIGALLIA (AN)

LOCANDA STRADA DELLA MARINA
Fam. Bedetti
Strada della Marina 265
60019 Senigallia (AN)
Tel. 07 16 60 86 33 - Fax 07 16 61 17 27
info@lsdn.com - www.locandastradalelamarina.it

 160€

Open all year • 9 double rm • Half-board €103 • Park, swimming pool, dogs not admitted in restaurant

 Menu €31/57

 The graceful rooms are named after wild flowers: lily, heather and broom.

Tucked away in an immense century-old park, the inn is located in a picturesque farmhouse, which was at one time the holiday home of the Becci family. Restored using salvaged materials such as bare beams and parquet floors, it is decorated with period furniture. Perfect to relax by the swimming pool or see a play or concert in the small theatre/concert hall, or just take things easy in the garden that overlooks the Adriatic sea. Look out for the old tobacco drier in the restaurant.

Access: Take the SS16 towards Rimini, before Cerano, turn left to Scapezzano

MARCHE

SERRUNGARINA (PU)

CASA OLIVA
 Sig. Baldelli
Via Castello, 19
61030 Serrungarina (PU)
Tel. 07 21 89 15 00 - Fax 07 21 89 15 00
casaoliva@casaoliva.it - www.casaoliva.it ♀♀75€

Closed 10-31 Jan • 2 single rm, 14 double rm, 2 suites • Half board €50 • Parking, no dogs in the restaurant

 Menu €25/43

 The views of the Marche hills from the ramparts.

The fortified village of Bargni is situated on Via Flaminia, the old Roman road that heads inland from Fano. As with so many settlements in the Marche, it originated as a lookout post and to this day it retains a forbidding aspect. Sitting at the foot of the village, the hotel has a stone facade with a raised entrance reached by a flight of steps. Inside, the carefully restored building has a spacious restaurant with large windows, and unfussy, well presented and comfortable accommodation.

Access: On the outskirts of the village

MARCHE

SERRUNGARINA (PU)

18

VILLA FEDERICI

Sig. Baldelli
Via Cartoceto, 4
61030 Serrungarina (PU)
Tel. 07 21 89 15 10 – Fax 07 21 89 15 10
info@villafederici.com – www.villafederici.com

 75-93€

Open all year • 5 double rm • Half-board €63-75 • Parking, garden, no dogs

 Menu €25/36

 We most liked   The rustic tranquillity of the hillside location among trees.

"Parva domus magna quies", states the brochure (small house, great tranquillity) for this peacefully situated late-17C patrician residence. Far from the hustle and bustle of urban life, the building sits between two copses, partially obscuring it and giving it an air of understated refinement. Inside, the lady of the house has created an ambience of elegance using antique family pieces to furnish the rooms in a simple rustic style. Fine views of the hillside landscape and the Metauro river running through it.

Access: Towards Cartoceto, along Via Bargni

MARCHE

SIROLO (AN)

LOCANDA RISTORANTE ROCCO

Sig. Tridenti e Fabiani
Via Torrione 1
60020 Sirolo (AN)
Tel. 07 19 33 05 58 – Fax 07 19 33 05 58
ifo@locandarocco.it – www.locandarocco.it

120-150€

Closed Jan and Feb • 7 double rm • Parking, dogs not admitted

 Menu €42/54

 Dining under a starlit sky in summertime.

An inn in the Middle Ages, where travellers and tradesmen could find food and a bed on the road to Conero, this small hotel, run by a warm friendly team, continues to greet guests cordially. Recently extended by a wing referred to as the "Rocco in campagna", the establishment is surrounded by a vast garden and is only two minutes from the beach of Stirolo. True to its traditions, the hotel's restaurant serves a full repertoire of meat and fish using local produce but with a distinctive creative note.

Access: Behind the town ramparts

MARCHE

SIROLO (AN)

20

MONTECONERO

Sig. Melappioni
Via Monteconero, 26
60020 SIROLO (AN)
Tel. 07 19 33 05 92 – Fax 07 19 33 03 65
info@hotelmonteconero.it
www.hotelmonteconero.it

 140-150€

Open all year • 5 single rm, 32 double rm, 12 suites • Half-board €89-98 • Parking, park, swimming pool, tennis court, dogs not admitted in restaurant

 Menu €29/40

 The high bare stone vaulted ceiling of the breakfast room.

This attractive complex is set in a secluded country site. The generous interior proportions of the abbey, built on the Conero headland, have been tastefully decorated in a deliciously discreet yet romantic style. The premises are ideal for receptions and meetings. The understated elegance of the rooms is enhanced by wooden furniture, made by 19C craftsmen. In the restaurant, you will be treated to the region's gastronomic traditions in a room whose vast bay windows overlook the coast and the park. Ideal for relaxing as you wander around the park's paths.

Access: Towards Ancône, after 3km turn left towards Badia di San Petro

MARCHE

TREIA (MC)

IL CASOLARE DEI SEGRETI

Sig. Lucamarini
Contrada San Lorenzo, 28
62010 Treia (MC)
Tel. 07 33 21 64 41 – Fax 07 33 21 81 33
info@casolaredeisegreti.it – www.casolaredeisegreti.it

🏃🏃 **65€**

Closed 3-19 Nov • 3 double rm • No breakfast • Parking, garden, swimming pool, dogs not admitted in restaurant

 Menu €27/36

 The ambience of an earlier age.

It is difficult to summarise the appeal of this solid rustic establishment, nestling among the undulating Marche hills. One of the attractions is the restaurant with lovely stonework in its arches and passageways, redolent of bygone times and making for a warm ambience. Traditional Marche cuisine is lovingly prepared by Signora Lucamarini using carefully selected produce, a hallmark of good quality.

Access: From Treia, on the left towards San Lorenzo

MARCHE

URBANIA (PU)

22

MULINO DELLA RICAVATA

Sig.ra Faggi
Via Porta Celle
61049 Urbania (PU)
Tel. 07 22 31 03 26 – Fax 07 22 31 03 26
info@mulinodellaricavata.com
www.mulinodellaricavata.com

 70-80€

Open all year • 4 double rm • Half board €60-70 • Parking, garden

 Set Menu €27 and 32

 A mill bearing witness to centuries of history on the banks of the Metauro.

Travellers along the banks of the Metauro in the 14C may well have encountered the occasional friar making his way with produce from his convent to this stone built mill. Now as then, it sits among trees by the riverside. A chance to see some old mill equipment, as the mill itself and the little cave with its underground spring, makes the journey all the more worthwhile. The flower bedecked façade also gives the place a certain charm.

Access: From Urbania, head towards Monte Soffio, continue for 1km, turn left towards Sassocorvaro

MARCHE

URBINO (PU)

23

CA' ANDREANA

Sig.ra Loschi e Sig. Ferrari
A Gadana - Località Cà Andreana
61029 URBINO (PU)
Tel. 07 22 32 78 45 – Fax 07 22 32 78 45
info@caandreana.com – www.caandreana.com

78-88€

Closed 9-27 Jan, 27 Sep-7 Oct • 6 double rm • Half-board €60-65 • Parking, garden, swimming pool, no dogs in the restaurant • Bicycles available, jam for sale

 Menu €27/39

 The Marche hills and the proximity to Urbino.

The verdant hills of the Marche seem to give colour to the pale stone and roof tiles of this old but well maintained farmhouse. Against this rustic backdrop, the cuisine is surprisingly sophisticated without compromising its authenticity, using carefully selected local produce (home grown wherever possible). During the summer months, meals are served in the cool courtyard, from where guests can survey the peaceful countryside, perhaps before setting off to discover Urbino, the quintessential Renaissance city.

Access: On leaving Gadana, continue for 2km towards Pieve di Cagna

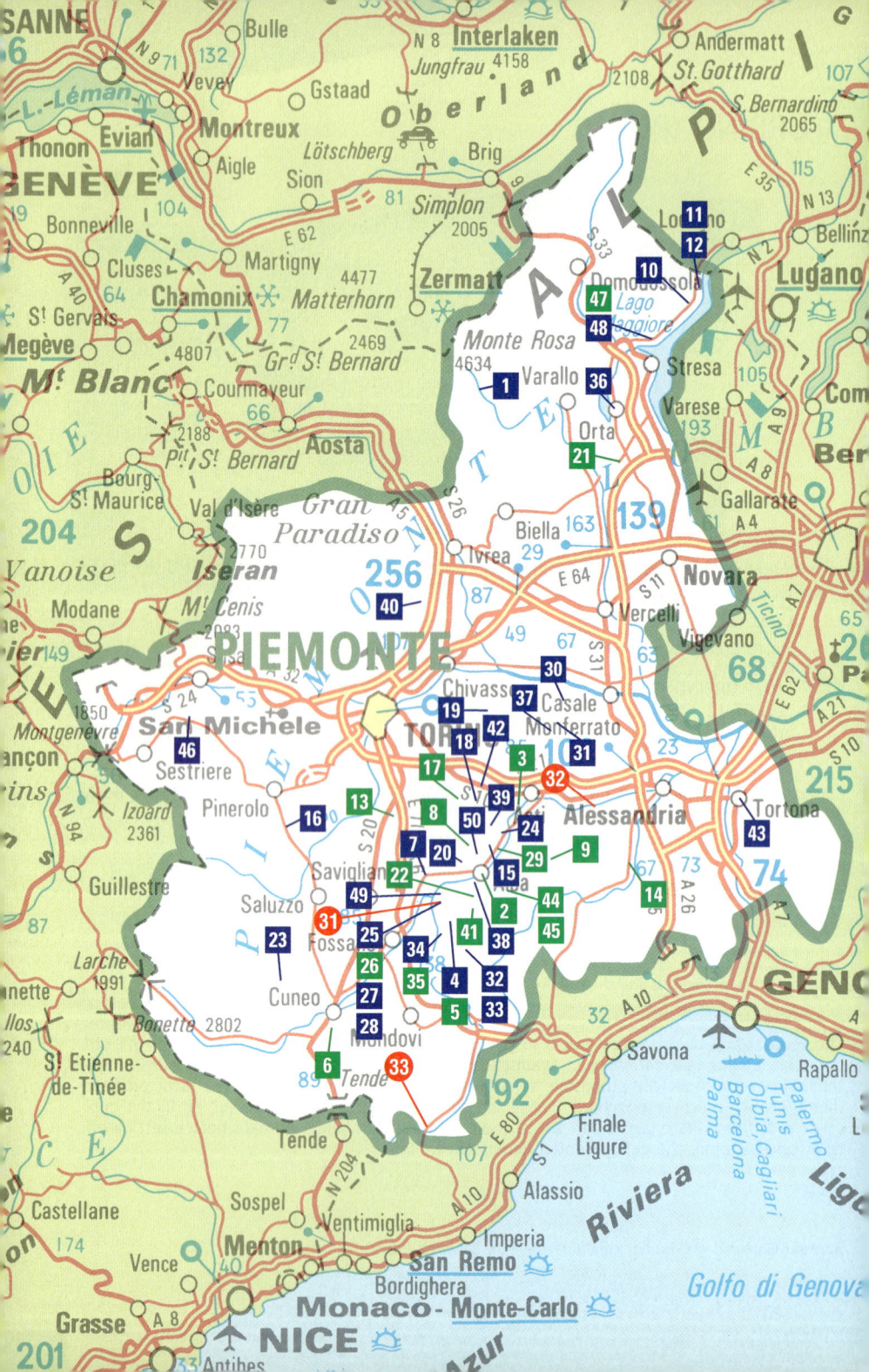

Piemonte

Piedmont is a region of mountains and rivers, hemmed in on three sides by the rugged profile of the Alps which gradually soften prior to rising as the foothills of the Apennines, beyond which lie Liguria and the sea. Water rushes down valleys from the spectacular snow capped peaks before joining the majestic river Po, flowing placidly past the farmland and towns which mark the boundaries of the Monferrato district. To the south, between the mountains and the plain, are the hills of the Langhe and the Roero, renowned for their prestigious wines such as Barbera and Barolo, the perfect accompaniment for a typical Piedmontese meat dish. The inhabitants of this land are a reserved and determined people whose forefathers were instrumental in the campaign to unify Italy. For centuries, Piedmont was ruled by Europe's most ancient dynasty, the House of Savoy; although French speakers, it was thanks to their resolve that the unification movement was born. Today, Italy is a Republic and Turin is undergoing a major facelift, but the regal splendour of bygone times is still to be seen at Stupinigi, Venaria and Racconigi, where a succession of state rooms, gardens and fine furnishings survive untarnished.

50 establishments

Recommended sites and circuits
Piemonte

> The majestic Alps provide a spectacular setting for Turin and its surrounding little market towns with their charming squares lined with handicrafts shops, restaurants and cafés. Posted like sentinels at the borders of Piemonte, the Alps also serve as the setting for the "paths of heaven", the routes taken by pilgrims in medieval times to reach Rome, Saint-Jacques-de-Compostelle and Jerusalem.

If you follow the Via Francigena you will come upon one of the symbols of Piemonte: **la Sacra di San Michele**. Located at the summit of Mount Pirchiriano, this ancient abbey dominates the Val Susa. It has witnessed the passing of history from the Romans to Napoleon, and has seen the inception of Piemonte and the House of Savoy. Here visitors can indulge in the asceticism of approaching the Zodiac Door, at the summit of the Stairway of the Dead, beyond which lies a better life in paradise.

The Val Susa is also home to another attraction: the **Fenestrelle** fort, an impressive military construction that is unique in Europe. A 3-km walkway nicknamed the "Wall of China" connects the buildings of the lower citadel with positions 635m higher up. In the past, the different forts were linked by (external) paths and long (internal) stairways that had a total of 4000 steps!

Further on, in a landscape modelled both by nature and by man, rounded hills covered with vines, which overshadow impregnable castles, alternate with small market towns to create a visual feast. Here in the vicinity of Candelo you can visit the medieval Ricetto, a fortified structure built by the local population in order to protect its wine and wheat.

Between Langhe and Roero is Cherasco, a charming town nicknamed "the star city". Napoleon, having admired its palaces, castle, churches and the ruins of the 16C ramparts declared it "the most beautiful part of Italy". In the windows of antique shops in the historic centre it is not unusual to find extemely valuable old objects. Indeed, for the last ten years, French and Italian antiques dealers and collectors have met here yearly at the lively secondhand market. Don't forget to visit the district Tower with its moon-dial, the Triumphal Arch of the Madonna of the Rosary and the Castle of the Viscontis, which boasts unsurpassable views over the hills of Novello, Vergne and La Morra. Within the La Morra vineyards you can admire the Barolo chapel, a small church built in homage to the famous wine and restored with much imagination by Sol Lewitt and David Tremlett.

A recipe to try, wines and... a nugget of information

Wines

_Barolo
_Barbaresco
_Dolcetto
_Barbera
_Arneis
_Nebbiolo
_Brachetto
_Grignolino

Local specialities

Chocolate, *gianduiotti* (typical hazelnut chocolates, the first to be wrapped), *Castelmagno* (made exclusively with milk from the Val Grana), *robiola di Roccaverano, bruss* (made from fermented scraps of old cheese), truffles, hazelnuts, rice, cherries, *Krumiri de Casale* (V-shaped wheat biscuits), *grissini*.

BONÈT

Ingredients
- 2 tablespoons sugar
- 2 tablespoons flour (or potato flour)
- 6 eggs yolks
- 5-6 *amaretti* (a couple more for decoration)
- 1 litre whole milk
- optional: 2 spoons bitter cocoa powder or a cup of coffee

Method
Beat the eggs with the sugar then add the milk. Mix well then add the flour and the finely crushed *amaretti*. If you want to increase the flavour, add the coffee or cocoa powder. Cook in the oven (in a bain-marie) for about 45 min. at 180°. Use a toothpick to check if the cake is cooked; if it comes out dry, you can take the cake out of the oven. Allow to cool then leave in the fridge for several hours. Decorate with the *amaretti* and serve.

Food for thought
In Piedmontese, *bonèt* is the word for the hat worn by men in the countryside, its round form being the same as that of the cake. The most plausible hypothesis regarding the origins of the word comes from Langhes (where the cake originates). Here, the *bonèt* cake was served at the end of the meal and was said to "cover" the other dishes just as a hat "covers" the head.

Our favourite places to eat

L'OSTERIA DEL VIGNAIOLO
Santa Maria (La Morra, CN) – Tel. 0173 50335
Closed Wed and Thu.
A la carte menu €2-32

 Discovering authentic regional flavours in a small country-house setting.
This osteria is located a few kilometres from La Morra, the high point of the region's spectacular wine-growing landscape. Inside this little brick house you can enjoy the understated atmosphere that is typical of trattorias in Langhe. The menu proposes simple Piemontian cuisine: its renowned raw meat antipasti, *tonno di coniglio* (marinated rabbit), terrines and vegetable flans, followed by fresh pasta and roasted meats that are much-acclaimed. As a final note, there are chocolate, hazelnut and sabayon desserts.

TRATTORIA LOSANNA
Via San Rocco 36 – Masio (AL) – Tel. 0131 799525
Closed 27 Dec-13 Jan, Aug, Sun eve and Mon.
A la carte menu €15-35

 Being transported back in time by the medieval tower and traditional Monferrato cuisine.
Perched on top of a hill from which you can admire the Tanaro Tiglione valleys, this restaurant benefits from an extremely pleasant location that is also easily accessible from the motorway. This trattoria hasn't given in to the fashion for overdoing things. Here you can still find an agreeable commotion, an informal family welcome, and traditional Monferrato cuisine. Among the most celebrated traditional dishes on the menu are the assortment of antipasti, the *agnolotti di carne* (pasta filled with meat), the selection of *bolliti* (a kind of stew), and, for dessert, the hazelnut *panna cotta*.

PONTE DI NAVA – DA BEPPE
Frazione Ponte di Nava 32 – Ponte di Nava (Ormea, CN) – Tel. 0174 399924
Closed Wed.
A la carte menu €19-33

 The backdrop – perfect for sampling regional produce.
This restaurant has been run by the same family since 1869. The establishment, located at the Ligurian border, offers superb panoramic views over the left bank of the Tanaro. Dishes reflect its ambiguous geographical situation, drawing inspiration as much from the traditions of Langhe as from the Ligurian hinterland. Try the vegetable flans and the *bagna caoda* (anchovy purée) and also the pesto and herb ravioli. The mountains make their presence felt too, with game, mushrooms and chestnuts.

PIEMONTE

ALAGNA VALSESIA (VC)

CASA PRATI

Sig.ra Castagnola
Frazione Casa Prati, 7
13021 Alagna Valsesia (VC)
Tel. 01 63 92 28 02 – Fax 01 63 92 26 49
casapratizimmer@libero.it
wwwzimmercasaprati.com

👤👤 **70-112€** ☕

Open all year • 6 double rm • Garden, dogs not admitted

The faultless welcome and hospitality amidst green or snow-covered fields.

What better place to find a refreshing spot in summer or go skiing in winter? An ideal establishment for a restful break to build up your strength on gentle (or energetic) walks through the woods of Valsesia. At an altitude of 1220m at the foot of the ski slopes and Mount Rosa, and 50m from the Nature Park of Alta Valsesia and the town centre, this chalet-style construction was once a stable, before it was restored with salvaged materials. A friendly family guesthouse and pleasant comfortable rooms in which wood is the prevailing feature. Each room is different, but they all command a panoramic view of the Alpine landscape.

Access: From the church square, head towards ski lifts, in the second bend, take the small road to Casa Prati

PIEMONTE

ALBA (CN)

2

VILLA LA MERIDIANA-CASCINA REINE

Sig. Giacosa
Località Altavilla, 9
12051 Alba (CN)
Tel. 01 73 44 01 12 – Fax 01 73 44 01 12
cascinareine@libero.it

♂♀ 85€

Open all year • 8 double rm, 1 suite • Parking, garden, swimming pool • Bicycles available, pétanque, archery, angling

The views over the old town and, on clear days, the Alps.

Situated on one of the hills outside Alba, this hotel is an attractive mix of genteel refinement and rustic idyll. The accommodation is divided between an old farmhouse and an Art Nouveau villa, on the façade of which is the sundial from which this establishment takes its name. The best rooms are those providing views over the surrounding countryside. Guests may enjoy a reading room, billiards, gym and the opportunity to go truffle hunting with dogs.

Access: Leave Alba and head towards Barbaresco

PIEMONTE

ANTIGNANO D'ASTI (AT)

3

LOCANDA DEL VALLONE

Sig. Lupica
Strada del Vallone, 9 a Gonella
14010 Antignano d'Asti (AT)
Tel. 01 41 20 55 72 – Fax 01 41 20 55 72
info@locandadelvallone.com –
www.locandadelvallone.com

🧍🧒 **75-85€**

Closed 10 Nov-31 Mar • 3 double rm • Parking, garden, swimming pool

 Breakfast served under the eaves of the former hen house during the summer months.

Situated among verdant gardens, this is a tastefully restored Piedmontese farmhouse. The limited accommodation is furnished in period style, with equally historic bathrooms to match. The tiled floor is original, dating from the 18C. Altogether more recent, and the only concession to contemporary pleasures, is the swimming pool, a welcome amenity for visitors during the summer months. A gem of a place at a reasonable price.

Access: Leave the village towards San Martino Alfieri, then turn left and follow the signs

PIEMONTE

BAROLO (CN)

4

CA' SAN PONZIO
Sig. Bianco
A Vergne ovest 3,5 km, via Rittane, 7
12060 Barolo (CN)
Tel. 01 73 56 05 10 – Fax 01 73 56 05 10
info@casaponzio.com – www.casanponzio.com

✶ ✝ 62-68€

Closed Jan • 6 double rm • Breakfast €8 • Parking, garden

Enjoying the sounds of the countryside from the comfort of the terrace.

Originally built in 1915 and in the hands of the same family ever since, this farmhouse has recently been carefully restored. An unexpected English-style lawn laid out between the hazelnut trees precedes the entrance, located beneath a typical Piedmontese balcony, accessible from some of the rooms. These are furnished in rustic style while those on the top floor have period pieces and are better proportioned. Young management team and guaranteed peace and quiet, bar the odd cockerel and church bell.

Access: 3km from the village towards Vergne

BAROLO (CN)

LA TERRAZZA SUL BOSCO

Sig. Camerano
Via Conforso, 5
12060 Barolo (CN)
Tel. 017 35 61 37 – Fax 01 73 56 08 12
laterrazzasulbosco@tiscali.it

🚹🚹 **70€**

Open all year • 5 double rm • Breakfast €5 • Parking • Horse riding, pétanque, bicycles available and sale of wine

 Being next door to the king of Italian wines.

Barolo is the centre of production for one of Italy's most important wines; opened in 2001, this establishment is next door to the castle, home of the town's wine museum. Occupying an 18C building, it lies along the old town walls and overlooks the countryside beyond. The rooms are simple, furnished with modern pieces and wrought iron beds. A great place to stay for all kinds of visitors, but particularly appropriate for wine buffs.

Access: Near the castle, which is also the wine museum

PIEMONTE

BOVES (CN)

6

LA BISALTA LOCANDA DEL RE

Sig. Cavallo
Via Tetti Re, 5
12012 Boves (CN)
Tel. 01 71 38 87 82 – Fax 01 71 38 87 82

60€

Open all year • 5 double rm • Breakfast €6; half board €47 • Parking, garden, tennis, mini-golf, no dogs

 Set Menu €23 and 31

 Snails on the menu for dinner - the owners are passionate about their snail farming operation.

There are countless reasons for staying at this friendly establishment. Dating from 1741, the well restored house sits at the foot of the Alps, and has a tennis court and crazy golf for younger visitors. The rooms are modern and spacious; the two most sought after retain their original 18C tiled floors and brick vaulted ceilings. Perhaps the most unusual feature of the place, though, is its organic snail farming operation; guests wishing to savour the house delicacy may do so in the restaurant.

Access: Go through the village and continue to Rivoira

PIEMONTE

BRA (CN)

7

L'OMBRA DELLA COLLINA

Sig. Chiesa
Via Mendicità Istruita, 47
12042 Bra (CN)
Tel. 017 24 48 84 – Fax 017 24 48 84
lombradellacollina@libero.it – www.lombradellacollina.it

👤👤**78€**

Open all year • 5 double rm • Parking

 The proprietor's genuine interest in days gone by.

In the historic centre of Bra, one of Piedmont's gastronomic centres, this charming establishment is set around an internal courtyard at the centre of which stands an imposing fig tree. Originally built in 1768, the building was subsequently embellished with the addition of a typical balcony. The owner's passion for antiques manifests itself not only in the adjoining toy museum, but also in the tasteful choice of furnishings.

Access: In the historic centre in a road that is perpendicular to Via Vittorio Emanuele

PIEMONTE

CANALE (CN)

8

VILLA CORNAREA

Fam. Bovone
Via Valentino 150
12043 Canale (CN)
Tel. 01 73 97 90 91 - Fax 017 19 58 99
info@villacornarea.com - www.villacornarea.it

👤👥 85-90€

Closed Jan • 9 double rm • Breakfast €6 • Parking, garden, swimming pool • Bicycles available, sale of wine

"In quiete salus" is more than a motto in this establishment, it is a way of life.

In 1908 a lawyer and mayor of the village for many years turned the original farmhouse into the existing graceful turreted villa on top of Cornarea hill. Seventy years later, the current owner, a wine specialist, acquired the property in order to replant a very ancient and little-known white wine: Arneis. This haven of peace and quiet decorated in a Liberty style continues to evoke the opulent lifestyle of Piedmont's rich middle classes. Each of the nine rooms is individually and subtly decorated with a tasteful colour scheme and period furniture. An unusual little foot bridge spans the swimming pool.

Access: Take Via Valentino to the right of San Bernardino Square, towards Monteu Roero-Carmagnola

PIEMONTE

CANELLI (AT)

LA CASA IN COLLINA

Sig. Amerio
località Sant'Antonio 30
14053 Canelli (AT)
Tel. 01 41 82 28 27 – Fax 01 41 82 35 43
casaincollina@casaincollina.com
www.casaincollina.com

90-110€

Closed Jan • 6 double rm • Parking, garden • Bicycles available, guided tours, sale of oil and regional produce

 The faultless elegance of the combination of stone, brick, earthenware and wrought iron.

As you draw up in front of this house, you may be reminded of the scene in Pavese's novel of the same name in which the protagonists seek refuge in a quiet peaceful place. This family winegrowing estate is comprised of an impressive farmhouse surrounded by vineyards as far as the eye can see. Relax in the plush interior, perfect for a few days' rest, as you read or chat with friends in the sitting room. The breakfast room overlooks the hills where wolves, hares and pheasant continue to live wild. All the very generously proportioned rooms are furnished with antiques. And what is the secret that binds Carlo to his wines? To find out, you'll have to pay him a visit!

Access: From the centre of Canelli, follow the signs to "regione Sant'Antonio"

PIEMONTE

CANNERO RIVIERA (VB)

10

IL CORTILE

Sig. Sgier
Via Massimo D'Azeglio, 73
28821 Cannero Riviera (VB)
Tel. 03 23 78 72 13 – Fax 03 23 78 72 13
cortilecannero@libero.it – www.cortile.net

 105-110€

Closed 1 Nov-14 Mar • 9 double rm

 Menu €40/61

 The central courtyard, from which the establishment takes its name.

Life here revolves around the courtyard, particularly during the summer months, when gourmet meals are served to the many visitors. Surrounding it is the first floor accommodation which Signor Sgier, originally from the Swiss canton of Grigioni, makes available to guests. This is a stylish and tastefully presented establishment, from its carefully selected furnishings to its creative cuisine, which will satisfy the demands of even the most exacting travellers.

Access: Park by the main road near the lake and follow the signposts

PIEMONTE

CANNOBIO (VB)

11

DEL LAGO

Sig. Albertella
Via Nazionale, 2
28822 Cannobio (VB)
Tel. 032 37 05 95 – Fax 032 37 05 95
enotecadellago@lycos.it – www.enotecalago.com

 95€

Closed Dec-Feb • 2 single rm, 11 double rm • Breakfast €10 • Parking, garden, beach, landing stage, no dogs in the restaurant

 Menu €41/70

 The ambience of the place, a homage to elegant relaxation.

This large establishment on the main road that runs along the lakeside is renowned principally for its restaurant and wine list. Its accommodation is also of a high standard, with spacious, well presented and elegant rooms. Particularly appealing are its balconies from which visitors can enjoy fine views of the lake, while enjoying a glass of wine in a comfortable armchair. What more could you ask for?

Access: Between Cannero Riviera and Cannobbio, by the lake

PIEMONTE

CANNOBIO (VB)

12

PIRONI

Sig. Albertella
Via Marconi 35
28822 Cannobio (VB)
Tel. 032 37 06 24 – Fax 032 37 21 84
info@pironihotel.it – www.pironihotel.it

130-160€

Closed 11 Nov-19 Mar • 12 double rm • Parking, dogs not admitted

 The walls and ceilings of the breakfast room adorned with Neoclassical frescoes.

A reminder of a bygone age, the ancient frescoes, period furniture, vaulted ceilings and medieval stone pillars are in fact perfectly at home with the modern, functional fixtures and fittings. This convent, formerly the home of a Franciscan community, was turned into a sophisticated aristocrat's abode before it became the charming small hotel it is today. It will delight guests who appreciate detail. In the heart of the historic centre, it is nonetheless peaceful, and the individually decorated rooms are furnished with 18C country-style pieces; some command a splendid view of the quiet lake and neighbouring pedestrian streets.

Access: In the historic centre, near Piazza Vittorio Emanuele

PIEMONTE

CARMAGNOLA (TO)

MARGHERITA

Sig. Roccia
Strada Pralormo, 315
10022 Carmagnola (TO)
Tel. 01 19 79 50 88 – Fax 01 19 79 52 28
info@girasoligolf.it – www.girasoligolf.it

🚶🚶 70€

Open all year • 12 double rm • Breakfast €8 • Parking, swimming pool, golf, no dogs in the restaurant • Angling, calcetto, sale of wine and jam

 Menu €20/30

 The gentle daily rhythm alternating between rounds of golf and relaxation.

A golfer's paradise, with 45 holes over three courses. This large farmstead has transformed itself over recent years, although agricultural traces remain in the form of rabbit farming and the rearing of other small farm animals. The main house has stone floors, brick walls and wooden roof beams; accommodation comprises a dozen rooms and several apartments suitable for longer stays. In addition to the golf club, there is also a restaurant.

Access: Leave the motorway and continue for 2km towards Pralormo

PIEMONTE

CASSINE (AL)

14

IL BUONVICINO

Sig.ra Peverati
Strada Ricaldone di Sotto, 40
15061 Cassine (AL)
Tel. 01 44 71 52 28 - Fax 01 44 71 58 42
ilbuonvicino@libero.it

👤👤 **70€**

Closed Aug • 1 single rm, 5 double rm • Parking, garden, no dogs • Guided tours, sale of jam and wine

 Set Menu €25

 The interesting and surprising nibbles available in the restaurant.

Look out for the barrel on the Ricaldone road which leads to this 19C Monferrato farmhouse, meticulously restored by its owners. Situated in a secluded spot, this is a working winery offering accommodation; six rustic style rooms with many of the original furnishings still in situ. All have a bird theme and painted decor to match; the Turkey and Duck rooms are perhaps the most attractive, the former on the top floor and the latter with open fireplace. The restaurant offers interesting dishes and does not restrict its menu to the local cuisine.

Access: From Cassine, take the road towards Ricaldone. A giant barrel indicates you have arrived!

PIEMONTE

CASTELLINALDO (CN)

15

IL BORGO

Sig.ra Ferrero
Via Trento, 2
12050 Castellinaldo (CN)
Tel. 01 73 21 40 17 – Fax 01 73 21 40 17
agriturismoilborgo@tiscali.it – www.ilborgoagriturismo.it

👤👤 **70€**

Open all year • 6 double rm • Parking, no dogs

 The changing view over the hills as the seasons progress.

Castellinaldo is a typical hill village of the Roero district, encircling the walls of a medieval castle. After negotiating sharp bends and steps, the visitor emerges in front of a splendidly restored building, its long history inextricably linked to that of the nearby castle; indeed the whole settlement sprung up here to supply it. Breakfast is served in the brick-vaulted old cellars, and characterful low passageways lead to the rooms, each named after a famous local wine. The attractive furnishings are all in tasteful period style.

Access: At the foot of the medieval castle

PIEMONTE

CAVOUR (TO)

16

LOCANDA LA POSTA

Sig.ra Mignola
Via dei Fossi, 4
10061 Cavour (TO)
Tel. 012 16 99 89 – Fax 012 16 97 90
info@locandalaposta.it – www.locandalaposta.it

80-120€

Closed 26 Jul-12 Aug • 20 double rm • Half board €60-80

 Menu €31/37

 The long established and traditional style Genovesio family management.

For five generations the Genovesio family has continued the tradition of hospitality for which this establishment, situated between Pinerolo and Saluzzo, has been renownd since the 18C. The rooms are ranged along the long balcony which overlooks the central courtyard, furnished in period style and offering every modern convenience, including air conditioning. The busy restaurant is particularly animated at the beginning of the summer season, when it hosts a gourmet convention.

Access: In the historic centre

PIEMONTE

CELLARENGO (AT)

17

CASCINA PAPA MORA

Sorelle Bucco
Via Ferrere, 16
14010 Cellarengo (AT)
Tel. 01 41 93 51 26 – Fax 01 41 93 54 44
papamora@tin.it – www.cascinapapamora.it

60-70€

Open all year • 6 double rm • Half board €55-65 • Parking, garden, swimming pool, horse riding, dogs not admitted • Sale of jam, wine, sauces and brandy

 Set Menu €20 and 30

 The English country house feel and the rooms under the eaves.

This early 20C Piedmont farmhouse is situated in open countryside with organic farming on all sides. It is named after the man who first built the place, the great-grandfather (nicknamed "il papà della mora" – the brunette's papa) of the current owners, the Bucco sisters. The warm welcome here makes it a popular place to stay; there are five rooms, a garden with a little lake, table tennis and mountain biking, plus a small restaurant offering home grown fruit and vegetables and classic Piedmont cuisine. Simple, authentic atmosphere.

Access: Take Via Ferrere, continue along a dirt track, go past the small bridge and the chapel of Maria Ausiliatrice

PIEMONTE

CISTERNA D'ASTI (AT)

18

GARIBALDI

Sig. Vaudano
Via Italia, 1
14010 Cisterna d'Asti (AT)
Tel. 01 41 97 91 18 - Fax 01 41 97 91 18
ilgaribaldi.vaudano@libero.it

👤👤 60€

Closed 16-31 Jan, 16-30 Aug • 3 single rm, 4 double rm • Half board €45

 Menu €20/28

 The restaurant, a perfect blend of history, local tradition and Piedmontese cuisine.

Was Garibaldi born here? Did he stay here, pass through, or fight a battle here? The answer sadly is no. The hotel was, however, founded by one of his followers in the last quarter of the 19C, and today it is a charming place to stay and absorb a little history, especially in its restaurant. The atmosphere is pleasant, characterful and unique, largely thanks to the efforts of Signor Vaudano and his family who have managed the place for more than half a century. The accommodation is less remarkable, but comfortable nonetheless.

Access: In the heart of the village, near the church of the Madonna dell'Ere

PIEMONTE

COCCONATO (AT)

19

LOCANDA MARTELLETTI

Sig.ra Romiti
Piazza Statuto, 10
14023 Cocconato (AT)
Tel. 01 41 90 76 86 – Fax 01 41 60 00 33
info@locandamartelletti.it – www.locandamartelletti.it

 **95€**

Open all year • 9 double rm • Garden

 Menu €27/34

 Breakfast served in the delightful hanging garden with fine views over the hills.

At the top of the village, located on the square where the town hall stands, this 18C structure was built on the foundations of a 13C castle, traces of which are still visible inside. Although the original occupants, the noble Martellati family, are long gone, the building's history is very much in evidence from the wine cellars to the four old wells. These days, however, the rooms are very comfortable. The first floor restaurant is laid out over three elegant but intimate rooms.

Access: On the square of the town hall

PIEMONTE

CORNELIANO D'ALBA (CN)

20

ANTICO CASALE MATTEI

Sig.ra Valfrè
Via Cristoforo Colombo, 8
12040 Corneliano d'Alba (CN)
Tel. 01 73 61 99 20 – Fax 01 73 61 99 20
info@casalemattei.com – www.casalemattei.com

67-80€

Open all year • 5 double rm • Parking, garden

 The original 19C wrought iron or wooden beds.

In the 18C the Mattei family built this fine farmhouse, with a typical Piedmontese balcony overlooking the inner courtyard. The property has been passed down through the generations to today's owners, who have converted it to offer superb accommodation without compromising the original structure. The simple rustic style, period furnishings, and excellent breakfast incorporating local produce add up to make this an attractive place to stay.

Access: In the heart of the village

PIEMONTE

CUREGGIO (NO)

LA CAPUCCINA

Sig.ra Fortina
Via Novara 19 b, località La Capuccina
28060 Cureggio (NO)
Tel. 03 22 83 99 30 – Fax 03 22 88 36 91
info@lacapuccina.it – www.lacapuccina.it

🚹🚸 75€ ☕

Open all year • 7 double rm • Half-board €60 • Parking, garden • Bicycles available, pétanque, cheese and jam for sale

Set Menu €22 and 24

Animals, fruit, vegetables and medicinal plants – life as it used to be.

It was here that the Questing Brothers set up their home before leaving Varallo Pombia for Vercellese in the 16C. At the beginning of the 20C the building was turned into a farm. Ideal for family holidays, this country house is a modern "old farm" whose farmyard animals, cows, horses and donkeys will delight youngsters. The small farmhouse has seven comfortable and attractively countrified guestrooms. The restaurant serves tasty regional dishes made from farm produce and homemade pasta, cheeses and jams.

Access: From the village, head towards Novara and follow the tourist information signs

PIEMONTE

DIANO D'ALBA (CN)

22

LA BRICCOLA

Sig.ra Olivero
Via Farinetti, 9
12055 Diano d'Alba (CN)
Tel. 01 73 46 85 13 – Fax 01 73 46 85 13
labriccola@virgilio.it - www.labriccola.com

70-85€

Closed Jan • 4 double rm • Half board €60-70 • Parking, garden • Wine and hazelnuts for sale

Menu €23/30

The fine views over vineyards from the rooms.

While her parents continue to tend their vines and hazel groves, wine expert Ivana has for some years run this establishment, a recently restored hundred year old farmhouse occupying a splendid location among the vines. The trattoria style restaurant has plenty of atmosphere with chandeliers, and bacchanalian frescoes, and accommodation is provided in four themed rooms: Diana, Cupid, Bacchus and Venus, the last of which has a four poster bed.

Access: On the minor 157 road to Diana D'Alba from Grinzane Cavour

PIEMONTE

DRONERO (CN)

23

CAVALLO BIANCO

Sig.ra Belliardo
Piazza Manuel, 18
12025 Dronero (CN)
Tel. 01 71 91 65 90 - Fax 01 71 91 65 90
cavallo-bianco@libero.it - www.ilcavallobianco.com

👤👤 60€

Open all year • 6 single rm, 9 double rm • Half board €40-50

 Menu €21/32

 The owners' collection of items on display.

This attractive building is located in the centre of Donero, a charming town in the province of Cuneo. Situated in a side street away from the traffic, its interior is filled with ephemera (principally textiles and gramophones) and antiques. The best rooms are on the first floor; some retain their original frescoes. Up on the second floor, the accommodation is more modern but provides romantic views over the rooftops. Classic local fare and pizzas in the restaurant.

Access: In the heart of the village

PIEMONTE

GOVONE (CN)

24

IL MOLINO

Sig. Minasso
Via XX settembre, 15
12040 Govone (CN)
Tel. 01 73 62 16 38 – Fax 01 73 62 16 38
info@ilmolinoalba.it – www.ilmolinoalba.it

75-90€

Closed Jan and Feb • 6 double rm • Parking, dogs not admitted

 The well-stocked library and collection of old farming tools.

This 19C flourmill, where the farm workers used to bring their harvest for milling, is now a welcoming sophisticated guesthouse located in the heart of the historic centre of this small town. Brick vaults, bare beams, marble fireplaces and an old stone staircase up to the rooms set the scene for the interior. Each of the elegant rooms is adorned with 18C furniture and boasts a balcony overlooking the hills and Alpine mountain range. The "weighing room" is now the breakfast room where you can enjoy local specialities.

Access: In the historic centre

PIEMONTE

LA MORRA (CN)

25

BRICCO DEI COGNI

Sigg. Bollano e Boggione
località Bricco Cogni 39
12064 La Morra (CN)
Tel. 01 73 50 98 32 - Fax 01 73 50 00 14
info@briccodeicogni.it - www.briccodeicogni.it

👤👤 **80-100€**

Closed Jan • 6 double rm • Breakfast €8 • Garden

Basking by the fireside or in the sunshine, depending on the season.

The owners of this impressive and elegant 19C aristocratic abode take great pleasure in welcoming guests. Located amidst mountains, hills and vineyards, the house has pleasant rooms painted in romantic colours and adorned with antiques and period objects. Outdoors, one never tires of gazing at the vast expanse of greenery all around from the flower-decked panoramic terrace.

Access: From La Morra, follow the signs to Rivalta and then for Bricco dei Cogni

PIEMONTE

LA MORRA (CN)

26

LA CASCINA DEL MONASTERO

Sig. Grasso
Cascina Luciani, 112/a - Fraz. Annunziata
12064 La Morra (CN)
Tel. 01 73 50 92 45 - Fax 01 73 50 08 61
info@cascinadelmonastero.it
www.cascinadelmonastero.it

👦👧 **90-95€**

Closed 15 Dec-15 Jan • 10 double rm • Parking, garden, small dogs welcome • Bicycles available, wine for sale, guided tours

 The splendid breakfast room decorated with farming implements.

This establishment dates from around 1600, when it was built as a dependent monastic farmstead to grow grapes for the monks' wine. Since then it has seen many come and go, including Pope Pius VII who in 1804 crowned Napoleon emperor. Staying here in October is particularly pleasant, when the grape harvest is in full swing and guests have a grandstand view of the action. The richly decorated interior is faultlessly cared for by the enthusiastic management team of Guiseppe and Velda. The play area and little lake will appeal to younger visitors.

Access: 28.5km from Asti on the SS 231 for 28.5km, then continue for 6km to La Morra and 2km to Annunziata

PIEMONTE

LA MORRA (CN)

27

CORTE GONDINA

Sig.ra Oberto
Via Roma 100
12064 La Morra (CN)
Tel. 01 73 50 97 81 – Fax 01 73 50 97 82
info@cortegondina.it – www.cortegondina.it

90-110€

Closed 2 Jan-3 Mar • 14 double rm • Parking, garden, swimming pool

The memory of the schoolteacher lingers on in her house.

This elegant, understated building is named after one of its inhabitants, Radegonda, nicknamed "Gondina" and it was here that she spent her early years as a schoolmistress. The family home stands in the historic centre of La Morra and is ideal for those wishing to visit the town's wine cellars. The house is comprised of a number of pleasant living rooms, including a reading room and unusual but tastefully decorated guestrooms in which tradition combines with modernity. On the breakfast table you will find organic yoghurts and jams as well as homemade cakes and biscuits.

Access: *In the village*

PIEMONTE

LA MORRA (CN)

28

VILLA CARITA

Sig.ra Carita
Viia Roma 105
12064 La Morra (CN)
Tel. 01 73 50 96 33
info@villacarita.it – www.villacarita.it

  110-120€

Closed Jan and Feb • 4 double rm, 1 suite • Parking, garden, dogs not admitted

> The splendid view of the castles and tiny villages surrounded by vineyards.

This recently restored small country home, on the edge of La Morra, is surrounded by the vineyards of Langhe del Barolo. The sophisticated Villa Carità is now home to five rooms, prettily decorated in shades of yellow, overlooking the hills. You can admire this matchless panorama from the belvedere in the garden, equipped with railings and wrought-iron chairs. At dawn or dusk it is the best place to enjoy the sight of the sun rising or setting over the village.

Access: In the heart of the village

PIEMONTE

MAGLIANO ALFIERI (CN)

CASCINA SAN BERNARDO

Sig.ra Raballo
Via Adele Alfieri, 31
12050 Magliano Alfieri (CN)
Tel. 017 36 64 27 - Fax 017 36 64 27
info@cascinasanbernardo.com
www.cascinasanbernardo.com

🕈🕈 80€

Closed 15 Dec-30 Jan • 6 double rm • Parking, garden, swimming pool, no dogs

 The manor-style association between the house and its surrounding landscape.

Built in 1887 and subsequently sold to the family which continues to own it today, this building has been carefully restored and is the archetypal patrician residence, with an imposing brick entrance and a setting providing stunning views over the hills and villages of the Roero district. The charming breakfast room is the former tool store although in summer, breakfast is taken outside to a backdrop of fruit orchards. The comfortable rooms have imposing wrought iron beds and modern bathrooms.

Access: In the heart of the village, past the castle

PIEMONTE

MOMBELLO MONFERRATO (AL)

30

CA' DUBINI

Sig. Dubini
Via Roma, 17
15015 Mombello Monferrato (AL)
Tel. 01 42 94 41 16 – Fax 01 42 94 49 28
info@cadubini.it – www.cadubini.it

👤👤 **75€** ☕

Closed 1-20 Aug • 4 double rm • Parking, garden

 The harmonious period furnishings.

In the heart of the tranquil Monferrato area and conveniently placed for excursions into the surrounding countryside and the hills around Turin, Asti and Alessandria, Mombello is a typical farming village part of which extends across a wooded hill. Once resplendent with vines, just a few vineyards survive nowadays; those that do produce an excellent, high-quality Barbera wine. Ca' Dubini is the perfect base from which to explore this fascinating region. The property is an old farmstead whose stylish public rooms are furnished with period pieces and traditional terracotta floors. The bedrooms here are simple, yet elegant.

Access: In the heart of the village

PIEMONTE

MONCALVO (AT)

31

LOCANDA DEL MELOGRANO

Sig. Cerruti
Corso Regina Margherita 38
14036 Moncalvo (AT)
Tel. 01 41 91 75 99 – Fax 01 41 91 75 99
info@lalocandadelmelograno.it
www.lalocandadelmelograno.it

Open all year • 9 double rm • Parking

The inlaid wooden doors of the old convent.

Although Moncalvo cannot claim to have any more than three thousand inhabitants at the most, it is nonetheless proud of its title of town, granted by the family of Savoie in the 18C. In the 19C the village inn welcomed cattle breeders and dealers come to take part in the cattle market. The restoration work sought to preserve the building's original structure and it is now home to large sitting rooms furnished in a modern style, a bright breakfast room and an immense portico with its original brick vaults. It makes an ideal basecamp for those wishing to explore the region and its nature parks on foot or by bicycle, or to re-enact the taking of Monferrato in May.

Access: In the village

PIEMONTE

MONFORTE D'ALBA (CN)

32

LE CASE DELLA SARACCA

Fam. Perin
Via Cavour 5
12065 Monforte d'Alba (CN)
Tel. 01 73 78 92 22 – Fax 01 73 78 97 98
info@saracca.Com – www.saracca.com

👤👤 **110€** ☕

Open all year • 6 double rm • Dogs not admitted

 An enchanting mixture of Medieval history and mystery.

Visitors have to climb up a steep hill to explore and discover the ancient secrets of Monforte. In the maze of picturesque streets in the historic centre that once led to the castle, you will come upon this stone edifice, characteristic of medieval architecture. You only have to venture over the threshold to find yourself immersed in a distant past. The stonewalls, wooden ceilings and Indian furniture of the six rooms, most of which boast a fireplace, are full of the legends and emotions of a thousand years of history. Rest assured however: tasteful modern fixtures and fittings have not been forgotten.

Access: In the heart of the village

PIEMONTE

MONFORTE D'ALBA (CN)

33

IL GRILLO PARLANTE

Sig. Staubli Jentgen
Frazione Rinaldi 47, Località Sant'Anna
12065 Monforte d'Alba (CN)
Tel. 01 73 78 92 28 - Fax 01 73 78 92 28
info@piemonte-it.com - www.piemonte-it.com

31-62€

Open all year • 6 double rm • Breakfast €8 • Parking, garden, small dogs welcome

The ideal atmosphere in which to enjoy country life.

The outlying property of a small hamlet reached by a dirt track, this colourful hotel's isolated setting is the perfect location from which to enjoy the Langhe countryside. Everything here is fresh and new, including the young management team. Simple yet tasteful furnishings in keeping with the rustic setting. Wonderful views from the breakfast area and some of the rooms, particularly in the morning.

Access: Leave Monteforte along Via Raddino

PIEMONTE

NOVELLO (CN)

34

B&B ABBAZIA IL ROSETO

Sig.ra Demichelis
Via Roma, 38
12060 Novello (CN)
Tel. 01 73 74 40 16 – Fax 01 73 74 40 16
info@abbaziailroseto.com
www.abbaziailroseto.com

👤👤 75€

Closed Jan • 6 double rm • Parking, garden, no dogs

 We most liked The spectacular view of Monviso from the balcony of room 3.

Located on the road heading into Novello, this 15C abbey was once renowned for its rose garden. Much has changed over the years although the building retains a great deal of its original charm. Six rooms are available to guests; all have open fireplaces and tastefully selected period style furnishings (rugs, wrought iron beds and wooden furniture). Breakfast is served in the characterful surroundings of the brick built former wine cellars.

Access: In the village

PIEMONTE

NOVELLO (CN)

IL NOCCIOLETO

Sig.ra Rigoni
Località Chiarene, 4
12060 Novello (CN)
Tel. 01 73 73 13 23 - Fax 01 73 73 12 51
info@ilnoccioleto.com - www.ilnoccioleto.com

 70€

Closed Jan • 1 single rm, 7 double rm • Half board €42 • Parking, garden, swimming pool • Bicycles available, hazelnuts and wine for sale

 Set Menu €25 and 30

 The children's area of the garden.

Set deep in the countryside, this attractive building provides comfortable spacious accommodation and pleasant grounds. A former barracks, it opened as an agriturismo a few years ago, following a sensitive restoration project. Vineyards and hazelnut trees surround the property, and there is a garden with swimming pool. Traditional Langhe cuisine in the restaurant, with home made pasta and a wide selection of meat dishes.

Access: From Via Circonvallazione, take Via Crosa for 2.5km

PIEMONTE

ORTA SAN GIULIO (NO)

36

LA CONTRADA DEI MONTI
Fam. Ronchetti
Via dei Monti, 10
28016 Orta San Giulio (NO)
Tel. 03 22 90 51 14 – Fax 03 22 90 58 63
lacontradadeimonti@libero.it
www.orta.net/lacontradadeimonti

110€

Closed Jan • 9 single rm, 8 double rm • Garden, small dogs welcome

 The room with sloping wood roof.

The village of Orta has a charm of its own, with its old centre of alleys and historic buildings, and stunning views over the mountains, the lake and the magical island of San Giulio. Located in the heart of Orta, this elegantly genteel and comfortable hotel is close to the picturesque Piazza Motta. Breakfast is served in an attractive room with beamed ceilings and stone walls, while the lobby has an open fireplace with comfortable armchairs and sofas.

Access: In the historic centre

PIEMONTE

PENANGO (AT)

RELAIS IL BORGO

Sig.ra Comollo
a Cioccaro, Via Biletta, 60
14030 Penango (AT)
Tel. 01 41 92 12 72 – Fax 01 41 92 30 67
ilborgodicioccaro@virgilio.it
www.ilborgodicioccaro.com

 120€

Closed 20 Dec-15 Jan • 12 double rm • Half board €110 • Parking, garden, swimming pool, no dogs

 Set Menu €40 and 60 for residents only

 Enjoying the scenery of hillsides and farms from the comfort of a poolside lounger.

This farmstead has been comprehensively restored with due respect to the region's architectural heritage; beyond the lobby is a small courtyard encircled by a balcony giving access to the rooms. Each of these is named after a plant species, and the elegance of the furnishings and attention to detail compare favourably to the area's most distinguished hotels. The public areas are thoughtfully laid out (TV room, library, meeting room), and the courtyard has an unusual circular swimming pool and garden furniture.

Access: Take the SS 457 towards Moncalvo, then turn right towards Cioccaro

PIEMONTE

RODDI (CN)

CASCINA TOETTO

Sig. Alluto
Località Toetto, 2
12060 Roddi (CN)
Tel. 01 73 61 56 22 - Fax 01 73 61 56 22
info@cascinatoetto.it - www.cascinatoetto.it

60-75€

Closed Aug • 5 double rm • Parking, garden, dogs not admitted

 The aroma of grilled meats wafting across the verdant garden.

The Roddi plain lies among Piemonte's Langhe hills, close to the spot where the tributary waters of the Talloria flow into the Tanaro river. Built in 1939, this farmstead was recently restored to provide accommodation in the shape of five welcoming and spacious rooms furnished in period style. To the front of the two buildings which make up this establishment (the farmhouse and the former hay barn) are the well kept gardens, offering barbecue facilities and archery. A good base from which to discover the area's gastronomic delights.

Access: In the country towards Pollenzo

PIEMONTE

SAN DAMIANO D'ASTI (AT)

CASA BUFFETTO

Fam. Lutold
Frazione Lavezzole 67
14015 San Damiano d'Asti (AT)
Tel. 01 41 97 18 08 – Fax 01 41 98 01 52
info@casa-buffetto.com
www.casa-buffetto.com

👫 120-120€

Open all year • 7 double rm • Parking, garden, sauna, swimming pool, dogs not admitted

 The Stöckli-Zimmer: formerly a silk farm, now an elegant guestroom.

This former winegrowing estate, overlooking Monferrato on the top of a hill surrounded by vineyards, is now an inn where guests can delight in the evening concert of crickets, frogs and nightingales. Seven elegant rooms with rib valuted windows command magnificent views of the Langhe hillsides. Period furniture in the rooms reminds guests of the building's historic past. The up-to-date fixtures and fittings are fully in tune with current demands. The peaceful shaded garden and swimming pool outdoors add to the establishment's appeal.

Access: In the countryside, towards San Martino Alfieri

PIEMONTE

SAN GIORGIO CANAVESE (TO)

40

FORESTERIA DEL CASTELLO

Sig. Pachiè
Via Piave, 4
10090 San Giorgio Canavese (TO)
Tel. 01 24 45 07 38 - Fax 01 24 45 05 98
info@foresteriadelcastello.it
www.foresteriadelcastello.it

130-150€

Open all year • 10 double rm • Parking, garden

 Tranquillity and elegance mingled with the souvenir of countless military expeditions.

Protected behind the strongholds that dominate the town, this fortress and its immense towers were built in feudal times to defend the territory. Old paintings depict the castle of the Counts of Biandrate, a famous family of Carolingian origins, whose descendants include the first king of Italy, Arduino of Ivrea and the Counts of Canavese. On the occasion of the 2005 Winter Olympics, the oldest part of the fort, the hostelry, was turned into a small comfortable and refined hotel, with personalised rooms furnished with antiques, each of which commands a matchless view of the Alps.

Access: In a wing of the castle

PIEMONTE

SINIO (CN)

41

LE ARCATE

Sig.ra Manzone
Località Gabutto, 2
12050 Sinio (CN)
Tel. 01 73 61 31 52 – Fax 01 73 61 31 52
learcate@yahoo.it – www.agriturismolearcate.it

65-68€

Closed 8 Jan-15 Feb • 8 double rm • Half board €48 • Parking • Sale of honey, hazelnuts and wine

Menu €16/21

The view from the picture windows of Monviso, beyond vineyards and hazelnut groves.

Situated on the banks of the river Talloria downstream from Alba, Sinio is a village of medieval origin, dominated to this day by its castle standing guard over the road heading south. From the large arched windows, guests enjoy spectacular views of the undulating hills rolling to the horizon, the stark profile of Monviso rising in the distance. Traditional Piedmontese cuisine features prominently in the restaurant; dishes such as bagnacauda, vitello tonnato and brasato are all naturally accompanied by fine wines from the Langhe or Roero.

Access: In the country towards Montelupo Albese

PIEMONTE

TIGLIOLE (AT)

42

VITTORIA

Sig.ra Strocco
Via Roma, 14
14016 Tigliole (AT)
Tel. 01 41 66 77 13 – Fax 01 41 66 76 30
giampieromusso@libero.it – www.ristorantevittoria.it

 150€

Open all year • 11 double rm • Half-board €120 • Parking, garden, swimming pool, dogs not admitted

 Menu €45/60

 We most liked The delightful staircase that leads down to the illuminated swimming pool.

This inn was formerly a stagepost for tradesmen en route to Turin by carriage or horseback. The former family tavern has since been turned into a restaurant and small hotel in which the authentic character of the Asti countryside blends in perfectly with modern comforts. Hotel Vittoria, on the main road, continues to flaunt its 18C façade, while the interior features modern, understated rooms. Local specialities enhanced by herbs from the cottage garden are served in two vaulted dining rooms. Don't miss the tarts and delicious biscuits at breakfast time.

Access: In the heart of the village

PIEMONTE

TORTONA (AL)

43

CASA CUNIOLO

Fam. Cuniolo
Via Amendola 6 (zona Castello)
15057 TORTONA (AL)
Tel. 01 31 86 21 13 – Fax 01 31 86 68 31
info@gabriellacuniolo.com - www.gabriellacuniolo.com

130€

Open all year • 4 double rm • Parking, garden, small dogs welcome

 This villa was inspired by the early 20C Lombardy style: modernism, classicism and rationalism.

Gigi Cuniolo, a 20C Piedmont landscape artist, enjoyed a well-deserved reputation for his art and also for his hospitality. On the hillside of the castle, this immaculate white villa, built according to the canons of rationalist architecture so popular during the 1930s, was the artist's home and workshop. Today the villa's elegant proportions are home to four rooms decorated with unusual furniture, designer touches and souvenirs of the artist, a Navy officer in his youth. In the spacious breakfast room, guests are served freshly pressed juices and homegrown produce.

Access: Near the castle

PIEMONTE

TREZZO TINELLA (CN)

44

ANTICO BORGO DEL RIONDINO

Sig. Poncellini
Via dei Fiori 12
12050 Trezzo Tinella (CN)
Tel. 01 73 63 03 13 – Fax 01 73 63 03 13

 105€

Closed 21 Dec-15 Mar • 8 double rm • Parking • Sale of wine

 Set Menu €36 and 41 for residents only

 Total peace and quiet for undisturbed rest and relaxation.

An ideal destination for those in search of a relaxing holiday and a chance to daydream while gazing at the beautifully peaceful landscape of the green hillsides, vineyards as far as the eye can see, meadows and forests, orchards and vegetable gardens that surround this 18C town whose medieval foundations are worthy of a fairy tale. The rooms are pleasant and well kept, down to the tiniest detail, despite the rather low ceilings. In the kitchen, Piedmont flavours will tantalise your palate and satisfy your gastronomic curiosity.

Access: 3.5km from the village, to the north-east in a medieval town

PIEMONTE

TREZZO TINELLA (CN)

CASA BRANZELE

Sig. Bianco
Via Cappelletto, 27
12050 Trezzo Tinella (CN)
Tel. 01 73 63 00 00 – Fax 01 73 63 09 07
branzele@casabranzele.com
www.casabranzele.com

 75-90€

Closed 7 Jan-15 Mar • 5 double rm • Parking, garden • Bicycles available

 Wandering among the hazelnut groves with the hillside views beyond.

Ideal for visitors seeking a peaceful hotel in the Langhe countryside, this fine 19C country residence has been comprehensively restored by its current owners, a friendly young couple who are psychologists by training. They are not the only people to have been charmed by this building sitting among vineyards and hazelnut groves. It has five simple yet charming rooms, some of which retain an old Piedmontese-style upper level. Also worthy of note is the excellent breakfast comprising local products.

Access: In the rural region of Monpiano

PIEMONTE

USSEAUX (TO)

LAGO DEL LAUX

Sigg. Canton e Aimo
via al Lago 7
10060 Usseaux (TO)
Tel. 012 18 39 44 – Fax 012 18 39 44
laux@mclink.it – www.hotellaux.it

106-126€

Open all year • 7 double rm • Half-board €74-84 • Dogs not admitted

 Menu €30/47

 The dining room: embroidered curtains, fireplace and bunches of cut flowers on each table.

Anyone who likes the snow or long walks in the woods, photography or just good Piedmont cooking cannot fail to be won over by the village of Laux. At an altitude of 1350m, this picturesque town overlooking a delightful small natural lake stands on a morainic pass. It is thought to have been built by a Waldenses community, forced to leave Provence in the 13C, who found refuge in this small valley. Equally steeped in history, this small retreat, in the heart of green pastures and meadows, remains full of hidden secrets. We can however reveal a few gastronomic clues: Piedmont and Occitan dishes, a wide range of regional cured meats, homemade pasta and polenta.

Access: Outside the village at the foot of the Rocca del Laux, on the banks of a natural lake

PIEMONTE

VERBANIA (VB)

47

IL MONTEROSSO

Fam. Minotti
Via Cima Monterosso, 30
28922 Verbania (VB)
Tel. 03 23 55 65 10 – Fax 03 23 51 97 06
ilmonterosso@iol.it – www.ilmonterosso.it

60-75€

Closed Jan, Feb • 1 single rm, 8 double rm • Half board €54-60 • Parking, garden

Set Menu €19 and 22

The view of the lake from the house, set among trees.

A ring of forested peaks surrounds the peaceful waters of the lake, making for fine views from the imposing stone tower of this 19C house. The accommodation offers total tranquillity, interrupted only by the occasional lowing of cattle or neighing from the adjacent stables, where horses may be hired for exploring the surrounding woodland.

Access: At Pallanza, take Viale Azzari and follow the signs

PIEMONTE

Verbania Pallanza (VB)

48

AQUADOLCE

Sig.ra Bartolucci
Via Cietti, 1
28922 Verbania Pallanza (VB)
Tel. 03 23 50 54 18 – Fax 03 23 55 75 34
info@hotelaquadolce.it – www.hotelaquadolce.it

80-105€

Closed 15 Jan-28 Feb • 1 single rm, 12 double rm • No dogs

 The views from the rooms on the upper floors.

A small gem in the centre of the old town, facing the lakefront in the elegant Verbano district. Far from the fashionable hustle and bustle of Stresa, but still facing the Isole Borromee, this 19C hotel has recently undergone sensitive renovation. Almost all the guestrooms have views of the lake and are furnished in arte povera style. A copious buffet breakfast is served in a light and spacious room next to reception. Aquadolce attracts a mix of Italian and foreign guests who are admirably taken care of by the young and enthusiastic staff.

Access: On the banks of Lake Pallenza

PIEMONTE

VERDUNO (CN)

49

REAL CASTELLO

Sig.ra Burlotto
Via Umberto I, 9
12060 Verduno (CN)
Tel. 01 72 47 01 25 - Fax 01 72 47 02 98
info@castellodiverduno.com
www.castellodiverduno.it

👤👤 **100-120€**

Closed 1 Dec-19 Mar • 18 double rm and 2 suites • Half-board €90-107 • Parking, garden, dogs not admitted

 Menu €37/51

 "Gamonedo", a cheese direct from the Asturias!

A former abode of the Counts of Savoie, the castle, near the hostellery and outbuildings, is today a luxury hotel, surrounded by a garden of century-old trees in the historic heart of the small village. The impressive edifice contains elegant rooms which are peaceful and quiet, and decorated with period furniture, original frescoes and countless family heirlooms. The cuisine is a mixture of good plain cooking and typical peasant dishes. The establishment also organises cooking and tasting courses, in addition to contemporary art exhibitions.

Access: In the castle

PIEMONTE

VEZZA D'ALBA (CN)

50

DI VIN ROERO

Sig.ra Borlengo
Piazza San Martino, 5
12040 Vezza d'Alba (CN)
Tel. 017 36 51 14 – Fax 01 73 65 81 11

 52€

Open all year • 4 double rm • Half board €30-40

 Menu €15/20

 The finest traditions of the Roero, namely good food and wine, united under one roof.

Given the area's reputation for producing fine red and white wines, this establishment's choice of name is unsurprising. Located among the Cuneo hills, the ambience is friendly and simple, with the walls painted a lively yellow throughout. Irresistible Piedmontese cuisine with particular emphasis on Roero specialities.

Access: In the upper part of the town

Puglia

In recent years, this region has experienced a reawakening of interest on the part of independent minded travellers. The attractions of its seaside resorts, particularly those of the Gargano peninsula and the south coast between Otranto and Gallipoli, most notably Santa Maria de Leuca, have played a large part in this, but visitors are increasingly heading inland to discover the delights of the real Puglia among its extensive olive groves. In addition to its natural beauty, the region's rich cultural heritage is remarkably evenly distributed, making some of its smaller towns just as interesting as the big cities. Thus, while the streets and alleys of Bari and Lecce clearly deserve exploration, so the lesser centres of Trani, Barletta, Lucera and Ostuni are also guaranteed to surprise and inspire those who seek them out. Other important landmarks include the *trulli* of Alberobello and Frederick II's castles.

Puglia's cuisine has also grown in reputation over the last few years. Drawing upon excellent natural produce, this simple fare is best savoured at one of the hundreds of little festivals held across the region, mainly in the summer months.

15 establishments

Recommended sites and circuits
Puglia

> Visitors cannot fail to be moved by the heady atmosphere of this magnificent region looking towards the mysterious African plains and Asia. From the enigmatic Gargano grottoes to the sun-drenched fields of Tavoliere, from the steppes of the Murgia to the silvery expanses of olive trees, the air is bursting with legends.

A few kilometres from **Andria**, the horizon meets with the imposing silhoutte of **Castel del Monte**. Behind the perfectly geometrical lines of its walls the secret of its function still lies intact, as if suspended between the sacred and the profane. Built by Federico II, it is an expression of medieval culture, marked by the esoteric tradition of sects that were initiated in the Mysteries of the Orient and practised the religion of the Templars. The number eight is omnipresent, and each element of the construction follows precise rules of algebra and astronomy: the octagonal plant is surrounded by eight towers, themselves octagonal, built on the points of each of its corners, the eight rooms of each floor give onto an octagonal court. Further on, the town of Trani, whose oldest part is plotted around the port and on a little peninsula. In the centre, the churches and palazzi call to mind its illustrious past. The imposing white cathedral, with highly complex architectonic forms, is reflected in the turquoise waters of the sea. **Santa Maria di Leuca**, a treasure of the heel of Italy, stands on a coast where cliffs give way to little sandy inlets. The grottoes and underwater riches are a veritable paradise for divers; but the charm of this village, carved out of the rock and cradled by the sea, is in part due to the beauty of its villas. Each of them has a different style, steeped in history and boasting a blend of Ionic, Gothic, French, Tuscan, as well as Pompeian, Moorish, Arab, and even Chinese influences. The most important monument is the Sanctuary dating from 1C AD. Located in the upper part of the town, it can be reached by car or by climbing the interminable stairs that lead to the square, from where it is possible to admire the coast from above and, weather permitting, Albania's mountains.

A recipe to try, wines and... a nugget of information

Wines

_Aleatico di Puglia
_Primitivo di Manduria
_Negro Amaro
_Malvasia Nera
_Moscato di Trani

Local specialities

Burrata (cheese with a buttery centre), Altamura bread, *friselle salentine* (durum wheat and barley bread), white wine *taralli* (biscuits), broad beans, olives, *carteddate* (doughnuts with honey, mulled wine and cinnamon), *lampasciuni* (wild onions for cooking in water and served with a salad), figs, orecchiette pasta, almonds.

CAVATELLI CON LE CIME DI RAPA

Ingredients

- 300g *cavatelli*
- 1kg turnip shoots
- 4 anchovy filets in oil
- 4-5 tablespoons of extra virgin olive oil
- bread without crusts
- garlic
- salt

Method

Clean the turnip shoots and remove the big leaves and hard parts, then rince. Bring to the boil a saucepan of water, and as soon as it starts to bubble add the shoots; wait until the water comes to the boil again and add the *cavatelli*.
Meanwhile, heat in the oil 2 or 3 garlic cloves with the skin, add the anchovies and crush them with a fork so that they break down. Take the stale bread, make it into crumbs and place under the grill. Drain the pasta and the turnip shoots. Away from the heat, put them back in the recipient and add the bread crumbs and the anchovy mixture. Mix well and serve.
The bread is optional but... try it at least once!

Food for thought

Lambascioni or *lampascioni* are wild onions with a slightly bitter taste that can be found by ploughing the ground but only picked after 4 or 5 years.

Our favourite places to eat

U.P.E.P.I.D.D.E.
Vicolo Sant'Agnese 2 – Ruvo di Puglia (BA) – Tel. 080 3613879
Closed 10 Jul-20 Aug and Mon.
A la carte menu €22-33
The skilful blend of tradition and innovation against a backdrop of 15C ramparts.
This restaurant is located in the city's magnificent historical centre. Its typical interior consists of a large oblong space, seemingly dug out of the rock, which opens unexpectedly onto several small adjacent rooms with brick vaults and wooden staircases. The cuisine is traditional, offering a selection of specialities ranging from fresh pasta to meat stews. The impressive cellars are located in the oldest part of the building, dating from the 15C, and house a remarkable selection of wines.

ANTICHI SAPORI
Piazza San Isidoro 10 – Montegrosso (Andria, BT) – Tel. 0883 569529
Closed 23 Dec-3 Jan, 5-25 Jul, Sat eve and Sun.
A la carte menu €22-31
The photos of the village and the display of everyday objects of rural life.
Mussolini founded Montegrosso as part of a scheme to build farmhouses for war veterans. As a result, nowadays, the village has many *masserie* (traditional farms) and typical restaurants. The gastronomic history of this trattoria dates back to the culinary traditions of the Murge hills – typical objets from this time enhance the festive atmosphere. But don't be distracted by the décor, for it is the food that reigns supreme. The menu offers a copious selection of antipasti, almost a meal in itself, as well as local produce accompagnied by grilled meats.

MEDIOEVO
Via Castello 21 – Monte S. Angelo (FG) – Tel. 0884 565356
Closed Mon except Jul-Sep.
A la carte menu €18-36
The irristible smell of the delicious local bread.
Steep and winding roads lead up to this charming village, where legend has it that the Archangel Michael appeared three times in a cave just beyond the houses. The local cuisine is equally remarkable, and is especially renowned for its delicious bread, available in specialist shops. Located a stone's throw from a Norman castle, this restaurant with a characteristic barrel-vaulted ceiling offers a selection of Puglian specialities, including some revived from local memory. The typical ingredients are broad beans and lamb.

PUGLIA

ALESSANO (LE)

MASSERIA MACURANO

Sig. Lugli
Contrada Macuran, 134
73031 Alessano (LE)
Tel. 08 33 52 42 87
info@masseriamacurano.com
www.masseriamacurano.com

👥 ☕ 70-100€

Open from 8 Mar-31 Oct • 5 double rm • Half-board €55-70 • Parking, no dogs • Organised trips, walking, oil and jam for sale

Set Menu €15 and 20

The charming high vaulted ceilings.

Situated in the southernmost part of the Salento, this 16C fortified farmhouse is roughly equidistant from the Adriatic and Ionian coasts. Sensitively restored without detracting from the original features, the building is a classic example of the domestic architecture prevalent in this far flung corner of the peninsula. The owner is a sculptor, originally from Modena, and the simply furnished rooms are remarkable for their size. Homely cuisine focusing on local dishes.

Access: 3km away, follow the signs to Macurano

PUGLIA

ANDRIA (BA)

BIOMASSERIA LAMA DI LUNA

Sig. Petroni
a Montegrosso
70035 Andria (BT)
Tel. 08 83 56 95 05 – Fax 08 83 59 31 34
info@lamadiluna.com – www.lamadiluna.com

👫 130€ ☕

Open from 1 Apr-30 Nov • 10 double rm • Parking, garden • Bicycles available, guided trips, sale of oil

 Pleasant walks among almond and cherry trees, orchids and giant fennel plants.

Reconciling mankind with nature is the aim of this farm, which combines thousand-year-old traditions with a modern Japanese philosophy devoted to rest and wellness. Built around a well that catches the rainwater, this house was a former farmers' home. Restored little by little according to organic architectural principles, it features light guestrooms with a fireplace and north-facing beds, a relaxation area with library and a veranda, where breakfast is served, made only from farm-grown organic produce of course.

Access: 18km away towards Castel del Monte

ANDRIA (BA)

TENUTA COCEVOLA

 Sig. Calvi
Strada Statale 170 al km 9,9 Contrada Cocevola
70031 Andria (BT)
Tel. 08 83 56 69 45 – Fax 08 83 56 97 06
info@tenutacocevola.com
www.tenutacocevola.com

 90-115€

Open all year • 24 double rm • Half-board €75-88 • Garden, dogs not admitted in restaurant

 Menu €30/45

 The immense garden is ideal for relaxing walks and grand receptions.

Built out of tuff rock, this 18C property stands out against a backdrop of blue sky and dark green olive groves. Once past its arched portico, you will discover a light interior and pleasant rooms of understated elegance, all of which are identical and fitted with wood furniture. In the intimate restaurant, you will be invited to sample a repertoire of local fare, which cleverly mingles tradition and sophistication, creating unusual combinations. The delicious wine and olive oil are both made on the estate.

Access: On the N170 towards Castel del Monte, at km 9.9, follow the signs to Tenuta Cocevola

PUGLIA

AVETRANA (TA)

4

MASSERIA BOSCO

Sig. De Padova
Via Stazione km. 1
74020 Avetrana (TA)
Tel. 09 99 70 40 99 – Fax 09 99 70 41 90
info@masseriabosco.it – www.masseriabosco.it

90-160€

Open all year • 12 double rm • Half-board €106-110 • Parking, park, dogs not admitted • Bicycles available, sale of oil, jam and honey

 Menu €25/35

 The four-metre-deep hole, right in the middle of the dining room.

Formerly encircled by a forest of oaks, this stone-built house is home to rooms with high tuff ceilings and adorned with lovely old well-polished furniture, creating a delightfully old-fashioned and welcoming ambience. A number of architectural features, such as openings in the roof to bring in the hay, and a sprinkling of farming implements, bear witness to the fact that the dining rooms were formerly the farm's haylofts. Tradition also prevails in the kitchen: vegetables and meat from the region, homemade pasta and the olive oil on the table comes from the olive trees surrounding the property.

Access: On leaving the village, head north for around 2km, take the last dirt track

PUGLIA

FASANO (BR)

MASSERIA NARDUCCI

Sig. Narducci
Via Lecce, 131
72016 Montalbano di Fasano (BR)
Tel. 08 04 81 01 85 – Fax 08 04 81 01 85
agriturismo_narducci@yahoo.com
www.agriturismonarducci.it

 70-90€

Open all year • 9 double rm • Half board €50-60 • Parking, garden, no dogs • Sale of jam and oil

 Menu €24/36

 The charming and welcoming dining room.

Part of the historical fabric of the landscape, this 19C building began as a post office and retains the typical characteristics of the region's farmhouses, namely functionality and simplicity. Today it is an oasis of peace and tranquillity, sited among gardens and surrounded by the Apulian countryside. Produce grown in the neighbouring fields can be purchased directly, or savoured in the restaurant, a gem of a place serving local specialities.

Access: On the old N°16 road between Ostuni and Fasano

GALATINA (LE)

PALAZZO BALDI
Turismo e Servizi S.r.l.
Corte Baldi 2
73013 Galatina (LE)
Tel. 08 36 56 83 45 - Fax 08 36 56 48 35
hbaldi@tin.it - www.hotelpalazzobaldi.com

👤👤 120€

Open all year • 2 single rm, 13 double rm • Garden

 Discreet luxury that continues into the 21st century.

In the early 16C, Galatina enjoyed a significant economic boom, mainly because of the tanning industry. As a result, this town in the heart of the Salento, attracted the Baldi counts and financiers, originally from Umbria and Tuscany, who had immense reception halls and stables for the horses and carriages built in and around their vast property. Nowadays the palace offers guests welcoming rooms, each of which is individually decorated and adorned with works of art and beautifully crafted objects. The orchard of citrus fruit and comfortable terrace are ideal to laze in the sun and spend long summer evenings.

Access: In the historic centre

PUGLIA

GRAVINA IN PUGLIA (BA)

7

MADONNA DELLA STELLA

Sig. Bosco
Via Madonna della Stella
70024 Gravina in Puglia (BA)
Tel. 08 03 25 63 83 – Fax 08 03 22 33 02
info@madonnadellastella.org
www.madonnadellastella.it

 70€

Open all year • 10 double rm • Half-board €50 • Parking, garden, dogs not admitted

 Menu €24/37

 Rock and tuff creatively combined in a magical atmosphere.

Initially makeshift refuges for the inhabitants of Gravina when the Vandals of Genserico laid the town to waste in 456, one of these natural caves is now a highly original pizza restaurant. The restaurant looks out over a village of immaculate houses, where everything reminds one of a former cave dwelling civilisation. This evocative setting is where you will be served traditional old recipes for lunch and dinner. Further on, a tuff building is home to unpretentious welcoming rooms where you will be awakened by the sounds of the countryside.

Access: In the archaeological zone

PUGLIA

LOCOROTONDO (BA)

SOTTO LE CUMMERSE

Sig.ra Salerno
Via Vittorio Emanuele 138
70010 Locorotondo (BA)
Tel. 08 04 31 32 98 – Fax 08 04 31 32 98
info@sottolecummerse.it – www.sottolecummerse.it

82-115€

Open all year • 9 double rm, 1 suite • Breakfast €3, half-board €83-93 • Small dogs welcome

 Stepping back in time into the traditions and history of this town.

This establishment provides comfortable private holidays in an unusual site. Offering a fascinating insight into history within the walls of an ancient property, without forgoing the convenience of modern comforts, it has found an innovative way of reviving buildings of great cultural and artistic value dotted around the old town. The pointed rooftops, characteristic of the houses of Locorotondo built in local stone, are home to eminently comfortable rooms and apartments, whose simple architecture is set off by "arte povera" furniture and hand-painted crockery.

Access: In the historic centre near the cathedral

PUGLIA

MAGLIE (LE)

CORTE DEI FRANCESI

Sig.ra Amato
Via Roma 172
73024 Maglie (LE)
Tel. 08 36 42 42 82 – Fax 08 36 42 42 83
info@cortedeifrancesi.it – www.cortedeifrancesi.it

👤👦 **60-100€**

Open all year • 6 double rm • Breakfast €5 • Dogs not admitted

An unusual insight into a profession in this enchanting house and patio.

Already known in Maglie at the dawn of the 19C, when two French tanners set up shop here, the "French Court" is ideal for anyone who would like to find out more about the region's folklore. This historic house is typical of Salento, with an inner courtyard where the tanning business was run until late in the 19C. The inn has, for its part, retained the same attachment to period building materials. The guestrooms are comfortable, overlooking the patio, and enhanced with colourful locally crafted furniture. The picturesque breakfast room is built over the tanning vats.

Access: In the heart of the historic centre

PUGLIA

NOCI (BA)

10

LE CASEDDE

Sig.ra Lacenere
Strada Provinciale 239
70015 Noci (BA)
Tel. 08 04 97 89 46 – Fax 08 04 97 89 46
info@lecasedde.com – www.lecasedde.com

👤👥 **68€**

Open all year • 8 double rm • Half board €54 • Parking, garden, tennis, no dogs • Organised trips, pétanque, bicycles available, sale of jam, oil and wine

 Set Menu €21 and 23

 The unique experience of spending the night in a trullo.

A genuine agriturismo where simplicity goes hand in hand with hospitality. Accommodation comes in the form of trulli, the well known characteristic dwellings of the Puglia region, decorated in a contemporary style and offering a comfortable ambience. A few other rooms and the public areas are in a larger building which has an imposing open fireplace. Strategically located in the centre of an area teeming with places of interest, and 20km from the sea.

Access: On the main road to Gioia del Colle, about 3km away

PUGLIA

OSTUNI (BR)

11

NOVECENTO

Sig. Cosimo
Contrada Ramunno
72017 Ostuni (BR)
Tel. 08 31 30 56 66 – Fax 08 31 30 56 68
hotelnovecento@tiscali.it
www.hotelnovecento.com

72-120€

Open all year • 16 double rm • Half-board €47-72 • Parking, park, swimming pool

 Set Menu €22 and 45

 The distinctive ambience created by an austere colour scheme and stone vaulted ceilings.

The façade and interior of this hotel match the prevailing colour of Ostuni, also known as the "White City", which dominates the farthest hillsides of the Murge. Surrounded by an immense park, this 18C residence was entirely rebuilt in the 19C. The architecture is classical with a few whimsical Liberty features, exuding the traditional hospitality and warmth of the south. Everything around you is an invitation to wind down and relax, from the large swimming pool tucked away in the green park to the comfortable bedrooms and cosy sitting rooms where you can read a good book or chat with friends. The traditional cuisine is prepared with produce from the family vegetable garden.

Access: Right in the country, 1km from Ostuni, on the Murge Pass

PUGLIA

POGGIORSINI (BA)

12

MASSERIA IL CARDINALE

Sig. Terribile
Località Contrada Capoposto
70020 Poggiorsini (BA)
Tel. 08 03 23 72 79 – Fax 08 02 46 41 78
info@ilcardinale.it – www.ilcardinale.it

 73€

Closed 7 Jan-28 Feb • 10 double rm • Half-board €60 • Parking, garden, swimming pool, tennis, dogs not admitted in restaurant • Horse riding, guided trips, angling, bicycles available, sale of vegetables in oil and jam

 Set Menu €27 and 35

 Relaxation, countryside and medieval souvenirs amidst the green hillsides of Murgia.

Do you know of a country guesthouse that already existed at the time of the first crusade? We do! Called the "Capoposta" in the Middle Ages, it stands by what was referred to as the "Flea-ridden path" (most of those who took part in the first crusade were poor) and it was here that the pilgrims returning from the Holy Land found food and a bed for the night. Renamed "Il Cardinale", it has been extended over the centuries to become the agritourism establishment it is today. Still a working farm, guests are treated to the coolest rooms and can also take a closer look at the cereal and winegrowing activities. A large fireplace takes pride of place in the picturesque dining room, where regional specialities are served.

Access: In the country, 5km from Contrada Capoposto

PUGLIA

TAVIANO (LE)

13

A CASA TU MARTINU

Sig. Macrì
Via Corsica, 97
73057 Taviano (LE)
Tel. 08 33 91 36 52 – Fax 08 33 91 36 52
info@acasatumartinu.com
www.acasatumartinu.com

👤👤 **80-100€**

Open all year • 11 double rm • Garden, garage, no dogs

 Menu €22/33

 The delightful garden illuminated at night.

One of the best places in the Salento, located in the historic heart of Taviano near the church of Santa Lucia. A classic 18C patrician palace, its simple façade is whitewashed to reflect the glare of the scorching sun. Well presented accommodation with period style furnishings, but the real gem here is the charming courtyard garden, a typical feature of the palaces of southern Italy, where the lucky few could relax in total privacy from the public eye.

Access: In the historic centre

PUGLIA

TRANI (BA)

14

SAN PAOLO AL CONVENTO

Sig.ra Lamacchia
Via Statuti Marittimi 111
70059 Trani (BT)
Tel. 08 83 48 29 49 – Fax 08 83 48 70 96
hotels.paolo@virgilio.it
www.sanpaoloalconvento.traniweb.it

👤👤 135-145€

Open all year • 33 double rm • Small dogs welcome

 For residents only

 Breakfast is served in a former chapel decorated with the Last Supper.

This hotel is located in an impressive listed building, the former monastery of Barnabiti Fathers dating from the 15C. Only five yards from the water's edge and wedged between the docks, the church devoted to the same patron saint and the town hall overlooking the sea, this establishment still has its original floors. Furnished with period pieces and paintings, the rooms command a sumptuous view of the port and the cloisters. The hotel also boasts a modern wellness centre and a comfortable sitting room, the Sala Paolina.

Access: In the sheltered dock between the town hall and Barnabiti church. In the convent of the same name

PUGLIA

UGGIANO LA CHIESA (LE)

15

MASSERIA GATTAMORA

Sig.ra Baldassarre
Via Campo Sportivo, 33
73020 Uggiano la Chiesa (LE)
Tel. 08 36 81 79 36 – Fax 08 36 81 45 42
info@gattamora.it – www.gattamora.it

100-105€

Closed Jan-Feb • 2 single rm, 9 double rm • Parking, garden, no dogs in restaurant

Menu €27/37

The coloured Lecce stone in the vaulted ceilings.

Situated on the outskirts of the village, this long 19C farmhouse has a whitewashed façade. Inside the look is altogether more striking; a vast structure, the walls of local stone supporting the vaulted roof. In the restaurant are two rows of columns supporting star vaults giving the appearance of a church rather than a converted stable block. The same style is in evidence in the rooms, their bare walls of hewn stone possessing an unusual charm.

Access: On the outskirts of the village

Sardegna

Nuraghic evidence suggests activity on the island as early as 1800 BC, from which point onwards Sardinia was subject to successive conquests by maritime powers, including the Phoenicians, Romans, Vandals, Byzantines, Saracens, Pisans, Genoese, Spaniards and Austrians. Traces of their presence are strewn across the island, but most notably in the coastal towns. Inland, the beautiful but wild landscape has been more resistant to conquest. Today, Sardinia is known throughout the world for its stunning coastline and archipelagos, which every summer draw huge numbers of visitors, including many big spenders. Despite this, it is still possible to avoid the famous resorts and instead seek out an unspoilt corner of natural paradise.

The cuisine is worthy of special mention: specialities include *carasau* (soft-doughed bread), *sebadas* (round doughnuts) and *papassinos* (desserts). Worthy of mention also are the Vermentino (white) and Cannonau (red) wines as well as the myrtle liqueur.

7 establishments

Recommended sites and circuits Sardegna

> Cradle of an ancient culture and a land of great traditions, Sardinia was born from the contact between the Earth and the Sea. This is an island of sun and nature, with the scents of Mediterranean flora, myrtle and rosemary, and the colours of a wild and unspoilt nature. Its ancient traditions and authentic character have enchanted visitors since the dawn of time.

The town of **Alghero** is one of Sardinia's most beautiful. A vibrant and unique place nicknamed "Italy's Catalan town" because its history and dialect reflect Catalonia. All along the ramparts of the old town, you will be immersed in the medieval atmosphere that lives on, and charmed by Alghero's numerous towers: the Torre del Portal, in the heart of the historical centre, from where the view is unbeatable, the Torre dell'Esperò, which is the oldest, the Torre di S. Jaume, the only one to have an octagonal layout, used in the past for kennels (whence, in all probability, its name *Torre dels Cutxcus*, "Tower of Dogs"). Strolling along the coast, you will come to the **Capo Caccia** promontory whose high and sheer sides, punctuated by natural grottoes and cliffs, offer a spectacle of rare beauty and still untamed nature where you can admire the elegant falcons and griffins in flight. Don't miss the **Grotta di Nettuno** (Neptune's Grotto), located at the western end of the promontory. You can reach it by foot via the **Escala del Cabirol** and its 656 steps overhanging the sea – the climb down is sure to get your adrenalin flowing. The grotto extends over 1200m of fairytale landscapes as only nature can create: magnificent lakes and narrow passages that open out onto wider spaces decorated by incredible limestone formations. Along the eastern coast, the beauty of the landscape is equally stupefying. Continue towards the heart of the **Costa Smeralda** (Emerald Coast) into a dreamily beautiful scenery of immaculate beaches, limpid waters and rocky promontories and inebriating scents. From **Porto Rotondo** to **Golfo Aranci** lies a succession of rocky little inlets that open out onto the sea. The name Golfo Aranci in fact comes from a cartographical mistake: the town owes its name to an inaccurate translation of an ancient term *granchi* (crabs) as *aranci* (oranges) – ironically enough there is not a single orange tree on the coast!

A recipe to try, wines and... a nugget of information

Wines
_Cannonau di Sardegna
_Vermentino di Gallura
_Girò
_Nuragus
_Vernaccia

Local specialities
Pecorino, fresa (one of the region's few soft cheeses), *porceddu* (spit-roast suckling pig), *malloreddus, culigione* (stuffed ravioli), *fregola* (little balls of semolina grilled and served in a meat or fish broth), fish eggs, *tonnina* (sausage made from tuna), chestnuts, mushrooms, honey, nougat, *carasau* bread, saffron.

MALLOREDDUS (gnocchetti sardi)

Ingredients
▸ 500g semolina
▸ 1 measure saffron
▸ salt
▸ tomato sauce
▸ grated Sardinian pecorino

Method
Make a well with the flour and dilute the saffron in a glass of warm water with a pinch of salt. Work the dough thus obtained until it has a firm, compact consistency, then cut it into cylinders approximately the width of three fingers and shape into little ropes that are long and thin like *grissini*. Cut the ropes into small bean-size pieces and roll them on the back of a fork to imprint them with lines, then press them into a concave shape. Leave them to dry on a lightly floured tea towel. Cook the little gnocchi in a large volume of salted water, drain them and add the tomato sauce and grated Sardinian pecorino.

Food for thought
Filo 'e ferru is a grappa made by distilling the marc from grapes used to make the island's most potent wines. The name comes from the necessity, in the past, to hide the recipients used in the clandestine distilling process; they were hidden inside pumpkins that were tied with a wire to indicate the presence of the grappa.

Our favourite places to eat

DA RICCARDO
Via Vittorio Emanuele 13/15 – Magomadas (NU) – Tel. 0785 35631
Closed 15-31 Oct and Tue.
À la carte menu €22-41
 The simplicity of the seafood dishes, in keeping with Sardinian tradition.
This family-run trattoria is housed in a former mansion in the heart of the village. Simplicity is their credo. The restaurant area occupies just one attractively decorated room with rustic-style tables, where they serve homemade seafood dishes. The owner, Signor Roberto, himself a fisherman, can personally vouch for the freshness of the cuisine. On the menu: seafood and shellfish soups, skate with garlic sauce, grilled catch of the day and the incomparable seadas (desserts made with honey and sheep's cheese).

SU GOLOGONE
Sorgente su Gologone (Oliena, NU) – Tel. 0784 287512
Open all year.
À la carte menu €35-50
 Enjoying the offerings of this gourmet palace on the terrace or by the huge fireplace.
It's hard to believe that at one time this gourmet restaurant made nothing but *panini*. Against the backdrop of the Barbagia forests, a stone's throw away from the limpid springs of the heights of Supramonte, the Palimodde family built their white-walled restaurant dedicated to Sardinian cooking. The inside is a veritable museum dedicated to island traditions; the restaurant houses a display of cooking utensils and a curious fireplace in which suckling pigs are roasted – one of the house specialities that will only render your choice of dishes all the more difficult.

AL TONNO DI CORSA
Via Marconi 47 – Ile de San Pietro (Carloforte, CA) – Tel. 0781 855106
Closed 7 Jan-28 Feb and Mon, except Jul-Aug.
À la carte menu €45-61
 Tasting their tuna specialities, and strolling in the narrow streets nearby.
Located in the upper town, in the heart of the historic district known as the *casinee*, this restaurant is just a few minutes from the seafront. The open kitchen provides a guarantee of quality and gives a foretaste of the mouthwatering dishes to come. The restaurant has two rooms and two outdoor terraces for summer dining, an ideal setting for discovering Carloforte's tradition of tuna, fished in adjacent tuna farms and prepared in all manner of ways. Fresh pasta and the best of the Mediterranean also feature on the menu.

SARDEGNA

AGGIUS (SS)

IL MUTO DI GALLURA

Sig. Serra
Località Fraiga
07020 Aggius (SS)
Tel. 079 62 05 59 – Fax 079 62 05 59
info@mutodigallura.com – www.mutodigallura.com   80€

Open all year • 1 single rm, 13 double rm • Parking, garden, swimming pool, no dogs • Horse riding, bicycles available, cheese and wine on sale

Set Menu €16 and 35

The heritage conserved in the choice of name.

In the mid 19C, a feud between the families of two young lovers resulted in more than 70 deaths around Aggius. To this day, local folklore recalls the muto di Gallura (the 'Gallura mute'), a hitman who has become a figure of romantic nostalgia. The spirit of the district is best discovered by walking or riding through the countryside, a timeless landscape as venerable as any Sardinian tradition.

Access: About 1km from the village towards Tempio Pausania

SARDEGNA

BOSA (NU)

SA PISCHEDDA

Sig. Pischedda
Via Roma, 8
08013 Bosa (NU)
Tel. 07 85 37 30 65 – Fax 07 85 37 20 00
info@hotelsapischedda.it
www.hotelsapischedda.it

 75-98€

Open all year • 6 single rm, 9 double rm • Half board €60-75 • Parking, garden, dogs not admitted in restaurant

 Menu €28/45

 The unusual interior, with frescoes and a strong Mediterranean feel.

Named after the owner (the term means a type of basket in local dialect), this establishment is a slice of the real Sardinia, where the island's sense of identity is alive and well. Situated in the centre of Bosa, one of the prettiest towns in the area, it occupies a 19C palazzo. This building also hosts a permanent exhibition of works of art by the painter Eugenio Scheler, whose frescoes adorn the lobby and some of the rooms, making a stay here an even more memorable experience.

Access: In the historic centre

CALASETTA (CA)

BELLAVISTA

Sig.ra Tregosti
Via Sottotorre, 7
09011 Calasetta (CA)
Tel. 078 18 89 71 – Fax 078 18 82 11
tregomar@tiscali.it
www.calasettabellavista.it

 84-94€

Closed 4 Nov-15 Dec • 2 single rm, 10 double rm • Breakfast €7, half board €79-85 • Garden, no dogs

 Menu €30/45

 Watching the sun go down over the island of San Pietro.

This is not the place for those few unmoved by Sardinia's culture of cuisine and the sea. This little hotel has a simple façade and is attractively situated on a low hill above the beach with views over the island of San Pietro, separated by a narrow strip of water from the peninsula of Sant'Antioco. The restaurant has two appealing features, namely its terrace and the traditional Sardinian cuisine, including some interesting cheeses.

Access: Very near the town, in the seaside area

SARDEGNA

QUARTU SANT'ELENA (CA)

SU MERIAGU

Fam. Laconi
Via Rimini, 1
09045 Quartu Sant'Elena (CA)
Tel. 070 89 08 42 – Fax 070 89 08 42
sumeriagu@tiscali.it

 80-100€

Open all year • 3 single rm, 5 double rm • Half board €60-70 • Parking, garden

 Menu €24/31

 The pride in all things Sardinian, especially matters culinary.

Sant' Andrea is a small settlement on the road which runs east from Cagliari along the gulf of Quartu. The hotel is close to the sea and derives its name from a local term meaning a shaded grazing area. Inside, the modern decor has a tasteful personal feel. Two pleasant rooms; one small and cosy with open fireplace, the other larger and circular with a single central column supporting the ceiling beams. The island's traditional crafts are evoked in the choice of decorative items.

Access: Outside the village, along the coast towards Villasimius

SAN PIETRO (ISOLA DI) - CARLOFORTE (CA)

HIERACON

Hieracon Srl
Corso Cavour, 32
09014 Carloforte (CA)
Tel. 07 81 85 40 28 – Fax 07 81 85 48 93
hotelhieracon@libero.it – www.hotelhieracon.com **85-100€**

Open all year • 3 single rm, 19 double rm, 2 suites • Breakfast €4; half board €70-80 • Garden

 Menu €30/52

 Enjoying the cool mornings beneath the garden's palm trees.

Hieracon was the Greek name for the island of San Pietro, and although this former private residence does not date back to ancient times, it has some history to it. The façade is in the decorated style of the early 20C, its austere upper storey profile broken up by floral detail surrounding the windows. There is a well planted inner courtyard garden where breakfast may be taken; the seafront is a stone's throw away, while the port and centre of town are also easily reached.

Access: By Caroloforte promenade, centrally located

SARDEGNA

SANTU LUSSURGIU (OR)

6

ANTICA DIMORA DEL GRUCCIONE

Sig.ra Belloni
Via Michele Obinu, 31
09010 Santo Lussurgiu (OR)
Tel. 07 83 55 20 35 – Fax 07 83 55 20 36
info@anticadimora.com – www.anticadimora.com

👤👤 76€

Closed 7-21 Jan • 3 single rm, 6 double rm • Half board €60 • Dogs not admitted

 Set Menu €25 and 30 for residents only

 The family's love of nature

Situated at an altitude of 500m in the Parco Naturalistico del Sinis-Montiferru, Santu Lussurgiu is a typical inland medieval village, located 30km from the sea, and is an ideal base for visitors wishing to explore this lesser-known part of Sardinia. The Antica Dimora is a stone mansion whose architecture shows clear evidence of Spain's former influence over the island. An imposing doorway leads to the internal courtyard, which is the perfect spot in which to sit and relax, surrounded by greenery and attractive climbing plants. The well-appointed rooms are discreetly comfortable, while the restaurant serves a selection of genuine Sardinian dishes.

Access: In the historic centre

SARDEGNA

STINTINO (SS)

DEPALMAS PIETRO

 Sig. Depalmas
Località Preddu Nieddu
07040 Stintino (SS)
Tel. 079 52 31 29
agriturismo.depalmas@tiscali.it
www.agriturismodepalmas.com

👤👤 52€

Open all year • 2 single rm, 4 double rm • Breakfast €4; half board €45 • Parking, garden, no dogs in the restaurant

 Set Menu €25

 Views of the sea to both east and west.

This establishment was a restaurant until recently enhanced by the addition of simple, welcoming accommodation from where guests may enjoy the tranquillity of their surroundings. The emphasis remains very much on food; most of the meat is reared by the proprietor and often cooked over the open fire in the dining room. Ideally situated near the famous beach at Pellosa, on the Stintino peninsula from where there are views of the gulf of Asinara and the Sardinian sea.

Access: 2km from the village, towards Porto Torres

Sicilia

Lying at the very heart of the Mediterranean, Sicily is a historical chronicle. Greeks, Romans, Arabs, Normans, Spaniards and French have left their mark here, among its incredibly varied landscape and extraordinarily hospitable people. From the alleys of Ortigia to the summits of its volcanic peaks, on its protected beaches, and in its little mountain villages perched on rocky outcrops, there is infinite variety which never fails to surprise the visitor. The numerous archipelagos skirting the island are especially popular with those who love the sea.

Sicily's cuisine is justly renowned, and the mere mention of a few of its dishes should get mouths watering. Specialities include *arancini di riso* (rice balls), *pasta alla Norma* (with aubergines, tomatoes and ricotta cheese), *sarde a beccafico* (sardines), *cannoli* (filled with ricotta and candied fruit) and *cassata* (partly-iced cream cake), ice cream and *granite*. Needless to say, these specialities are best accompanied by a glass of the local wine: Alcamo, Etna Rosso, Malvasia delle Lipari, Moscato di Pantelleria and Marsala to name but a few.

21 establishments

Recommended sites and circuits
Sicily

> Sicily is a veritable museum of art and history under an open sky, a melting pot of civilisations and cultures that has made this incredible sun-drenched island a place of dramatic contrasts in which Mediterranean identity has been enriched with Arab and Norman influences.

In **Sciacca**, Norman and Arab civilisations intermingle in the Moorish atmosphere of the little streets and courtyards. The imprint of history is omnipresent from the Norman cathedral, at the heart of the densely packed little streets, to the 15C Bertolino Palazzo, the port, or the Enchanted Castle, whose gardens are scattered with hundreds of sculpted stone figures. Sciacca is also known for its ceramics and its thermal springs, which have been celebrated by many illustrious figures (Plutarch, Diodorus, Cicero, Pliny, Strabo). The earthenware of **Caltagirone** is also renowned; they have been making it here since the dawn of time and numerous boutiques enliven the streets with the tiles, plates and vases that worthily represent this ancestral art form. The *cannatari* have perfected a decorative technique without altering the Moorish motifs and traditional colours. In the churches and opulent palaces you can sense the influence of past peoples (Genoese, Normans, Aragonese and Spanish). The Scala di Santa Maria del Monte, a stairway of 143 steps, of an overall height of 50m, which connects the higher part of the town with the lower part, is certainly worth a detour. Entirely covered with multicoloured earthenware, it rates as the town's principal attraction.

Don't forget to visit **Erice**, the "windy town", whose centre has preserved intact the charm of an ancient fortified market town with its typical boutiques (the local pastries made behind the silent walls of the convents are exquisite!). You should also visit the castle of Venus, built by the Normans upon the ruins of an old temple dedicated to the eponymous goddess. Further on, **San Vito Lo Capo**, located at the summit of a promontory at the extreme west of the island, is a small fishing village whose beautiful flora and habitations cannot fail to delight. To get to it, take the little winding road that runs along the side of the low hills, through olive trees, isolated market towns, vineyards and fields. Here the sea and beaches are excellent: 3km of golden sands to rival any tropical paradise. Between San Vito Lo Capo and **Scopello** is the **nature reserve of Zingaro** with its 1700ha of untainted nature, clear waters and cliffs that descend to the sea, forming inviting rocky inlets with white pebbles.

A recipe to try, wines and... a nugget of information

Wines
_Alcamo Bianco
_Cerasuolo di Vittoria
_Corvo red and white
_Donnafugata
_Etna
_Marsala
_Zibibbo

Ingredients
- 300g plain flour
- 30g butter
- 30g caster sugar
- 30g pistachios
- 400g ricotta
- 200g icing sugar
- 100g candied fruit (orange, cedar, squash)
- 50g chocolate slivers
- 1 egg
- dry Marsala (or dry white wine)
- frying oil
- ground cinnamon

Local specialities
Pasta with sardines, *pasta alla Norma* (in homage to Bellini's masterpiece), ricotta, *primosale, sfinciuni* (tomato and onion pizza), *schiacciate* (flat breads that can be stuffed), oranges, medlars, pomegranates, arbutus-berries, Damascus grapes, *minnulata* (water with almond milk), grenadine, *rosolio* (liqueur), *cassata* (pastry with fromage frais and candied fruit), *caponata* (of Persian origin).

CANNOLI ALLA SICILIANA

Method
Mix together the flour, egg yolk, sugar, melted butter, a pinch of salt, and the Marsala until you obtain a smooth and supple consistency. Cover and leave for 2hr. Mix the icing sugar into the ricotta, add the diced candied fruits, the roughly chopped pistachios and the chocolate and mix well. Roll out the pastry and cut it into thin squares measuring 10-12cm each side; brush with the beaten egg white and roll them around cylindrical moulds. Fry and then leave on absorbent kitchen paper, take off the moulds and fill with ricotta. Sprinkle over the vanilla icing sugar and cinnamon.

Food for thought
In Sicily it is inconceivable to eat a meal without bread! Each village has dozens of different types, of varying composition, shape, and rising and cooking time; bread has hundreds of names, and there are also types of bread that are especially prepared solely on the occasion of religious and non-religious festivals.

Our favourite places to eat

MAJORE
Via Martiri Ungheresi 12 – Chiaramonte Gulfi (RG) – Tel. 0932 928019
Closed Mon and Jul.
A la carte menu €15-21
 One hundred years of experience in the art of preparing pork.

History takes pride of place in this restaurant. Located in a medieval market town, it is renowned for the savoir-faire of a family that has been in the restaurant business for more than a century. The appeal of the place lies in its unfussy food and in the simplicity of the décor. The restaurant's motto, "Here, we exalt pork", hung on the wall of one of the two rooms, will give you a hint of what to expect. Homemade sausage, ravioli with pork-based sauce and grilled or stuffed pork ribs (the house speciality) are on offer. Other suggestions include various risottos and *macaroni alla Norma* (with aubergine and ricotta).

LA CAMBUSA
Via Garibaldi 72 – Lipari (ME) – Tel. 349 4766061
Open 20 Mar-Oct.
A la carte menu €26-36
 Sampling the Sicilian and Eolian seafood specialities.

This restaurant, located in the centre of the village, has just one room that is decorated with original objects and photos, and set out with small, closely arranged tables. It's a family-run place: the lady of the house works in the kitchen and her husband works the front of house. Simple and rustic seafood specialities vary according to the day's catch and reflect the island's dual Eolian and Sicilian traditions. We recommend the *capricci siciliani* (an assortment of antipasti) for starters, then *macaroni alla Norma*, spaghetti or the catch of the day, and to finish, *cassata siciliana* (a local pastry with fromage frais and fruit conserve).

NOEMI
Via Manzoni 8 – Gallodoro (ME) – Tel. 0942 37338
Closed 25 Jun-15 Jul and Tue.
A la carte menu from €25-28
 Sicily in all its glory: feast your eyes and titillate your palate.

This restaurant has extraordinary panoramic views over the coast, which you can appreciate all the more from the outdoor seating area during the summer months. The owners extend a warm family welcome and offer a delightful taste of traditional Sicilian cuisine. You can choose between several different menus that propose fixed selections of antipasti and main dishes. The typically Sicilian food served is a happy marriage of quantity and quality.

SICILIA

AVOLA (SR)

MASSERIA SUL MARE

Sig. Conigliaro
Contrada Gallina
96012 Avola (SR)
Tel. 09 31 56 01 01 – Fax 09 31 56 01 01
info@masseriasulmare.it
www.masseriasulmare.it

140-160€

Open all year • 1 single rm, 21 double rm • Half-board €85-95 • Parking, beach, dogs not admitted in restaurant

Set Menu €17 and 25

Creeks, coves and jetties paint the picture of this splendid private beach.

Founded in 1693 by order of Prince Nicolò Aragona Pignatelli following the destruction of ancient Abola by a massive earthquake, the town is today a busy agricultural hub, devoted above all to almonds, citrus fruits and wine. The region is also rich in cottage gardens, olive groves and wheat fields. The main wing of the farm, set in the heart of this natural patchwork, dates from the early 20C, offering beautiful rooms, fitted out in the former stables, outbuildings and little cottages dotted around the estate. The former barn, where the almonds used to be dried, is now the restaurant which makes it a point of honour to serve local produce that does full justice to the island's gastronomic heritage.

Access: On the Siracusa-Nota road at km marker 391.600

SICILIA

CALTAGIRONE (CT)

2

VILLA TASCA

Sig.ra Tasca
Contrada Fontana Pietra
95041 Caltagirone (CT)
Tel. 093 32 27 60 – Fax 09 33 35 12 69
info@villatasca.it – www.villatasca.it

100-148€

Open all year • 10 double rm • Half-board €80-120 • Parking, park, garden

 Menu €24/34

 Waiting patiently on the sundeck for the sun to rise or set.

Treat yourself to a break and a few days' rest: a dip in the pool, a bicycle ride along the tree-lined cycling path that runs alongside the old railway line from Caltagirone to Piazza Armerina, or a horseback trek. On your return, this 18C farmhouse will be waiting to welcome you with open arms. Located in a quiet spot off the main tourist track, this country house offers comfortable rooms, all overlooking the garden and a small sitting room adorned with period furniture, ideal for a quiet read or chat with friends. The restaurant, open to guests only, features good plain cooking that upholds Sicilian culinary traditions.

Access: 3km from the village towards Mirabella Imbaccari

SICILIA

CARLENTINI (SR)

3

TENUTA DI ROCCADIA

Sig.ra Ferrauto
Contrada Roccadia
96013 Carlentini (SR)
Tel. 095 99 03 62 – Fax 095 99 03 62
info@roccadia.com – www.roccadia.com

👤👤 **100€**

Open all year • 20 double rm • Parking, garden, swimming pool, no dogs in the restaurant • Sale of cheese, oil and jam, guided trips, horse riding

 Set Menu €20 and 40

 The home grown produce, ripened in the Sicilian sun.

No corner of Sicily is without traces of the island's long history, and this district is no exception. This agriturismo is located in an archaeological area where excavations have revealed an ancient necropolis. Today's landscape is agricultural, producing olives and citrus fruits which are used for making jams and liqueurs as well as for immediate consumption. The simple rooms are decorated in rustic style. Activities include swimming, riding and archery.

Access: *4km from the village towards Villasmundo*

SICILIA

CATANIA (CT)

4

LA VECCHIA PALMA

Sig. Calvino
Via Etnea, 668
95128 Catania (CT)
Tel. 095 43 20 25 – Fax 095 43 11 07
info@lavecchiapalma.com
www.lavecchiapalma.com

100-110€

Open all year • 1 single rm, 10 double rm, 1 suite • Small dogs welcome

 The patrician elegance of this villa in old Catania.

Located on via Etnea, the street which runs through the centre of Catania towards the summit of Mount Etna, this hotel is an elegant 19C villa retaining its original interior layout and small courtyards. The period ambience is especially strong in the rooms, furnished with antique pieces and decorated with frescoes and original stucco work on the ceilings.

Access: In the centre of the town on the main road

SICILIA

EOLIE (Isole) Filicudi (ME)

LA CANNA

Sig.ra Merlino
Contrada Rosa
98050 Filicudi (ME)
Tel. 09 09 88 99 56 – Fax 09 09 88 99 66
info@lacannahotel.it – www.lacannahotel.it

62-140€

Closed Nov • 14 double rm • Breakfast €10, half-board €98 • Parking, swimming pool, dogs not admitted

 Menu €28/33

 The island's countryside is as tempting to the eye as it is to the palate.

Formerly known as "Phoenicusa" because of its lush green vegetation of ferns and palm trees, the wild unspoilt isle of Filicudi is the least known of the Eolian archipelago. Perfect for all those in search of a seaside holiday, it is also greatly appreciated by those who enjoy quiet walks in the country. This old house surrounded by greenery has retained its original structure. A swimming pool, large terrace with a sundeck and a cafeteria for breakfasts or a nightcap before bed are available to guests. Traditional flavours and simple recipes take pride of place on the menu. Fishing boats can be hired to explore the island.

Access: Near the port, panoramic view

SICILIA

MODICA (RG)

PALAZZO FAILLA

Dr. Failla
Via Blandini 5
97015 Modica (RG)
Tel. 09 32 94 10 59 - Fax 09 32 94 10 59
info@palazzofailla.it - www.palazzofailla.it

125-160€

Open all year • 2 single rm, 5 double rm • Half-board €90-115 • Garage, dogs not admitted

 Menu €31/55

 Elegance and attention to detail set the scene for this happy blend of the charm of yesteryear and modern comforts.

In the upper part of the town, where the houses seem to cling to the rock face, a few yards from the cathedral and the counts' castle, this hotel has kept intact the atmosphere of the 17C aristocratic palace in which it is located. The rooms are comprised of vaulted or fresco-painted ceilings and are decorated with earthenware and ceramic craftwork, all of which in a happy spirit of opulent antiquity and modernity. The warm and cordial staff is tirelessly on the lookout to satisfy your every whim, from breakfast time, when you have an immense choice of homemade sweet and savoury specialities, to dinnertime, a creative adaptation of traditions, served in the Gazza ladra restaurant.

Access: At Modica Alta, near San Giorgio Cathedral

SICILIA

NICOSIA (EN)

BAGLIO SAN PIETRO

Sig.ra Greco
Contrada San Pietro
94014 Nicosia (EN)
Tel. 09 35 64 05 29 – Fax 09 35 64 06 51
info@bagliosanpietro.com – www.bagliosanpietro.com   80€

Closed 30 Oct-30 Nov • 9 double rm • Half board €58 • Parking, garden, swimming pool, no dogs

Menu €18/26

The flavours and colours of the Sicilian countryside.

Surrounded by leafy oak and hazel trees and grazing sheep, this stone walled farmstead is composed of a 17C main house and farm workers' hovel with inner courtyards. The restaurant is in the old hay barn and serves simple fare incorporating genuine local products grown under the Sicilian sun, a far cry from the elaborate dishes of city hotels.

Access: On the way out of the village towards Palermo

SICILIA

NOTO (SR)

MASSERIA DEGLI ULIVI

F.lli Salvatore
Contrada Porcari
96017 Noto (SR)
Tel. 09 31 81 30 19 – Fax 09 31 81 30 19
info@masseriadegliulivi.com
www.masseriadegliulivi.com

👤👤 **90-150€**

Closed 10 Nov-28 Feb • 16 double rm • Half-board €100-105 • Parking, garden, swimming pool, tennis, dogs not admitted

 Set Menu €25 and 30

 The wood ceilings, terracotta tiled floors and traditional furniture made on the island.

This establishment is ideally situated for those wishing to see the main tourist sites of the region, including Palazzolo Acreide, famous for its Greek theatre, the natural reserves of Cava Grande and its small lakes linked by mini waterfalls, and the ruins of Pantalica. This plush late 19C residence, lost in a landscape of olive groves, old roses and Mediterranean essences, is ideal for a well-earned rest, offering spacious, comfortable and well-equipped rooms. In the dining rooms, whose characteristic roofs are made from bundles of reeds and plaster, you will be treated to a menu that continues to uphold the region's gastronomic traditions.

Access: Around 8km from the village towards Palazzolo Acreide

SICILIA

PETTINEO (ME)

9

CASA MIGLIACA

Sig.ra Allegra
Contrada Migliaca
98070 Pettineo (ME)
Tel. 09 21 33 67 22 - Fax 09 21 39 11 07
info@casamigliaca.com - www.casamigliaca.com

Open all year • 8 double rm • Half board only €75 • Parking, garden, pétanque, no dogs

 For residents only

 The view from the courtyard over the ancient ruins of Alesa to the azure sea beyond.

Close to Pettineo, the entrance to this property is flanked by pillars, beyond which a dirt track winds through olive trees. After 100m or so it reaches this 17C olive press, entirely surrounded by peaceful farmland which to this day is engaged in cultivation of the olive, the true symbol of the nations of the Mediterranean. Olive processing remains the principal activity of this establishment, although for some years it has also offered accommodation, allowing guests to enjoy stunning views over the valley to the shores of the Tyrrhenian.

Access: At the entrance to the village on the SP 113

SICILIA

PIANA DEGLI ALBANESI (PA)

10

MASSERIA ROSSELLA

Sig. Dara
contrada Rossella
90037 Piana degli Albanesi (PA)
Tel. 09 18 46 00 12 – Fax 09 18 46 00 12
info@masseria-rossella.com
www.masseria-rossella.com

👤👤 100-120€

Closed 6 Jan-28 Feb • 10 double rm • Half-board €73-83 • Parking, garden, swimming pool, dogs not admitted in restaurant • Paragliding, bicycles available, oil and jam for sale

Set Menu €25 and 35

The ancient stone arch above the entrance to the restaurant.

In a region famous for its roses since time immemorial, this magnificent hunting lodge, built by Prince di Belmonte at the start of the 19C, is a fine example of simple elegance down to the tiniest details. In the heart of the Sicilian countryside, this establishment offers guests rooms with independent access, fitted out with hand-crafted antiques, engravings on the walls and opulent fabrics, in addition to a library. Local flavours and produce from the farm estate (cheese, wine, olive oil and fruit) can be sampled in a large dining room. Gigantic white mulberry trees surround the swimming pool complete with parasols and loungers.

Access: At Ficuzza-Piana Albanesi crossroads, take the n°5 minor road towards Piana for 8km

SICILIA

RAGUSA (RG)

11

IL BAROCCO

Sig. Cabibbo
Via S. Maria La Nuova , a Ibla
97100 Ragusa (RG)
Tel. 09 32 66 31 05 – Fax 09 32 22 89 13
info@ilbarocco.it – www.ilbarocco.it

100-120€

Open all year • 3 single rm, 12 double rm • Half-board €68-80

 Menu €19/26

 *The joiner's workshop has been converted into a hotel, an imaginative blend of old and new.*

This unusual late 19C edifice stands on the Ibla, a hill inhabited by the Sicilians as early as the 14C BC. The property, made up of two buildings laid out around an inner courtyard, is now home to Il Barocco Hotel, in tribute to the Baroque art façades on many of the town's houses. The interior, adorned with frescoes that depict the town's main monuments, is both stylish and simple, furnished in an "arte povera" style. Nearby, an aristocratic palace is home to a pizza restaurant of the same name with an informal atmosphere that is ideal for savouring dishes whose aromas evoke both art and history.

Access: Near San Giorgio Cathedral

SICILIA

RANDAZZO (CT)

L'ANTICA VIGNA

Sig.ra Zuccarello
Località Montelaguardia
95036 Randazzo (CT)
Tel. 095 92 40 03 – Fax 095 92 33 24
info@anticavigna.it – www.anticavigna.it

 66-70€

Closed 10 Jan-10 Feb • 10 double rm • Half board €50-60 • Parking, garden, tennis, no dogs • Bicycles available, oil and wine for sale

 Set Menu €20 and 25

 The view of Mount Etna, a sleeping giant dominating the horizon.

Randazzo is on the road leading from the sea to the island's hinterland, running from the parkland of the Nebrodi in the north to that of Etna in the south. Not far from the town, this agriturismo blends into a surrounding landscape shaped by centuries of volcanic activity. From the low white farmhouse, guests can explore the countryside, in which it is easy to imagine bygone times of feudal farming activity, when the wider world beyond Sicily's shores would have been unknown to the population.

Access: 4km from the village on the edge of Nebrodi Park

SICILIA

SAN MICHELE DI GANZARIA (CT)

13

GIGLIOTTO

Sig. Savoca
Contrada Gigliotto
94015 Piazza Armerina (CT)
Tel. 09 33 97 08 98 – Fax 09 33 97 08 98
gigliotto@gigliotto.com – www.gigliotto.com

80-100€

Closed Nov • 14 double rm • Half-board €65-85 • Parking, garden, swimming pool, dogs not admitted

 Set Menu €25 and 35

 The swimming pool with sundeck that dominates the hillsides of eastern Sicily.

In the heart of an estate planted with cereal crops, olives, vineyards and figs, this 14C farmstead, surrounded by the picturesque baglio siciliano, has been treated to a facelift. The rooms are decorated in warm southern colours and adorned with terractotta tiled floors and attractive furniture. The elegant dining room, with a wood ceiling and stone arcades, is the meeting place of traditional Sicilian scents and flavours, made from organic produce grown on the estate. Guests are invited to take riding lessons, go for long rides in the countryside, take part in the farm's daily activities or simply explore the surrounding towns and country.

Access: About 8km from the village towards Piazza Armerina

SICILIA

SCIACCA (AG)

14

VILLA PALOCLA

Sig.ra Venezia
Contrada Raganella
92019 Sciacca (AG)
Tel. 09 25 90 28 12 – Fax 09 25 90 28 12
info@villapalocla.it – www.villapalocla.it

👤👤 115-150€

Closed 1-15 Nov • 10 double rm • Half-board €80-100 • Parking, garden, swimming pool, dogs not admitted

 Menu €32/50

 Tranquillity, flowers, citrus fruits and architecture: Sicily in a nutshell.

Surrounded by farmland and citrus fruit trees, the Villa Palocla is a fine example of the rural architecture of western Sicily. This country property, whose immaculate walls date from the end of the Baroque period, offers eight elegant rooms with vaulted ceilings, frescoes and antique furniture, each of which is named after a flower. On the ground floor a spacious area tiled in Sicilian terracotta tiles has been created for cultural and leisure activities, and for meals served outdoors. The property also boasts three dining rooms with crystal chandeliers and a winter garden ideal for receptions, banquets and business lunches.

Access: Right out in the country, 3km from the town

SICILIA

SCOPELLO (TP)

TRANCHINA

Sig. Tranchina
Via A. Diaz, 7
91014 Scopello (TP)
Tel. 09 24 54 10 99 – Fax 09 24 54 12 32
pensionetranchina@interfree.it

76-100€

Open all year • 6 single rm, 4 double rm • Half board €57-73 • No dogs

 For residents only

 The location in a typical old Sicilian village.

This small family run guesthouse is in the heart of Scopello, a small village surrounded by the scrubland that characterises the local landscape, on a rocky outcrop from where there are fine views out over the gulf of Castellammare and the verdant craggy hills of Sicily. Simple accommodation which is well presented, and courteous service from the owners.

Access: In the town centre

SICILIA

SIRACUSA (SR)

16

DOLCE CASA

Sig.ra Regolo
Via Lido Sacramento, 4
96100 Siracusa (SR)
Tel. 09 31 72 11 35 – Fax 09 31 72 11 35
contact@bbdolcecasa.it – www.bbdolcecasa.it

👤👤 **65-85€**

Open all year • 8 double rm • Parking, garden

 Walking among the garden's palm trees in the cool evenings.

Here is a real B&B in the English tradition, the result of the experiences of the proprietor's daughter, who after several years in the UK decided to convert this large family home into accommodation for guests. The house is surrounded by spacious gardens, almost a park in fact, where various exotic plant species are grown. The large well presented rooms have a family ambience, as does the bright and airy lounge, supported by arched structures, a pleasant spot in which to while away the time. Within easy reach of the sea and Syracuse with its famous archaeological remains.

Access: Around 3km from the historic centre, opposite the Giove Olimpico Temple

SICILIA

SIRACUSA (SR)

GIUGGIULENA

Sig.ra Perasole
Via Pitagora da Reggio 35
96100 Siracusa (SR)
Tel. 09 31 46 81 42 - Fax 09 31 46 81 42
info@giuggiulena.it - www.giuggiulena.it

👤👤 **90-95€** ☕

Open all year • 6 double rm

The warm relaxed welcome is both natural and spontaneous.

Sesame seeds, sugar, honey, orange peel, cinnamon and a liberal sprinkling of Sicilian culinary talent. It might seem like a magic potion, but these are, in fact, just a few of the ingredients that are essential to the dessert of Arabic origins after which the house is named. Two minutes from Ortigia, the famous historic centre of Syracuse, Giuggiulena is a Mediterranean villa overlooking the Ionian sea. The sea-view rooms are flooded in light, as is the spacious dining room and the panoramic terrace-sundeck. Direct access to the sea down a flight of steps carved out of the rock.

Access: 1km from Ortigia bridge, near the Latomia dei Cappuccini

SICILIA

SIRACUSA (SR)

18

GUTKOWSKI

Sig.ra Pretsch
Lungomare Vittorini, 26
96100 Siracusa (SR)
Tel. 09 31 46 58 61 - Fax 09 31 48 05 05
info@guthotel.it - www.guthotel.it

 85-100€

Open all year • 3 single rm, 23 double rm

 The setting; the sea to the front and history on all sides.

The island of Ortigia is Syracuse's original site of settlement, a Greek colony which became one of the most powerful cities in the Mediterranean under its famous tyrant Dionysos. Even today, the evidence of those times remains in the form of the extensive archaeological remains which successive generations have not succeeded in erasing. Many people have been captivated by their charm including the English lady who, together with a local friend, runs this B&B in an old fisherman's house. The accommodation is very simple, but the views of the sea and the convenience of its location make this a place well worth knowing about.

Access: In the centre of Ortigia on the shore of the Levante

SICILIA

SIRACUSA (SR)

LA PERCIATA

Sig. Monello
Via Spinagallo, 77
96100 Siracusa (SR)
Tel. 09 31 71 73 66 – Fax 09 31 71 74 12
perciata@perciata.it – www.perciata.it

75-99€

Open all year • 1 single rm, 12 double rm • Half board €61-73 • Parking, garden, swimming pool, tennis, no dogs • Horse riding, bicycles available, jam and oil for sale

Menu €23/31

The contrasting colours of the vegetation and the rocky scenery.

Set at the foot of a small and rugged hill where the Mediterranean scrub clings to the bright white stones. The modern main building with swimming pool is partially hidden by trees which separate it from the stables and surrounding farmland. A mere 11km from Syracuse, this is a good alternative to staying in town. Among the local sights to be discovered are the Monello caves, where the calcareous stone has been gradually eroded by water action over the ages.

Access: 10km from the town towards Canicattini

SICILIA

TRAPANI (TP)

BAGLIO FONTANASALSA

Sig.ra Burgarella
A Fontanasalsa - Via Cusenza, 78
91100 Trapani (TP)
Tel. 09 23 59 10 01 – Fax 09 23 59 10 01
fontanasalsa@hotmail.com – www.fontanasalsa.it

 100€

Open all year • 2 single rm, 7 double rm • Half board €80-85 • Parking, garden, swimming pool, dogs not admitted in restaurant • Bicycles available, guided trips, sale of oil and wine

 Set Menu €25 and 35

 The olive groves and the citrus trees: two symbols of Sicily.

Phoenicians, Greeks, Romans, Arabs, Normans, Angevins, Aragonese.... the list of peoples who have enriched Sicily's history with their monuments and works of art is a lengthy one. Few things have remained unchanged over the ages, but one of them is the olive, the cultivation of which dominates the landscape between mount Erice and the sea. Fontanasalsa is a long established farm which recently diversified into providing accommodation in the shape of seven rooms with rustic wood furnishings and wrought iron beds. The cuisine focuses on local dishes, and in summer may be enjoyed outdoors, wafted by the fragrance of citrus trees. Good standards of service from a management team running this place for love rather than money.

Access: 8km from the town between the slopes of Monte Erice and Stagnone Laguna

SICILIA

VENTIMIGLIA DI SICILIA (PA)

21

CRAPA LICCA

Sig. Cassata
Località Contrada Traversa km. 15,600
90020 Ventimiglia di Sicilia (PA)
Tel. 09 18 20 21 44 – Fax 09 18 20 28 78
amministrazione@crapalicca.it – www.crapalicca.it

110€

Closed 8-25 Jan • 6 double rm • Half-board €68 • Parking, swimming pool, dogs not admitted • Horse riding, archery, bicycles available

 Set Menu €22

 The unusually shaped swimming pool in a natural pool in the rocks.

Once upon time, there lived a greedy naughty little goat who used to sneak into the estate's kitchens and steal the farmer's dinner. Such is the tale that inspired this country house, whose interior decoration reveals a creative and imaginative talent. Ideal for a quiet break in the country, the former farm is comprised of two elegant rustic buildings. The rooms are welcoming and graced with period furniture and there is an elegant veranda where you can relax or take breakfast in summertime. In the restaurant with bare rock walls and a wood ceiling, you will sample typical fare of the Sicilian hinterland.

Access: On n°16 minor road towards Bagheria at Km marker 15.600

Toscana

Florence, Siena, Arezzo, Lucca... Tuscany has so many cities of beauty, memories of them can be evoked by many a visitor years after seeing them. Breakfast in Siena's Piazza del Campo, a morning stroll to Florence's Uffizi museum, a picnic in the woodlands of the Casentino, an early afternoon walk across Chianti's hillsides followed by a dip off Elba's rocky shores, a relaxing thermal bath at Montecatini, an aperitif watching the sun set over the Ponte Vecchio, and a splendid *fiorentina* steak for dinner... such would be a perfect day in Tuscany. With a whole week's holiday, visitors can enjoy a more relaxed itinerary, taking in some of the less well known sites, the incredibly varied countryside, and of course the excellent food and wine. The many who will find it difficult to leave will understand the reasons behind the "Chianti-shire" phenomenon.

90 establishments

Recommended sites and circuits
Tuscany

> Few regions can boast of an artistic heritage grounded in its own land and culture as Tuscany can. As a region that is conscious of having been one of the beacons of the western Christian world and where a wealth of historical, cultural and artistic variety presents itself to the tourist, Tuscany cannot be understood in a single visit, but to fall in love with it, just one look will suffice.

You will be astounded by the symbiosis of countryside and culture, rural and urban. You only have to think of the universality of the imprint left by the Renaissance on **Florence** and of the eclectic genius of the movement's protagonists, who left their mark on the little market towns as much as on the large cities. Thus we find the bridge of **Buriano** behind Leonardo da Vinci's *Mona Lisa* and Castelfranco di Sopra in the background of the *Virgin of the Rocks*.

To discover for yourself the spirit of this region, just walk through the hills and see rising up before you, from the countryside of the Val d'Elsa, the silhouette of *San Giminiano*, remarkable for the beauty of its thirteen towers constructed by the town's noble families in order to highlight their prominence. Don't miss the Museo Civico, the Museum Spezieria di Santa Fina and, not for the faint-hearted, the Museum of Torture. Located on a hilltop not far from San Giminiano, Volterra dominates the surrounding countryside. History has left a deep mark here; in the historical centre, the magic and mystery of the medieval period permeates the ramparts, the maze of little streets and the tower-dwellings.

The hills, too, have their mysteries: the legend of San Galgano and the sword in the stone, for example. The ruins of the San Galgano abbey lie inside a dense wood, but the sword is preserved in the little church of Monte Siepi, a neighbouring high point. The history of this area goes back to the 12C. Galgano, a descendant of a noble family, loved adventure and the absence of constraints. According to the legend, he converted when the Archangel Michael appeared to him in a dream and in order to renounce his past life, the young man thrust his sword into the rock. The young hermit knight's fame grew and in around 1185 a small circular church was built around the rock. The tale of the young man is a singular one and the name Monte Siepi has ancient origins most probably linked to pagan rituals. The circles of the church roof recall Celtic symbology, also used by the Templers, and the name Galgano evokes Galvano, one of the knights of King Arthur. The coincidences are numerous in this region that holds many other secrets.

A recipe to try, wines and... a nugget of information

Wines

_Brunello di Montalcino
_Candia dei Colli Apuani
_Chianti
_Rosso di Montepulciano
_Vernaccia

Local specialities

Colonnata bacon, olives, *pecorino*, chestnuts, Treschietto onions, vegetables, spelt, *brigidini di Lamporecchio* (wafers), *cantuccini de Prato, panforte di Siena, sgabei* (strips of dough fried and eaten with cold meats), *panigacci di Podenzana* (unleavened bread), *testarolo* (pastry cooked under ashes).

CACIUCCO ALLA LIVORNESE

Ingredients

- 500g octopus
- 500g squid or small cuttlefish (or both)
- 300g Spanish lobster or gambas or langoustines (or all three)
- 300g dogfish
- 200g fish for soup
- 12 mussels
- 500g very ripe tomatoes
- 1 tablespoon tomato purée
- 1 glass extra virgin olive oil
- 1 glass red wine
- 4 cloves garlic
- onion
- chilli
- celery
- sage
- 8 slices dense rustic bread

Method

In a large pot, cook two cloves of garlic, the sage and chilli in half a glass of oil. Cut the octopus into sections; as soon as the garlic browns, add it to the pan and keep cooking over a low heat for 20min, then add the squid and the cuttlefish. Continue cooking with a little wine and the tomato purée. While it is cooking, in a frying pan, brown off the onion, celery and the two remaining cloves of garlic in the rest of the oil, add the fish for soup, tomatoes and a little water. Boil for 20min then transfer everything to the other pot, add the fish, cut into chunks, the shellfish and crustaceans. As the cooking finishes, grill the bread and rub it over with a little garlic then put the slices in the dishes and pour the Spanish lobster over them.

Food for thought

Bread is the most representative foodstuff of the region. Here people eat it *sciocco*, that is, without salt, and that is why it so perfectly complements all kinds of recipes, from antipasti to desserts. There was a time when bread replaced pasta, which was not widely eaten in Tuscany, except for *pici senesi* (long pasta) and *pappardelle* with hare.

Our favourite places to eat

OSTERIA MAGONA
Piazza Ugo 2/3 – Bolgheri (Castagneto Carducci, LI) – Tel. 0565 762173
Closed 15-31 Jan, Nov and Mon.
A la carte menu €31-48

 The Tuscan cuisine that varies with the seasons.

Located in the heart of one of Italy's most famous wine-producing areas, this osteria is one of the region's treasures, along with its ancient castles and cypress-lined roads. You will find it in the historical centre of Bolgheri, a market town that still abounds with memories of G. Carducci, the famous 19C Tuscan poet. In a simple and lively environment, the chefs propose delicious Tuscan cuisine with authentic flavours. On offer are cold meats selected from among the best producers, soups, fresh egg pasta and meats acquired from the region's most renowned butchers.

OSTERIA POGGIO DI SOTTO
Via Galliano 15/a – Galliano (Barberino di Mugello, FI) – Tel. 055 8428654
Open year-round.
A la carte menu €21-28

 The relaxing rural setting, enlivened by the vitality and originality of the owner.

A welcoming osteria that has managed to combine rustic elements with more elegant and refined features. In summer you can take advantage of the summerhouse and enjoy your meal in the calm of the Mugello countryside. The owner of the place is also its greatest asset. A restaurateur by vocation, he livens things up considerably. His credo is to serve quality food made from regional produce. The choice is great: *bruschetta*, thick tomato soup, a choice of Tuscan meats, *or tortelli di patate* (pasta stuffed with potatoes) with a duck-based sauce.

DEL FAGIOLI
Corso Tintori 47 r – Florence (FI) – Tel. 055 244285
Closed Sat, Sun and Aug.
A la carte menu €24-30

 The simplicity of a restaurant located in the very heart of Italian artistry.

This family-run trattoria is situated a short distance from the River Arno between Santa Croce Basilica and the Piazza della Signoria. The atmosphere is simple and understated, with a rustic wood interior, paintings and closely arranged tables. The cuisine is a mixture of Florentine and Tuscan: *crostini*, cold meats, *ribollita* (bread-based vegetable soup) and *pappa al pomodoro* (thick tomato soup), followed by meat dishes and cod-based dishes. Finish your meal with homemade pastries or *cantucci* (almond biscuits).

TOSCANA

ARCIDOSSO (GR)

RONDINELLI
Sigg. Ragnini
Località i Rondinelli, 32
58031 Arcidosso (GR)
Tel. 05 64 96 81 68 – Fax 05 64 96 81 68

  70€

Open all year • 11 double rm • Breakfast €7; half board €60 • Parking, garden, swimming pool, dna • Horse riding, pétanque, sale of oil

 Set Menu €18 and 25

 Riding through the woods.

The façade of this 19C building reflects the history of this area, its austere functionality suggesting a fertile yet unforgiving landscape, in which gentle foothills give way to the rugged Amiata mountains, and chestnut woods provide the district with its colour and aromas. This establishment offers simple but welcoming hospitality; the spacious rooms contrast with the more limited public areas where the lounge area and dining room merge into one. Most important, however, is the surrounding natural beauty of the landscape, providing a stunning backdrop for visitors to explore.

Access: 5km from the village towards Zancona

TOSCANA

AREZZO (AR)

2

CASA VOLPI

Sig. Volpi
Via Simone Martini, 29
52100 Arezzo (AR)
Tel. 05 75 35 43 64 – Fax 05 75 35 59 71
posta@casavolpi.it – www.casavolpi.it

👤👤 95€

Open all year • 1 single rm, 13 double rm, 1 suite • Breakfast €9 • Parking, garden, no dogs

 Menu €22/32

 The fine view of Arezzo across the verdant parkland.

The medieval backdrop of the centre of Arezzo is readily visible from the windows of this 19C aristocratic residence situated in parkland. The view and surrounding greenery are far from the only features of this hotel. Its 15 stylish, well furnished rooms offer charming accommodation, the public areas and restaurant are elegant and, during the warmer months, guests may dine under a pergola in the garden. An excellent base from which to discover the district's numerous great works of art by Piero della Francesca and others.

Access: Near the stadium and Giotto Park

AREZZO (AR)

I PORTICI

Sig. Beatrice
Via Roma 18
52100 Arezzo (AR)
Tel. 05 75 40 31 32 – Fax 05 75 30 09 34
info@hoteliportici.com
www.hoteliportici.com

👤👤 **100-155€** ☕

Open all year • 6 double rm, 2 suites

 The family heirlooms dotted about the rooms.

This hotel, only a few yards from the famous frescoes painted by Piero della Francesca, as well as the Crucifix by Cimabue and Piazza Vasari, is located on the fourth floor of a 19C palace in the heart of the town. A family home until the beginning of the last century, the current young owners, Alessandro and Claudi, who were born here, decided to turn their home into a hotel. Decorated with Tuscan-style furnishings and family mementoes, each bedroom has its own individual colour scheme, echoed in the furniture and colours of the marble bathrooms.

Access: Near the railway station and San Francesco church

TOSCANA

BARBERINO VAL D'ELSA (FI)

4

LA TORRE DI PONZANO

Sig. McAuley
Strada di Ponzano, 8
50021 Barberino Val d'Elsa (FI)
Tel. 05 58 05 92 55 – Fax 05 58 07 11 02
torre_di_ponzano@hotmail.com
www.ponzano.wide.it

👤👤 89-145€ ☕

Closed 25 Dec-30 Jan • 6 double rm • Parking, garden, no dogs

 We most liked The Anglo-Italian management, giving the place a style unique in the area.

This part of Tuscany was once the battlefield where the armies of Florence and Siena would regularly meet to resolve their differences. On the ridge of a hill once stood a Florentine farmstead which was destroyed by the Sienese. Of that original structure only the tower remains. This houses one of the rooms, the rest being in the 16C farmhouse next door. Rustic elegance, with the emphasis on quality rather than ostentation.

Access: On the main road between Tavarnelle and Ponzano

TOSCANA

BIBBIENA (AR)

5

RELAIS IL FIENILE

Sig.ra Marini
località Gressa
52011 Bibbiena (AR)
Tel. 05 75 59 33 96 - Fax 05 75 56 99 79
info@relaisilfienile.it - www.relaisilfienile.it

👤👤 **88-108€**

Closed Nov-Mar • 6 double rm, 1 suite • Parking, garden, swimming pool, dogs not admitted

The enticing odour of homemade bread, pies and buns that greets you in the mornings.

An ideal destination if you fancy a short spring or autumn break. Stop off in Casentino and forget your daily routine for a few days. Book a room in this 18C farmhouse and contemplate the silent beauty, colours and scents of the landscape. An elegant and friendly atmosphere reigns throughout the pleasant interior of this establishment, proud of its ancient tradition of hospitality. The property is a picture of charm, from each of the rooms, named after the villages and towns that can be seen from the windows, to the dining room, where the lady of the house organises courses devoted to local savours by the fireside.

Access: 5km from the village, towards Chiusi della Verna, at the Gressa crossroads

TOSCANA

BORGO SAN LORENZO (FI)

6

CASA PALMIRA

Sig.ra Fiorini
Località Feriolo-Polcanto via Mulinaccio, 4
50032 Borgo San Lorenzo (FI)
Tel. 05 58 40 97 49 – Fax 05 58 40 97 49
info@casapalmira.it – www.casapalmira.it

80-85€

Closed 20 Jan-10 Mar • 1 single rm, 5 double rm • Parking, garden, no dogs

 Reading a book in a comfortable armchair, bathed in natural light from the skylight.

England or Tuscany. Although not quite in Chiantishire, the tasteful style in which this property has been restored and furnished evokes the culture of the English country house. Also evident, though, are strong links to the area's rich history; the oldest part of the building, originally a hay barn, date from the 12C. On the ground floor are the public areas including bar and open kitchen where breakfast is served, while upstairs are the rooms, each individually designed and incorporating furniture collected by the owner.

Access: On the SS 302, 9km from the centre of Fiesole towards Mugello

TOSCANA

CAMPIGLIA D'ORCIA (SI)

CASA RANIERI

Sig.ra Ranieri
Podere la Martina
53023 Campiglia d'Orcia (SI)
Tel. 05 77 87 26 39 – Fax 05 77 87 26 39
naranier@tin.it – www.casaranieri.com

 70-80€

Open all year • 7 double rm, 1 suite • Half board €65-70 • Parking, garden, swimming pool, dogs not admitted • Horse riding, pétanque, oil and jam for sale

 Set Menu €25 and 30 for residents only

 Riding through the glorious Tuscan countryside.

The period furnishings in the rooms and the covered riding school are but two of the many attractions of this place, transformed from a simple farm into an agriturismo retaining strong links with its heritage. The frills of hotel luxury are absent; instead a characterful rustic elegance pervades. During the summer months guests can cool off in the pool, sited in a panoramic spot with fine views over the green hills of the Orcia valley. Traditional Tuscan cuisine in the restaurant, which also lays on cookery courses.

Access: From the village continue for 2km along the SS 2

TOSCANA

CAPALBIO (GR)

8

GHIACCIO BOSCO

Sig.ra Olivi
Strada della Sgrilla, 4
58011 Capalbio (GR)
Tel. 05 64 89 65 39 – Fax 05 64 89 65 39
info@ghiacciobosco.com
www.ghiacciobosco.com

👤👥 **75-110€** ☕

Open all year • 15 double rm • Parking, swimming pool, garden, dogs not admitted • Oil and jam for sale

 The charming bathrooms.

Far from the typical atmosphere of the Maremma, with its butteri cowboys and rural traditions, the village of Capalbio has long been a fashionable retreat for Italy's political and cultural elite. An attractive village, surrounded by countryside and yet close to the sea, it is now home to the Ghiaccio Bosco agriturismo, which offers elegant accommodation to satisfy the most demanding clientele. Uniformed staff, green lawns reminiscent of England, a swimming pool, comfortable guest rooms and a friendly management all add to the elegant atmosphere.

Access: From the centre of the village, take the SP 75 to Pescia Fiorentina, and then the SP 101 towards Manciano

TOSCANA

CASTELLINA IN CHIANTI (SI)

9

FATTORIA TREGOLE

Sig.ra Kirchlechner
località Tregole 86
53011 Castellina in Chianti (SI)
Tel. 05 77 74 09 91 – Fax 05 77 74 19 28
fattoria-tregole@castellina.com
www.fattoria-tregole.com

130€

Closed 16 Nov-28 Feb • 1 single rm, 3 double rm, 1 suite • Parking, garden, swimming pool, dogs not admitted

The lovely bedrooms decorated in an English style by the lady of the house.

Overlooking the hillsides of Chiantigiano, whose forests, vineyards and olive groves hide a wealth of country homes and mansions, but above all a historic and cultural legacy that should not be missed, this farmstead is a haven of peace and quiet where you can savour and taste the traditions of a bygone era. The scene is set first by the bare beams, terracotta floors and fireplace. This is combined with a passion for wholesome country produce that can be tasted in the wine, brandy and olive oil produced by the owners. What's more, a delightful surprise awaits guests in the immense garden in the form of an unusual swimming pool, the work of a highly imaginative Italian designer.

Access: 4km from the town, towards the SS 222 road to Sienne, at the Tregole crossroads

TOSCANA

CASTELLINA IN CHIANTI (SI)

10

SALIVOLPI

Sig. Orlandi
Via Fiorentina 89
53011 Castellina in Chianti (SI)
Tel. 05 77 74 04 84 – Fax 05 77 74 09 98
info@hotelsalivolpi.com – www.hotelsalivolpi.it

✝✝75-95€

Open all year • 1 single rm, 18 double rm • Parking, garden, swimming pool

---

 Stretching out in the shade of an old mulberry tree when the sun is at its zenith.

If you're looking for a base camp for a trip to the seaside and a chance to explore the historic towns and museums of Tuscany and Umbria, but are not averse to peace and quiet in the silence of the Tuscan hillside, Salivolpi is just what you need. On a hilltop, the site of the former Etruscan Castellina and within easy reach of the historic heart of Castellina in Chianti, this hotel is encircled by a landscape of olive groves and cypress trees which stretches across the entire Elsa Valley from Monteriggioni as far as San Gimignano. Treat yourself to a trip back in time as you admire the refined setting of antique furniture and wrought-iron beds. Cordial welcome.

Access: Outside the village, towards San Donato

CASTELLINA IN CHIANTI (SI)

VILLA CRISTINA

Sig. Landini
Via Fiorentina, 34
53011 Castellina in Chianti (SI)
Tel. 05 77 74 11 66 – Fax 05 77 74 29 36
info@villacristina.it – www.villacristina.it

73-76€

Closed 25 Jan-20 Mar, 20 Nov-26 Dec • 5 double rm, 1 suite • Parking, garden

 The tower room, providing a unique perspective on the surrounding landscape.

This early 20C villa is conveniently located close to the centre of Castellina; a private house for most of its history, it retains its quirky residential layout. The rooms are simple yet well equipped, and to the rear is a terrace garden which is particularly pleasant early in the day or after dusk. Good, generous breakfasts are served to prepare visitors for days exploring Chianti country.

Access: A few kilometres from the town towards San Donato

TOSCANA

CASTIGLION FIORENTINO (AR)

12

CASA PORTAGIOIA

Sig. Betts
a Pieve di Chio 56
52043 Castiglion Fiorentino (AR)
Tel. 05 75 65 01 54 – Fax 05 75 65 01 54
info@tuscanbreaks.com
www.tuscanbreaks.com

140-160€

Closed Dec-Feb • 5 double rm • Parking, garden, swimming pool, dogs not admitted

 The magnificent view of the countryside from each room.

Surrounded by cypress trees, olive groves, vineyards, oak and evergreen trees, the town is ideally located for a quiet country holiday, devoted to discovering local gastronomic traditions and the treasures of the many famous historic and artistic towns in the vicinity. In the same spirit, this country house aims to make you feel at home in its rustic but elegant interior, whose bare beams are characteristic of Tuscan architecture. The outdoor picture is equally appealing, especially in summertime, when an appetising breakfast buffet is laid in the well-tended garden.

Access: From the centre, drive for 5km towards Pieve di Chio

TOSCANA

CERTALDO (FI)

13

OSTERIA DEL VICARIO

Sig.ra Conforti
Via Rivellino, 3
50052 Certaldo (FI)
Tel. 05 71 66 82 28 - Fax 05 71 66 82 28
info@osteriadelvicario.it
www.osteriadelvicario.it

80-120€

Open all year • 1 single rm, 4 double rm • Dogs not admitted

 Menu €60/95

 The charming restaurant terrace.

This is Boccaccio country; the great writer was born in Certaldo, a hill town where cars are forbidden and the atmosphere of the Middle Ages still prevails. It is at its busiest in July, when it hosts a theatre festival. Whatever time of year, this is the ideal hotel in which to stay; a characterful ambience with much woodwork in evidence, period furnishings, fine views and a warm welcome.

Access: At Certaldo Alto, in the heart of the historic centre

TOSCANA

CHIUSDINO (SI)

IL MULINO DELLE PILE

Sig. Burchianti
Località Mulino delle Pile
53012 Chiusdino (SI)
Tel. 05 77 75 06 88 – Fax 05 77 75 06 86
info@agriturismoilmulino.com
www.agriturismoilmulino.com

100-140€

Closed Jan-Mar • 8 double rm • Half-board €80-90 • Parking, garden, swimming pool, dogs not admitted

 Menu €26/34

 Country traditions and the site of a creative advertising campaign.

The Sienna countryside, whose earth has long been devoted to cereal crops, pulses and grapes, is the site of this stone wheat mill with an hydraulic wheel that was for many years the main feature of a TV commercial for one of Italy's leading brands! Built in the Middle Ages by the monks from the neighbouring abbey of Serena, it was in operation until the late 1970s, but it is now home to a country guesthouse with a children's play area, a swimming pool surrounded by greenery and a restaurant crowned with beams and semicircular arches.

Access: Right out in the country on the SS 141 road, near the Luriano crossroads

CHIUSI (SI)

LA CASA TOSCANA
Sig. Valeriani
Via Ermanno Baldetti, 37
53043 Chiusi (SI)
Tel. 05 78 22 22 27 - Fax 05 78 22 38 12
casatoscana@libero.it - www.valerianigroup.com

80-100€

Closed 15-30 Jan • 2 single rm, 4 double rm

 Breakfast on the terrace, among the perfumes of the flowers.

This tastefully restored palazzo in the centre of Chiusi is a gem; a limited number of rooms, each individually furnished and all bright and charming, with elegant modern bathrooms. At the rear is a planted terrace overlooking the church of San Francesco. A perfect base from which to explore the borderlands between Tuscany and Umbria, especially given the excellent road and rail links.

Access: In a narrow street in the historic centre, two minutes from Piazza del Duomo

TOSCANA

CIVITELLA IN VAL DI CHIANA (AR)

16

L'ANTICO BORGO

Sig.ra Gualdani
Via Don Alcide Lazzeri 22
52040 Civitella in val di Chiana (AR)
Tel. 33 97 95 16 74
info@antborgo.it – www.antborgo.it

👤👤95€ ☕

Open all year • 6 double rm • Dogs not admitted

 A stay in an old country house to savour the lifestyle of a bygone era.

The traces of a distant past are still visible in the narrow streets of this town where time seems to have stood still. This 19C palace on the main square was built on the foundations of an older construction set in the first ramparts. You cannot fail to be won over by the medieval atmosphere that reigns throughout this elegant restored property, decorated with old wood furniture and antiques. Traditional country dishes, originally presented, are served in the discreet and intimate setting of the dining room with bare stone walls.

Access: On the main square of the former town «Vallis clanarum»

TOSCANA

CORSIGNANO (SI)

17

CASA LUCIA
Sig.ra Formisano
Località Corsignano Vagliagli
53019 Corsignano (SI)
Tel. 05 77 32 25 08 – Fax 05 77 32 25 10
info@casalucia.it – www.casalucia.it

79-89€

Closed 10 Jan-28 Feb • 14 double rm • Breakfast €5 • Parking, garden

 The memory of a country past lingers on in two pretty cottages.

In a peaceful Siena hamlet in the heart of the silent countryside dotted with woods and vineyards, Cas Lucia, a happy marriage of wood and stone, is made up of two old buildings. A beautifully restored barn and a terracotta kiln are now home to delightful sitting rooms and pleasant rooms with original ceilings, wooden furniture and a sprinkling of period objects. Ideally situated for a quiet rest in the country yet conveniently close to Siena.

Access: Drive for 7km towards Vagliagli, in Corsignano

TOSCANA

CORSIGNANO (SI)

18

FATTORIA DI CORSIGNANO

Sig.ra Gallo
Località Corsignano - Vagliagli
53010 Castelnuovo Berardenga (Siena)
Tel. 05 77 32 25 45 – Fax 05 77 32 24 07
info@tenutacorsignano.it – www.tenutacorsignano.it

70-90€

Open all year • 10 double rm • Breakfast €7 • Parking, garden, swimming pool • Organised trips, bicycles available, sale of wine, oil and grappa

Set Menu €25 and 35

The large swimming pool in the grounds.

Situated in the southern Chianti region, in the splendid district of Castelnuovo Berardenga, the Fattoria di Corsignano is an attractive farmstead which specialises in the production of wine and olive oil. Guests stay in three buildings housing a total of ten apartments, each of which is equipped with kitchen, elegant rooms and antique furniture. The peaceful location, panoramic views and the friendly, efficient staff combine to offer a holiday in true Chianti style.

Access: From Siena take the road towards Vagliagli

TOSCANA

FIRENZE (FI)

ANTICA DIMORA FIRENZE
Sig.ra Gulmanelli
via Sangallo 72
50100 Firenze (FI)
Tel. 05 54 62 72 96 – Fax 05 54 63 44 50
info@anticadimorafirenze.it
www.anticadimorafirenze.it

130-145€

Open all year • 6 double rm • Dogs not admitted

Listening to classical music on a comfortable sofa with a cup of tea.

Next door to Palazzo Pandolfini, designed by Raphael in the early 16C, the property has retained the charm of the ancient city after which it is named. The elegant guestrooms are individually decorated in pastel colours, lavish quantities of marble, handmade fabrics, four-poster beds and period furniture. The breakfast buffet is served in a small sitting room which is also home to a library and a substantial film library for the use of guests. However, in addition to visiting the historic city of Florence, the hotel can also reserve excursions to other historic and artistic high spots, such as the bottega del Giambologna, today a modern workshop.

Access: Next to San Marco Museum

TOSCANA

FIRENZE (FI)

20

LOCANDA DI FIRENZE

Sig. Lagorio
via Faenza 12
50123 Firenze (FI)
Tel. 055 28 43 40 - Fax 055 28 43 52
lanfra.lagorio@tiscali.it
www.locandadifirenze.it

👤👤 **105-120€**

Open all year • 6 double rm • Dogs not admitted

We most liked Within easy reach of the museums, churches and Medici chapel.

This inn is located on the third floor of an 18C palace in the heart of the historic and picturesque market square of San Lorenzo. The spacious and comfortable guestrooms are decorated with antique furniture; breakfasts are very generous. Ideally located for the main historic and artistic treasures of Tuscany's capital: the Renaissance cathedral of Santa Maria del Fiore and Fortezza da Basso, built following political revolts and now the scene of cultural and trade events.

Access: Near the station and the Medici Chapels

TOSCANA

FIRENZE (FI)

RESIDENZA APOSTOLI

Sig.ra Panetta
borgo Santi Apostoli 8
50123 Firenze (FI)
Tel. 055 28 84 32 - Fax 055 26 87 90
info@residenzapostoli.it
www.residenzapostoli.it

90-130€

Open all year • 1 single rm, 4 double rm • Dogs not admitted

Emailed

Stay in the heart of Florentine history to better unveil its secrets.

If you find yourself close to Accialioli on the banks of the Arno, you will no doubt be tempted to cross over the Ponte Vecchio, kingdom of craftsmen and goldsmiths in the Middle Ages, to visit the Palazzo della Signoria. Founded by order of Arnolfo di Cambio, it was the headquarters of the Republican government and home to the Gonfaloniere di Giustizia and the Priori delle Arti. Pause for a minute and admire the austere Palazzo del Siniscalco in the district of Santi Apostoli. The first floor of this edifice is home to the Residenza, which offers airy pastel-coloured rooms in a welcoming family atmosphere. The hotel also has a practical booking service for excursions and museums.

Access: On the quayside of the Arno, between the Ponte Vecchio and that of the Santa Trinità, next to the historic centre

TOSCANA

FIRENZE (FI)

22

RESIDENZA GIULIA

Sig. Torrini
Via delle Porte Nuove, 19
50144 Firenze (FI)
Tel. 05 53 21 66 46 – Fax 05 53 24 51 49
anna@residenzagiulia.com
www.residenzagiulia.com

👤👤78-110€

Open all year • 6 double rm

 Enjoying the delightful views of the hills over breakfast.

Situated on the fifth floor, this B&B close to Santa Maria Novella station has stunning views over the Florentine hills. With this scenic backdrop, guests can enjoy breakfast served in the room; the accommodation is simply furnished and well presented by the friendly and helpful young management.

Access: Near the Porta al Prato square

TOSCANA

FIRENZE (FI)

23

RESIDENZA HANNAH E JOHANNA

Sig.ra Gulmanelli
Via Bonifacio Lupi, 14
50129 Firenze (FI)
Tel. 055 48 18 96 – Fax 055 48 27 21
lupi@johanna.it – www.johanna.it

 **95€**

Open all year • 2 single rm, 9 double rm • No dogs

 The friendly welcome in this unusual and elegant establishment.

The choice of hotel is key to the success of a holiday and its ambience is often one of the most memorable aspects that guests recall long after returning home. The friendly atmosphere of this small establishment makes it feel more like a private house than a city hotel. Situated in an old palazzo with an austere façade (and inner courtyard providing parking), the interior is surprisingly welcoming. Great attention to detail is evident in the elegant rooms, which are tastefully furnished and intimate in feel.

Access: Between Piazza della Libertà and the Fortezza da Basso

TOSCANA

FIRENZE (FI)

24

RESIDENZA JOHANNA

Sig.ra Gulmanelli
Via Cinque Giornate, 12
50129 Firenze (FI)
Tel. 055 47 33 77 – Fax 055 47 33 77
cinquegiornate@johanna.it – www.johanna.it

👤👤 85€

Open all year • 6 double rm • Parking, no dogs

The successful combination of domesticity and elegance.

This establishment stands out among the city's hotels on account of its traditional ambience. An informal yet courteous welcome awaits guests; the intimate and refined interior shows great attention to detail, creating a genteel elegance unmatched in the city at this price. This hotel's quality and the competence of its management make it a place well worth knowing.

Access: Near the Fortezza da Basso

TOSCANA

FIRENZE (FI)

25

TOURIST HOUSE GHIBERTI

Sig. Baroni
via Bufalini 1
50122 Firenze (FI)
Tel. 055 26 11 71 – Fax 055 26 41 70
thghiberti@tiscali.it
www.touristhouseghiberti.com

110-153€

Open all year • 5 double rm

 A friendly family atmosphere combined with cutting-edge technology.

Imagine a hotel in the heart of Florence that combines friendliness, technology and well-being with a passion for contemporary art! Located just behind the Duomo, the interior is bathed in sunlight and decorated in a characteristic Florentine style, enhanced by artist Fabio Calvetti's work and Florentine artist Angela Ceri's mosaics. It is also equipped with state-of-the-art equipment: computer and internet, flat-screen TV, DVD and CD player for films and music, speakers set in the bedside tables and headphones. A wealth of activities to keep you busy.

Access: Behind the cathedral

TOSCANA

FIRENZE (FI)

26

VILLA LA SOSTA

Sig. Fantoni
via Bolognese 83
50139 Firenze (FI)
Tel. 055 49 50 73
info@villalasosta.com – www.villalasosta.com

110-130€

Open all year • 5 double rm • Parking, garden, dogs not admitted

 We most liked Visiting the wine cellars and tasting the wines and local produce.

Did you know that Via Bolognese in Florence is the oldest road suitable for motor vehicles through the Florentine Alps? Such is the story behind the name of this elegant property built in the 19C. On the hillsides surrounding the historic centre, it is ideally located for a holiday spent exploring the town and its region. The guestrooms are peaceful and comfortable, and the attic room commands a splendid view of the landscape. On the leisure side, take the time to relax in the garden under the ivy trellis, where breakfast is served in the summer months.

Access: Very near the centre, on the road to Pratolino

FIRENZE (FI)

VILLINO IL MAGNIFICO

Sig.ra Luigetti
via Orcagna 24/26
50122 Firenze (FI)
Tel. 05 56 26 60 53 – Fax 055 67 42 83
info@villinoilmagnifico.com
www.villinoilmagnifico.com

90-110€

Open all year • 6 double rm, 1 suite • Dogs not admitted

 Strategically located for visiting a legendary Italian city.

This establishment is ideally located for visits to the capital of Renaissance Italy. The hotel is a stone's throw from the historic centre that is home to the city's major cultural and tourist sites. Thus its name, taken from the famous Florentine patron of the arts. Located inside a 19C pavilion, the guesthouse offers pleasant practical rooms decorated in an understated elegant style with period furniture and equipped with modern fixtures and fittings. Guests may also use the private parking facilities and the kitchen by request.

Access: Near ACI offices

TOSCANA

FIVIZZANO (MS)

28

IL GIARDINETTO

Sig. Mercadini
Via Roma, 151
54013 Fivizzano (MS)
Tel. 058 59 20 60 – Fax 058 59 20 60
hotelilgiardinetto@libero.it

👤👤47€

Closed 4-30 Oct • 7 single rm, 10 double rm • Breakfast €3.70; half board €41.50 • Garden, no dogs

 Menu €15/25

 The blend of historic backdrop and contemporary comfort.

Since 1882, this establishment has provided accommodation for travellers crossing the Apuan Alps here in Fivizzano, a historic crossroads between the regions of Emilia, Liguria and Tuscany. The tradition of hospitality which has developed over the years is jealously guarded, and guests may be sure of a warm welcome. Portraits of famous visitors decorate the walls, a fitting archive chronicling the distinguished heritage of this venerable hotel.

Access: Near Piazza Teatro

GAIOLE IN CHIANTI (SI)

29

BORGOLECCHI

Sig. Borsotti
Via San Martino, 50
53010 Lecchi (SI)
Tel. 05 77 74 69 03 – Fax 05 77 74 68 14
info@borgolecchi.com   www.borgolecchi.com

👫 98-120€ ☕

Closed Jan-Apr • 6 double rm, 1 suite • Parking

The attractive combination of grey stone and verdant olive groves.

Located in a charming stone-built village on the so-called castle route, a series of lookout posts originally built to protect Siena from Florentine incursions. Here in Borgolecchi, the tower dates from 1100 while the hotel is situated on the main street; its public areas are simple and its rustic style rooms have attractive furnishings and modern bathrooms. Almost all have terraces giving onto the tranquil hillside.

Access: *10km from Siena on the SS 408 then towards Lecchi*

TOSCANA

TOSCANA

GROSSETO (GR)

30

POGGIO DEGLI ULIVI

Sig. Morucci
strada Vallemaggiore 174
58010 Rispescia-Grosseto (GR)
Tel. 05 64 40 51 34 – Fax 05 64 40 58 33
grifodoc@tin.it – www.poggiodegliulivi.it

 60-110€

Open all year • 6 single rm • Parking, garden, swimming pool, dogs not admitted • Bicycles available, pétanque

 The small artificial lake where you can observe birds that are indigenous to the Maremma region.

The name of this country guesthouse brings to mind the scents, colours and tranquility of the surrounding countryside. Tucked away in the green landscape of Maremma, it stands in the heart of a family-run farm estate, devoted primarily to olives. However it is also just a few minutes away from the trendy and lively seaside resorts of Talamone, Marine di Grosseto, Castiglione della Pescaia and Monte Argentario. The establishment offers comfortable guestrooms with a small kitchen, and guests also have the run of an immense garden and swimming pool, a children's play area, a barbecue and a wood-fired oven.

Access: On the Aurelia main road, at km marker 712.80, Vallemaggiore exit

TOSCANA

LUCCA (LU)

LA CAPPELLA

Sig. Monticelli
a Cappella via dei Tognetti 469, località Ceccuccio
55060 Lucca (LU)
Tel. 05 83 39 43 47 - Fax 05 83 39 58 70
lacappella@lacappellalucca.it
www.laccappellalucca.it

👥 90-120€

Open all year • 4 double rm, 1 suite • Parking, garden, swimming pool

Regional produce takes pride of place in the gargantuan breakfasts served in the main hall.

Not far from the antique Via Francigena that pilgrims from France and Spain used to follow to Rome, this 18C convent is now an intriguing tourist complex. "La Cappella", entirely restored by the current owners, is ideal for anyone eager to explore regional art and history, or indeed for anyone in need of a well-earned break. Cooking enthusiasts can attend Tuscan, and particularly Luccan, cookery lessons organised by the lady of the house.

Access: Around 10km from the town, follow the signs to Camaiore

TOSCANA

LUCCA (LU)

32

ALLA CORTE DEGLI ANGELI

Sig. Bonino
Via degli Angeli 23
55100 Lucca (LU)
Tel. 05 83 46 92 04 – Fax 05 83 99 19 89
info@allacortedegliangeli.com
www.allacortedegliangeli.com

 130-150€

Open all year • 6 double rm

 The brightly coloured guestrooms from yellow to pale blue, a cheerful magical blend.

If you're looking for a well-kept establishment with a romantic elegant interior and within easy reach of the town's main historic and cultural sites, whilst not on a main road, this is the place for you. Behind the ramparts, Corte degli Angeli is a treasure trove of modern comforts hidden in an historic property, with guestrooms whose colour scheme matches a flower to create a cheerful setting. Splendid view of the rooftops and towers of the town's historic buildings from the windows.

Access: Near San Frediano church

TOSCANA

LUCCA (LU)

33

ALLA DIMORA LUCENSE

Sig.ra Scicchitano
Via Fontana 17/21
55100 Lucca (LU)
Tel. 05 83 49 57 22 – Fax 05 83 44 12 10
dimoralucense@libero.it – www.dimoralucense.it

👤👤 **110-125€**

Open all year • 8 double rm • Breakfast €9 • Dogs not admitted

 The inner courtyard is ideal to savour the quietude of the magical town.

Ready to take a leap back in time to the Tuscan Renaissance era? All you have to do is venture across the threshold of Dimora Lucense, a small family hotel within easy reach of the ramparts and piazza dell'Anfiteatro. This is a perfect opportunity for you to wind down and relax as you relish the quality of life of a bygone era. A 16C atmosphere prevails throughout the entire establishment, from the last carriage of Lucca standing in a shed to the names of the town's streets and squares on each bedroom door.

Access: Near San Frediano church

TOSCANA

LUCCA (LU)

LA ROMEA

Sigg. Calissi e Ristori
Vicolo delle Ventaglie 2
55100 Lucca (LU)
Tel. 05 83 46 41 75 – Fax 05 83 47 12 80
info@laromea.com – www.laromea.com

110-130€

Open all year • 1 single rm, 4 double rm

 Contemporary art exhibitions adorn the walls of the elegant breakfast-sitting room.

Old and new combine delightfully in this peaceful, family-style establishment run by a friendly and attentive staff. The first floor of this late 14C property, on the edge of the historic centre, will enable you to savour the charm and appeal of the delightful medieval town of Lucca, whilst relaxing in premises that are perfect down to the tiniest detail. All of the rooms, of which there are very few, are different both in size and architecture; one stands in the shade of the Torre delle Ore, another is in an ancient tower of the palace, while yet another has a stone portal.

Access: Near Piazza Anfiteatro and Via Fillungo

TOSCANA

LUCCA (LU)

35

VILLA ALESSANDRA

Sig. Tosca
via Arsina 1100/b
55100 Arsina Lucca (LU)
Tel. 05 83 39 51 71 – Fax 05 83 39 58 28
villa.ale@mailcity.com
www.villa-alessandra.it

125-135€

Open all year • 6 double rm • Garden, swimming pool

Culture, sport and relaxation are on the bill for this establishment.

If you would like to combine lying on the beach with your passion for literature, music and cooking, then the Villa Alessandra is exactly what you're looking for. This elegant 18C property stands on a gentle hillside surrounded by vineyards and olive groves that have been a feature of the fertile landscape for centuries. A cordial welcome awaits you inside, where you can admire the attractive and original furniture in the sitting room with fireplace, light airy library and attractive rooms. The establishment organises concerts of classical music and literary meetings, and holds bridge and cookery lessons.

Access: Around 5km from the town, follow the signs to Camaiore and then Arsina

TOSCANA

LUCCA (LU)

36

VILLA ROMANTICA

Sig. Favilla
via Barbantini 246, località Stadio
55100 Lucca (LU)
Tel. 05 83 49 68 72 – Fax 0583 95 76 00
info@villaromantica.it – www.villaromantica.it

 130€

Open all year • 6 double rm • Parking, garden, swimming pool, dogs not admitted

 The greenery and sweet-smelling flowers around the refreshing swimming pool.

The name of this establishment, just a few minutes from the town centre, is in perfect keeping with its ambience. Shaded by century-old trees, this late 19C cosy villa, which exudes a distinctive family atmosphere, is home to a well-cared-for interior decorated in light colours in an English style. The breakfast buffet is served in summertime in the Liberty-style veranda that opens onto the garden, or in a sitting room warmed by a log fire in winter, ideal for a nightcap. Sundeck and swimming pool.

Access: Near the stadium

MANCIANO (GR)

GALEAZZI

Sig. Galeazzi
Località Spinicci, 250
58010 Marsiliana (GR)
Tel. 05 64 60 50 17 – Fax 05 64 60 50 17
info@agriturismogaleazzi.com
www.agriturismogaleazzi.com

60-65€

Open all year • 1 single rm, 8 double rm, 3 suites • Parking, garden, swimming pool, no dogs • Bicycles available, fishing, archery, oil and wine for sale

The tranquil experience of fishing among the olive groves.

This establishment is very much a working farm, and the agricultural backdrop makes for a relaxing ambience. Although an undistinguished modern building, everything is very clean and tidy, with the simple furnishings in mint condition. Facilities include a fine swimming pool, and a small lake providing carp and tench fishing.

Access: Take the Albinia road for around 15km

TOSCANA

MANCIANO (LU)

38

LE PISANELLE

Sig. Maurelli
sulla strada provinciale 32 per Farnese
58014 Manciano (LU)
Tel. 05 64 62 82 86 - Fax 05 64 62 58 40
info@lepisanelle.it - www.lepisanelle.it

 95-102€

Closed 15-30 Nov, 20-25 Dec and 7-31 Jan • 7 double rm, 2 suites • Half-board €83-88 • Parking, garden, swimming pool, dogs not admitted

 Menu €32/38 for residents only

 Cypress trees, roses, oleanders and broom fill the garden with scent and colour.

Etruscan, Romanesque and medieval remains are still visible in the town, on the former "salt route", while more recent souvenirs adorn the walls of this 19C property, an authentic architectural and historic legacy. Nestling in green fields of olive groves and fruit orchards above the valley of Fiora, this farm has been turned into a discreetly elegant country guesthouse after restoration work was carried out to enhance the original structure. The interior style is very pleasant, and each of the comfortable rooms with "arte povera" style furniture is decorated in a different colour scheme. In the evenings you will sit down to tasty Tuscan dishes.

Access: 4km along the n°32 minor road towards Farnese

TOSCANA

MANCIANO (GR)

POGGIO TORTOLLO

Sig.ra Paggetti
Località Poggio Tortollo
58014 Manciano (GR)
Tel. 05 64 62 02 09 - Fax 05 64 62 09 49
poggiotortollo@hotmail.com
www.poggiotortollo.it

✝✝55-80€

Closed 10 Jan-10 Feb • 1 single rm, 4 double rm • Parking, garden, swimming pool • Organised trips, bicycles available, honey and oil for sale

 The direct access to the rooms from outside.

Passionately run by Signora Poggetti, this small agriturismo has consistently improved over the years, making it a comfortable place to stay. Simplicity is the key here, entirely in keeping with the rural setting. The building is surrounded by greenery, being part of a farm which has fine views over fields, woodland and hills. Guests can lounge by the pool or explore the area on mountain bikes. A perfect base from which to discover the Maremma, and close to the thermal baths at Saturnia.

Access: Drive for around 4km on the SP 32 to Farnese

TOSCANA

MARCIANO DELLA CHIANA (AR)

40

IL QUERCIOLO

Sig. Fani
Località Badicorte Via Bosco Salviati, 5
52010 Marciano della Chiana (AR)
Tel. 05 75 84 50 00 – Fax 05 75 84 50 00
info@ilquerciolobadicorte.com
www.ilquerciolobadicorte.com

100-120€

Closed Jan, Feb • 4 double rm • Breakfast €8 • Parking, garden, swimming pool • Bicycles available, jam, oil and wine for sale

 The period washbasins in some of the rooms.

The origins of this farmhouse date back to the 13C, although its present appearance owes much to structural alterations undertaken in the 19C. Recent renovation work has carefully highlighted many of the building's architectural features. In addition to the drawing rooms, fireplaces, wooden beams and stone arches, the bedrooms are striking for their refined period furniture and original ornaments dating from the mid-19C to the Belle Epoque period of the early 20C, all of which belonged to the owner's family. The house is surrounded by an attractive garden, with the hills, olive groves and sunflower fields of the Valdichiana in the distance.

Access: At the Monte San Savino exit off the A1, head towards Marciano della Chiana

MASSA MARITTIMA (GR)

PODERE RIPARBELLA

Sig.ra Malzacher
località Sopra Pian di Mucini
58024 Massa Marittima (GR)
Tel. 05 66 91 55 57 – Fax 05 66 91 55 58
riparbella@riparbella.com – www.riparbella.it

98€

Closed 1-24 Dec and 2 Jan-14 Mar • 3 single rm, 8 double rm • Half-board €69-79 • Parking, garden, dogs not admitted • Sale of oil, grappa and jam

 Set Menu €22 and 28 for residents only

 The view of the olive groves and vineyards stretching as far as the medieval town of Massa Marittima.

Riparbella is ideal if you like relaxing, reading, walking and practising your linguistic skills. Surrounded by woods and organic crops, such as aromatic herbs, vineyards and olive groves, this old manor house restored from top to toe according to organic architectural principles, is now home to a minimalist modern interior with numerous whimsical details including designer lamps and brightly coloured quilts on the beds. On the ground floor there is a pleasant sitting room with fireplace and a dining room, in which you can try the healthy, inventive dishes in which game and farm produce take pride of place.

Access: Around 6km away, towards Prata near Monterotondo crossroads

TOSCANA

MONTAIONE (FI)

42

VECCHIO MULINO

Sig. Ciulli
Viale Italia, 10
50050 Montaione (FI)
Tel. 05 71 69 79 66 – Fax 05 71 69 79 66
info@hotelvecchiomulino.it – www.vecchiomulino.it

65-90€

Open all year • 5 single rm, 10 double rm • Parking, garden, dogs not admitted

The stonework in evidence throughout.

Montaione is a delightful village equidistant (60km) from Florence, Siena and Pisa, set in a landscape remarkable for both its natural beauty and rich history. Built into the old ramparts, this hotel today shows little trace of its original function; all the milling machinery is long gone, replaced by characterful accommodation in the form of fifteen fine rooms, furnished with antique pieces and wrought iron beds. Panoramic views, family management, a garden and small breakfast room complete the picture.

Access: In the historic centre of the village

MONTALCINO (SI)

43

IL PODERUCCIO

Sig. Girardi
Via Poderuccio, 52
53020 Sant'Angelo in Colle (SI)
Tel. 05 77 84 40 52 - Fax 05 77 84 41 50
poderuccio.girardi@virgilio.it

Closed 1 Dec-7 Apr and 1-31 Jul • 6 double rm • Parking, garden, swimming pool, no dogs • Pétanque, oil, grappa and wine for sale

The attractive garden filled with colourful flowers.

With its panoramic location near the vineyards, this agriturismo is perfect for wine enthusiasts who wish to tour the Montalcino area, which is renowned for its high-quality Brunello wines. The house is simple and classical in style, with a harmonious and symmetrical appearance. Surrounded by a green meadow and a delightful garden carefully tended by the owners, the property also boasts a swimming pool situated slightly away from the house to ensure a quiet and peaceful stay for guests. The rooms are furnished with rustic pieces which perfectly match the overall flavour of the property.

Access: 10km from the town on the road to the sea, near Monte Amiata

TOSCANA

MONTECARLO (LU)

44

ANTICA CASA DEI RASSICURATI

Cooperativa Peperosa
Via della Collegiata, 2
55015 Montecarlo (LU)
Tel. 05 83 22 89 01 – Fax 058 32 24 98
info@anticacasadeirassicurati.it
www.anticacasadeirassicurati.it

👤👤 **68-80€**

Open all year • 2 single rm, 4 double rm • Small dogs welcome

 Breakfast, served either in the lounge with open fireplace, or on the patio outside.

Not to be confused with the capital of Monaco, the small medieval village of Montecarlo is situated among the olive groves and vineyards of the Lucchesia, offering a rather more understated experience for visitors against the backdrop of its historic Tuscan buildings. Antica Casa dei Rassicurati is the ideal spot for those seeking peace, relaxation and unspoilt beauty. Passionately and competently run by an all female team, the rooms are elegant and breakfast is enhanced by the inclusion of homemade jams and pastries.

Access: In the heart of the historic centre, near Sant'Andrea church

MONTECARLO (LU)

45

ANTICA DIMORA PATRIZIA

Merckx Boudewijn
via Carmignani 10/12
55015 Montecarlo (LU)
Tel. 058 32 21 56 – Fax 05 83 22 94 98
info@anticadimorapatrizia.com
www.anticadimorapatrizia.com

 70-80€

Open all year • 6 double rm • Half-board €42-60

 Menu €22/37

 The tranquillity of the picturesque historic centre perched on an isolated hilltop.

The Teatro Comunale dei Rassicurati, built in the early 18C by the "Accademia degli Assicurati", a group of affluent merchants and aristocrats, is right in the heart of the historic centre of Montecarlo on Via Carmignani. To this day it has remained a significant cultural and theatrical centre. A little further on, at the foot of the fortress, a palace from an earlier period is home to a cosy interior, whose ceilings are adorned with frescoes and enriched by objets d'art. On the ground floor there is an immense hall with a sitting room and piano, in addition to a traditional restaurant, for guests only, that serves Tuscan cuisine.

Access: In the heart of the historic centre

TOSCANA

MONTECARLO (LU)

46

LA NINA

Fam. Lazzareschi
Via San Martino, 54
55015 Montecarlo (LU)
Tel. 058 32 21 78 – Fax 058 32 21 78
infolanina@libero.it – www.lanina.it

55€

Open all year • 10 double rm • No breakfast • Parking, garden, no dogs

 Menu €25/39

 The large, elegant and well presented rooms.

This is an attractive yellow house overlooking the countryside from a verdant location on the outskirts of the village of Montecarlo. The excellent accommodation is tastefully furnished, spacious and shows much attention to detail. No breakfast available (although this may be taken in any of the several bars nearby) but there is an adjacent restaurant of the same name offering robust Tuscan cuisine.

Access: On the way out of the village towards Lucca

TOSCANA

MONTECATINI TERME (PT)

47

PETIT CHÂTEAU

Sig.ra Gemignani
viale Rosselli 10
51016 Montecatini Terme (PT)
Tel. 05 72 90 59 00 - Fax 05 72 90 58 06
info@petitchateau.it - www.petitchateau.it

👤👤 **92-132€**

Open all year • 6 double rm • Garden

 The individually decorated luxurious rooms.

This elegant, Liberty-style property with a pink and white façade was built in the 1920s in the heart of Tuscany. The interior of this archaeological and historic monument of great value has been renovated from top to toe. Ideally situated for guests wishing to take the waters or indulge in a shopping spree, this small hotel offers handsome, individually decorated rooms enhanced by high-quality furniture and matching fabrics, and a small meeting room next door. Breakfasts are served inside or under the arbour in the refreshing garden.

Access: In the town centre, near the spa

TOSCANA

MONTECATINI TERME (PT)

48

VILLA LE MAGNOLIE

Sig. Meucci
Viale Fedeli, 15
51016 Montecatini Terme (PT)
Tel. 05 72 91 17 00 – Fax 057 27 28 85
info@hotelmichelangelo.org
www.michelangelo-hotel.it

👤👤 100€

Open all year • 6 double rm • Parking, garden

 The top floor room with wooden ceiling, a must for incurable romantics.

Montecatini is a renowned spa town and consequently there are many hotels from which to choose. Those looking for something a little different without wishing to spend a fortune should seek out this establishment, an early 20C Art Nouveau villa run by the Meucci family in a caring and tasteful fashion. There are six charming rooms, plus an attractive lounge and breakfast room. Guests have access to all the facilities of the neighbouring Hotel Michelangelo (gym, swimming pool, tennis court).

Access: Two minutes from the centre, near the golf course and spa

TOSCANA

MONTEMERANO (GR)

49

LE FONTANELLE
Sig. Perna
Località Poderi di Montemerano
58050 Montemerano (GR)
Tel. 05 64 60 27 62 - Fax 05 64 60 27 62
le.fontanelle@tiscali.it - www.lefontanelle.net

👣👣 78€

Open all year • 12 double rm • Parking, garden, no dogs in the restaurant • Fishing

 Set Menu for residents only

 Getting close to the local flora and fauna.

Perfect for those in quest of the unspoilt, this agriturismo harmoniously co-exists with its natural surroundings, which teem with wildlife. Composed of several stone buildings, there are around a dozen rooms in all which are simple yet welcoming. In summer, the guests only restaurant serves its tasty cuisine beneath a delightful gazebo.

Access: *3km from the village towards Manciano*

TOSCANA

MONTERIGGIONI (SI)

50

BORGO GALLINAIO

Sig. Izzo
strada del Gallinaio 5
53035 Monteriggioni (SI)
Tel. 05 77 30 47 51 - Fax 05 77 30 47 93
info@gallinaio.it - www.gallinaio.it

👤👤 120-150€

Closed 4 Nov-31 Mar • 1 single rm, 11 double rm • Half-board €88-103 • Parking, garden, swimming pool, park, dogs not admitted

 Set Menu €28 for residents only

 The old water tank, now a swimming pool, is where water was drawn in former times.

Perched on a hilltop held sacred by the Etruscans, only two minutes from Monteriggioni, Borgo Gallinaio is a small hamlet of buildings dating from the 15C, whose stone walls, terracotta tiled floors and chestnut wood rafters are characteristic of regional farmhouses. The interior features pleasant rooms that are named after the property's architectural features. In summertime, take a seat in the vast courtyard and enjoy a breakfast of local specialities. The restaurant, for guests only, serves carefully prepared Tuscan dishes.

Access: Around 2km from the village towards Siena

TOSCANA

MONTERONI D'ARBIA (SI)

51

CASA BOLSININA

Sig. Mazzotta
località Casale Caggiolo
53014 Monteroni d'Arbia (SI)
Tel. 05 77 71 84 77 - Fax 05 77 71 84 77
bolsinina@bolsinina.com - www.bolsinina.com

105-120€

Closed 15 Jan-15 Mar • 5 double rm, 1 suite • Half-board €80-90 • Parking, garden, swimming pool, dogs not admitted

 Set Menu €30 and 35 for residents only

 The tranquil landscape and warm family greeting – a home away from home.

Siena's hillsides, once a shallow ocean covered in tumuli and dunes, form the backdrop to this elegant property, restored from top to toe. The ground floor of the 18C farm is home to an immense sitting room, with a fireplace and billiards table, ideal for evenings spent in the company of friends. Outdoors the cool garden and refreshing swimming pool with deck chairs, loungers and parasol are equally attractive. Warm, friendly welcome.

Access: Around 6km from the village towards Buonconvento

TOSCANA

MONTEVARCHI (AR)

52

RELAIS LA RAMUGINA-FATTORIA DI RENDOLA

Fam. Bucciarelli
località Rendola 89
52025 Montevarchi (AR)
Tel. 05 59 70 77 13 – Fax 05 59 70 74 75
info@fattoriadirendola.it – www.fattoriadirendola.it 👫 89-99€

Closed Jan • 10 double rm, 1 suite • Parking, swimming pool, dogs not admitted in rooms

 Menu €35/48

 The chance to stay in a historic residence full of the scents of the countryside.

Montevarchi, a small town founded in the 12C around the castle of the same name, was the scene some six centuries later of the lavish reign of Leopoldo di Lorena, Grand Duke of Tuscany. This Leopoldian-style farmhouse, immersed in a typical Tuscan landscape of olive groves and vineyards, has been turned into a small but elegant posthouse that is home to brightly coloured personalised guestrooms, each of which is decorated with antique furniture. The restaurant specialises in classical Tuscan cuisine with a number of modern inspirations.

Access: 4km from the village towards Mercatale

MONTIERI (SP)

LA MERIDIANA-LOCANDA IN MAREMMA

Sig.ra Crippa
strada provinciale 5 Le Galleraie Sud-Est : 2,5 km
58026 Montieri (GR)
Tel. 05 66 99 70 18 – Fax 05 66 99 70 17
direzione@lameridiana.net
www.lameridiana.net

110-160€

Closed 8 Jan-28 Feb • 13 double rm • Half-board €100 • Parking, garden, swimming pool, dogs not admitted • Horse riding, guided trips, sale of jam and honey

Set Menu €30 and 38

The small sitting room in the stables where a log fire burns in winter.

Whatever the season, the experience and scents of this establishment are as varied as they are pleasant: pause and listen to the silence, breathe in the odour of roasted chestnuts or take a refreshing dip in the small lake. Such is the appeal of the region of Maremma, the setting of this property. The 17C cottage has been transformed into a welcoming country guesthouse where you can recharge your batteries while you take a break from your daily routine. The spacious rooms are furnished with wrought-iron beds, and a fireplace adorns the small sitting rooms. Fresh homemade pasta and locally-reared meat take pride of place on the menu in the delightful restaurant overlooking the valley. Outdoors there is a swimming pool and a fitness track.

Access: 3km from the village towards Gabellino

TOSCANA

MONTIERI (GR)

54

RIFUGIO PRATEGIANO

Sig. Paradisi
località Prategiano 45
58026 Montieri (GR)
Tel. 05 66 99 77 00 – Fax 05 66 99 78 91
info@prategiano.com – www.prategiano.com

 80-130€

Closed 6 Nov-19 Mar • 4 single rm, 20 double rm • Half-board €56-85 • Parking, garden, swimming pool, dogs not admitted in restaurant

 Set Menu €17 and 20

 Relating your adventures of the day in front of a log fire or under the starlit sky.

This property is not only full of the rustic charm of Tuscany's country homes, but is also set in the beautiful Maremma countryside. It is very popular with lovers of wide-open spaces, and daily hikes, bicycle and horseback rides are organised into the Mediterranean hinterland and along the stunning coast. Also close at hand are countless old castles and the silver and copper mines which raised the Montieri to fame in the Middle Ages. Excursions are organised daily to different spots and accompanied by delicious picnics and excellent company. In the evening, you will sit down to a delicious array of local produce.

Access: 1km from the village right out in the country

TOSCANA

MONTOPOLI IN VAL D'ARNO (PI)

55

QUATTRO GIGLI

Sig.ra Puccioni
piazza Michele da Montopoli 2
56020 Montopoli in Val d'Arno (PI)
Tel. 05 71 46 68 78 – Fax 05 71 46 68 79
info@quattrogigli.it – www.quattrogigli.it

85-95€

Open all year • 2 single rm, 22 double rm • Half-board €63-68 • Garden, dogs not admitted

 Menu €37/63

 The restaurant's ancient recipes served in earthenware dishes.

Among its many edifices of great historic interest, Montopoli, built against a slope of tuff rock, boasts an 8C castle, referred to as the "eminent castle" by Boccaccio himself due to its impressive fortifications. The hotel, built in the heart of the historic town on a quiet panoramic spot, extends a gracious welcome to guests, offering comfortable guestrooms with a distinctive Tuscan influence. The high spot of the establishment is the restaurant, located in the former barns of the Podesteria. Tourists and gourmets alike flock here to enjoy traditional Renaissance specialities.

Access: In the heart of the small town

TOSCANA

PALAZZUOLO SUL SENIO (FI)

56

LE PANARE

Sig. Minardi
Località Scheta
50035 Palazzuolo sul Senio (FI)
Tel. 05 58 04 63 46
lepanare@tin.it – www.lepanare.it

👤👥 40-65€

Closed Nov-Apr • 4 double rm • Half board €30-45 • Parking, garden, no dogs in the restaurant

 Set Menu €10 and 20 for residents only

 The young and enthusiastic management.

Situated among Tuscany's unspoilt Mugello hills, this old farmstead offers limited but characterful accommodation with wood beamed sloping ceilings, stone walls and rustic furnishings. Meals are served in a dining room dominated by a large open fireplace and a single horseshoe shaped table. An unusual feature of the place is its small collection of arms and armour.

Access: 5km from the village towards Piedimonte

TOSCANA

PELAGO (FI)

57

LOCANDA TINTI
Sig. Tinti
Via Casentinese 65 a Diacceto
50060 Pelago (FI)
Tel. 05 58 32 70 07 - Fax 05 58 32 78 28
info@locandatinti.it - www.locandatinti.it

👤👤 80€

Open all year • 6 double rm • Breakfast €8 • Dogs not admitted

 Relive a page of history as you discover the traditions of a tiny village tucked away in the hillsides.

The tiny village of Diaccetto, hidden in the heart of the Florentine Levant amid vineyards and olive groves, is the home of this delightful red-fronted property with green shutters. This sophisticated establishment, whose warm welcome cannot be faulted, has retained the picturesque charm of old posthouses where travellers used to stop for the night before continuing on their road. Bare exposed beams, terracotta floors and Roman stone doors set the scene for the bedrooms decorated with 19C wood furniture and wrought-iron bedsteads. A terrace with sundeck and two small breakfast rooms are available to guests.

Access: From the town, drive for 3km along the SS 70

TOSCANA

PERGINE VALDARNO (AR)

FATTORIA DI MONTELUCCI

Sig. Cipolletti
a Montelucci
52020 Pergine Valdarno (AR)
Tel. 05 75 89 65 25 – Fax 05 75 89 63 15
info@montelucci.it – www.montelucci.it

 120-140€

Closed Jan-Feb • 1 single rm, 32 double rm, 2 suites • Half-board €89-99 • Parking, park, swimming pool, dogs not admitted in restaurant • Guided trips, sale of oil, wine, cured meat, cheese and jam

 Menu €33/50

 A real rest in Infernaccio – without television or telephone.

"Mountain of light" is the significance of this ancient establishment's name. Montelucci, originally a fort on the hills between Arezzo, Siena and Florence, was destroyed in the Middle Ages during battles between the Florentines and the Arrezians. The farm has since been rebuilt and extended over the centuries and is now comprised of a main house and several outbuildings; a perfect spot to rest and commune with nature or find out more about the region's history in a tranquil setting. The restaurant, located where the grapes were formerly pressed, serves traditional fare that varies with the seasons.

Access: Around 3km from the town, in the countryside

POGGIO MURELLA (GR)

59

IL CANTUCCIO

Sig. Camilli
via Termine 18
58050 Poggio Murella (GR)
Tel. 05 64 60 79 73 – Fax 05 64 60 79 73
camilli.rossano@tiscali.it – www.cameresaturnia.it   **60-90€**

Open all year • 1 single rm, 5 double rm • Garden, dogs not admitted

 A faultless example of hospitality and cordiality.

The small town of Poggio Morella, dating back to the Middle Ages, lies a few kilometres from the thermal spa of Saturnia and contains houses of modest proportions. It is no doubt the Pagus Lucretio cited by the Latins in Antiquity. An ideal destination for those in search of tranquillity and relaxation, this enchanting and beautifully cared for guesthouse offers comfortable rooms, all decorated with hand-painted features, wooden furniture and brightly coloured bedspreads. Ancient family recipes feature prominently on the breakfast table every morning and you will be treated to bread with oil, fruit or cream pies, croissants, pizzas, etc.

Access: In the centre of the village, near the Saturnia thermal baths

TOSCANA

PONTREMOLI (MS)

60

CÀ DEL MORO
Fam. Bezzi
Via Casa Corvi, 9
54027 Pontremoli (MS)
Tel. 01 87 83 22 02 – Fax 01 87 83 22 02
info@cadelmoro.it – www.cadelmororesort.it

102-116€

Open all year • 5 double rm • Half board €108 • Parking, garden, golf practice range, dogs not admitted in restaurant

 Menu €26/34

 The chestnut woods that surround the farm.

Pontremoli is the capital of the Lunigiana, the delightful district bordered by the parkland of the Apuan Alps, the Versilia riviera down to the southern tip of the Ligurian coast, and the Tuscan-Emilian Apennine watershed. Three kilometers from the town, the perfectly restored Cà del Moro occupies a typical farmstead. The rooms in the former hay barn are tastefully furnished and well equipped. The restaurant is in the old converted cellars. Lovely outdoor summer terrace and four-hole golf course.

Access: Just 3km from the centre, right out in the country

PONTREMOLI (MS)

COSTA D'ORSOLA

Sig. Bezzi
Località Orsola
54027 Pontremoli (MS)
Tel. 01 87 83 33 32 – Fax 01 87 83 33 32
info@costadorsola.it – www.costadorsola.it

👫 86-114€

Closed Nov and Jan • 14 double rm • Half board €58-72 • Parking, swimming pool, tennis, dogs not admitted in restaurant • Bicycles available, oil for sale

 Menu €25/33

 The horses grazing around the house.

This stone built settlement is surrounded by verdant countryside with wooded hillsides rising in the distance. The peace and quiet here is broken only by the rustling of leaves in the breeze and birdsong. Inside, the ambience is tastefully understated and the furnishings simple. Friendly and helpful family management.

Access: 2km from the centre in the heart of the small town of the same name

TOSCANA

RADDA IN CHIANTI (SI)

CASTELVECCHI

Sig. Catania
Verso Volpaia
53017 Radda in Chianti (SI)
Tel. 05 77 73 80 50 – Fax 05 77 73 86 08
castelvecchi@castelvecchi.com – www.castelvecchi.com

 98€

Closed from 1 Dec-31 Mar • 1 single rm, 10 double rm • Half-board €64 • Parking, garden, swimming pool, dogs not admitted • Sale of wine

 Menu €23/35

 The old millstone in the inner courtyard.

You only have to cross the threshold of this medieval town to enjoy the simple pleasures and authentic landscapes of Chianti, surrounded by the scents and silence of the countryside. The main house and former cottages of a former winegrowing estate now welcome guests to an interior that varies from rustically informal to plush and elegant. The restaurant, open to guests only, is located in the old pressing room under a tangled mass of brick arches and exposed beams; traditional regional dishes.

Access: Some 6km from the town towards Volpaia

TOSCANA

RADDA IN CHIANTI (SI)

63

PODERE TERRENO

Sig.ra Haniez
53017 Radda in Chianti (SI)
Tel. 05 7773 83 12 – Fax 05 7773 84 00
podereterreno@chiantinet.it – www.podereterreno.it

45€

Closed 20-27 Dec • 1 single rm, 5 double rm • Half-board only €95-120 • Parking • Angling, pétanque, bicycles available, sale of oil, wine and grappa

 Set Menu for residents only

 Exchanging tales and adventures as you sit down in the company of other guests around the large table.

This friendly 16C farmhouse stands against a characteristic Tuscan landscape of olive groves, oak trees, vineyards and broom bushes. The original terracotta floors and old wooden beams are still visible and the establishment has a few well-kept guestrooms, decorated with period furniture, for those who are eager to get back to grass roots and/or go walking, horse-riding or bicycling. The former kitchens are now home to a rustic dining room with a fireplace, where the owners' hospitality can be appreciated to the fullest.

Access: Some 5km from the town towards Volpaia

TOSCANA

RADICONDOLI (SI)

65

FATTORIA SOLAIO

Sig.ra Carabba Serafini
Località Solaio
53030 Radicondoli (SI)
Tel. 05 77 79 10 29 - Fax 05 77 79 10 15
info@fattoriasolaio.it - www.fattoriasolaio.it

👤👤 75-90€

Closed 7 Jan-15 Mar, 5 Nov-26 Dec • 8 double rm • Parking, swimming pool, dogs not admitted in restaurant • Oil, honey and wine for sale

 Set Menu €20 for residents only

 The combination of patrician elegance and rustic simplicity.

This agriturismo encapsulates the agricultural history of the Sienese countryside in microcosm. The earliest buildings date from the 15 and 16C, retaining their original simple demeanour which is decidedly rustic. The main house is of a later date, by which time the traditional rural architecture had given way to a more elegant style befitting a patrician residence. Guests can enjoy an ambience little changed since the 18C, when the resident gentry would have walked here among their verdant gardens.

Access: Around 12km from the town towards Castelnuovo Val di Cecina

TOSCANA

SAN CASCIANO IN VAL DI PESA (FI)

66

SALVADONICA

Sig. Baccetti
a Mercatale via Grevigiana 82
50024 San Casciano in Val di Pesa
Tel. 05 58 21 80 39 - Fax 05 58 21 80 43
info@salvadonica.com - www.salvadonica.com

113-119€

Closed 7 Nov-14 Mar • 5 double rm, 10 suites • Parking, garden, swimming pool, tennis court • Sale of oil and wine

 Vaulted ceilings and splendid views from all sides.

This spot is as well suited to relaxation and meditation as it is to physical exercise. Salvadonica is home to a delightful country guesthouse, located halfway between Siena and Florence in the green Tuscan countryside. Treat yourself to a dip in the pool in the shade of the olive groves, a horse ride through the hills or quite simply the chance to take it easy and enjoy the peace and quiet. The establishment also has a massage centre, so relax and let yourself be pampered by wellness specialists.

Access: From the centre, drive for 3km towards Mercatale

TOSCANA

SAN GIMIGNANO (SI)

67

IL CASALE DEL COTONE

Sig. Martelli
Località Cellole, 59
53037 San Gimignano (SI)
Tel. 05 77 94 32 36 – Fax 05 77 94 32 36
info@casaledelcotone.com – www.casaledelcotone.com   108€

Closed 2 Nov-23 Dec • 14 double rm • Parking, garden, swimming pool, no dogs in the restaurant • Oil and wine for sale

 Set Menu €40 for residents only

 The little 17C chapel with its stucco work decoration.

One of Tuscany's most striking landscapes, the countryside around Siena is a characteristic ochre colour. This natural beauty, coupled with the district's tranquillity, makes a country hotel more appealing than staying in town, especially when it is a late 17C farm with its own chapel and hectares of surrounding olive groves and vineyards. This establishment is decorated in period style with antique furniture; around the property peace reigns supreme among the trees, allowing guests to get away from it all

Access: From the centre drive for 2km towards Certaldo

TOSCANA

SAN GIMIGNANO (SI)

68

FATTORIA POGGIO ALLORO

F.lli Fioroni
Località Ulignano - Via Sant'Andrea, 23
53037 San Gimignano (SI)
Tel. 05 77 95 01 53 – Fax 05 77 95 02 90
info@fattoriapoggioalloro.com
www.fattoriapoggioalloro.com

76-90€

Closed 6-31 Jan • 10 double rm • Half board €66-75 • Parking, garden, swimming pool, no dogs • Oil, wine, pasta, honey and saffron for sale

 Set Menu €30 and 36 for residents only

 The view of San Gimignano in the distance, like a mirage in the evening light.

To spend time here is to shut the door on the outside world. The view is over the rolling Sienese hills, planted with cereal crops, olive groves and saffron, and dotted with livestock farms. From this landscape, the local cuisine sources its raw materials, the most distinguished of which is the renowned Chianina beef, used for Fiorentina steak. Gazing from the terrace towards the extraordinary skyline of San Gimignano, guests might be tempted to prolong their stay indefinitely.

Access: 5km from the village towards Certaldo

SAN GIMIGNANO (SI)

69

PODERE VILLUZZA

Sig.ra Crocchini
Località Strada, 25
53037 San Gimignano (SI)
Tel. 05 77 94 05 85
info@poderevilluzza.it – www.poderevilluzza.it

Open all year • 6 double rm • Parking, garden, swimming pool, no dogs • Extra virgin olive oil for sale

The San Gimignano towers dominating the view with the Sienese landscape rolling away in the distance

Built in pale stone, this easily reached farmhouse occupies an isolated position atop a hill. From here the views stretch for miles, encompassing vineyards, olive groves, citrus orchards and the walls of San Gimignano, encircling the town's extraordinary cluster of medieval towers. Inside, this establishment has an ambience of bygone times with wood beamed ceilings and brick arches; the elegant rooms show the feminine touch of the owner, the courteous Signora Sandra.

Access: On leaving the village head towards Certaldo as far as Strada

TOSCANA

SAN GIMIGNANO (SI)

70

IL ROSOLACCIO

Sig. Ingrid Music
località Capezzano
53037 San Gimignano (SI)
Tel. 05 77 94 44 65 - Fax 057 7 94 44 67
music@rosolaccio.com - www.rosolaccio.com

108€

Closed from 1 Nov-14 Mar • 1 single rm, 5 double rm • Half-board €79 • Parking, garden, swimming pool

 For residents only

 The steep uphill walk is the price to pay for the splendid view of the hills and countryside.

The establishment was named after a medicinal plant from the poppy family used as a sedative. This country guesthouse, of relaxing virtues but without any unwanted secondary effects, is located in an old stone farmhouse perched on top of a hill between Siena and Florence. The farm has been extended over the years to house the growing farming families. Now restored, its comfortable guestrooms vary in size but all have lovely brick ceilings and timber rafters. The pleasant sitting room is heated by a log fire in winter, and the rustic dining room is full of the characteristic charm of the Tuscan countryside.

Access: On leaving the village towards Certaldo, drive for 8km and follow the signs before the white bridge

TOSCANA

SAN GIOVANNI D'ASSO (SI)

71

LA LOCANDA DEL CASTELLO

Sig.ra Ratti
Piazza Vittorio Emanuele II, 4
53020 San Giovanni d'Asso (SI)
Tel. 05 77 80 29 39 – Fax 05 77 80 29 42
info@lalocandadelcastello.com
www.lalocandadelcastello.com

100-150€

Closed 15 Jan-28 Feb • 6 double rm, 3 suites • Half board €85-100 • Small dogs welcome

 Menu €26/41

 Dining against the stone backdrop of the olive press, wafted by the scent of truffles.

San Givanni d'Asso sits in the ochre scenery of the Sienese countryside, a small medieval village sited in the shadow of one of the many castles which to this day stand guard over the landscape. The white truffle is one of this area's great natural jewels, and this establishment's restaurant, occupying the old olive press, employs it liberally in its cuisine. Two floors up, in a section of the building dating from the 18C, the rooms are colourful and well furnished, demonstrating the owner's feminine touch at work.

Access: On the main square near the castle

TOSCANA

SAN GIOVANNI D'ASSO (SI)

72

LA LOCANDA DI MONTISI

Sig. Crocenzi
a Montisi Via Umberto I°, 39
53020 San Giovanni d'Asso (SI)
Tel. 05 77 84 59 06 – Fax 05 77 84 58 21
info@lalocandadimontisi.it
www.lalocandadimontisi.it

Closed 10 Jan-10 Feb • 7 double rm • Half-board €65-85

 Menu €21/31

> The rooms are named after existing districts and historic events in the village.

Montisi, in the heart of the Siena hillsides, covered in forests and popular with walkers since time immemorial, is home to this small inn in the historic town centre, in a neighbourhood whose fame stems from the San Giovanni d'Asso truffle fair held every year in November. The 18C property has retained the rustic charm of country houses and its seven delightful guestrooms combine romanticism and practicality, while the picturesque dining room is laid out in the cellars, which boast their original chalk and clay walls.

Access: In the historic centre of Montisi

TOSCANA

SAN MINIATO (PI)

73

VILLA SONNINO
Sig. Rosselli Campigli
via Castelvecchio 9/1 località Catena est : 4 km
56027 San Miniato (PI)
Tel. 05 71 48 40 33 – Fax 05 7148 51 75
villa@villasonnino.com – www.villasonnino.it

86-96€

Open all year • 13 double rm • Half-board €69-75 • Parking, park, dogs not admitted

 Menu €26/38

 The vast park and drive lined by cypress trees that leads to the villa.

A small town steeped in history and a property where many famous families have lived; and a unique chance to relive a page of local history almost as if you were there. San Miniato, a village of Roman origin in the heart of the region, is rich in splendid panoramic views and history, such as the Rocca di Federico II and the edifice in which the hotel is located. The building was the home of several high-ranking families over the centuries, including the Sonnino family, of Jewish origins, who were granted the title of Baron by Umberto I. Today the establishment features a comfortable romantic interior, spacious classically furnished guestrooms and a vaulted dining room where Mediterranean cuisine takes pride of place.

Access: On the road to Pisa, after 100m, take Via San Giovanni

TOSCANA

SAN QUIRICO D'ORCIA (SI)

74

LA LOCANDA DEL LOGGIATO

Sig.ra Marini
a Bagno Vignoni, piazza del Monetto 30
53027 San Quirico d'Orcia (SI)
Tel. 05 77 88 89 25 - Fax 05 77 88 83 70
locanda@loggiato.it - www.loggiato.it

130-150€

Open all year • 8 double rm • Dogs not admitted

 The large sitting room with fireplace, mezzanine, piano and treats for the sweet-toothed.

Thirty inhabitants and an enormous basin filled with water that used to be a thermal swimming pool: such are the characteristics of Bagno Pignoni, a tiny town of ancient origins. By the square, the inn is located in one of the 14C buildings. It is a peaceful establishment, ideal for reading, writing, painting or just resting. Each of the several romantic rooms, decorated individually with a colour and a detail that evokes the past, is enhanced by objets d'art. The generous, tasty breakfast table is laid in the wine bar, or when the weather is very hot, by the thermal basin.

Access: In the spa resort of Bagno Vignoni

TOSCANA

SAN QUIRICO D'ORCIA (SI)

75

IL RIGO
Sig. Cipolla
Località Casabianca
53027 San Quirico d'Orcia (SI)
Tel. 05 77 89 72 91 – Fax 05 77 89 82 36
ilrigo@iol.it – www.ilrigo.com

100-110€

Closed 10 Jan-13 Feb • 15 double rm • Half board €72-78 • Parking, garden • Oil for sale

 Set Menu €15 and 23 for residents only

 The air of times gone by here and in the surrounding landscape.

The coat of arms adorning this 16C farmhouse is that of the Hospital of Santa Maria della Scala in Siena, once a significant landowner in this area. The landscape has changed little in the intervening years, although a second house of red brick was subsequently built to house the tenant farmers who tilled the surrounding fields. Today, the accommodation these buildings provide is for guests, for whom there awaits unspoilt countryside, well presented rooms and cordial service from the owners, who dine in company with their visitors. Cookery courses are also available, run in a friendly and relaxed style.

Access: On the outskirts of the village towards Bagni San Filippo

TOSCANA

SANSEPOLCRO (AR)

76

RELAIS PALAZZO DI LUGLIO

Sig. Tofanelli
frazione Cignano 35
52037 San Sepolcro (AR)
Tel. 05 75 75 00 26 – Fax 05 75 75 98 92
info@relaispalazzodiluglio.com
www.relaispalazzodiluglio.com

110-130€

Closed 10-20 Jan • 4 double rm, 10 suites • Parking, park, swimming pool, dogs not admitted

 Set Menu €35 and 50 for residents only

 Walks or horseback rides through the forest or canoeing down the rapids.

Three kilometres from Sansepolcro, birthplace of Piero della Francesca, this impressive 17C farm was formerly the summer home of noble families. Today it is surrounded by greenery, but also close to tourist and cultural sites and the spa resorts; an ideal establishment to pamper yourself, get back to grass roots or set out to explore the region's historic and gastronomic treasures. As for the menu, take a seat under the dining room's stone arches and treat your taste buds to a festival of flavours.

Access: 3km from the village on the Rimini road

TOSCANA

SARTEANO (SI)

77

LE ANFORE

Sig.ra Balzarini
via Oriato 2/4
53047 Sarteano (SI)
Tel. 05 78 26 55 21 – Fax 05 78 26 55 21
leanfore@priminet.com – www.balzarini.it

65-75€

Closed 15 Nov-15 Dec • 9 double rm, 1 suite • Parking, garden, swimming pool • Bicycles available, guided trips, sale of oil and wine

 Set Menu €23 for residents only

 Rediscovering the simple way of life of a bygone era and the rhythm of the countryside.

Known for its thermal springs and its famous Saracen Joust, Sarteano lies hidden in the peaceful landscape of Tuscany's hills. Enveloped in a distinctive, rustic yet refined atmosphere, this comfortable country guesthouse is located in a restored farmhouse, whose rooms are named after thoroughbred horses that have won various horse races. It will delight all those who long to get back to grass roots. Even the meals possess a holiday spirit with traditional dishes made from farm grown produce.

Access: 3km from the centre eastbound

TOSCANA

SATURNIA (GR)

78

VILLA CLODIA
Sig. Bonanni
Via Italia, 43
58050 Saturnia (GR)
Tel. 05 64 60 12 12 – Fax 05 64 60 13 05
villaclodia@laltramaremma.it – www.hotelvillaclodia.com

👫 95€

Closed 10 Jan-1 Feb • 1 single rm, 9 double rm • Garden, swimming pool, no dogs

 The little garden surrounded by trees and hedgerows.

Situated in the centre of Saturnia, this quiet little hotel has been converted from a private residence. A family atmosphere prevails without compromising the high standards of the place, which has refined touches such as trompe l'oeil wall decoration in some of the rooms, a few of which also benefit from a large terrace, from where the view takes in the ribbon of trees which encircles the house and its lawn (swimming pool).

Access: In the spa resort

SIENA (SI)

ANTICA RESIDENZA CICOGNA

Sig.ra Trefoloni
via dei Termini 67
53100 Siena (SI)
Tel. 05 77 28 56 13 – Fax 05 77 28 56 13
info@anticaresidenzacicogna.it
www.anticaresidenzacicogna.it

👦👧 **80-100€**

Open all year • 1 single rm, 4 double rm • Dogs not admitted

 The charm and mystery of a home steeped in history, dreams and heirlooms.

Clever restoration work has revealed the missing links in the long history of this palace near the cathedral. A fireplace and frescoes dating from the 19C endow the interior with the romantic aura of former centuries, a blend of mystery and thrills. The property, which dates back to the Middle Ages, features five pleasantly and individually decorated guestrooms with lions painted on the walls, a four-poster bed, a rustic style characteristic of Tuscany, bunches of roses and cornflowers or a portrait of a female angel winging her way to Siena with two babes in her arms.

Access: In the centre two minutes from Piazza del Campo and the cathedral

TOSCANA

SORANO (GR)

80

DELLA FORTEZZA

Sig. Caruso
piazza Cairoli
58010 Sorano (GR)
Tel. 05 64 63 20 10 – Fax 05 64 63 32 09
info@hoteldellafortezza.it – www.hoteldellafortezzal.it

130€

Closed from 7-31 Jan • 2 single rm, 12 double rm, 1 suite • Parking, small dogs welcome

Treat yourself to a stay in the fort of an aristocratic antique Roman family.

It is one of the most significant testimonials to military architecture of the Middle Ages, although all that remains of the orginal Orsini fort is the outer structure as part of the interior has given way to a modern hotel. You will be staying in the heart of an Etruscan archaeological area of great historic interest, where the memory of its former inhabitants and battles seems to linger on. Guests can relax in the rooms dotted along the narrow corridors, characteristic of this type of architecture, and in the fine guestrooms where you will admire the splendid antique ceilings and bare beams.

Access: In the heart of the historic centre, inside Fortezza Orsini

SOVANA (SI)

81

PESNA

Sig.ra Vetrano
via del Pretorio, 9
58010 Sovana (SI)
Tel. 05 64 61 41 20 - Fax 05 64 63 73 74
info@pesna.it - www.sovana.it

👤👤 **70-90€**

Open all year • 2 single rm, 4 double rm • Dogs not admitted

 The restrained setting of this haven of peace and quiet devoted to the memory of a hero – and to holidays.

Amid the peaceful clearings and green hills of the limestone plateau of Sovano, you might still be able to hear the echo of a historic battle in which the brave Etruscan warrior Posna distinguished himself. This small, welcoming establishment is a tribute to the memory of this figure of local history. In the heart of the historic town centre, the former palace has retained its original floors and bare beams. The rooms are simple but comfortable and decorated with wooden furniture. At breakfast you can choose between a pleasant room indoors or the outdoor terrace furnished with wrought-iron tables and chairs.

Access: In the heart of the village

TOSCANA

SUBBIANO (AR)

LA CORTE DELL'OCA

Sig. Donati
Viale Europa 16
52010 Subbiano (AR)
Tel. 05 75 42 13 36 - Fax 05 75 42 04 12
info@cortedelloca.it - www.cortedelloca.it

62€

Open all year • 1 single rm, 10 double rm, 2 suites • Breakfast €4, half-board €62

 Menu €27/35

 Like a black and white film, time seems to have magically stopped here.

The property owes its name to an old sign uncovered in the former joiner's workshop, while the interior reveals the owner's Fellinian dream. A pleasant period structure houses this establishment where visitors can still admire the picturesque Cantina di Quintilo, whose barrels, casks and various wooden utensils continue to withhold the secret of the grape pressing, fermentation and must processing. The Corte is also home to intimate and refined rooms furnished in a period style. What's more, the Osteria dell'Oca serves delicious local dishes: tortellini, stew and homemade pasta, while the owner will invite you to taste a vintage or two at the bar.

Access: In the centre of the village near Piazza Castello

TOSCANA

SUBBIANO (AR)

83

RELAIS TORRE SANTA FLORA

Sigg. Lombardi e Soldini
località Il Palazzo 169
52010 Subbiano (AR)
Tel. 05 75 42 10 45 - Fax 05 75 48 96 07
info@santaflora.it - www.santaflora.it

110-130€

Open all year • 1 single rm, 13 double rm, 1 suite • Parking, garden, swimming pool, dogs not admitted

 Menu €37/45

 Former halt for legionaries and passing travellers.

This ancient country property stands in the heart of Tuscany on the banks of the Arno and it is proud of its thousand-year-old history. The tower was the work of the Lombards in the 8C, after which, some 400 years later, Benedictine monks of Santa Flora and Lucilla moved here, offering food and accommodation to riders and travellers. Present-day tourists will find attractively decorated Tuscan-style rooms adorned with period objects and a picturesque dining room flanked by a small wine-cellar in the former stables.

Access: In the centre of the village towards Ponte Caliano

TOSCANA

SUVERETO (LI)

84

BULICHELLA

Sig.ra Miyakawa
località Bulichella 131
57028 Suvereto (LI)
Tel. 05 65 82 98 92 – Fax 05 65 82 95 53
info@bulichella.it – www.bulichella.it

 86€

Open all year • 2 single rm, 12 double rm • Half-board €63-68 • Parking, garden • Bicycles available, angling, guided trips, sale of jam, oil and wine

 Set Menu €20 and 50 for residents only

 Tuscany and Japan join forces for a 100 % organic stay.

In the heart of the Val di Cornia and surrounded by a peaceful garden and pond in the shade of vineyards and olive groves, this farm is entirely devoted to organic agriculture and also offers guests the chance to find out more about local traditions. The farm's two wings are comprised of small comfortable rooms with Tuscan terracotta floors and a wine-tasting room next to the cellar. The restaurant will delight lovers of fine wines and good food. On the leisure side, you can visit the area and explore its cultural sites either on foot, on horseback or by boat.

Access: In the countryside, 1km from the centre

TOSCANA

TAVARNELLE VAL DI PESA (FI)

85

ANTICA PIEVE

Sig. Bacci
strada della Pieve 1
50028 Tavarnelle Val di Pesa (FI)
Tel. 05 58 07 63 14 – Fax 05 58 07 65 22
info@anticapieve.net – www.anticapieve.net

90-120€

Open all year • 6 double rm • Garden, swimming pool

 Menu €15/45 for residents only

 Cooking and relaxation lessons amid sweet-scented vineyards

On Via Cassia, a famous ancient road that used to link Florence to Rome, this farm in the Chianti region is surrounded by an immense garden and is ideally located to explore the region. The lovely rooms with terracotta floors and bare beams are simply decorated with period furniture. During the day you can relax by the swimming pool, go on excursions or pay a visit to the neighbourhood wine cellars. A wide choice of leisure activities and ample opportunity to take things easy.

Access: Outside the centre, right in the countryside

TOSCANA

VADA (LI)

86

VILLA GRAZIANI

Fam. Graziani
via per Rosignano 14
57018 Vada (LI)
Tel. 05 86 78 82 44 – Fax 05 86 78 59 98
info@villagraziani.com
www.villagraziani.com

👫 110-140€

Open all year • 4 double rm, 2 suites • Parking, garden, dogs not admitted • Bicycles available, horse riding sale of oil

 Set Menu €25 and 30

 Cereals, olive oil and wine produced on the estate and horseback rides.

If you would like to treat yourself to a short break that combines the charms of the past with those of horses, then you're in the right place! The Graziani farm, built in the 19C, offers guests the run of its handsome interior, decorated with unusual furniture and knick-knacks that relate the daily life and history of a former era. The flower-decked gardens contain Roman remains. Impressive staircases and a museum of peasant life are other attractions. If you feel like something more energetic, saddle up and go for a gallop in the hinterland or on the beach. At dinnertime, all the guests sit down at the same large table to share the evening meal together.

Access: In the centre of the village near Piazza Garibaldi

VAGLIAGLI (SI)

87

CASALI DELL'AIOLA

Sig. Campelli
Località l'Aiola
53010 Vagliagli (SI)
Tel. 05 77 32 27 97 – Fax 05 77 32 25 09
casali_aiola@hotmail.com – www.aiola.net

👫 **95€** ☕

Open all year • 8 double rm • Parking, garden, no dogs

Tasting the local produce against the backdrop of the old hay barn.

Here the eternal rivalry between Siena and Florence is evident; the medieval castle which once occupied this site was razed to the ground in the 16C after Siena was defeated by her rival in alliance with the Emperor Charles V. Today, only traces of its imposing boundary walls survive, around which the farm buildings which today make up this agriturismo were subsequently built. The interiors retain a rustic feel with stone walls and wooden roof beams. The old livestock shed has become the breakfast room, while the former hay barn is a relaxing lounge where guests can while away the hours gazing out over the Tuscan hills.

Access: 12km from the village towards Vagliagli

TOSCANA

VILLAFRANCA IN LUNIGIANA (MS)

88

GAVARINI

Sig.ra Folloni
Mocrone - Via Benedicenti, 50
54028 Villafranca in Lunigiana (MS)
Tel. 01 97 49 55 04 - Fax 01 87 49 57 90
info@locandagavarini.it - www.locandagavarini.it

70-80€

Closed 7-30 Nov • 7 double rm, 1 suite • Half board €50-60 • Parking, garden

 Menu €20/40

We most liked The brickwork in the dining room with the open fireplace.

Easily reached from either the motorway or the main road, Locanda Gavarini is in the village's medieval quarter, near the church of San Maurizio. Originally a trattoria, it now also offers accommodation in the form of six new rooms which are comfortable and welcoming. Meals are served in two large rooms, one of which has an open fireplace and imposing brick arches, or outside among the flowers of the garden in summer.

Access: On the Filattiera road, drive for 2km then turn right towards Mocrone

TOSCANA

VINCI (FI)

TASSINAIA

Sig. Ciani
Via di Petroio, 15
50058 Vinci (FI)
Tel. 34 78 27 39 62
info@tassinaia.it – www.tassinaia.it

65-75€

Open all year • 5 double rm • Parking, garden, no dogs

 Echoes of Leonardo against the backdrop of the countryside.

It is likely that Leonardo frequented these parts before going on to dazzle the great courts of the Renaissance with his creative genius. Vinci has dedicated a museum to its most famous son which display many models from his vast oeuvre. The landscape is little changed from the 15C, as guests may observe from the terrace of this B&B occupying an 18C house with tile and wood sloping roof. The rustic style interior is in keeping with the tone of the building, with a fine pietra serena open fireplace in the breakfast room, hewn from the same stone in which Brunelleschi and Michelangelo worked.

Access: 4km from Vinci on the hillside

TOSCANA

VOLTERRA (PI)

90

VILLA RIODDI

Sig. Scudellari
Località Rioddi - Strada Monte Volterrano
56048 Volterra (PI)
Tel. 058 88 80 53 – Fax 058 88 80 74
info@hotelvillarioddi.it – www.hotelvillarioddi.it

88-93€

Closed 15 Jan-2 Mar, 3 Nov-27 Dec • 13 double rm • Parking, garden, swimming pool, no dogs

 The timeless atmosphere of this former post house.

During the period of the Grand Duchy of Tuscany, this 15C building was a post house. Five centuries later it is a peaceful hotel, benefiting from rooms with chestnut furniture, and boasting vaulted ceilings in the former coach house that now makes up the public area. The passage of time has not diluted the charm of this ancient building which is surrounded by extensive gardens and has panoramic views of the Etruscan walls of Volterra and the Cecina valley.

Access: Outside the village towards Cecina

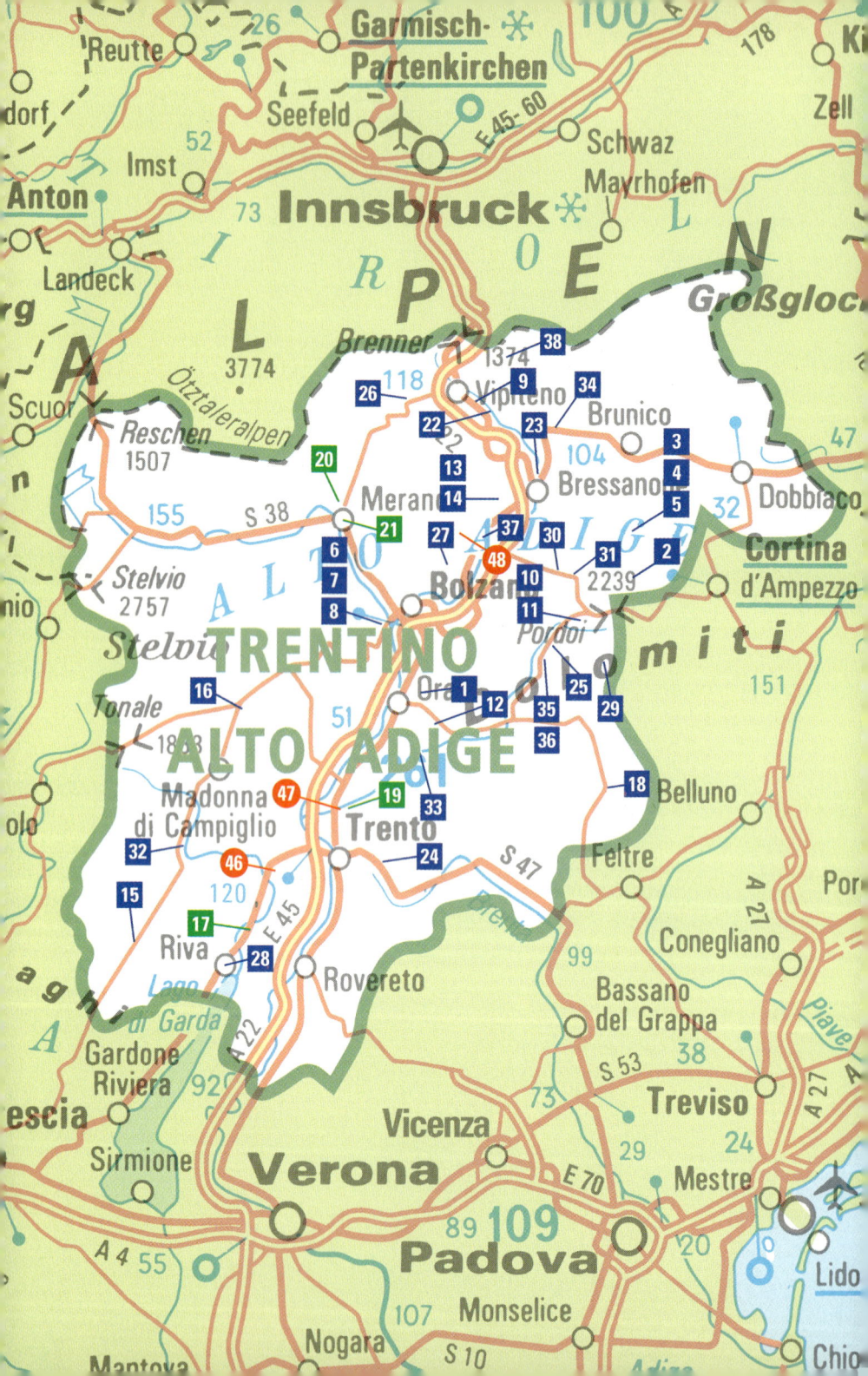

Trentino Alto Adige

At dusk, when the sun's rays turn the landscape pink, the Dolomites cease to be inanimate rock and come alive, as captured in countless pictures of the Val di Fassa, Valgardena or the Val Badia. The road winding down from the peaks towards the plain takes in many spots of historical importance; the Holy Roman Emperor passed by here on his way to negotiate with the Italian city states, the German bishops gathered here to participate in the Council of Trent following Luther's reforms, and here Otzi, the mummified herdsman from 3000 BC was found, now on display in Bolzano's archaeological museum. To this day, the region remains a meeting place between cultures, the German and Ladin speaking minorities being the most notable. Historical and cultural diversity has resulted an impressive artistic heritage, encapsulating both the Italianate style of Trento's cathedral and the austere northern style of the cathedrals of the Bolzano area. Its cuisine also reflects this variety of influences: strudel, knödel and Müller-Thurgau contrast with Marzemino d'Isera, carne salada and "strangolapreti".

38 establishments

Recommended sites and circuits
Trentino Alto Adige

> Trentino is a mountainous and rocky region. Its natural beauty and mysterious ancestral traditions are expressed in stone. Stone was the material used in the construction of its castles and houses; and it is in stone that the Roman epigraphs and capitals, the Renaissance doorways and the Baroque archways were sculpted. They are all precious vestiges of the past that the present has fortunately not forgotten.

The ancient origins of **Merano** can also be traced in stone, as testified to by the many medieval-era edifices, the ramparts, towers and the ruins of Castel San Zeno. During the 19C, the town was one of the largest health resorts in Central Europe, highly valued by the Austrian aristocracy as well as its Prussian, English, French and Russian counterparts. Today the town is once more a charming spa resort with elegant architecture, gardens and opulent parks. In the environs of this fascinating town you can explore the splendid castles that are ideal destinations for short visits and excursions.

On the road which runs from Merano to Lana, buried between the vineyards and the orchards, lies **Cermes**, a delight at any time of year. In spring you can watch as nature awakens, in summer you can enjoy the town in flower and the beauty of the surroundings, and, in autumn, a landscape ablaze with red colours. The setting is dominated by the imposing silhouette of the Ledenberg residence. This old manor is well worth a visit, especially for its valuable furnishings (furniture, paintings, tile stoves, etc.). The furnishings include original (17C) elements and period pieces found exclusively in the region by the owners. The knights' room is of particular interest; here you can see a table outlining the family tree of the current proprietors, with over 250 members of this noble house.

On to **Gargazzone**, a charming little Tyrolian village. With its town centre and festive fountains, its church, ancient *masi* and surrounding country houses, it is the perfect place to unwind after the stress of frenetic urban life.

Alongside the ancient stone stand modern infrastructures designed to facilitate the daily life of the region's inhabitants. The big park, along with other smaller ones, is fitted out with children's recreational facilities that have won the town the title of "child-friendly community". The grown-ups can have fun too as the town has diverse sporting facilities.

A recipe to try, wines and... a nugget of information

 Wines

_Teroldego Rotaliano
_Marzemino Trentino
_Spumante Trento D.O.C.
_Moscato giallo
_Moscato rosa
_Vino Santo Trentino D.O.C.

Ingredients
- 1kg Reinette apples
- 100g butter
- 150g raisins
- 100g pine kernels
- 100g walnuts
- the zest of half a lemon
- 2 tablespoons ground hazelnuts
- 1 tablespoons breadcrumbs
- 400g flour
- 70g butter
- 1 egg
- a pinch of ground cinnamon

Local specialities

Cheeses: Asiago, Grana Trentino, Casolet, Puzzone di Moena. Apples, bacon (cold meats), honey, *ciuiga* (sausage), cherries, strawberries, blueberries, grappa, rye bread, *krapfen*, *canederli* (bread gnocchi whose consistency and taste alter according to the ingredients: bacon, spinach, ricotta, cheese).

STRUDEL DI MELE

Method

Tip the flour onto a work surface and make a well in the centre; put the softened butter and four tablespoons of warm water into it. Work the ingredients together until you have a dense and elastic dough and leave to rest for 30min in a preheated pot. Peel the apples and cut them into thin rounds, add the raisins, pine kernels, chopped walnuts, zest, sugar and cinnamon. Lightly flour a work surface, roll out the dough and brush it over with melted butter. Spread a layer of ground hazelnuts and breadcrumbs over the dough, then add a layer of apples, strew sugar over it all and roll up the dough, making sure you seal it properly at the ends. Put it in the oven (180°C) for 1hr. Serve the strudel warm, sprinkled with icing sugar.

Food for thought

Strudel is just one variety of *Baclava*, an ancient Turkish sweet. The recipe left its homeland to arrive in Europe in around 1526 when Sultan Suleiman the Legislator won the battle of Mohacs, defeating the Hungarians (whose land was soon to be annexed by the Turks). The recipe for Baclava was however modified, with the addition of a new basic ingredient: apples.

Our favourite places to eat

DA CIPRIANO
Via Graziadei 13 – Calavino (TN) – Tel. 0461 564720
Closed Wed and lunchtime (except Sun and public holidays).
A la carte menu €20-26

 The cordiality of the owner and the hugely varied menu.

Da Cipriano has its premises in the very centre of historical Calavino, in a residence dating from the 16C. The decor in its small rooms is at once rustic and modern; but whether you are seated next to the fireplace or in the restaurant's more elegant room, the owner will treat you with extreme courtesy. The menu's diversity is equally pleasing: apart from the house speciality there is also an exceptional selection of grilled trout and meats, ham, fresh pasta and homemade pastries.

TRATTORIA LA VECCHIA SORNI
Piazza Assunta 40 – Sorni (Lavis, TN) – Tel. 0461 870541
Closed 3 weeks between Feb and Mar, Sun eve and Mon.
Booking advisable.
A la carte menu €29-35

 The panoramic seating area for unforgettable al fresco suppers.

Located in a small hamlet, close to the church square, this family-run restaurant enjoys an excellent position looking out over the Adige valley and the surrounding vineyards. For a candlelit dinner, ask to be seated in the small room with the earthenware stove. When it comes to the menu, the owners have broadened their horizons: beyond the regional specialities there are also fish dishes discerningly enhanced with aromatic herbs.

AUENER HOF
Località Prati 21 – Sarentino (BZ) – Tel. 0471 623055
Closed Mon.
A la carte menu €28-44

 The regional produce and inventive approach to traditional cuisine.

The Schneider family's restaurant is to be found just a stone's throw from the village of Sarentino, after a long but pleasant ascent. It is ideally placed for walks or horse-riding thanks to its tranquil forest location and incredible view over the Dolomites. The enchanting setting, however, is just a foretaste of the pleasure to come once inside. First there is the meticulously decorated room, with its beautifully laid tables, then there is the food: rustic regional cuisine with traditional elements behind a modern facelift that makes for lighter dishes.

TRENTINO ALTO ADIGE

ALDINO (BZ)

KRONE

Sig. Franzelin
piazza Principale 4
39040 Aldino (BZ)
Tel. 04 71 88 68 25 – Fax 04 71 88 66 96
info@gasthof-krone.it – www.gasthofe-krone.it   **122-148€**

Closed 10 Nov-24 Dec • 13 double rm • Half-board €73-94 • Dogs not admitted in restaurant

Menu €32/41

The sun-drenched terrace overlooking the Adige valley is the perfect place to relax and wind down.

Old vaulted ceilings, a welcoming interior and lovely earthenware stoves set the scene for this hotel run by the Franzelin family since 1720. Opposite the village's main square, it used to accommodate pilgrims en route to the Convent of the Madonna di Pietralba. Today it has retained an understated charm and period style with old furniture, marble and country fabrics, in addition to an impressive range of modern fixtures and fittings. Tasty regional specialities take pride of place in the simple stube with dishes from the upper Adige such as speck and cheeses made according to ancestral traditions.

Access: In the village

TRENTINO ALTO ADIGE

ALTA BADIA (BZ)

2

ALPENROSE

Fam. Alfreider
Strada Agà, 20
39033 Corvara in Badia (BZ)
Tel. 04 71 83 62 40 – Fax 04 71 83 56 52
garni.alpenrose@rolmail.net
www.garnialpenrose.com

50-84€

Closed 9 Apr-31 May and Nov • 1 single rm, 4 double rm • Parking, dogs not admitted

 The friendly management style and ambience.

On the border of Alto Adige and the Veneto, Corvara is situated in one of the most spectacular and charming parts of the Dolomites. A break here offers something for everyone, be it walking through woodland and meadows, or the excitement of skiing; either way the scenery is beautiful. What better base from which to discover the area than this small, pleasant B&B, with a family atmosphere and enjoying a quiet, sunny location?

Access: In the centre

TRENTINO ALTO ADIGE

ALTA BADIA (BZ)

CIASA MONTANARA

Sig. Bernardi
La Villa - Strada Plaon, 24
39030 Badia (BZ)
Tel. 04 71 84 77 35 - Fax 04 71 84 77 35
ciasa@montanara.it - www.montanara.it

55-76€

Open all year • 1 single rm, 12 double rm • Parking

 The combination of traditional style and modern comfort.

The main road through town can get busy in the summer months so this establishment, tucked away up above in the old quarter, enjoys a pleasant location. In addition to its tranquil and panoramic setting, it also offers a comfortable, pleasant ambience and friendly service, making for an unforgettable stay. Built in 1999, this establishment is traditional in style yet incorporates every modern convenience, while its smooth running is assured by the professional management of the Bernardi family.

Access: In the village

TRENTINO ALTO ADIGE

ALTA BADIA (BZ)

4

LA CIASOTA

Sigg . Rattonara e Pitscheider
La Villa - Strada Colz, 118
39030 Badia (BZ)
Tel. 04 71 84 71 71 – Fax 04 71 84 57 40
laciasota@rolmail.net – www.garnilaciasota.it   👤👤 62-84€

Closed 20 Apr-25 Jun, 25 Sep-1 Dec • 2 single rm, 13 double rm • Parking, garden, no dogs

 The wooden balconies, decked with colourful flowers in summer.

This large attractive family house has been transformed by a well known local champion skier into a pleasant and welcoming establishment, equally suitable for skiing holidays and summer breaks. Pale pine wood panels cover most of the walls, and the accommodation is full of character and comfortable. The restaurant is also attractive, although its size means that the other public areas are a little cramped. There is a basement gym, and of course the opportunity to have skiing lessons direct from the owner.

Access: On La Villa Corvara road

TRENTINO ALTO ADIGE

ALTA BADIA (BZ)

5

TAMARINDO
Sig. Bernardi
La Villa - Via Plaon, 20
39030 Badia (BZ)
Tel. 04 71 84 40 96 – Fax 04 71 84 49 06
tamarindo@rolmail.net – www.tamarindo-lavilla.it

54-80€

Closed 21 Apr-31 May and Nov • 1 single rm, 8 double rm • Parking, dogs not admitted

 The friendly and spontaneous personality of the owner.

This new building is in the old part of town, shrouded in the silence which seems to roll in from the woods to envelop the castle and church. The gregarious nature of the management is surprising, particularly given the reputation of the locals for being reserved. The open terrace offers inspiring views of the valley and surrounding mountains, and is the perfect spot in which to sit with a book and enjoy the sunshine. The spacious rooms have sparklingly modern bathrooms.

Access: In the village

TRENTINO ALTO ADIGE

APPIANO SULLA STRADA DEL VINO (BZ)

6

ANSITZ TSCHINDLHOF

Fam. Moerl
a San Michele via Monte 36
39057 Appiano sulla Strada del Vino (BZ)
Tel. 04 71 66 22 25 – Fax 04 71 66 36 49
info@tschindlhof.com – www.tschindlhof.com

100-159€

Closed 6 Nov-28 Mar • 4 single rm, 11 double rm, 2 suites • Half-board €87 • Parking, garden, swimming pool, dogs not admitted in restaurant

 For residents only

 The fragrant scent of grapes and the majestic mountain view from the windows.

Treat yourself to a stay that combines elegance with peace and quiet. You may however consider taking a few language lessons when you know that you will be greeted by the Mörl von Pfalzen zu Mühlen und Sichelburg family (no less!), but rest assured, despite their impressive ancestry, your hosts will do everything to make you feel at home. Guests have the run of immense outdoor spaces, an interior in which wood prevails, cosy guestrooms, each with a Germanic sounding name, and a delightful restaurant where the cuisine is distinctly Italian in flavour.

Access: 1km from the village towards Monte Berg

TRENTINO ALTO ADIGE

APPIANO SULLA STRADA DEL VINO (BZ)

7

BAD TURMBACH

Sig. Worndle
Via Rio della Torre, 4
39057 Appiano sulla Strada del Vino (BZ)
Tel. 04 71 66 23 39 – Fax 04 71 66 47 54
gasthof@turmbach.com – www.turmbach.com

 66-84€

Closed 22 Dec-20 Mar • 1 single rm, 14 double rm • Half board €45-54 • Parking, garden, swimming pool, garage, no dogs in the restaurant

 Menu €41/50

 The classic local cuisine, passionately prepared and served.

Located on a high plateau at an altitude of 500m in the delightful Oltradige district, the town of Appiano sulla Strada del Vino, ideal whatever the season, is splendidly located against a backdrop of vineyards, fruit orchards, ancient abodes and old manor houses. This simple yet charming hotel in the upper part of the town boasts a restaurant with a fine gastronomic reputation. Diners can also enjoy wines produced by the owners themselves.

Access: Towards Monte on the pass

TRENTINO ALTO ADIGE

APPIANO SULLA STRADA DEL VINO (BZ)

8

SCHLOSS AICHBERG

Fam. Khuen-Belasi
Via Monte, 31 a San Michele
39057 Appiano sulla Strada del Vino (BZ)
Tel. 04 71 66 22 47 – Fax 04 71 66 09 08
info@aichberg.com – www.aichberg.com

👤👤 99€

Closed 16 Nov-28 Feb • 10 double rm, 2 suites • Parking, garden, swimming pool, no dogs

 The vineyards and orchards surrounding the old house.

As the name suggests, this really is a castle with all the features one might expect; crenellated tower, fortified residence, plus some more recent buildings providing the accommodation. Rich in history, this is a remarkable place to stay, even though the interior has recently been renovated. The large gardens and heated pool, plus the hospitality of the owners make for an enjoyable ambience, especially for those in quest of traditional culture and gastronomic delights.

Access: After San Michele, on the road to Appiano/Monte, on the left

TRENTINO ALTO ADIGE

CAMPO DI TRENS (BZ)

BIRCHER
Sig.ra Rayd Werth
Località Maria Trens
39040 Campo di Trens (BZ)
Tel. 04 72 64 71 22 - Fax 04 72 64 73 50
info@hotelbircher.it - www.hotelbircher.it

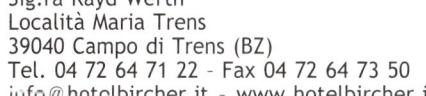 69-94€

Closed 3 Nov-26 Dec • 4 single rm, 28 double rm • Half board €50-62 • Parking, swimming pool, sauna, small dogs allowed in rooms

 Menu €28/41

 The warm, generous family hospitality.

Halfway between Bressanone and the Austrian border, 1000m up in the Isarco valley, Campo di Trens is a small village on the edge of woodland, whose houses are all perfect examples of the regional architectural style. Enthusiastically run by a family management team (fourth generation), the Bircher hotel has been extensively improved and enhanced, both in terms of decor and facilities, which include an indoor swimming pool and fitness facilities. Generous, mouth-watering buffet breakfast.

Access: In the village

TRENTINO ALTO ADIGE

CANAZEI (TN)

10

STELLA ALPINA

Sig. Goller
via Antermont 6
38032 Canazei (TN)
Tel. 04 62 60 11 27 – Fax 04 62 60 21 72
info@stella-alpina.net – www.stella-alpina.net

72-130€

Closed 5-27 May and 9 Oct-4 Dec • 5 double rm, 2 suites • Dogs not admitted

 The first floor veranda – if you close your eyes you can almost imagine you're swooping down the slopes.

A gentle awakening in a comfortable ladine-style bedroom and a tasty buffet breakfast served in the picturesque stube will ensure that you are ready to make the most of the busy day ahead of you. Lovers of this region inevitably spend their time between skiing, perhaps including the fabulous "Sellaronda" circuit, and exploring the paths that crisscross the Dolomites landscape of snow-capped mountains. Nothing, however, prevents you from making the most of the establishment's excellent sauna and hydromassage bath, or simply taking the time to read and daydream on the comfortable veranda.

Access: In the village

TRENTINO ALTO ADIGE

CANAZEI (TN)

11

AL VIEL
Fam. Bernard
Streda de Ciampac, 7
38032 Canazei (TN)
Tel. 04 62 60 00 81 – Fax 04 62 60 62 94
garnialviel@virgilio.it

60-98€

Closed May and Oct-Nov • 12 double rm • Parking, no dogs

 The woodwork creating a warm ambience throughout.

Of recent construction, this building has a grey-pink façade and incorporates a great deal of wood in characteristic mountain style. Peacefully located a short walk from the centre and the ski lifts, this hotel has an informal ambience more readily associated with a private house, thanks to the owners' friendly management style.

Access: In the village

TRENTINO ALTO ADIGE

CARANO (TN)

12

MASO EL GIATA

Sig.ra Locatin
località Aguai 3
38033 Carano (TN)
Tel. 04 62 23 14 56
info@masoelgiata.it - www.masorlgiata.it

👤👤 120€

Closed Oct-Nov • 3 double rm, 1 suite • Parking, garden, dogs not admitted

 The breakfast room located in the former stables whose low ceiling is adorned with stone vaults.

This happy marriage of old and new is inspired by the meeting of the ladina tradition with that of the trentina. Located in the Val di Fiemme, prolongation of the Val di Fassa, but with a name that changes from one dialect to another, this quiet peaceful site is home to a few rare stone and wood buildings set in a landscape of meadows, small cottage gardens and surrounded by forests. Head for the delightful maso typical of the 18C, whose date carved in the timber frame is the only clue to guide anyone interested in tracing the history of this still little-known region.

Access: Outside the village towards Ora, near the main road

TRENTINO ALTO ADIGE

CHIUSA (BZ)

ANSITZ FONTEKLAUS

F.lli Gfader
Località Fraina
39043 Chiusa (BZ)
Tel. 04 71 65 56 54 – Fax 04 71 65 50 45
info@fonteklaus.it – www.fonteklaus.it

72-82€

Closed Dec-Mar • 10 double rm • Half board €48-55 • Parking, garden, swimming pool, dogs not admitted in restaurant

Menu €26/53

Swimming in the small lake, a panoramic natural pool.

This 14C fairytale house with red and white shutters and a sloping roof, surrounded by fir trees and green meadows, commands some of the best sweeping views in the Alto Adige. This is the backdrop against which the Gfader family enthusiastically runs this charming establishment which, in addition to its fantastic location, is noteworthy for its attractive mountain-style décor and furnishings and its gastronomic delights. The ideal spot for romantic weekends or longer family breaks.

Access: Outside the village at an altitude of 897m. In Fraina, 3km from the crossroads, near a small natural lake

TRENTINO ALTO ADIGE

CHIUSA (BZ)

14

UNTERWIRT

Fam. Haselwanter
Località Gudon
39043 Chiusa (BZ)
Tel. 04 72 84 40 00 – Fax 04 72 84 40 65
info@unterwirt-gufidaun.com
www.unterwirt-gufidaun.com

50-56€

Closed 7 Jan-2 Feb and 18-30 Jun • 3 double rm • Breakfast €15 • Parking, garden, swimming pool

 Menu €39/58

 The restaurant, which could not be more typically local in style.

This simple residence is in the pleasant little village of Gudon, not far from the motorway. Surrounded by gardens, it has a pool for those hot summer months. Inside there are seven simple yet comfortable rooms, some with cooking facilities. The restaurant focuses on local specialities, with an interesting and varied menu, and has a cosy feel with antique "stuben" which are characteristic of the local architecture.

Access: In the village

TRENTINO ALTO ADIGE

CIMEGO (TN)

AURORA
Fam. Tomlumm Pormoos
Località Casina dei Pomi, 139
38082 Cimego (TN)
Tel. 04 65 62 10 64 – Fax 04 65 62 17 71
graziano@hotelaurora.tn.it – www.hotelaurora.tn.it **46-70€**

Open all year • 1 single rm, 18 double rm • Half board €45-48 • Parking, garden, swimming pool, no dogs in the restaurant

 Menu €23/32

 The infectious enthusiasm of the owners.

Situated 600m up in the Chiese valley, Cimengo is an old town where history is ever present, most notably in the narrow alleyways of the ancient Quartinago quarter with its Venetian-style architecture. Located conveniently if not idyllically on a road, this hotel is readily recognisable by its mountain style and painted façade, giving it a chocolate-box air. Inside, there is a chalet feel, with a lot of woodwork in evidence, particularly in the rooms under the eaves and the dining room; renowned for local specialities.

Access: On the main road

TRENTINO ALTO ADIGE

DIMARO (TN)

16

KAISERKRONE

Sig. Meneghini
Piazza Serra, 3
38025 Dimaro (TN)
Tel. 04 63 97 33 26 – Fax 04 63 97 30 16
info@kaiserkrone.it – www.kaiserkrone.it

70-110€

Closed 10-20 May • 7 double rm

 The largest rooms, almost on the scale of an apartment.

In the centre of Dimaro, at the foot of the majestic Sasso Rosso, this hotel is named after the Emperor Franz Joseph who once stayed here. Little has changed since his time. This is a classic Austrian-style building, its façade a light pink, with two tone shutters and a sloping roof. Inside, there is much woodwork in evidence, making for a warm, intimate ambience. The remarkable rooms are spacious and decorated with pale wood furnishings. The public areas, although somewhat cramped, include a bar where the buffet breakfast is served.

Access: In the village

TRENTINO ALTO ADIGE

DRO (TN)

17

MASO LIZZONE

Sig. Brighenti
Via Lizzone, località Ceniga
38074 Dro (TN)
Tel. 04 64 50 47 93 – Fax 04 64 50 47 93
info@masolizzone.com – www.masolizzone.com

83-90€

Closed Nov-Feb • 1 single rm, 4 double rm • Parking, garden, swimming pool, dogs not admitted • Honey, oil and wine for sale

 The well equipped kitchen, available to guests.

Water, air, iron, earth and fire. Not mythology or science, but the names of the splendid rooms in this fine country house to the north of Lake Garda, situated in a peaceful spot surrounded by olive groves and vineyards. The accommodation, occupying the first floor, is tasteful and simple. Downstairs is the large vaulted kitchen for the use of guests, a breakfast room and library. There are also seven camping pitches occupying the terraced area.

Access: Outside the village towards Ceniga

TRENTINO ALTO ADIGE

FIERA DI PRIMIERO (TN)

18

CHALET PIERENI

Sig. Zagonel
località Piereni 8, a Val Canali
i 38054 Fiera di Primiero (TN)
Tel. 043 96 23 48 – Fax 043 96 47 92
info@chaletpiereni.it – www.chaletpiereni.it

 60-85€

Closed 10 Jan-8 Apr • 2 single rm, 21 double rm • Half-board €45-65 • Parking, dogs not admitted in restaurant

 Menu €20/32

 A delightful retreat for lovers of the countryside and unforgettable landscapes.

A series of tight bends through forests and landscapes of never-ending horizons, dotted here and there with tiny old refuges, takes you up to Pale di San Martino. This mountain-top landscape is home to countless walks that range from relaxing strolls to energetic alpine hikes. The road leads to a cul-de-sac at the end of which stands this picturesque alpine retreat, whose immaculate wall and wooden balconies are decked in flowers. The interior features a traditional chalet-style flavour, which extends to the cuisine, where authentic regional produce, fresh homemade pasta, game, mushrooms and desserts take pride of place.

Access: Towards Val Canali-Agordo, then follow the deviation to Piereni to the left

TRENTINO ALTO ADIGE

GIOVO (TN)

MASO POMAROLLI

F.lli Franch
Località Maso Pomarolli, 10
38030 Palù di Giovo (TN)
Tel. 04 61 68 45 71 – Fax 04 61 68 45 70
info@agriturmasopomarolli.it
www.agriturismomasopomarolli.it

70€

Closed 11 Jan-15 Feb • 3 single rm, 5 double rm • Half board €50 • Parking, garden, no dogs in the restaurant • Organised trips, bicycles available

 For residents only

 The breathtaking views from some of the rooms.

The Cembra valley with its orchards and terraced vineyards forms the backdrop for this characteristic alpine agriturismo, restored and refurbished by the Franch brothers to provide accommodation for around fifteen guests. The rooms have typical wood furniture of good quality; the two most sought after have stunning views. Breakfast and dinner are served in a charming dining room; incorporating home grown ingredients, the cuisine focuses on local specialities and is not to be missed.

Access: Outside the village towards San Michele-Faedo, in the vineyards

TRENTINO ALTO ADIGE

LAGUNDO (BZ)

20

PLONERHOF
Fam. Pohl
Via Peter Thalguter, 11
39022 Lagundo (BZ)
Tel. 04 73 44 87 28 – Fax 04 73 49 12 20
info@plonerhof.it – www.plonerhof.it

👤👤 48-56€ ☕

Open all year • 2 single rm, 4 double rm, 3 suites • Parking, garden, swimming pool • Wine for sale

 The wooden balconies bedecked with flowers.

This 14C building is not far from the town centre; occupying a sunny and verdant location, it is decorated with typical Tirolese inscriptions in gothic characters which line the staircase and the little dining area. The rooms have a simpler feel, with small but well equipped bathrooms. The swimming pool and garden planted with fruit trees are very welcome features in the summer months.

Access: Near the village

TRENTINO ALTO ADIGE

MERANO (BZ)

SITTNERHOF

Sig. Brunner
Via Verdi, 60
39012 Merano (BZ)
Tel. 04 73 22 16 31 – Fax 04 73 20 65 20
info@bauernhofurlaub.it
www.bauernhofurlaub.it

70-80€

Closed 16 Nov-28 Feb • 6 double rm • Parking, garden, swimming pool, no dogs • Jam for sale

 A bucolic ambience surprisingly close to the heart of Merano.

In a quiet and shady residential street, this agriturismo occupies a splendid building of 11C origin which has undergone numerous alterations down the centuries; today its facade combines dark wood with religiously inspired fresco painting. Inside, the most charming room is the characteristic stube where breakfast is served. The accommodation is less striking and furnished with modern pieces. Around the house is the family vineyard, which guests may visit, and the garden with a splendid swimming pool.

Access: Turn onto Via delle Corse, near the centre

TRENTINO ALTO ADIGE

MULES (BZ)

22

STAFLER

Fam. Stafler
Mules
39040 Mules (BZ)
Tel. 04 72 77 11 36 – Fax 04 72 77 10 94
romantikhotel@stafler.com – www.stafler.com

 100-140€

Closed Nov • 7 single rm, 25 double rm, 4 suites • Half-board €75-113 • Parking, park, swimming pool, tennis court, sauna

 Menu €29/58

 A child's dream come true between farmyard adventures and exploring the park's secrets.

A delightful park complete with benches and chairs and a small lake full of water lilies and cheerful ducks is the scene of this mountain site. Breathe in the crisp mountain air as you savour the romantic aura of this former post house anchored in the past, once an inn and now an elegant hotel. Ideal for magical winter festivities or just for a few days' rest to get back to grass roots. In the pleasant stube, which features wooden benches and traditional objects, you can sample original and highly creative dishes.

Access: On the main road

TRENTINO ALTO ADIGE

NOVACELLA (BZ)

23

PONTE-BRÜCKENWIRT

Sig. Zanol
Via Abbazia, 2
39040 Novacella (BZ)
Tel. 04 72 83 66 92 – Fax 04 72 83 75 87
brückenwirt@tin.it – www.brueckdnwirt@tin.it

👤👤 **82-90€** ☕

Closed Feb • 3 single rm, 9 double rm • Half board €51-56 • Parking, garden, heated swimming pool, no dogs

 Menu €23/28

 The tranquillity which prevails throughout.

Well situated close to the famous Novacella abbey, this fine 12C building offers traditional local hospitality courtesy of its family management team. Order and cleanliness reign in both the accommodation – the top floor rooms are especially attractive – and the public areas, composed of the bar, restaurant and the characteristic stube. Outside there is a large garden with swimming pool and wooden tables set out under ancient shady trees.

Access: Near the abbey

TRENTINO ALTO ADIGE

PERGINE VALSUGANA (TN)

24

CASTEL PERGINE

Sig.ra Neff e Sig. Schneider
Via del Castello, 10
38057 Pergine Valsugana (TN)
Tel. 04 61 53 11 58 – Fax 04 61 53 13 29
verena@castelpergine.it – www.castelpergine.it

Closed 5 Nov-4 Apr • 4 single rm, 17 double rm • Half board €50-73 • Parking, garden, no dogs in the restaurant

 Menu €30/39

 The contemporary artwork exhibited in the garden.

Those wishing to step back in time should choose this hotel for their holiday, a charming medieval castle dating from the 13C which has been well restored and is competently run by Verena and Theo, an enthusiastic couple who were previously a translator and an architect. Gourmets will enjoy the elegant restaurant which serves generous portions of Trentino cuisine and has an excellent wine list.

Access: Follow the signs to the Cappella dei Masetti and the Castello, around 2.5km from the village

TRENTINO ALTO ADIGE

POZZA DI FASSA (TN)

25

ANTICO BAGNO

Sig. Zulian
Via Antico Bagno
38036 Pozza di Fassa (TN)
Tel. 04 62 76 30 51 - Fax 04 62 76 32 32
info@hoteltermeanticobagno.it
www.hoteltermeanticobagno.it

👫 **72-82€** ☕

Closed 5 Oct-4 Dec • 23 double rm • Half board €47-80 • Parking, garden, no dogs

 Set Menu €24 and 37

 The hotel's spa, set on the edge of woodland among mountains.

For centuries, this spot has attracted visitors on account of its sulphurous spring waters and their curative powers. Today the tradition continues thanks to this hotel, founded by the current owner's father, who wanted to create an establishment appropriate for a thermal resort. Pleasantly situated on high ground a little out of town, it is flanked by woods which extend down the slopes, while the view of the village church is enhanced by the backdrop of high mountain peaks beyond.

Access: From the centre, follow the river along Via Danie for 1km

TRENTINO ALTO ADIGE

RACINES (BZ)

26

SONKLARHOF

Sig. Leider
località Ridanna alt. 1342
39040 Racines (BZ)
Tel. 04 72 65 62 12 – Fax 04 72 65 62 24
sonklarhof@web.de – www.sonklarhof

👫 105-140€

Closed 6 Nov-18 Dec and 10 Apr-8 May • 50 double rm, 5 suites • Half-board €59-70 • Parking, garden, swimming pool, tennis court, dogs not admitted in restaurant

 Set Menu €15 and 21

 Sipping a glass of good wine in the Tyrolean-inspired cellar.

Paradise on earth for enthusiastic skiers, lovers of excursions or simply anyone who wants to relax in the sunshine, Val Ridanna is set in the peaceful landscape of the Alps, eager to extend a warm welcome to holiday-makers in search of a break from the frenetic pace of modern life. The Leidetr family will be delighted to invite you to sample the quality of their ancient tradition of hospitality and their hotel's many leisure activities: relaxation, swimming, reading or chatting in the winter garden, without forgetting the wellness centre, before finishing the evening in the pleasant rustic-style restaurant.

Access: On the main road

TRENTINO ALTO ADIGE

RENON (BZ)

27

BEMELMANS POST

Fam. Senn
Via Paese 8
39054 Collalbo Renon (BZ)
Tel. 04 71 35 61 27 – Fax 04 71 35 65 31
info@bemelmans.com. – www.bemelmans.com

100-150€

Closed 4 Mar-8 Apr • 5 single rm, 45 double rm, 6 suites • Half-board €66-99 • Parking, garden, swimming pool, sauna, fitness, tennis court, dogs not admitted in restaurant

 For residents only

 The first floor overlooking the unforgettable Sciliar.

The muted, irresistible atmosphere of late 19C hotels, the subtle balance between past and present in the interior and the warm welcome extended by this family-run establishment all set the scene for a picture of a well-earned holiday rest. The father of the psychoanalyst, after whom the establishment is named, was a regular at this hotel, which is surrounded by countryside to be explored on foot or by bicycle. The elegant, spacious modern-style guestrooms, in which every detail is carefully thought out, all overlook the Alpine range. In the dining room and delightful stube, you will be served authentic traditional cuisine.

Access: Near the town hall on the main square

TRENTINO ALTO ADIGE

RIVA DEL GARDA (TN)

28

VILLA MIRAVALLE

Sig. Marchi
via Monte Oro 9
38066 Riva del Garda (TN)
Tel. 04 64 55 23 35 – Fax 04 64 52 17 07
info@hotelvillamiravalle.com
www.hotelvillamiravalle.com

120-150€

Closed 2-20 Nov • 2 single rm, 29 double rm • Parking, garden, swimming pool, dogs not admitted

 Menu €32/48

We most liked — Meat grilled over hot embers in the dining room, the Villa's speciality.

In the shelter of the town's ramparts, this lovely villa was converted into a hotel in 1930 when the Marchi family decided to turn their home into a guesthouse. Some 70 years later the original eight bedrooms have increased two-fold, but the owners have preserved the warm welcoming atmosphere of yesteryear. Villa Miravalle, set in an immense park with swimming pool, offers a spacious sitting room together with a veranda that are ideal for reading or quiet chats among friends. The rooms are simple but very pleasant, and a series of photographs depicting the Riva del Garda adorns the dining room where you will be served a mixture of surf and turf dishes.

Access: In the village

TRENTINO ALTO ADIGE

SAN PELLEGRINO (PASSO DI) (TN)

RIFUGIO FUCIADE
Sig. Rossi
Località Fuciade
38030 Soraga (TN)
Tel. 04 62 57 42 81 – Fax 04 62 57 42 81

 80€

Closed 8 Apr-14 Jun, 16 Oct-23 Dec • 7 double rm • Half board €70 • Garden, dogs not admitted

 Menu €35/56

 The exceptional mountain location.

Keen walkers can reach this establishment on foot through woodland; should the snows have come, a snowmobile will be necessary. Situated nearly 2000m up (1982m, to be specific) the views over the surrounding countryside are stunning, taking in meadows, woods, mountains and sky, with very little else except the odd alpine dwelling in wood and stone. Up here, the world beyond the Dolomites does not impinge at all. In the restaurant, the cuisine is tasty and simple mountain fare, served to guests at solid refectory tables.

Access: On the SS 346, take the dirt track up the pass

TRENTINO ALTO ADIGE

SANTA CRISTINA VALGARDENA (BZ)

30

GEIER

Sig. Geier
Via Chemun, 36
39047 Santa Cristina Valgardena (BZ)
Tel. 04 71 79 33 70 – Fax 04 71 79 33 70
garni-geier@valgardena.com
www.garnigeier.com

 64-106€

Closed Dec-Apr • 8 double rm • Gym, no dogs

 The high peaks of the Dolomites soaring above the valley.

Travellers passing through Santa Cristina cannot fail to notice this traditional mountain building, its stark white ground floor walls surmounted by the wooden structure of the upper storey and beamed sloping roof. The façade is suggestive of a warm and comfortable alpine residence, and once inside this is confirmed. The accommodation and public areas, including sauna and solarium, are modern yet welcoming in feel, with much pale woodwork in evidence. From the balcony there are fine views of the Dolomites stretching into the distance.

Access: In the village near the town hall

TRENTINO ALTO ADIGE

SELVA DI VALGARDENA (BZ)

31

VILLA PRA RONCH
Sig.ra Rabanser
Via La Selva, 80
39048 Selva di Valgardena (BZ)
Tel. 04 71 79 40 64 – Fax 04 71 79 40 64
praronch@valgardena.it
www.val-gardena.com room/praronch

 76-100€

Closed Nov • 5 double rm • Parking, garden

 The scent of wood from the Tirolese furnishings.

Previously a private house, this charming B&B is in a panoramic location looking out over the surrounding mountains, vast natural watchtowers impervious to time and the elements. Against this rugged backdrop, the traditional architecture of this alpine building is particularly elegant, its stone walls covered in white plaster surmounted by the wooden beams of the upper storey and roof. Inside, woodwork is also prominent throughout; the rooms are variously decorated, but all possess a characteristic style typical of the area.

Access: In the outskirts of the village on the main road towards Santa Cristina, take the deviation to the road to Selva

TRENTINO ALTO ADIGE

SPIAZZO (TN)

32

MEZZOSOLDO

Sig. Lorenzi
Località Mortaso
38088 Spiazzo (TN)
Tel. 04 65 80 10 67 – Fax 04 65 80 10 78
info@mezzosoldo.it – www.mezzosoldo.it

👤👤 **65-85€**

Closed 16 Apr-14 Jun, 26 Sep-4 Dec • 2 single rm, 24 double rm • Half board €45-70 • Parking

Set Menu €26 and 37

The Trentino heritage evident in the cuisine and the decor.

The Mezzosoldo family have run this establishment for four generations and over a century. The accommodation is furnished with antique pieces which give each room a distinctive style, ranging from rustic to polished mahogany. In the restaurant, diners may choose between four room, one romantic, another rustic, the third like a hay barn and finally the light and airy winter garden style room. An ideal spot for those in search of the real Trentino.

Access: On the main road in the village

TRENTINO ALTO ADIGE

VALFLORIANA (TN)

33

FIOR DI BOSCO

Fam. Lozzer
località Sicina 55
38040 Valfloriana (TN)
Tel. 04 62 91 00 02 - Fax 04 62 91 00 02
graziano.lozz@libero.it
www.girovagandointrentino.it

👫 60-70€

Closed 9 Apr-30 May and 1 Oct-6 Dec • 1 single rm, 10 double rm • Half-board €43 • Parking

 Menu €28/35

 Getting up early in the morning to milk the cows and discover what life was like in a bygone era.

After a few years spent in an old shepherd's refuge beating cream to make butter and cheese, your hosts, Graziano and Isabella, have since opened this modern, comfortable country guesthouse behind the stables and their dairy farm. The dairy produce is still made according to tradition using ancestral gestures, techniques and tools. On the table you will be treated to 100 % organic, traditionally prepared farm produce. Each of the guestrooms, named after a flower, is rustic in style and decorated primarily in wood.

Access: On the main road in Sicina

TRENTINO ALTO ADIGE

VANDOIES (BZ)

34

TILIA

Sig. Oberhammer
via Weisskircher 33, località Vandoies di Sopra
39030 Vandoies (BZ)
Tel. 04 72 86 81 85 – Fax 04 72 86 98 89
info@chris-oberhammer.com – www.tilia.bz

 100€

Closed 24 Jun-15 Jul • 3 double rm • Parking

 Menu €52/69

 The profusion of butterflies, flowers and small animals that adorn the hand-painted plates.

May we present the Tilia – a gigantic ornamental plant, a 17C edifice, formerly home to the Law Court and a modern, innovative restaurant. Poised between botany and history, we are interested above all in the current interior of this establishment in the Val Pusteria, which is home to two rooms pleasantly decorated with paintings and contemporary wooden statues. In the charming late 19C stube, the cuisine is a masterful creative concoction, right from the morning, as the enticing smell of fresh baking and fresh fruit salads greet your nostrils. A few guestrooms, decorated in a chalet style in which wood prevails, are also available.

Access: On the main road

TRENTINO ALTO ADIGE

VIGO DI FASSA (TN)

35

MILLEFIORI

Sig. Mariano
Strada de la Vila 16
38039 Vigo di Fassa (TN)
Tel. 04 62 76 90 00 – Fax 04 62 76 90 00
info@hotelmillefiori.com – www.hotelmillefiori.com

90€

Closed 20 Jun-1 Jul, 4 Nov-4 Dec • 1 single rm, 11 double rm • Half board €45-60 • Parking, garden, no dogs in the restaurant

Menu €16/30

The panoramic view of the Dolomites from the terrace.

Vallonga is a small village on the Passo di Costalunga road, perched on a slope among the woods of the mountain valleys. The hotel is in a sunny and panoramic spot; in summer it is instantly identifiable on account of the flowers which bedeck its wooden balconies. Tiled staircases and corridors lead to the rooms, furnished in alpine style. The owner, Signor Cecco, oversees the kitchen personally and in summer guests are served on the terrace.

Access: Outside the village on the road to Costalunga pass

TRENTINO ALTO ADIGE

VIGO DI FASSA (TN)

36

OLYMPIC
Sig. Pellegrin
strada Dolomites 4, località San Giovanni
38039 Vigo di Fassa (TN)
Tel. 04 62 76 42 25 – Fax 04 62 76 46 36
info@hotelolympic.it – www.hotelolympic.it

👫 **79-138€**

Closed 15 May-30 Jun and 15 Oct-30 Nov • 26 double rm • Half-board €55-77 • Parking, garden, fitness facilities, dogs not admitted

 Menu €23/36

 Waking to the bright morning sunshine after a refreshing night's sleep.

The many appeals of this establishment include the scents of the surrounding forests and flowers, a cordial welcome on the part of efficient staff, comfortable guestrooms lined in light-coloured wood and the characteristic ladine stube with a stove and a mixture of regional and innovative dishes, without forgetting the superb wellness centre with a sauna and Turkish bath. Such is the signification of the five Olympic circles that adorn the hotel's façade with the distinctive panorama of the Val di Fassa in the background. One could even add a sixth circle – an interior designed to make the stay as unforgettable for children as for adults!

Access: On the main road near San Giovani church

TRENTINO ALTO ADIGE

VILLANDRO (BZ)

37

ANSITZ ZUM STEINBOCK

Sig. Rabensteiner
Santo Stefano 38
39040 Villandro (BZ)
Tel. 04 72 84 31 11 – Fax 04 72 84 34 68
steinbock@dnet.it – www.zumsteinbock.it

👤👤 **80-112€**

Closed 10 Jan-10 Feb • 1 single rm, 19 double rm • Half-board €69-75 • Parking

 Menu €37/62

 The appeal of yesteryear, far from the bustle of modern life.

How about a trip back in time to an era steeped in romance? That of mysterious castles rich in charm and magic where troubadours were invited to sing and play to a noble assembly of gracious ladies and brave knights. As you reach Val d'Isarco, pause and look for this 18C abode that you can recognise by its sign depicting an ibex perched on a rock. Relax and nap in the welcoming guestrooms or head outdoors for a more energetic sleigh ride, before you end your day with a gastronomic treat in the cosy stube where recipes from the upper Adige are combined with Tuscan influences.

Access: In the village

TRENTINO ALTO ADIGE

VIPITENO (BZ)

KRANEBITT
Fam. Totsch
Val di Vizze - Località Caminata alt. 1441 (Est: 16 km)
39040 Vizze (BZ)
Tel. 04 72 64 60 19 – Fax 04 72 64 60 88
info@kranebitt.com – www.kranebitt.com

92-116€

Closed 18 Apr-21 May, 30 Oct-25 Dec • 4 single rm, 24 double rm • Half board €51-61 • Parking, garden, swimming pool, no dogs in the restaurant

 Menu €23/36

 The mountains which rise skywards from the wooded valley.

Flanked by fir trees, this hotel overlooks a valley dotted with the pale outlines of alpine houses. Recently renovated, it now boasts a health club with sauna, spa bath and solarium. Also on offer are various spa treatments including a hay, algae or milk bath. The overriding attraction however remains the mountains, ideal for winter skiing and summer breaks in one of Italy's most beautiful landscapes.

Access: Outside the village, on SS 508, continue for 14km to Caminata

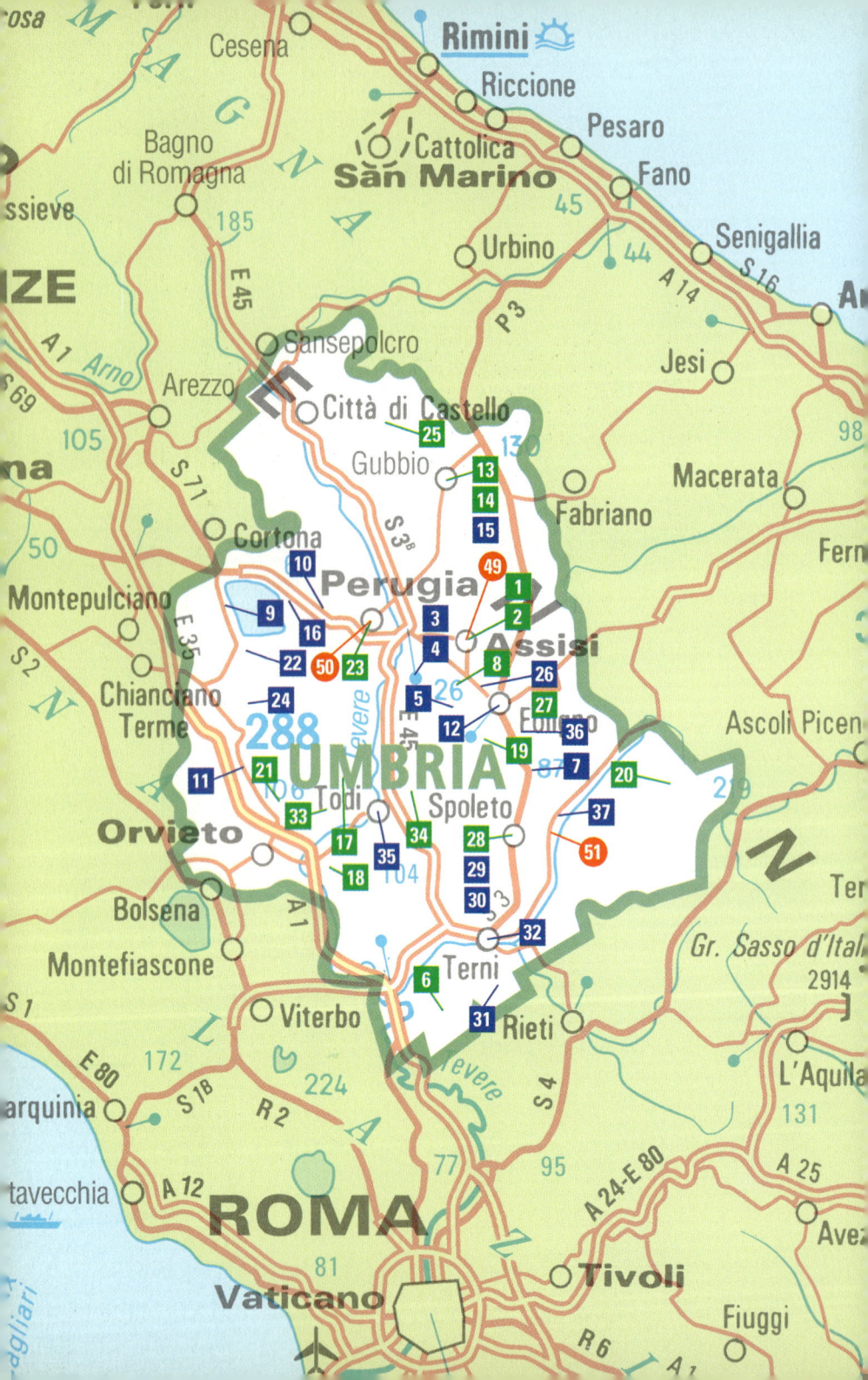

Umbria

Hilly and lush, Umbria is central Italy's only landlocked region, a fact unlikely to bother visitors given its myriad attractions. Not that water is scarce; it has the large lake Trasimeno, the smaller Piediluco and the river Tiber.

Its gentle scenery and vast pasturelands have been celebrated since Antiquity, and it comes as no surprise that the region has spawned many artists, poets and great men like St Francis of Assisi.

Churches, palaces, streets and squares characterise the historic centres of its cities, such as Gubbio, Orvieto, Spoleto, Spello and Foligno. Its capital, Perugia, sits in a panoramic spot and is one of the most important historical centres as well as being the seat of an ancient and renowned university.

The cuisine includes tasty pasta dishes thanks to the variety of local specialities, almost all of which are meat based. Wine buffs cannot fail to be impressed by the selection available, including Torgiano, Sagrantino di Montefalco and Orvieto.

37 establishments

Recommended sites and circuits
Umbria

> Known for being the green heart of Italy, Umbria is in reality much more than that. Here the works of nature and man are in utter harmony. You will see evidence of it in the market towns and villages, where traditions have always formed an integral part of daily life.

Todi is located at a great height, from which it overlooks the Tiber valley. Thanks to its small churches, austere palaces and tranquil recesses it has retained a medieval charm. Inside the Duomo, erected on the ruins of a Roman temple, there is an exquisite choir; not far from there is the church of San Fortunato, with its magnificent gothic doorway, crypt and tomb of the poet Jacopone da Todi.

Orvieto is another example of the integration of man and nature. The silhouette of the Duomo invites you to go on foot to the fortress (although there is a funicular railway). The Torre del Moro, the highest point in the town, offers spectacular views. Then there is the lowest point in the town at the bottom of the San Patrizio well (62m deep), which you can get to via two spiral stairways (248 steps) that never cross.

The beauty of **Gubbio** is not to be overlooked! Its Roman theatre, located outside the city ramparts, attests to its ancient origins, whereas the Palazzo dei Consoli, the Piazza Pensile and the Palazzo Pretorio date from the start of the 14C. Watch out for the Fountain of Madmen; legend has it that whoever walks around it three times will lose his mind. There are also macabre tales surrounding the "Door of Death", entranceways of certain houses not far from the Via dei Consoli that were once believed to be affected by the passage of coffins, but are today considered to have fulfilled a defensive function.

Following Umbria's central road you come to the delightful Basilica of St Francis, which seems to rise directly out of the rock of Mount Subasio. Around here everything seems to pertain to the humble monk and his "Lady Poverty". The origins of Assisi go back to Etruscan times, but it was only in the Middle Ages that it acquired its current urban character. Renowned for having fathered the patron saint of Italy, it is also home to various works of art: the Rocca Maggiore, the Roman amphitheatre, the Basilicas of St Francis and St Clara. Lower down, on the plain, is the Basilica of St Maria degli Angeli, built to protect the Cappella della Porziuncola, a humble meeting point for Franciscan monks. Assisi is a city whose beauty, enriched by the mystical atmosphere particular to a place rendered unique by history and faith, is far greater than the sum of its works of art.

A recipe to try, wines and... a nugget of information

 **Wines**
- Torgiano Rosso Riserva
- Montefalco Sagrantino
- Sangiovese
- Rosso Orvietano

Local specialities

Lentils from the Castelluccio plain, truffles, oil, *mazzafegati* (liver sausages, sweet and savoury, to be enjoyed fresh or dried), *corallina di Norcia* (sausage), *mortadella umbra*, *budellacci affumicati* (smoked pig intestines), Norcia raw ham, *sanguinaccio* (pork blood pudding, white wine, spices and orange peel), cold venison meats, *umbricelli* (pasta made from flour and water), *scafata* (broad bean soup), Marsciano peaches, chestnuts, Monteleone spelt, saffron.

ZUPPA DI FARRO

Ingredients
- 200g spelt
- 4 potatoes
- 4 courgettes
- 100g green beans
- 200g white beans
- 300g cabbage, carrots (and other vegetables of your choice)
- 100g thin bacon slices
- 3 cloves garlic
- chilli
- extra virgin olive oil
- salt

Method
Chop the vegetables into chunks and cook separately with the spelt in water. In a large frying pan, soften the garlic and bacon then add the spelt, vegetables, salt and chilli and allow it all to infuse with flavour for a minute or so. Serve the soup with boiled or grilled meat (in which case make a thicker soup) or as a main dish with a thick slice of toasted rustic bread at the bottom of each dish, a dash of herb-flavoured oil and chilli.

Food for thought
The form of a truffle depends principally on the nature of the soil: if it is loose, the truffle will be rounded and smooth whereas if it is dense, the growth of the truffle is impeded and it will therefore have a warty exterior. The most prized black truffle, almost bronze in colour, grows in cool soil beneath lime trees.

Our favourite places to eat

 ### LA FORTEZZA
Vicolo della Fortezza 2/b – 06081 Assisi (PG) – Tel. 075 812418
Closed Christmas, lunchtime, except Sat and Sun.
A la carte menu €21-26

We most liked *A heavenly selection of regional specialities behind an inconspicuous little door.*
La Fortezza has the advantage of being located in the town centre, just a few steps from the town hall square, while remaining off the tourist track due to its inconspicuous entrance at the top of a flight of stairs. Once inside this magnificent medieval edifice built upon Roman foundations, you can enjoy the warm family welcome and the fast and attentive service. The rustic dining room has a vaulted ceiling, and the regional cooking celebrates Umbria's traditional specialities, from ham and fresh pasta to lamb and pigeon.

 ### GIÒ ARTE E VINI
Via Ruggero D'Andreotto 19 – Perugia (PG) – Tel. 075 5731100
Closed Sun eve and Mon lunchtime.
A la carte menu €23-29

We most liked *The superb selection of wines and the chef's extraordinary creative flair.*
Located on the outskirts of the city, inside the hotel of the same name, this restaurant's clientele stretches way beyond its hotel guests. A large room with a few rustic touches, situated on the first floor of a modern building, serves as the setting for your meal. The service is highly professional. The food, principally Umbrian, is elevated by the creative genius of the chef, whose culinary skills cannot be beaten when it comes to regional produce. Enjoy a culinary tour of fresh pasta, soups, lamb and pigeon.

 ### DEL PONTE
Via Borgo 15 – 06040 Scheggino (PG) – Tel. 0743 61253
Closed Mon.
A la carte menu €21-28

We most liked *The passion for regional produce that spans three generations.*
You could almost believe you were in a fairy tale, with the little footbridges spanning the river Nera, whose waters are so clear you can easily make out the trout swimming in them. This is the enchanting setting for the Del Ponte restaurant. For three generations, this family's knowledge of regional produce has remained undiminished, as the simple traditional preparation of the trout and the black truffles makes clear. The growing notoriety of the restaurant has in no way altered the deliberate simplicity of the décor, dominated by cheerful pastel colours.

UMBRIA

ASSISI (PG)

IL GIARDINO DEI CILIEGI

Sig.ra Covarelli
Via Massera, 6
06081 Assisi (PG)
Tel. 07 58 06 40 91 – Fax 07 58 06 90 70
giardinodeiciliegi@libero.it – www.ilgiardinodeiciliegi.it

70-90€

Closed 8-31 Jan • 8 double rm • Half board €70 • Parking, garden, swimming pool, dogs not admitted • Bicycles available, oil for sale

Set Menu €20 and 30 for residents only

The family atmosphere, making all guests feel at home.

Against the agricultural backdrop of olive growing and wine making, visitors may go walking or cycling, visit local vineyards, or enjoy a game of bowls or table tennis. This is the perfect spot for those seeking a peaceful and relaxing break, cared for by expert hosts. Comfortable rooms, a charming restaurant, and tasteful period style furnishing throughout.

Access: On a road parallel to the express highway, 4km from Viole

UMBRIA

ASSISI (PG)

MALVARINA

Sig. Fabrizi
Pieve Sant'Apollinare, 32 località Viole
06081 Assisi (PG)
Tel. 07 58 06 42 80 – Fax 07 58 06 42 80
info@malvarina.it – www.malvarina.it

 93€

Open all year • 12 double rm, 3 suites • Half board €72 • Parking, garden, swimming pool, no dogs • Horse riding, jams and oil for sale, cookery lessons

 Set Menu €25 and 30

 Enjoying the glories of nature from the saddle.

This establishment occupies three buildings surrounded by olive groves, with pool and sun deck for the summer, and stables for those who wish to explore the area on horseback. Situated in a peaceful spot, the place is professionally run with uniformed staff, great attention to detail and fastidious cleanliness. The rustic style rooms are well equipped and the restaurant has a set menu offering home made specialities.

Access: 4km from Assisi near Piieve di Sant'Apollinare in Viole

BETTONA (PG)

3

IL POGGIO DEGLI OLIVI

Sig.ra Mannelli
a Passaggio in località Montebalacca
06080 Bettona (PG)
Tel. 07 59 86 90 23 – Fax 07 59 86 90 23
info@poggiodegliolivi.com
www.poggiodegliolivi.com

80-120€

Closed 8 Jan-10 Feb • 12 double rm • Half-board €65-85 • Parking, garden, swimming pool, tennis court, dogs not admitted

 Menu €28/39

 The warm greeting is accompanied by the scent of grapes and olives.

To reach this oasis of tranquillity, you will have to drive uphill for a few kilometres through a green landscape. The hospitable country home, built in the heart of a large park with a fitness track, is rustic in style and each of its pleasant guestrooms, where wood takes pride of place, is named after a flower. The highlight of the establishment, however, is the cuisine. The restaurant, which enjoys a panoramic view of the main cultural sites, offers a vast choice of dishes including fish and meat ranging from classical regional specialities to highly inventive creations.

Access: Take the road to Passaggio for 3km, then head south for 1km

UMBRIA

BETTONA (PG)

TORRE BURCHIO

 Il Burchio s.r.l.
località Torre Burchio
06084 Bettona (PG)
Tel. 07 59 88 50 17 - Fax 075 98 71 50
torreburchio@tin.it - www.torreburchio.it   104€

Closed 7 Jan-14 Feb and 21-28 Dec • 1 single rm, 16 double rm • Half-board €75 • Parking, garden, swimming pool, tennis court, dogs not admitted in restaurant

 Set Menu €21 and 23

 Getting back to grass roots through walks and culinary traditions.

Country lovers will not be disappointed by Torre Burchio, which is surrounded by meadows as far as the eye can see and ideal for enjoyable horseback rides along delightful country lanes through medieval towns or enriching mountain-bike excursions to find out more about Umbria's wildlife. After a hard day's roaming around the countryside sampling a host of adventure and leisure activities, you will be ready to relax in simple, rustic-style rooms and in the evenings you will be invited to sample tasty dishes. Imagine the enticing smell of freshly baked crusty bread, piping hot dishes straight from the oven and a mouth-watering choice of jams!

Access: Drive for 7km on a dirt track with the same name as the estate, then follow the signs

BEVAGNA (PG)

POGGIO DEI PETTIROSSI

il poggio dei Pettirossi s.r.l.
Vocabolo Pilone, 301
06031 Bevagna (PG)
Tel. 07 42 36 17 44 - Fax 07 42 36 92 38
info@ilpoggiodeipettirossi.it
www.ilpoggiodeipettirossi.it

 70-90€

Open all year • 29 double rm • Half board €60-70 • Parking, garden, swimming pool, no dogs in the restaurant

 Menu €28/48

 Sunbathing by the pool while enjoying the fantastic view.

Those worried about staying in a boarding house pretending to be an agriturismo, or finding themselves sandwiched in a viewless bumgalow between a railway line and motorway, can discard their concerns. Here the promotional material is all true; vineyards and olive groves ring the property, the views take in half of Umbria, the accommodation is extremely comfortable, and the situation is perfect, being a short hop from Assisi, Foligno, Spoleto, Perugia, and Bevagna.

Access: South of Bevagna drive for 3km, in Vocabolo Pilone

UMBRIA

CALVI DELL'UMBRIA (TR)

6

SANTA BRIGIDA

Sig.ra Pannullo
Località Santa Brigida, 3
05032 Calvi dell'Umbria (TR)
Tel. 07 44 71 03 86 – Fax 07 44 71 03 75
info@bioagriturismo.it – www.bioagriturismo.it

👤👤 75€

Closed Dec-Feb • 6 double rm • Breakfast €5; half board €65 • Parking, swimming pool, garden • Oil and jam for sale

 Menu €19/33

 The charming terraced pool with fine views over the valley.

Halfway between Assisi and Rome, Calvi sits on a rocky outcrop at the southernmost tip of the province of Terni, close to the Lazio border. This typical stone built establishment is peacefully located a little out of town; in the main house is the accommodation in the form of rooms and two apartments, while the restaurant is in an adjacent building. The atmosphere is charming, with homely furnishings that are warm yet functional. Also worthy of note are the fine views over the surrounding countryside, and the home made cuisine incorporating meat from animals raised on the adjoining farm

Access: 3km from the village in Santa Brigida

CAMPELLO SUL CLITUNNO (PG)

LE CASALINE

Sig. Zeppadoro
Località Casaline
06042 Campello sul Clitunno (PG)
Tel. 07 43 52 11 13 - Fax 0 43 27 50 99
casaline@libero.it - www.lecasaline.it

 65€

Open all year • 1 single rm, 6 double rm • Half board €55-65 • Parking, garden, dogs not admitted

Menu €32/49

The authentic rural ambience.

Situated 500m up, halfway between Foligno and Spoleto, this building started life as a mill in the 18C before being used as a cowshed in the 19C. Opened as a hotel in 1972, the place retains a strong agricultural feel, with all manner of animals roaming around the perimeter, making for a delightfully rustic setting.

Access: Drive for 4km towards Sivigliano

UMBRIA

CANNARA (PG)

8

LA FATTORIA DEL GELSO

Sig. Rulli Bonaca
Via Bevagna, 16
06033 Cannara (PG)
Tel. 074 27 21 64 – Fax 074 27 21 64
info@lafattoriadelgelso.com
www.lafattoriadelgelso.com

 90-95€

Open all year • 8 double rm • Half board €65-70 • Parking, garden, swimming pool, dogs not admitted in restaurant • Organised trips, bicycles available, oil and wine for sale

 Set Menu €20 and 25

 The lively decorative scheme and well planted garden.

The ideal base from which to explore Umbria's charming towns, this well presented establishment is located just outside the village, and offers pleasant spacious accommodation with personal touches. The owners pride themselves on this haven of peace and quiet, and, in this respect, the hotel is probably not best suited to young families. Situated in a panoramic spot, the pool provides welcome relief during the hot summer months.

Access: Drive for 1km towards Campofondo

UMBRIA

CASTIGLIONE DEL LAGO (PG)

LOCANDA POGGIOLEONE

Sig. Luigetti
Via Indipendenza, 116/B
06061 Castiglione del Lago (PG)
Tel. 075 95 95 19 – Fax 075 95 96 09
locandapoggioleonel@libero.it
www.locandapoggioleone.it

80€

Closed 15 Jan-15 Mar • 4 single rm, 8 double rm • Half board €65 • Parking, garden, swimming pool, no dogs

 Set Menu for residents only

 The wrought iron beds, lending a touch of class to the accommodation.

The owner, Signor Luigetti, has fled a white collar existence to fulfill a long standing ambition; ably assisted by his sister, he runs this homely, comfortable establishment with a personal touch. The rooms are furnished in period style, the bathrooms are smart, and the public areas spacious and welcoming, as is the garden with pool, particularly during the summer. The residents-only restaurant specialises in Umbrian and Tuscan cuisine.

Access: *Drive for around 8km towards Montepulciano, in Pozzuolo*

UMBRIA

CORCIANO (PG)

10

LOCANDA SOLOMEO

Sig. Cavicchi
piazza Carlo Alberto Dalla Chiesa 1
06073 Corciano (PG)
Tel. 07 55 29 31 19 – Fax 07 55 29 40 90
solomeo@tin.it – www.solomeo.it

125€

Closed 10 Jan-28 Feb • 12 double rm • Half-board €88.50 • Parking, garden, swimming pool, fitness facilities, dogs not admitted

Menu €23/29

 The village women take turns cooking in this establishment!

The modest town of Solomeo stands on the top of a small hill. According to the Roman historian, Livy, the peasants of this village contributed to supplying wheat when Perugia decided to help Rome during the second Punic war. However, on a more contemporary note, the inn is decorated in a Liberty-style that provides a pleasant setting for the happy marriage between old and new. In the handsome dining room you can sample delicious specialities from the Umbrian region prepared with produce from the estate.

Access: 8km from Corciano in the centre of Solomeo

FICULLE (TR)

11

LA CASELLA

Sig. Menna
località La Casella
05016 Ficulle (TR)
Tel. 076 38 66 84 – Fax 076 38 60 75
lacasella@tin.it – www.lacasella.it

👤👤 **120-140€** ☕

Open all year • 2 single rm, 30 double rm • Half-board €95-100 • Parking, garden, swimming pool, dogs not admitted in restaurant

 Menu €25/35

 The house organises horseback outings and riding lessons.

The immense woodlands of oaks and green oaks between Umbria and Tuscany provide the backdrop for this authentic country estate dating from the 19C, which is ideal for a few days' break in a comfortable, relaxing atmosphere. The former main wing of the farm has been converted into rustic-style guestrooms and public areas in which the stone, brick and exposed timberwork is characteristic of ancient constructions. The memory of the past also fills the dining room where guests are invited to sample simple, carefully prepared dishes made from healthy and tasty produce.

Access: Drive for 7km towards Fabro Scalo, then towards Parrone, and then towards Casella, the last 6km are along a dirt track

UMBRIA

FOLIGNO (PG)

12

VILLA RONCALLI
Sig. Scolastra
Via Roma, 25
06034 Foligno (PG)
Tel. 07 42 39 10 91 – Fax 07 42 39 10 01

 75-85€

Closed 9-19 Jan • 2 single rm, 8 double rm • Half board €75-85 • Parking, swimming pool, no dogs

 Menu €40/50

We most liked The sumptuous surroundings of the breakfast room.

Just outside Foligno, this historic residence retains its timeless charm. Surrounded by verdant parkland, it is at its best in summer when the swimming pool is open and guests are served their meals outside. The family management team has created a warm and informal ambience, with a strong feminine touch in evidence in the large and clean rooms. The restaurant is popular with regulars and tourists alike, and serves local dishes which vary according to seasonal availability.

Access: Drive through Foligno and continue for 1km on Via Roma

UMBRIA

GUBBIO (PG)

13

CASTELLO DI PETROIA

Sig. Sagrini
località Scritto
06020 Scritto Gubbio (PG)
Tel. 075 92 02 87 – Fax 075 92 01 08
castellodipretoia@castellodipretoia.com
www.castellodipetroia.com

 130-140€

Open 1 Apr-31 Dec • 3 double rm, 3 suites • Half-board €100-125 • Parking, garden, golf practice range, dogs not admitted in restaurant

 Set Menu €28 and 36 for residents only

 The restaurant commemorates the exploits of the Duke of Montefeltro.

Between Gubbio and Perugia, the castle of Petroia, which dominates the entire Valle del Chiascio, is closely associated with the historic events that marked the Middle Ages. The most well-known event is no doubt the birth of Duke Federico da Montefeltro, who became a condottiere at the age of 16 and was responsible for the palace around which the village of Urbino grew up. The manor, surrounded by forest, vineyards and wheat fields, is just as fascinating today and continues to extend a warm welcome to guests. The cuisine makes it a point of honour to uphold local traditions and flavours. The evening meal is served at 8.30pm sharp, most often in the company of other guests and the owners themselves!

Access: Towards Perugia on the N 298, after 14km in Scritto

UMBRIA

GUBBIO (PG)

LE CINCIALLEGRE

Sig.ra Coffer De Robertis
Frazione Pisciano
06024 Gubbio (PG)
Tel. 07 59 25 59 57 – Fax 07 59 27 23 31
cince@lecinciallegre.it – www.lecinciallegre.it

👤👤 96€

Closed 15 Dec-15 Mar • 1 single rm, 6 double rm • Half board €70-75 • Parking, garden, no dogs in the restaurant • Bicycles and quads available, honey, jam and cured meat for sale

 Set Menu €30 and 40 for residents only

 The dining room's light and panoramic veranda.

The view from here changes with the seasons, with meadows of daisies in spring, and leaves of every colour in autumn. The house itself is stone built, occupying a delightfully isolated site tucked away in the hills, although guests will be reassured to know that it is well signposted. The warm interior shows great attention to detail; in the dining room, the emphasis is on home grown produce and traditional local recipes.

Access: Drive for 8km along the N 219 towards Umbertide, at Mocaiana head towards Nerbisci and continue for 5km

UMBRIA

GUBBIO (PG)

15

LOCANDA DEL GALLO

Sig.ra Moro
località Santa Cristina
06024 Gubbio (PG)
Tel. 07 59 22 99 12 – Fax 07 59 22 99 12
info@locandadelgallo.it
www.locandadelgallo.it

112-122€

Closed 7 Jan-31 Mar • 10 double rm • Half-board €75-80 • Parking, garden, swimming pool, dogs not admitted

Set Menu for residents only

The unusual contrast of medieval architecture and oriental furniture.

The town of Santa Cristina was the site of a castle that was fought over by the Eugubinians and the Perugians during the entire Middle Ages until its destruction was ordered by the latter. It was only two centuries later when a nobleman from Florence, Cosimo del Grillo, married a Perugian girl, Francesca della Penna, that this stone country house was built. Now it is up to you to find out what led to the construction of the small church many years afterwards, and in a far more recent period, why the ancient property has been decorated with Indonesian furniture and objects! Pause and enjoy a gastronomic meal as you elucidate the mystery. Olive oil, home-grown vegetables, aromatic herbs and homemade bread take pride of place on the menu.

Access: *22km from Gubbioin, in the countryside around Santa Cristina*

UMBRIA

MAGIONE (PG)

16

BELLA MAGIONE

Sig. Scattini
viale Cavalieri di Malta 22
06063 Magione (PG)
Tel. 07 58 4730 88 – Fax 07 58 47 30 88
info@bellamagione.it – www.bellamagione.it

75-93€

Open all year • 6 double rm • Parking, garden, swimming pool

 Tranquil hillsides, cruises on Lake Trasimeno and utter peace and quiet.

Magione, a delightful little Umbrian town three kilometres from the eastern shore of Lake Trasimeno, which commands a splendid view of the picturesque fishing villages, is surrounded by acres of peaceful farmland, dotted with picturesque medieval towns. At the gate to the town, opposite the Castle of the Knights of Malta, look for the pink façade of this welcoming guesthouse, whose spacious colourful interior features a reading room with a small library. Countless outdoor leisure activities including a garden, swimming pool, tennis courts, horse riding and excursions in the region.

Access: In the centre near the castle

MONTE CASTELLO DI VIBIO (PG)

FATTORIA DI VIBIO

Sig. Saladini
a Doglio, località Buchella 9
06057 Monte Castello di Vibio (PG)
Tel. 07 58 74 96 07 – Fax 07 58 78 00 14
info@fattoriadivibio.com – www.fattoriadivibio.com

Open all year • 14 double rm • Half-board €90-110 • Parking, garden, swimming pool, tennis court, dogs not admitted in restaurant • Horse riding, wellness centre, mountain bikes, small lake for angling, cookery lessons, sale of oil

 Menu €37/47

 The swimming pool surrounded by sweet-scented, silent hillsides.

Ideal for those in search of an establishment that combines wellness with sport in a setting steeped in history, yet without having to forgo modern comforts. The old farmhouse has been renovated and turned into a sophisticated country guesthouse with a cheerful interior enhanced by wall hangings, knick-knacks and brightly coloured furniture. Physical exercise and relaxation take place in a large building that is home to a well-equipped fitness and wellness centre, at an extra charge. At mealtimes, farm-grown produce, homemade bread, oil, pasta and cured meats will garnish your plate.

Access: Head towards Doglio for 10km, Buchella is nearby

UMBRIA

MONTECCHIO (TR)

18

POGGIO DELLA VOLARA

Sig. Tordi
Via Volara, 1 - Località Volara
05020 Montecchio (TR)
Tel. 07 44 95 18 20 – Fax 07 44 95 18 20
info@poggiodellavolara.it
www.poggiodellavolara.it

👤👤 80-100€

Closed Jan-Feb • 14 double rm • Half board €57-70 • Parking, garden, swimming pool • Oil, jam and wine for sale

 Set Menu for residents only

 The large and inviting swimming pool, perfect for hot summer afternoons.

Located 400m up, this establishment has fine views over its surrounding hills. This is classic Umbrian scenery, a verdant landscape which invites exploration on foot or by mountain bike. The simple and orderly house is not huge, but comfortably provides accommodation in the form of six rooms, decorated in local style with wooden furniture and wrought iron beds. The guests-only restaurant is overseen personally by the owners and serves traditional Umbrian cuisine.

Access: Drive for around 5km northbound to Volara

UMBRIA

MONTEFALCO (PG)

CAMIANO PICCOLO

Sig. Fabrizi
Località Camiano Piccolo, 5
06036 Montefalco (PG)
Tel. 07 42 37 94 92 – Fax 07 42 37 10 77
camiano@bcsnet.com
www.camianopiccolo.com

62-100€

Open all year • 8 double rm • Parking, garden, swimming pool, dogs not admitted in restaurant • Oil and wine tasting

 Set Menu €22 and 30 for residents only

 The gardens, complete with vegetable plot, alongside the swimming pool.

In open countryside, yet only a stone's throw from the walls of Montefalco, this agriturismo is located in a charming little farming settlement. The stone buildings house accommodation in the form of rooms and apartments, public areas and a small guests only restaurant. The tone is no frills simplicity, but entirely adequate given the rustic setting. There are some luxuries, though, including breakfast which in summer is served outside, and the swimming pool with parasols and loungers, sufficiently distant to ensure that guests are not disturbed.

Access: A few hundred metres outside the ramparts

UMBRIA

NORCIA (PG)

20

CASALE NEL PARCO DEI MONTI SIBILLINI

Sig.ra Mensurati
Località Fontevena
06046 Norcia (PG)
Tel. 07 43 81 64 81 – Fax 07 43 81 64 81
agriumbria@casalenelparco.com
www.casalenelparco.com

80-90€

Closed 10 Jan-10 Feb • 13 double rm • Half board €60-70 • Parking, garden, swimming pool, no dogs • Horse riding, bicycles available, rafting, cured meat and cheese tasting and sale

 Menu €24/38

 Admiring the natural beauty of the countryside from the saddle.

Opened as an agriturismo at the end of the last decade, this restored farmhouse is situated a little out of town in a panoramic and peaceful spot. It has ten attractive and well presented rooms, while outside there is a large and pleasant garden with swimming pool. Horses may be hired from the neighbouring stables for rides through the countryside. The restaurant serves authentic and tasty cuisine using home grown organic ingredients.

Access: 1km from the centre right out in the countryside

ORVIETO (TR)

BORGO SAN FAUSTINO

Sig. Perotti
Borgo San Faustino 11/12
05010 Morrano (TR)
Tel. 07 63 2 53 03 – Fax 07 63 21 57 45
borgosf@tin.it – www.agriturismosanfaustino.it

👥 80-100€

Closed 9-31 Jan • 13 double rm • Parking, garden, swimming pool, fitness facilities, no dogs in the restaurant • Horse riding, pétanque, bicycles available, sale of jam, oil, cheese, cured meat and wine

Menu €18/25

The rustic furnishings in the rooms.

San Faustino is a small farming settlement in the hills outside Orvieto, composed of two picturesque stone buildings which have been painstakingly restored over the years to offer accommodation in the form of a dozen rooms. The setting provides greenery and peace in abundance, while the establishment itself is passionately run by the family management team. In summer the garden and swimming pool come into their own; all year round the restaurant serves dishes incorporating home grown produce.

Access: Head towards Arezzo as far as the Morrano crossroads, turn right and continue as far as Km marker 7 200

UMBRIA

PANICALE (PG)

VILLA LEMURA

Sig.ra Cornish
località Villa le Mura 1
06064 Panicale (PG)
Tel. 075 83 71 34 – Fax 075 83 71 34
villalemura@libero.it villalemura@libero.it
www.villalemura.com

100-120€

Open all year • 4 double rm, 2 suites • Parking, garden, swimming pool, dogs not admitted

 Strolling by the fountains as you admire the sunset over the hilltops.

This summer residence once belonged to a high-ranking family from Perugia and everything today continues to evoke its aristocratic past, from the 19C frescoes on the ceilings and the delightful Italian-style garden to the majestic stone staircase that leads upstairs. Forget the present and the future and give into the magic of this elegant interior. Treat yourself to a delicious breakfast in the greenhouse planted with lemon trees, a walk down the park's shaded paths or a dip in the swimming pool hidden by olive groves. Among the guestrooms available are the restful yellow room, the dreamlike poet's room or the romantic and historic countess's suite.

Access: 1km northbound from the centre

UMBRIA

PERUGIA (PG)

23

SAN FELICISSIMO

San Felicissimo s.r.l.
Strada Poggio Pelliccione, 5
06077 Perugia (PG)
Tel. 07 56 91 94 00
info@sanfelicissimo.net
www.sanfelicissimo.net

👤👤 45-98€

Open all year • 10 double rm • Parking, garden, swimming pool • Sale of oil

 The panoramic and relaxing patio-veranda.

Just outside Perugia yet already deep in the hilly countryside, this classic farmhouse surrounded by olive groves has been tastefully converted into a charming agriturismo. Directly accessed from outside, the rooms are well presented and comfortable, as are the public areas, while the carefully tended garden has a swimming pool. The stunning views extending as far as the eye can see make for an unforgettable backdrop.

Access: 5km towards Ponte Felcino and Umbertide

UMBRIA

PIEGARO (PG)

24

CA' DE PRINCIPI

Sig. Crociani
Via Roma 43
06066 Piegaro (PG)
Tel. 07 58 35 80 40 - Fax 07 58 35 80 15
cadeprincipi@dimorastorica.it - www.dimorastorica.it

👤👤 **114€** ☕

Open 1 Apr-30 Nov • 20 double rm

The concert hall in the converted pressing room.

Piegaro, a sleepy town tucked away in the Umbrian hills that resounded with the praises of Jacopone da Todi and the sermons of St Francis of Assisi, and was also the birthplace of Raphael's work, has been an important agricultural and glassmaking centre for many centuries. Today, justly proud of its ancient past, it has remained intact and unspoilt behind its ramparts, adorned with countless beautiful edifices such as the noble palace and summer residence of the landowning Marquesses of Pallavicini. Today the edifice is home to an elegant interior decorated with splendid frescoes, period furniture and objets d'art. What better way to savour the splendour of a glorious past?

Access: In the village

PIETRALUNGA (PG)

25

LA CERQUA E LA BALUCCA
Sig. Martinelli
Località San Salvatore, 27
06026 Pietralunga (PG)
Tel. 07 59 46 02 83 – Fax 07 59 46 20 33
info@cerqua.it – www.cerqua.it

75-90€

Closed Jan-Feb • 19 double rm • Half board €55-70 • Parking, garden, swimming pool • Horse riding, organised trips, bicycles available, archery, jam for sale

 Set Menu €20 and 30

 The rustic accommodation with wooden ceilings, exposed stonework and open fireplaces.

In an unspoilt natural setting, this establishment is surrounded by stunning Umbrian countryside which retains its beauty on account of the profound commitment to organic farming and ecological principles of those who manage it. This establishment provides simple and genuine hospitality in a largely outdoor setting, offering swimming, riding, country walks and a children's play area. After a day in the fresh air, guests will be more than ready to tuck into the generous and authentic cuisine.

Access: 2km from the village, follow the signposts

UMBRIA

SPELLO (PG)

26

LABASTIGLIA

Fam. Fancelli
via Salnitraria 15
06038 Spello (PG)
Tel. 07 42 65 12 77 – Fax 07 42 30 11 59
fancelli@labastiglia.com – www.labastiglia.com

155€

Closed 7-31 Jan • 33 double rm • Heated swimming pool, dogs not admitted

 Menu €55/71

> The terraces overlooking the Chiona valley and the mountains.

In the vicinity of Mount Subasio, the mountain where Saint Francis of Assisi used to retreat to commune with Christ, you will find this former mill converted into a hotel by enthusiastic owners. Be prepared for an unforgettable stay as you enjoy magical, restful moments in welcoming rooms that overlook the picturesque Umbrian countryside. Old recipes made with regional produce and a modern presentation take pride of place on the table. During the daytime, sign up for cookery lessons or relax in the heated swimming pool. A tranquil site that is perfect for anyone in need of rest and relaxation.

Access: In the upper part of the historic centre

UMBRIA

SPELLO (PG)

27

LE DUE TORRI

Sig. Ciri
Via Torre Quadrano, 1
06038 Spello (PG)
Tel. 07 42 65 12 49 – Fax 07 43 27 02 73
info@agriturismoleduetorri.com
www.agriturismoleduetorri.com

66-80€

Closed 15 Jan-15 Feb • 4 double rm • Parking, garden, swimming pool, pétanque, no dogs • Bicycles available, oil, jam, honey and wine for sale

 Set Menu €20 and 30 for residents only

 The symmetrical severity of the solitary tower.

The imposing tower was once part of a network of fortifications which delineated the territories of Foligno and nearby Rocca Deli. Today's more peaceful times mean that it overlooks nothing more threatening than olive groves, vineyards and these two farmhouses which provide accommodation. Recently renovated, they retain their wood beamed ceilings, tiled floors and atmosphere of rustic simplicity. Guests can enjoy delightful walks through the surrounding farmland, with views over the Umbrian hills towards the white stone outline of Assisi.

Access: Head towards Cannara for around 5km as far as Limiti

UMBRIA

SPOLETO (PG)

28

CONVENTO DI AGGHIELLI

Sig. De Simone
frazione Pompagnano
06049 Spoleto (PG)
Tel. 07 43 22 50 10 – Fax 07 43 22 50 10
info@agghielli.it – www.agghielli.it

👥 120-150€

Open all year • 10 double rm, 6 suites • Half-board €83-98 • Parking, garden, dogs not admitted

 Menu €33/41

 Three- to seven-day breaks will enable you to get back to grass roots and commune with nature.

This former convent of the Order of Clares (or Poor Ladies) surrounded by silent forests, is now devoted to rest and gastronomy. Peace of mind and body are catered to in this establishment inspired by organic and biodynamic farming principles. In a bid to revive flagging spirits and tired bodies, the hotel organises walks in the woods, sporting activities, cookery and nutritional courses and relaxation sessions in the wellness centre. A picturesque restaurant with fireplace and panoramic terrace awaits you with a menu devoted to traditional Umbrian fare made from organic produce.

Access: To the right of the main road, head towards Terni for 4km

UMBRIA

SPOLETO (PG)

29

PALAZZO DRAGONI

Sig. Diotallevi
via Duomo 13
06049 Spoleto (PG)
Tel. 07 43 22 22 20 – Fax 07 43 22 22 25
info@palazzodragoni.it
www.palazzodragoni.it

👤👤 **125-150€** ☕

Open all year • 15 double rm • Dogs not admitted

 A fascinating romantic past in an authentic setting.

This period residence, built in the heart of the old town, belonged to a famous family that owed its wealth to its agricultural activities. The interior retains traces of a variety of periods, such as in the upper floors where a 16C atmosphere can be felt in the elegant rooms, some of which boast four-poster beds, in the dining room overlooking the medieval town and in the antique furnished sitting rooms, which are also suitable for meetings and conferences. The cellars are built level with the town's narrow lanes; but beneath them are passages that enabled the inhabitants to flee when the town was besieged.

Access: In the historic centre near the cathedral

SPOLETO (PG)

30

SAN SEBASTIANO IN SPOLETO

Sig. Cellamare
a Madonna di Baiano, via Acquasparta 4
06040 Baiano di Spoleto (PG)
Tel. 07 43 53 98 05 – Fax 07 43 53 99 61
albergosansebastiano@libero.it

 70-90€

Open all year • 1 single rm, 10 double rm, 1 suite • Half-board €60-80 • Parking, dogs not admitted

 Menu €35/45

 Peace and quiet mingled with history in a 17C mill.

On the road to Acquasparta, a town renowned for its major historic festivals, this old stone mill, set in the peaceful Umbrian countryside, has been masterfully restored in order to preserve the characteristic stone rafters and brick arches of the ceilings as much as possible. The mill is now a modest country residence decorated with early 19C furniture. The simple but spacious rooms, cosy dining room, inviting library with fireplace and general tranquillity of the spot offer a perfect setting to find out more about local culture and traditions.

Access: Head towards Acquasparta for 7km to the village of Madonna di Baiano

UMBRIA

STRONCONE (TR)

31

LA PORTA DEL TEMPO

Sig.ra Russo
via del Sacramento 2
05039 Stroncone (TR)
Tel. 07 44 60 81 90 – Fax 07 44 60 90 61
info@portadeltempo.com
www.portadeltempo.com

70-120€

Open all year • 1 single rm, 7 double rm

 A trip back in time, far from the worries of the present.

This 16C palace is built on the top of a hill in the heart of an ancient town whose narrow lanes are lined with stone houses. The expertly restored country guesthouse invites visitors to travel back in time and forget the stress of modern life. Each of the comfortable bedrooms is decorated in a different shade of pastel-coloured furniture and adorned with countless knick-knacks. You may choose to brush up your culinary talents and take a cookery course or head outdoors for more energetic leisure activities. Art therapy courses are also organised to develop and encourage an instinctive, beneficial approach to artistic expression. Homemade treats on the breakfast table.

Access: In the medieval town

UMBRIA

TERNI (TR)

32

LOCANDA DI COLLE DELL'ORO

Fam. Iaculli
strada di Palmetta 31
05100 Terni (TR)
Tel. 07 44 43 23 79 – Fax 07 44 43 78 26
locanda@colledelloro.it – www.colledelloro.it

70-90€

Open all year • 11 double rm • Parking, garden, swimming pool

A tranquil country house on the lower hillsides.

This inn surrounded by lush green hillsides is ideal to escape the hurly-burly of urban life for a while. The modern pink-coloured cottage was built using materials from a number of 19C edifices. The family touch can be felt in the attentive service, attention to detail and cordial welcome extended to guests. The spacious, comfortable interior is decorated in warm rich colours and sophisticated fabrics, enhanced by pretty hand-painted furniture full of the charm of yesteryear. Each of the rooms also benefits from a personal touch. Large swimming pool and splendid view of the valley.

Access: Take the Terni-Orte connection and then the road to Palmetta

UMBRIA

TITIGNANO (TN)

33

FATTORIA DI TITIGNANO

Sig. Fontani
05010 Titignano (TR)
Tel. 07 63 30 80 22 – Fax 07 63 30 80 02
info@titignano.com – www.titignano.com

 90€

Open all year • 15 double rm • Half-board €57 • Parking, garden, swimming pool, dogs not admitted in restaurant • Bicycles available, pétanque, sale of oil, wine and biscuits

 Set Menu €15 and 25

 The enticing scent of grapes and olives fills this ancient town.

This old family farmstead stands at the end of long dirt track on the top of a mountain that dominates the countryside on the banks of Lake Corsara. The thriving estate, which produces wine and olive oil, is home to a sumptuous stone castle inside of which is a large high-ceilinged dining room with fireplace where guests are served delicious farm produce. The rooms are simpler in style with terracotta tiled floors and wooden furniture, although the bathrooms do sport marble finishings. The estate offers countless leisure activities including a swimming pool, walks in the wood and relaxing naps on the banks of the lake.

Access: In the town of Titignano

517

UMBRIA

TODI (PG)

34

CASALE DELLE LUCREZIE

Sig. Adanti
Frazione Duesanti - Vocabolo Palazzaccio
05020 Todi (PG)
Tel. 07 58 98 74 88 – Fax 07 58 98 74 88
info@casaledellelucrezie.com
www.casaledellelucrezie.com

 70-80€

Closed 15-31 Jan • 13 double rm • Half board €55-60 • Parking, garden, swimming pool, dogs not admitted • Bicycles available, oil and wine for sale

 Menu €21/31

 The view of Todi.

This traditional stone farmstead is built in typical Umbrian style. Founded by the Romans, over-run by the Etruscans (an arch remains from this period) and then occupied by the Lucretian nuns in the 13C, the property enjoys a magnificent location deep in the hills, with splendid views of Todi from the bedroom windows. Guestrooms here are new and simply furnished, with modern bathrooms. The restaurant specialises in typical dishes of the region.

Access: Head towards Duesanti for around 5km

UMBRIA

TODI (PG)

35

SAN LORENZO TRE

Sig.ra Morena
via San Lorenzo 3
06059 Todi (PG)
Tel. 07 58 94 45 55 – Fax 07 58 94 45 55
lorenzotre@tin.it – www.sanlorenzo3.it

👫 95-110€

Closed Jan and Feb • 6 double rm • Dogs not admitted

 The chance to mix with the locals in the heart of a bustling historic town.

Far from the lush green landscapes of Umbria, ever synonymous with inner peace of mind and an invigorating climate that were the inspiration to many great artists, this period castle is unusually located in the heart of the town just two minutes from the main square. The interior is however steeped in charm and elegance, carefully enhanced by the soothing and tasteful dark wood furniture from the early 20C.

Access: In the town a few minutes from the main square

UMBRIA

TREVI (PG)

36

TREVI

Sig. Bellucci
via Fantosati 2
06039 Trevi (PG)
Tel. 07 42 78 09 22 - Fax 07 42 78 07 72
info@trevihotel.net - www.trevihotel.net

👤👶 **95-129€**

Closed 8 Jan-8 Feb • 11 double rm • Dogs not admitted

We most liked — The panoramic terrace that commands a splendid view of the green olive groves.

Treat yourself to a chance to relax and recharge your batteries in the wellness centre of this old palace, a mixture of medieval and Renaissance architecture with timber rafters and stonewalls, on the edge of the historic town. Palazzon Natalini, located in a quiet spot, is an impressive stone edifice whose interior is steeped in history, offering comfortable rooms of varying sizes, each decorated individually, but all enjoying the same fantastic sweeping view of the valley. In summer, the buffet breakfast is served on a green terrace – a perfect way to start your day.

Access: In the historic centre

UMBRIA

VALLO DI NERA (PG)

37

LA LOCANDA DI CACIO RE

Sig. Brunelli
Località i Casali
06040 Vallo di Nera (PG)
Tel. 07 43 61 70 03 – Fax 07 43 61 72 14
caciore@tin.it – www.caciore.it

 70-80€

Closed Jan and Nov • 8 double rm • Parking, garden, no dogs in the restaurant

 Menu €30/53

 The local heritage and cuisine.

The castle in this medieval village was once the defensive lynchpin for the entire valley, and many buildings were erected around it to benefit from the protection it offered. Among them was this farmhouse, which has changed little over the last five centuries. But here in the Nera valley, the architecture is not alone in having a long history; the local cuisine has an equally proud heritage. Truffles, barley, lamb and sausages are all standard fare which guests can enjoy in the restaurant, and indeed purchase to take home.

Access: In the medieval town

Valle d'Aosta

The woodland and valleys of the Gran Paradiso National Park are a haven for chamois, marmots and ibex, a classic alpine landscape sitting at the head of the long Dora Baltea valley. To the north lies Switzerland beyond the Gran San Bernardo, to the west Mont Blanc marks the border with France, so it comes as no surprise that both Italian and French are spoken here. The region has always been an important crossroads; for many years the local population resisted Roman incursion, but they eventually succumbed. The conquerors founded Augusta Praetoria, today known as Aosta. Monuments from this era were succeeded by many castles in the medieval period, among the finest in Italy. Natural beauty, however, is the overriding attraction of the Val d'Aosta; names such as Courmayeur, La Thiule and Greesney are familiar to lovers of winter sports and alpine ramblers. The local hospitality is best experienced at the dining table, around a fondue accompanied by coffee laced with Genepy, the local liqueur.

6 establishments

Recommended sites and circuits
Aosta Valley

> Mute sentinels of a past that has seen battles, economic exchanges, dominion, festivals and court intrigues, the ancient castles and sumptuous noble residences testify to the complex feudal history of this region surrounded by the imposing alpine mountain range.

There are more than a hundred castles in the region, perched on impregnable buttresses and watching over the valleys. They constitute a solid defensive network rich in history that provides the ideal pretext for exploring the incredible countryside all around. Climb up to the summits of the Aosta valley, where fairy tales, art and architecture all contribute to the charm of these fascinating giants. Welcoming you is **Bard Fort**, a practically impregnable masterpiece of military art. Napoleon was the only one who managed to conquer it after a sixteen-day siege. It was reconstructed in 1830 with 283 rooms designed to house up to 416 men. **Issogne Castle** is rather different; its influences, both Gothic and Renaissance, make for a harmonious whole composed of an equilateral main structure, angular towers and cross-bar windows. Inside you will discover a sumptuous decor, frescoes, panelled ceilings and period furnishings, and in the courtyard, the famous Grenada Fountain. The most pleasing decor is to be found, however, in **Fenis Castle**, the most imposing in the region. Unlike all the other castles, which were built for defensive purposes, this one is not located at a great height, but on a small hill. Its position tells us that the castle had no purpose other than to enhance the prestige of the Challant family. The double row of ramparts is embellished by angular and cylindrical towers and the interior is decorated with taste and finesse. All of the authentic and valuable furniture dates back to the 15C and 16C. **Saint-Peter Castle** could almost outdo even Fenis Castle. Despite having been restructured, this very old edifice looks like it came straight out of a fairy tale. The central structure has had four little circular towers added to it that make for a spectacular effect. In reality, however, the changes made to the structure are not that different from those undergone by other castles.

Savoia Castle, another of these fairytale places, is a residence made unique by its five pointed towers that dominate the structure. Don't miss its botanical garden, in which mountain plants originating from the Alps and from all over the world are grown amongst the rocks.

A recipe to try, wines and... a nugget of information

 Wines

_Muller-Thurgau
_Gamay
_Pinot
_Nus rouge
_Donnes
_Blanc de Morgex
_Arnad-monjovet

Ingredients
- 200g Aosta Valley fontine cheese
- 1 glass milk
- butter
- 1 tablespoon flour
- 4 egg yolks
- white pepper

Local specialities

Fontine cheese, cabbage, rye bread, Valpellinentze soup (made with bread, cabbage and fontine, then browned in the oven), chestnuts, *carbonade* (beef cut into strips and cooked in red wine), blancmange, Mont Blanc (chestnut purée in the form of a mountain with sugar, cocoa, milk and rum, topped with whipped cream), apple cake made with breadcrumbs.

FONDUTA

Method
Cut the fontine into cubes and leave it to marinate for about half an hour in a container holding half a glass of milk. In a saucepan, thin down the egg yolks with a spoonful of flour and the rest of the milk, add the fontine and the milk in which it has been soaking. Cook over a moderate heat and stir with a wooden spoon until creamy.
Don't forget that a fondue must not boil! Take it off the heat and add a pinch of white pepper and a few knobs of butter. Serve very hot.

Food for thought
In the past black bread was made once a year. The whole family would take part and when the bread came out of the oven there would be a big party. Once dried the bread was very hard so, to cut it, it was necessary to use a *copapàn*, an iron knife that can still be found today in traditional handicraft shops. In order to soften the bread it would be soaked for a few minutes in soup, milk, or, for lack of anything else, in water.

Our favourite places to eat

HOSTELLERIE DE LA POMME COURONNÈE
Frazione Resselin 3 – Aosta, Gressan (AO) – Tel. 0165 251010
Closed Tue and Wed lunchtime.
A la carte menu €29-47
 The open courtyard, a second stage for the display of culinary creativity.
From the outside, the stone and wood structure of this remodeled farmhouse identifies it as typical of the area; the inside is decorated with warm colours and rustic objects. The establishment is a family affair: the Mamma prepares apple-based specialities, accompanied by meat carpaccio or cheese, or made into jam to garnish black pudding. The succession of original dishes and creative combinations is topped off by the unbeatable homemade apple tart.

LA CLUSAZ
Località La Clusaz NW: 4,5km – Gignod (AO) – Tel. 0165 56075
Closed Tue and lunchtime except Sat, public hols and Aug.
A la carte menu €32-40
 The ancient path, the stone arches, and the memory of the pilgrims.
To reach this restaurant, take the road leading to the Great Saint-Bernard pass and stop at the cluster of buildings with an ornate façade. Here, you will find yourself in a singular place, where the rustic atmosphere lent by the stone vaults is allied with a decor of silver and crystal. The cuisine has its roots in local tradition and regional products, but the chef adds his personal touch, resulting in lighter dishes than the traditional versions and appetising, original presentations.

AL MANIERO
Frazione Pied de Ville 58 – Issogne (AO) – Tel. 0125 929219
Closed Mon, except in Aug and last two weeks in Jun.
A la carte menu €23-33
 The simple local dishes and the fittingly traditional atmosphere.
A narrow street leads you to this restaurant located in an old villa. Wood panelling and tightly packed little tables recreate the atmosphere of a typical village trattoria. The food is the star here. For starters, a tasty selection of cold meats, followed by calorific main dishes such as filled polenta and Valledao fondue. The meat dishes, ranging from *carbonada* (meat stew) and Valledao-style cutlets, are also typical of the region; the fish must be ordered in advance. The desserts are unpretentious and homemade.

VALLE D'AOSTA

CHAMPOLUC (AO)

LE VIEUX RASCARD

Sig.ra Vuillermet uillermet
rue des Guides 35
11020 Champoluc (AO)
Tel. 0 1 25 30 8746 – Fax 01 25 30 87 46
info@levieuxrascard.com

58-108€

Open 7 Dec-10 Apr and 15 Jun-30 Sep • 6 double rm • Parking

 The view of the old town of Champoluc.

Immaculate walls, a predominance of wood and the scent of flowers that fills the balconies, all of which in a refreshing green setting – such is the picture of hospitality in the Alps. A little removed from the bustle of the historic centre, this 17C raccard (granary) has been restored and converted into a small, pleasant guesthouse wih a welcoming family atmosphere. The few delightful rooms have been masterfully decorated in a local style, offering guests the chance to take full advantage of the pervading tranquillity. The small breakfast room commands a view of the sunny meadows and Monte Rosa.

Access: Near the centre

VALLE D'AOSTA

COGNE (AO)

LA BARME
Sig. Herren
Località Valnontey, 8
11012 Cogne (AO)
Tel. 01 65 74 91 77 – Fax 01 65 74 92 13
labarme@tiscali.it – www.hotellabarme.com

 65-106€

Closed Oct-Nov • 3 single rm, 13 double rm • Half board €47-63 • Garden, no dogs

 Menu €18/31

 The mountains, a striking backdrop to any visit.

Peace and quiet reign supreme in the little village of Valnontey, deep in the Gran Paradiso national park. This 18C building has been sensitively restored and reborn as a hotel providing comfortable accommodation without compromising its classic architectural style. The main section houses the smart public areas, namely the restaurant, games room and sauna. The well presented rooms have pine furnishings and are simple yet attractive. Sun lovers can bask all year round in the spacious sun-lounge.

Access: Once in Cogne, turn right and continue for 3km to Valnontey

VALLE D'AOSTA

SAINT PIERRE (AO)

LA MERIDIANA DU CADRAN SOLAIRE

Sig.ra Pozzini
località Chateau Feuillet 17
11010 Saint Pierre (AO)
Tel. 01 65 90 36 26 – Fax 01 65 90 98 63
info@albergomeridiana.it
www.albergomeridiana.it

 90-130€

Open all year • 18 double rm • Parking

 Menu €41/69

 The cellar is perfect to sample a glass of the local vintage.

If you are interested in nature, keen to find out more about the traditions and major events of the past and want to explore the Aoste Valley, then you could not do better than stop for a while in the small village of Saint Pierre, surrounded by magnificent mountain ranges and castles that date back to the beginning of time. This natural setting, rich in history, is home to the Meridiana, a family-run stone and wood property which offers rooms that are pleasantly decorated in a valdostano style and a charming restaurant whose experienced chef adores letting his imagination run wild.

Access: Very near the centre in Chateau Feuillet

VALLE D'AOSTA

SARRE (AO)

4

L'ARC EN CIEL

Sig. Fasolis
Frazione Vert, 1
11010 Sarre (AO)
Tel. 01 65 25 78 43 – Fax 01 65 25 78 43
www.agriturismolarcenciel.it

62-66€

Open all year • 5 double rm • Half board €47 • Parking, garden, no dogs • Cured meat and goat's cheese for sale

 Set Menu €14 and 22

 The view of the valley stretching skywards.

The name means rainbow and not without good reason. Guests may well get the feeling that they are up in the sky as they admire the breathtaking views over the Aosta valley and surrounding hillsides with the Ruitor glacier providing an impressive backdrop to the whole scene. Having got over the view, guests can enjoy the restaurant which serves dishes prepared using authentic local produce.

Access: A few hundred metres from the hamlet of Vert

VALLE D'AOSTA

VALSAVARENCHE (AO)

L'HOSTELLERIE DU PARADIS

Sig. Gianni
Località Eau Rousse, 21
11010 Valsavarenche (AO)
Tel. 01 65 90 59 72 – Fax 01 65 90 59 71
info@hostellerieduparadis.it – www.hostellerieduparadis.it

 90€

Closed 8-31 Jan and Nov • 5 single rm, 25 double rm • Breakfast €8; half board €70-80 • Parking, indoor swimming pool, dogs not admitted in restaurant

 Set Menu €20 and 40

 The snowbound alpine refuge.

A classic mountain refuge in appearance, this building of stone and wood with its slate roof seems to invite heavy snowfall in order to provide it with a fairytale setting. Winter is not the only season in which to visit, however, since summer guests can enjoy walking in the woods, some light climbing, or merely strolling in the peaceful surroundings of this national park. Although recently built, the accommodation is largely in wood, very much in keeping with local tradition.

Access: 3km in Eau Rousse

VALLE D'AOSTA

VERRAYES (AO)

6

LA VRILLE

Sig. Deguillame
Hameau du Grandzon, 1
11020 Verrayes (AO)
Tel. 01 66 54 30 18
lavrille@gmail.com
www.lavrille-agriturisme.com

👫 **70-84€**

Open all year • 6 double rm • Half-board €50-60 • Parking, garden, bowls, no dogs • Jam and wine for sale

 Set Menu €18 and 22 for residents only

 The generous breakfast served against a backdrop of stone and woodwork.

La Vrille is a typical mountain building in wood and stone, situated among vineyards within sight of Mounts Avic and Emilius. Its location is peaceful, yet convenient for the ski slopes. The quality of the local produce is evident in the hearty breakfasts, where there is no shortage of choice. The area's gastronomic heritage is celebrated in many local events, a good excuse for visitors to explore the mountains and villages of Val d'Aosta.

Access: 6km from the village, in Grandzon surrounded by vineyards

Veneto

It is impossible to describe the Veneto without mentioning Venice, its unique character, art and history having made it the seat of a commercial and cultural empire and subsequently a place of gilded decay. But there is a great deal more to the region than Venice; the rose coloured cathedrals of Dolomites' Cadore district, the evocative Roman remains of Verona, the houses on Treviso's canals, Giotto's frescoes in Padova, not forgetting the smaller towns such as Conegliano and Montagnana, little artistic jewels untouched by the passage of time. The Veneto's landscape of wheat fields on the plains and vineyards in the hills is dotted with the elegant outlines of Palladian villas, reminders of the age when Venice's nobility would retreat to the rural tranquillity of their country residences.

Land and sea are equally represented in the region's cuisine; the traditional peasant staples of *polenta* and rice feature alongside the famous *baccalà alla vicentina* (salted cod) and *sardelle in saor* (sardines in brine).

Soave, Bardolino and Amarone are some of the Veneto's great wines, all of which are a pleasure to get to know.

31 establishments

Recommended sites and circuits
Veneto

> A unique region with a glorious past that perfectly marries historical relevance and natural landscapes, medieval sights and Palladian villas. There are several smaller sites whose charm will appeal to visitors' senses, in addition to more traditional itineraries through the artistic centres.

Asolo, nestling amidst olive trees, vineyards and cypress trees, offers visitors sights of major historical, artistic and cultural value. The poet Carducci called it "the city of a hundred horizons" and it is its plethora of attractions (narrow streets, doorways, palazzi…) that make up its charm and beauty. Everything here reflects the city's ancient past. Its age-old appeal is in evidence in the ramparts, dominated by the fort. In the heart of the city is Piazza Garibaldi, where you can begin a tour of the principal monuments (the castle, medieval cathedral and remains of the Roman aqueduct). In a wine shop on Via Browning, inconspicuously placed behind the counter, is a clock which recounts the history of the city from its beginnings at the start of the 19C. Eleonora Duse, who stayed here towards the end of her career, described the city as "a land of lace and poetry".

Arquà Petrarca, a market town that has also managed to preserve an intensity and melancholy consistent with times past, is known for having been home to the poet Petrarch at the end of his life. His house, tucked away in a little cobbled street, is open to visitors. Its structure has been altered but the atmosphere that made it so unique remains unchanged. As does the atmosphere of the market town, whose many little streets are a continuous source of surprises: frieze panels, balconies, doorways. In the historical centre there are still houses dating from the 14C, washeries and palazzi, the most famous of which is Contarini Palace, which belonged to the Doges of Venice. Petrarch's body is at rest in the St Maria Assunta Church.

Marostica is a magnificent fortified medieval city dominated by two forts that offer fantastic views and surrounded by ramparts that descend down into the valley. Each year a giant game of chess is held on the main square. The origins of this tradition go back to 1454, when two noble warriors fell in love with the castellan's beautiful daughter and, as was the custom at the time, challenged each other to a duel. The castellan wanted to rescue the young men's friendship and forbade the duel, deciding that his daughter would marry whichever of the two won a game of chess, while the loser would marry the castellan's youngest daughter.

A recipe to try, wines and... a nugget of information

 Wines

_Bardolino
_Bianco di Custoza
_Valpolicella
_Soave
_Merlot
_Pinot
_Tocai italico
_Verduzzo

Ingredients

▶ 400g calf's liver
▶ 400g onions
▶ 30g butter
▶ 5 tablespoons extra virgin olive oil
▶ salt
▶ pepper
▶ chopped parsley

Local specialities

Vialone nano rice from Verona, *radicchio variegato di Castelfranco Veneto* (red and white endives), *radicchio*, Garda olive oil, Venetian ham, *bigoli* (thick spaghetti made with wholemeal flour or durum wheat). Cheeses: *taleggio, montasio, asiago, Grana Padano, ricotta affumicata* (smoked), *embriago* cheese.

FEGATO ALLA VENEZIANA

Method
Chop the onions finely (keep wetting the blade of the knife if you want to avoid tears), and soften them gently in the oil and butter, taking care not to let them brown. Add salt and pepper. Cut the liver into strips and add it to the onion. Cook over a high heat for a few minutes. Add salt to taste and, if desired, sprinkle with chopped parsley. Serve immediately.

Food for thought
In this region, close to Arquà Petrarca, the expression "swoon with pleasure" is synonymous with "jujube liqueur". This may sound strange but can be explained. Here, the jujube (a sweet fruit that is very rich in vitamin C) grows abundantly. Nowadays it takes on various forms: jujube in grappa, *giuggiolotti* (exquisite chocolates), *giuggiolosa* (a type of cake). And of course you can't leave without "swooning with pleasure" over the *brodo di giuggiole*, a sweet liqueur to be enjoyed at the end of a meal.

Our favourite places to eat

LA ROSINA
Via Marchetti 4 Nord: 2km – Valle San Floriano (Marostica, VI)
Tel. 0424 470360
Closed Mon and Tue.

A la carte menu €25-36

The memory of a kind-hearted woman, and the taste of cod – just how it should be.
This secluded restaurant nestled in a landscape of rolling green hills is a local institution. Run by the same family for nearly a century, in memory of the grandmother, who used to give a bowl of soup to soldiers passing through, the simplicity of the spacious interior remains intact. The majestic fireplace is not only aesthetic but also functional. On the menu: traditional grills, *bigoli* (fresh Veneto pasta), polenta, cheeses and, of course, the tasty *baccalà alla vicentina* (cod with polenta).

MERICA
Via Rezzola 93, Palazzo: 1,5km E of Sommacampagna (VR)
Tel. 045 515160
Closed Mon.

A la carte menu €28-35

The unpretentious and wholesome cuisine, reflecting the tastes of the past.
Arriving from the town of Sommacampagna by car, it is quick to get to Merica, a villa nestled in the Veronese countryside. The warm, family welcome has certainly done no harm to the restaurant's success with a local and international clientele, who are won over by the authentic and wholesome dishes. Healthy products go into the rich local specialities prepared by the ingenius chef and served in a spacious dining area, where the classic atmosphere is tempered by more rustic details.

AL BORGO
Via Anconetta 8 – Belluno (BL) – Tel. 0437 926755
Closed 15-30 Jan, Mon eve and Tue.

A la carte menu €26-32

The timeless taste of Val Belluna herbs and game from the mountainside.
Don't give up if you have trouble finding this restaurant. Your perseverance will be rewarded by a warm family welcome on arrival at the charming little 18C villa with ornate carved stone features and a well-kept garden affording an unbeatable view over the Dolomites... Nor will you be disappointed by the food: typical specialities prepared almost exclusively with homegrown products and meat, and accompanied by a selection of oils and balsamic vinegars.

VENETO

ALBAREDO D'ADIGE (VR)

LOCANDA ARCIMBOLDO
Fam. Guidorizzi
Via Gennari, 5 a Coriano Veronese
37041 Albaredo d'Adige (VR)
Tel. 04 57 02 53 00 – Fax 04 57 02 52 01
info@locandadellarcimboldo.it
www.locandadellarcimboldo.it

  80-100€

Closed 1-20 Aug • 4 double rm • Half board €80-90 • Parking, garden, dogs not admitted

 Menu €33/61

 **The sumptuous rooms, well presented down to the finest details.**

This comprehensively restored 19C house is conveniently situated on the road, yet looks onto its garden and parking area, making for a peaceful ambience. The enterprising and hospitable Guidorizzi family has emphasised quality over quantity; the limited number of rooms are elegantly rustic in style and well equipped. The restaurant is also worthy of note, serving local specialities in warm and welcoming surroundings.

Access: 5km southbound from the village in Coriano

VENETO

BELLUNO (BL)

NOGHERAZZA

Sig. Miari Fulcis
Via Gresane 78 località Castion
32024 Belluno (BL)
Tel. 04 37 92 74 61 – Fax 04 37 92 58 82
amiarif@tin.it – www.nogherazza.it

80-100€

Closed Feb • 6 double rm • Parking, garden

 Menu €25/33

 We most liked The woodwork, making for a warm ambience throughout.

This pleasant spot is difficult to pigeonhole; a welcoming ambience combined with convenient location halfway betweeen Venice and the Dolomites giving access to the delights of the Veneto and some of the most impressive alpine scenery. The wood panelled rooms are attractive, and there are also sports facilities including riding, football and volleyball, plus the restaurant offering local specialities as well as Tuscan and Umbrian dishes.

Access: 3km south-east from Belluno to Castion

VENETO

CAERANO DI SAN MARCO (TV)

3

COL DELLE RANE

Sig.ra Stefani
Via Mercato Vecchio, 18
31031 Caerano di San Marco (TV)
Tel. 042 38 55 85 – Fax 04 23 65 06 52
info@coldellerane.it – www.coldellerane.it

63-65€

Open all year • 14 double rm • Parking, garden, no dogs • Bicycles available, honey, jam and wine for sale

> Breakfast, composed of healthy natural products, looking out over the surrounding countryside.

Halfway between Asolo and Treviso, this comprehensively restored late 18C farmhouse is the ideal base from which to explore the area's famous Palladian villas. At one end of the house is the large breakfast area, also used for functions, overlooking the surrounding countryside through ample windows. The simple yet comfortable rooms are decorated in rustic style. All around are vineyards and orchards, ensuring a ready supply of home made jams.

Access: Outside the village on the SS 248

541

VENETO

CARRE' (VI)

4

LOCANDA LA CORTE DEI GALLI

Sig. Franceschi
via Prà Secco 1/a
36010 Carrè (VI)
Tel. 04 45 89 33 33 - Fax 04 45 89 33 18
lacortedeigalli@tiscali.it
www.lacortedeigalli.it

👤👤 130-160€

Open all year • 7 double rm • Parking, garden

 We most liked Green predominates everywhere from the climbing plants in the garden to the interior decoration.

Located in the barn of a 17C farm, where the farm tools and food used to be stored, this pleasant inn is immersed in the silence and greenery of a town steeped in history and tradition. The property, on the edge of the historic town of Carrè, belonged to the Thiene family for over a century. Restored from top to toe and turned into an inn, it is now home to pleasant and elegant rooms adorned with objets d'art, throughout which reigns a romantic atmosphere.

Access: Very close to the historic centre

VENETO

CASTELNUOVO DEL GARDA (VR)

LA MERIDIANA
Sig. Martinelli

Via Zamboni, 11 Località Sandrà
37010 Castelnuovo del Garda (VR)
Tel. 04 57 59 63 06 – Fax 04 57 59 63 13

ŤŤ68€

Closed 27 Dec-9 Jan • 2 single rm, 11 double rm • Half board €52 • Parking, garden, dogs not admitted in restaurant

 Menu €22/33

 The sloping wooden ceilings in some of the rooms.

This attractive farmhouse sits in open countryside to the south of Garda, in an area well known for its wines. In addition to its attractive surroundings, it is also well located for access to Lake Garda and the great artistic centres of Verona, Mantova, Padova and Venice, while several natural and theme parks are also nearby. In the main house, there is the tasteful accommodation, showing great attention to detail and personal touches throughout, while the former hay barn now houses the highly regarded restaurant.

Access: In Sandrà, drive for 3km along the main road to Pastrengo

VENETO

CAVASO DEL TOMBA (TV)

6

LOCANDA ALLA POSTA

Sig. Visentin
Piazza 13 Martiri, 13
31034 Cavaso del Tomba (TV)
Tel. 04 23 54 31 12 – Fax 04 23 54 31 12

Closed 10-31 Jan • 7 double rm

 Menu €24/34

> The characteristic sign which beckons the arriving guests.

A veritable institution in the district, this building appears in the earliest photos of Cavaso, taken a century ago. Ever since it has provided hospitality to travellers; the bar is popular with the locals, while the accommodation and restaurant cater for tourists. This is a welcoming spot, its rooms mostly refurbished with a personal touch and decorated in a homely style with antiques.

Access: On the village square

VENETO

DOLO (VE)

7

VILLA GOETZEN
Fam. Minchio
Via Matteotti, 6
30031 Dolo (VE)
Tel. 041 5102300 - Fax 041 412600
info@villagoetzen.it - www.villagoetzen.it

 80€

Open all year • 2 single rm, 10 double rm • Parking, garden, no dogs

 Menu €35/50

 The pleasant new terrace overlooking the river.

Although not the work of Palladio, this hotel is an attractive 18C villa on the river, albeit a little close to the road. It has a charming genteel ambience, is run by family management and offers well laid out, if somewhat compact, accommodation. In the main house are ten rooms, with another two in the former stable block. All are welcoming, with Venetian-style furnishings and every modern convenience. The elegant restaurant specialises in fish dishes.

Access: On the main road by Brenta canal

VENETO

FARA VICENTINO (VI)

8

LE COLLINE DELL'UVA

Sig.ra Barausse
Via Alteo, 15
36030 Fara Vicentino (VI)
Tel. 04 45 89 76 51 – Fax 04 45 89 76 51
lecollinedelluva@hotmail.com
www.lecollinedelluva.com

120€

Open all year • 5 double rm • Parking, garden, small dogs welcome

 Set Menu €20 and 30 for residents only

 The healthy and generous home made breakfast.

Opened in October 2001, this restored farmhouse is out of town and up in the hills and is ideal for visitors, be they tourists or business travellers, in search of elegance and simplicity. The creative management has successfully mixed family pieces with modern objects to create a harmonious minimalist look. In addition to the fine rooms, there is a pleasant breakfast room, a small bar and an attractive garden.

Access: 1.5km towards Salcedo-Asiago

FOLLINA (TV)

DEI CHIOSTRI

Sig. Zanon
piazza 4 Novembre 20
31051 Follina (TV)
Tel. 04 38 97 18 05 – Fax 04 38 97 42 17
info@hoteldeichiostri.com – www.hoteldeichiostri.com

👫 155€

Closed 7 Jan-13 Feb • 2 single rm, 13 double rm • Parking

 The Chinese trunks that enhance the interior decoration and evoke a passion for travel.

This unusual and unexpected hotel, in the heart of Marca Trevigiana and surrounded by the vineyards of Prosecco, combines the romanticism of 18C Italy with a minimalist modern design. While modern, Dei Chiostri is nonetheless laden with historic and artistic souvenirs. Located in the walls of an old palace, the guestrooms, all different in colour and style, have large windows and are whimsically decorated with objets d'art, exotic features and equipped with cutting-edge technology. An establishment that remains as popular with businessmen as it does with tourists eager to discover the Veneto region and its enchanting towns.

Access: In the village

VENETO

FOLLINA (TV)

10

VILLA GUARDA
Sig. Traina
Via San Nicolò, 47 a Pedeguarda
31050 Follina (TV)
Tel. 04 38 98 08 34 – Fax 04 38 98 08 54
info@villaguarda.it – www.villaguarda.it

👤👤 75€

Open all year • 4 single rm, 16 double rm • Breakfast €5 • Parking, garden

The gushing fountain at the centre of the charming garden.

This large white house is of long and irregular layout. Rising four storeys, it features covered terraces, a wooden gallery, a number of verandas and colonnades. In essence, an unusual and dynamic structure with asymmetrical dimensions and garden blends, it well into the hilly Trevisan landscape. Access to the rooms is by external staircases, which might leave visitors unsure as to the efficiency of the service here, but they need not worry. The management's high standards should satisfy even the most exacting guest. Parking for about twenty cars.

Access: 3km from Pedeguarda, towards Pieve di Soglio

LONGARE (VI)

LE VESCOVANE

Sig.ra Savoia
Via San Rocco, 19
36040 Longare (VI)
Tel. 04 44 27 35 70 – Fax 04 44 27 32 65
info@levescovane.com – www.levescovane.com

75-86€

Open all year • 8 double rm, 1 suite • Half board €58-63 • Parking, small dogs welcome • Bicycles available, organised visits, sale of jams, cured meat and wine

Menu €22/31

The wood and stone porch leading to the restaurant.

The road to this typical farmstead is located a few kilometres the other side of Vicenza – guests are advised to consult the website or call for directions before leaving the town. Originally built as a hunting lodge in the 16C, the attractive stone farmhouse is now surrounded by a well-tended garden and the peace and quiet of the Monti Berici. Although the style of the house is not as grand as that of a Palladian villa, there is still an elegant, country-house feel to the property. The agriturismo also boasts a busy restaurant which serves a selection of regional cuisine, some of which is produced on the farm.

Access: Towards Vicenza past the metal bridge, follow the signs to Villa Balzana-San Rocco

VENETO

MESTRE (VE)

12

CA' NOVA

Sig. Zanon
Via Bagaron, 1 località Campalto
30030 Mestre (VE)
Tel. 041 90 00 33 – Fax 04 15 42 04 20
ca-nova@tiscali.it

👤👤 80-100€

Closed Jan • 2 single rm, 4 double rm • Breakfast €5 • Parking

 The convenient location close to Venice.

Well situated for access not only to Venice itself, but also to the airport and motorway. This 18C villa has been completely restored boasting a genteel cream facade with contrasting blue shutters and surmounted by a classical style cornice. Its small rooms are tastefully furnished and welcoming. Managed in friendly fashion by the Zanon family, who also run the trattoria next door.

Access: 5km from Campalto towards the airport

VENETO

MIRA (VE)

RIVIERA DEI DOGI

Riviera dei Dogi Srl
Via Don Minzoni, 33
30034 Mira Porte (VE)
Tel. 041 42 44 66 – Fax 041 42 44 28
info@rivieradeidogi.com – www.rivieradeidogi.com

70-120€

Open all year • 6 single rm, 37 double rm • Breakfast €7.50 • Parking, no dogs

The wooden beams supporting the ceilings throughout.

For four hundred years, this house has watched the waters of the Brenta flow by, and seen generations of visitors come and go. Originally the counts Contarini used it as a weekend retreat, then it became an inn and by the end of the 19C it was the foremost hotel on the Brenta. It subsequently fell into disuse before being brought back to life about ten years ago; the rooms are large and welcoming (although the bathrooms are a little cramped), there is an attractive garden and the public areas have wooden ceilings and floors.

Access: In the village

VENETO

MIRANO (VE)

14

PARK HOTEL VILLA GIUSTINIAN

Sig. Agostini
via Miranese 85
30035 Mirano (VE)
Tel. 04 15 70 02 00 – Fax 04 15 70 03 55
info@villagiustinian.com
www.villagiustinian.com

 104-129€

Open all year • 10 single rm, 28 double rm, 2 suites • Parking, park

 Festivals and romantic weekends under the auspices of a famous ancestor.

Located within the famous Roman centuria, a testimonial to historic means of communication, this impressive 18C building used to belong to Lorenzo Giustinian, a Venetian patriarch. It is now home to a hotel that will enchant lovers of elegance and refinement with its damask fabrics, gilt work and "arte povera" style furniture that enrich the interior, both in the main wing and in the outbuildings. Outside is an immense park with a chalet that is used for parties and family get-togethers.

Access: Near the hospital

VENETO

MIRANO (VE)

15

VILLA PATRIARCA

Sig. Bortolato
via Miranese 25
30035 Mirano (VE)
Tel. 041 43 00 06 – Fax 04 15 70 20 77
info@villapatriarca.com – www.villapatriarca.com

70-98€

Open all year • 11 single rm, 14 double rm • Parking, garden, swimming pool, dogs not admitted

Aquagym lessons in a splendid old aristocratic residence.

A holiday residence of the 18C Venetian aristocracy, this immaculate property stands in an immense garden and is home to comfortably relaxed interior. An intimate breakfast room, refined reading room and guestrooms bathed in light and furnished in an "arte povera" style. Outdoors you can have a game of tennis or futsal. The swimming pool plus hydromassage, surrounded by greenery, boasts a sundeck, ideal for sunbathing, chatting with friends or nibbling a snack in the shade of the two arbours. Aquagym sessions in summer.

Access: Near the hospital

VENETO

PIEVE DI SOLIGO (TV)

16

DA LINO

Sig. Toffolin
a Solighetto via Brandolini 31
31053 Pieve di Soligo (TV)
Tel. 043 88 21 50 – Fax 04 38 98 05 77
dalino@tmn.it – www.locandadalino.it

👤👤 90€

Closed Jul • 2 single rm, 8 double rm, 7 suites • Parking

  Menu €38/53

> **We most liked** — Feeling at home in an establishment frequented by culinary and showbiz stars.

Inaugurated by the talented chef Lino Toffolin, this inn initiates its guests into the wealth of Venetian cuisine whilst also offering them the surprise of a distinctive setting. The dining rooms, bathed in the soft shimmer of candlelight, are adorned with objets d'art and hundreds of copper saucepans. The local gastronomy is inspired by the recipes of mothers, grandmothers and aunts with a generous sprinkling of creativity. The rooms and suites, tastefully decorated in a variety of modern and classical styles, have accommodated many famous figures. Ideal for a good rest or an exploration of the vineyards of Prosecco.

Access: At Solighetto, drive for 2km towards Follina

VENETO

PONTE DI PIAVE (TV)

17

CÀ DE PIZZOL
Sigg. De Pizzol
Via Vittoria, 92
31047 Ponte di Piave (TV)
Tel. 04 22 85 32 30 – Fax 04 22 85 34 62
info@cadepizzol.com - www.cadepizzol.com

 50€

Open all year • 1 single rm, 4 double rm • Parking, gym, no dogs • Sale of cured meats and wine

 Menu €19/32

 The authenticity of the cuisine and the hospitality alike.

In the finest rural guesthouse traditions, this typical farmhouse is located right next to the home of its owners. It is surrounded by greenery and colourful flowers, beyond which are the vineyards responsible for stocking the cellars with Pinot Bianco, Pinot Grigio, Prosecco and Refosco, to name but a few. The five rustic style rooms are warm and welcoming, while the dining room, which takes up the entire ground floor, serves cuisine largely composed of home grown produce.

Access: Drive for 3km along the Piave-Oderzo road to Levada-Busco

VENETO

PONTE DI PIAVE (TV)

18

RECHSTEINER

 Sig. Von Stepski Doliwa
Via Montegrappa, 3 - Località San Nicolò
31047 Ponte di Piave (TV)
Tel. 04 22 80 71 28 – Fax 04 22 75 21 55
rechsteiner@rechsteiner.it – www.rechsteiner.it

 55-63€

Open all year • 1 single rm, 10 double rm • Half board €47-49 • Parking, small dogs welcome • Bicycles available, sale of wine, cured meat and grappa

 Menu €17/24

 The clean and tidy presentation of the establishment.

In keeping with the local style, this large and austere farmhouse has been restored to provide accommodation in the shape of ten rooms. Public areas are composed of the garden, and inside a lounge-cum-dining room with imposing open fireplace. The rooms are given a warm feel by their wooden floors and ceilings, and rustic style furnishings. The estate-produced wines are worth tasting.

Access: In San Nicolò, drive for 3.5km following the signs to Salgareda

VENETO

QUARTO D'ALTINO (VE)

19

VILLA ODINO
Sig. Pasini
Via Roma 146
30020 Quarto d'Altino (VE)
Tel. 04 22 82 31 17 – Fax 04 22 82 32 35
info@villaodino.it – www.villaodino.it

👤👤 **144-158€**

Closed 23 Dec-6 Jan • 1 single rm, 26 double rm, 3 suites • Parking, garden, swimming pool

 The lush green garden on the banks of the Sile.

Villa Odino, an elegant hotel in which you can still sense the tranquillity and refinement of former eras, stands on the right bank of the Sile on the doorstep of Venice in a century-old park. The residence of emissaries of the bishopric of Torcello and occasionally a place of refuge for the Venetian aristocracy, it was turned into a country home in the early 18C and has since managed to preserve its former charm whilst adding the comfort of modern conveniences. Sumptuous Venetian fabrics, marble floors and original coffered ceilings are some of the features you will find in the richly decorated guestrooms and public areas.

Access: Very close to the A4 motorway intersection

VENETO

SAN MARTINO BUON ALBERGO (VR)

20

MUSELLA

Sig.ra Raber
località Monte del Drago 1 a Ferrazzette
37036 San Martino Buon Albergo (VR)
Tel. 045 97 33 85 – Fax 04 58 95 62 87
paulo@musella.it – www.musella.it

👤👤 130€ ☕

Closed 15 Dec-15 Feb • 1 single rm, 9 double rm • Parking, swimming pool • Bicycles available, sale of oil and wine

The visit to the cellars followed by a tasting session of wine, cheese and bread.

In the heart of an immense park of countless streams, vineyards and farms, this establishment is set round a 16C courtyard where the cowsheds usd to be, while next door is a villa built in the following century. Today the stables have become a thriving agricultural estate and the farmers' homes a pleasant country guesthouse. Treat yourself to a romantic break and go for walks in the woods or discover ancient traditions. The rooms are all pleasant and decorated individually according to the countryside, seasons or floral scents.

Access: 2km from the centre in Ferrazzette, follow the signs to Monte del Drago

VENETO

SAN POLO DI PIAVE (TV)

21

LA LOCANDA GAMBRINUS
Fam. Zanotto
Via Roma, 20
31020 San Polo di Piave (TV)
Tel. 04 22 85 50 43 - Fax 04 22 85 50 44
lalocanda@gambrinus.it - www.gambrinus.it

90€

Closed 8-18 Aug • 2 single rm, 2 double rm • Half board €80 • Parking, no dogs

 Menu €38/48

 The villa's pink tower partially obscured by trees.

On sunny days, the contrast between the verdant lawn and the pink exterior of this house viewed through the foliage of its surrounding trees is particularly striking. Elegantly simple, its period feel has not been impaired by restoration. Named after flowers, the six rooms are well presented and each has its individual style, allowing guests to choose between the yellow tones of Sunflower and the gauzy drapery of Violet. Whatever the selection, atmosphere is guaranteed across the board.

Access: In the centre of the village

VENETO

SAPPADA (BL)

22

CRISTINA

Sig. Galler
Borgata Hoffe, 19
32047 Sappada (BL)
Tel. 04 35 46 94 30 – Fax 04 35 46 97 11
info@albergocristina.it – www.albergocristina.it

👤👤 **100€**

Closed 10 May-25 Jun and Oct-Nov • 10 double rm • Breakfast €9; half board €70-80 • Parking, no dogs

 Menu €23/38

 The woodwork of the upper floor, blending equally with winter snow and summer pasture.

This hotel's ten rooms occupy a former hay barn with a striking facade of plastered stone and wood, which in summer is further enhanced by the flowers bedecking its balconies. Inside there is a warm and welcoming alpine feel entirely in keeping with the exterior. Situated in a sunny and peaceful spot which will make any visitor's stay all the more memorable.

Access: In the heart of the valley, near the ski lifts

VENETO

SAPPADA (BL)

23

HAUS MICHAELA

Sig. Piller
Borgata Fontana, 40
32047 Sappada (BL)
Tel. 04 35 46 93 77 – Fax 043 56 61 31
info@hotelmichaela.com – www.hotelmichaela.com

70-110€

Closed 1 Apr- 19 May, Oct-Nov • 14 double rm, 4 suites • Breakfast €11; half board €60-93 • Parking, garden, swimming pool, gym, no dogs

 Menu €32/45

 The vast choice of facilities available.

One of the most comprehensive and appealing hotels in the area, this establishment remains very popular despite its location some distance away from the centre. Its strength lies in the wide variety of amenities it offers guests. In addition to the swimming pool, there is a solarium, fitness centre offering a sauna, spa bath and massage facilities, plus a well equipped gym where trained staff can help guests get back into shape. All this against a delightful backdrop of fir trees which cling to the rocky slopes of the mountains.

Access: Near the centre of the village, a short walk from the pine forest

VENETO

SUSEGANA (TV)

24

MASO DI VILLA

Sig.ra Barel
via Col di Guarda 15, località Collalto
31058 Susegana (TV)
Tel. 04 38 84 14 14 – Fax 04 38 98 17 42
info@masodivilla.it – www.masodivilla.it

120-160€

Open all year • 6 double rm • Parking, garden, dogs not admitted

 The carved wooden floral motifs on the headboards.

The outline of the hills of Treviso, romantic Provençal atmosphere and attention to detail, "arte povera" style furniture, multicoloured silks and satins, craftwork and antique objects picked up left, right and centre… The scene is set for this maso, in which the main protagonist is colour: ochre yellow in the sitting room, old pink in the hall and burgundy in the rooms in tribute to grapes and everything to do with wine. Breakfasts are equally ritualised with homemade desserts in which you will taste unusual combinations: rhubarb and strawberry, apples and roses, pomegranate, figs and nuts.

Access: 5km away in Collalto

VENETO

TORRI DI QUARTESOLO (VI)

25

LOCANDA LE GUIZZE

Sig. Passarin
Via Guizze, 1
36040 Torri di Quartesolo (VI)
Tel. 04 44 38 19 77 – Fax 04 44 38 19 92
info@leguizze.it – www.leguizze.it

65-110€

Open all year • 6 double rm • Half board €55-75 • Parking, garden, no dogs

 Menu €24/40

Rustic simplicity in the heart of the Veneto countryside.

Set in the midst of the Veneto plain, this brightly coloured farm is typical of rural buildings in this area with an asymmetrical sloping roof covering the central construction. It is not difficult to imagine it as it used to be, with livestock in the stables and peasants returning from tilling the fields. Although modern and functional, the interior is redolent of the rural setting and its attendant tranquillity. The same care lavished on restoring this establishment is evident in the kitchen, where the excellent local cuisine is prepared for guests to enjoy outside under the pavilion.

Access: In Lerino at the hamlet of Torri di Quartesolo take the road to the church of Alture

VENETO

TREVISO (TV)

IL CASCINALE
Sig. Dotto
Via Torre d'Orlando, 6/b
31100 Treviso (TV)
Tel. 04 22 40 22 03 – Fax 04 22 34 64 18
info@agriturismoilcascinale.it
www.agriturismoilcascinale.it

48-50€

Closed 7-18 Jan, 16 Aug-3 Sep • 2 single rm, 12 double rm • Breakfast €8 • Parking, garden, dogs not admitted in rooms • Bicycles available

Menu €21/25

The farmhouse garden with views of Treviso.

Not far from the banks of the river Sile, this establishment is composed of two recently restored buildings, their white facades contrasting with the verdant backdrop of the surrounding landscape. The spacious and modern rooms make for very comfortable accommodation, while parents of young children will be pleased to know that there is a play area. The hotel's pleasant pavilion is the ideal spot to while away the evenings, cooled by a gentle breeze blowing across the garden.

Access: On the outskirts near Sile

VENETO

TRISSINO (VI)

27

CÀ MASIERI

Sig.. Zarantonello
località Masieri 16
36070 Trissino (VI)
Tel. 04 45 96 21 00 – Fax 04 45 49 04 55
info@camasieri.com – www.camasieri.com

👤👤 **100-130€** ☕

Closed Feb • 2 single rm, 10 double rm • Parking, swimming pool

 Menu €38/53

 Enjoying the tranquillity as you collapse after a busy day of sightseeing.

The origins of the small town remain shrouded in mystery: according to some specialists, Trissino was the name of a tribe from Northern Italy, while others consider it be of German origins, linked to peasant activity after the year 1000. Whatever, the hillsides surrounding Vicence remain full of the stillness of a bygone era, particularly at Cà Masieri, whose understated welcoming interior will transport you back in time without however depriving you of modern comforts. Today the farm is home to comfortable guestrooms and the former manor house to three dining rooms, where guests are treated to creative dishes that vary with the seasons.

Access: Take Via Verona from the centre of Trissino

VENETO

VALEGGIO SUL MINCIO (VR)

28

FACCIOLI

Sig. Faccioli
Località Borghetto - Via Tiepolo, 8
37067 Valeggio sul Mincio (VR)
Tel. 04 56 37 06 05 – Fax 04 56 37 05 71
www.valeggio.com/faccioli

90-105€

Closed 6-16 Jan • 2 single rm, 12 double rm, 1 suite • Parking

The sloping wooden ceilings in some of the rooms.

Situated in the fertile countryside around Verona, on the border between the provinces of Mantova and Brescia, this village is also conveniently located for exploring the Lake Garda region. Its picturesque setting on the banks of the River Mincio gives the village a film-set appearance. The Albergo Faccioli is a typical country house, with its old stables and hay barn still standing. The rooms here are warm and comfortable, with rustic furniture, wooden ceilings and modern bathrooms. The reception rooms are not particularly large, but are attractively furnished with wicker furniture.

Access: In the town

VENETO

VENEZIA (VE)

29

CASA REZZONICO

Sig. Veronese
fondamenta Gherardini 2813, Dorsoduro
30123 Venezia (VE)
Tel. 04 12 77 06 53 – Fax 04 12 77 54 35
info@casarezzonico.it – www.casarezzonico.it

👤👤 **80-150€**

Open all year • 1 single rm, 5 double rm • Dogs not admitted

 Taking a break in the peaceful garden to read or chat with friends.

While "Cà Rezzonico" is a 17C palace home to a museum of 17C Venice, "Casa Rezzonico" is a small hotel in the historic town centre that is ideally located for explorations of the Venetian capital, its calli and historic palaces that have marked history. Decorated in an austere style with antique wood furniture, the inn offers spacious light rooms, some of which overlook the garden where breakfast is served in summertime.

Access: In the Dorsoduro neighbourhood opposite Santa Barbara canal

VENETO

VENEZIA (VE)

30

LOCANDA GAFFARO

Sig. Giangaspero
corte del Gallo 3589, Dorsoduro
30123 Venezia (VE)
Tel. 04 12 75 08 97 – Fax 04 12 75 03 75
info@gaffaro.com – www.locandagaffaro.com

 110-145€

Open all year • 2 single rm, 4 double rm • Dogs not admitted

 Waking in the heart of the town and breakfasting in the courtyard.

Heaven on earth for all those who have always dreamt of discovering the world's most romantic city and strolling along its campi and campielli. Ideally located opposite Corte del Gallo, this small inn is right in the heart of Venice. So lay back and admire the simple, light and modern rooms before you ask the owners for tips about how to live Venice as the Venetians do, and then set out with no further ado. The Bridge of Sighs, Piazza San Marco, the Galleria dell'Accademia, or a pause to study the history of Venetian art "live" at the famous Guggenheim collection created by Peggy Guggenheim from a wealth of works by contemporary masters: all await you!

Access: Very near to piazzale Roma, and not far from Tolentini church

VENETO

VITTORIO VENETO (TV)

ALICE-RELAIS NELLE VIGNE
Sig. Cosmo
via Giardino 94, località Carpesica
31029 Vittorio Veneto (TV)
Tel. 04 38 56 11 73 – Fax 04 38 92 07 54
info@alice-relais.com – www.alice-relais.com

👤👤 125-145€

Open all year • 10 double rm • Garden, dogs not admitted • Organised trips, sale of cheese and wine

The interior bathed in sunlight thanks to the southern aspect.

Welcome to "Alice" where the dreams and emotions of Lewis Carrol's young heroine come to life in a mixture of tranquil landscape and fantasy world. At daybreak, go for a walk along the rows of vines, which stretch as far as the eye can see, on the lookout for squirrels, hares or pheasants. This posthouse, of definite literary inspiration, is located in the buildings of an old farmhouse. The owner's passion for fairy stories and hospitality has transformed the barns, cowsheds and attics into a modern country guesthouse which is a happy blend of local tradition, modern comforts and Indian furniture; the rooms are named after the characters of the famous tale.

Access: Outside the village, behind the A27 motorway between Carpesica and Manzana

ACTIVITY BREAKS

Feel like getting away from it all? Ready for a change of scenery? Want to get into the countryside and work off some stress or extra pounds? The hotels and country guesthouses listed below offer at least one sporting activity (swimming, cycling, horse-riding, golf, tennis, gym, rambling, etc.).

ABRUZZO & MOLISE
Loreto Aprutino
Le Magnolie — 16

BASILICATA
Bernalda
Relais Masseria Cardillo — 26

CALABRIA
Morano Calabro
La Locanda del Parco — 39
Nocera Terinese
Vota — 41
Pianopoli
Le Carolee — 42
Torre Di Ruggiero
I Basiliani — 44

CAMPANIA
Agropoli
La Colombaia — 51
Ceraso
La Petrosa — 55
Fisciano
Barone Antonio Negri — 58
Massa Lubrense
Piccolo Paradiso — 63
Melizzano
Mesogheo — 64
Paestum
Seliano — 68
Perdifumo
La Mimosa — 69
Pozzuoli
Villa Giulia — 70

EMILIA-ROMAGNA
Castel D'Aiano
La Fenice — 85
Ferrara
Locanda della Luna — 91
Misano Adriatico
Locanda i Girasoli — 95
Ostellato
Villa Belfiore — 97

ACTIVITY BREAKS

Salsomaggiore Terme
Antica Torre — 102

Santarcangelo di Romagna
Locanda Antiche Macine — 103
Verrucchio Le case rosse — 107

FRIULI VENEZIA GIULIA
Dolegna Del Collio
Venica e Venica - Casa Vino e Vacanze — 113

Medea
Kogoj — 114

Santa Maria la Longa
Villa di Tissano — 116

LAZIO
Canino
Cerrosughero — 126
Civita Castellana Relais Falisco — 128

Grotte di Castro
Castello di Santa Cristina — 129

Orte
La Locanda della Chiocciola — 131

Picinisco
Villa il Noce — 132

Rieti
Park Hotel Villa Potenziani — 133

San Donato Val di Comino
Villa Grancassa — 137

Tarquinia
Pegaso Palace Hotel — 139

Velletri
Da Benito al Bosco — 141

LIGURIA
Cenova
Negro — 151

Imperia
Relais San Damian — 153

LOMBARDIA
Bascapé
Tenuta Camillo — 167

Cervesina
Il Castello di San Gaudenzio — 173

Cologne
Cappuccini — 174

Ganna
Villa Cesarina — 177

Gardone Riviera
Bellevue — 178

Gravedona
La Villa — 179

Iseo
Relais Mirabella — 180
Montorfano Santandrea Golf Hotel — 181

San Felice del Benaco
Bella Hotel e Leisure — 185

San Giovanni in Croce
Locanda Ca' Rossa — 186

Sirmione
Bolero — 188
Ideal — 189

Tremezzo
Villa Marie — 190

MARCHE
Macerata
Le Case — 202

Montelparo
La Ginestra — 205

ACTIVITY BREAKS

San Costanzo
Locanda la Breccia — 208

San Lorenzo In Campo
Giardino — 209

San Severino Marche
Locanda Salimbeni — 210

Senigallia
Antica Armonia — 211
L'Arca di Noè — 212
Bel Sit — 213
Locanda Strada della Marina — 214

Sirolo
Monteconero — 218

Treia
Il Casolare dei Segreti — 219

Urbino
Ca' Andreana — 221

PIEMONTE

Alba
Villa la Meridiana-Cascina Reine — 228

Antignano D'Asti
Locanda del Vallone — 229

Boves
La Bisalta Locanda del Re — 232

Canale
Villa Cornarea — 234

Carmagnola
Margherita — 239

Cellarengo
Cascina Papa Mora — 243

La Morra
Corte Gondina — 253

Magliano Alfieri
Cascina San Bernardo — 255

Novello
Il Noccioleto — 261

Penango
Relais il Borgo — 263
San Damiano d'Asti casa Buffetto — 265

Tigliole
Vittoria — 268

PUGLIA

Avetrana
Masseria Bosco — 288

Noci
Le Casedde — 294

Ostuni
Novecento — 295

Poggiorsini
Masseria il Cardinale — 296

SARDEGNA

Aggius
Il Muto di Gallura — 305

SICILIA

Caltagirone
Villa Tasca — 320

Carlentini
Tenuta di Roccadia — 321

Eolie (isole) Filicudi
La Canna — 323

Nicosia
Baglio San Pietro — 325

ACTIVITY BREAKS

Noto
Masseria degli Ulivi — 326

Piana degli Albanesi
Masseria Rossella — 328

Randazzo
L'Antica Vigna — 330

San Michele Di Ganzaria
Gigliotto — 331

Sciacca
Villa Palocla — 332

Siracusa
La Perciata — 337

Trapani
Baglio Fontanasalsa — 338

Ventimiglia di Sicilia
Crapa Licca — 339

TOSCANA

Barberino Val D'Elsa
La Torre di Ponzano — 348

Bibbiena
Relais il Fienile — 349

Campiglia D'Orcia
Casa Ranieri — 351

Capalbio
Ghiaccio Bosco — 352

Castellina In Chianti
Fattoria Tregole — 353
Salivolpi — 354

Castiglion Fiorentino
Casa Portagioia — 356

Chiusdino
Il Mulino delle Pile — 358

Corsignano
Fattoria di Corsignano — 362

Grosseto
Poggio degli Ulivi — 374

Lucca
La Cappella — 375
Villa Alessandra — 379
Villa Romantica — 380

Manciano
Galeazzi — 381
Le Pisanelle — 382
Poggio Tortollo — 383

Marciano della Chiana
Il Querciolo — 384

Montalcino
Il Poderuccio — 387

Monteriggioni
Borgo Gallinaio — 394

Monteroni d'Arbia
Casa Bolsinina — 395

Montevarchi
Relais la Ramugina-Fattoria di Rendola — 396

Montieri
La Meridiana-Locanda in Maremma — 397
Rifugio Prategiano — 398

Pergine Valdarno
Fattoria di Montelucci — 402

Pontremoli
Cà del Moro — 404
Costa d'Orsola — 405

Radda in Chianti
Castelvecchi — 406

Radicondoli
Fattoria Solaio — 409

ACTIVITY BREAKS

San Casciano in Val di Pesa
Salvadonica — 410

San Gimignano
Il Casale del Cotone — 411
Fattoria Poggio Alloro — 412
Podere Villuzza — 413
Il Rosolaccio — 414

Sansepolcro
Relais Palazzo di Luglio — 420

Sarteano
Le Anfore — 421

Saturnia
Villa Clodia — 422

Subbiano
Relais Torre Santa Flora — 427

Tavernelle Val di Pesa
Antica Pieve — 429

Volterra
Villa Rioddi — 434

TRENTINO ALTO ADIGE

Appiano Sulla Strada Del Vino
Ansitz Tschindlhof — 446
Bad Turmbach — 447
Schloss Aichberg — 448

Campo Di Trens
Bircher — 449
Carano Maso el giata — 452

Chiusa
Ansitz Fonteklaus — 453
Unterwirt — 454

Cimego
Aurora — 455

Dro
Maso Lizzone — 457

Lagundo
Plonerhof — 460

Merano
Sittnerhof — 461

Mules
Stafler — 462

Novacella
Ponte-Brückenwirt — 463

Racines
Sonklarhof — 466

Renon
Bemelmans Post — 467

Riva del Garda
Villa Miravalle — 468
Vigo di Fassa Olympic — 476

Vipiteno
Kranebitt — 478

UMBRIA

Assisi
Il Giardino dei Ciliegi — 485
Malvarina — 486

Bettona
Il Poggio degli Olivi — 487
Torre Burchio — 488

Bevagna
Poggio dei Pettirossi — 489

Calvi Dell'Umbria
Santa Brigida — 490

Cannara
La Fattoria del Gelso — 492

Castiglione Del Lago
Locanda Poggioleone — 493

Corciano
Locanda Solomeo — 494

ACTIVITY BREAKS

Ficulle
La Casella — 495

Foligno
Villa Roncalli — 496

Gubbio
Castello di Petroia — 497
Locanda del Gallo — 499

Magione
Bella Magione — 500

Monte Castello di Vibio
Fattoria di Vibio — 501

Montecchio
Poggio della Volara — 502

Montefalco
Camiano Piccolo — 503

Norcia
Casale nel Parco dei Monti Sibillini — 504

Orvieto
Borgo San Faustino — 505

Panicale
Villa Lemura — 506

Perugia
San Felicissimo — 507

Pietralunga
La Cerqua e la Balucca — 509

Spello
LaBastiglia — 510
Le Due Torri — 511

Terni
Locanda di Colle dell''Oro — 516

Titignano
Fattoria di Titignano — 517

Todi
Casale delle Lucrezie — 518

VALLE D'AOSTA

Valsavarenche
L'Hostellerie du Paradis — 531

VENETO

Mirano
Park Hotel Villa Giustinian — 552
Villa Patriarca — 553

Quarto d'Altino
Villa Odino — 557

San Martino Buon Albergo
Musella — 558

Sappada
Haus Michaela — 561

Trissino
Cà Masieri — 565

LOCAL PRODUCE BREAKS

The Country Guesthouses listed below offer tasting sessions where you can sample local wines, olive oils, jams, home-made pasta, pesto, sun-dried tomatoes and other delicacies. They also often sell regional produce from the local area.

ABRUZZO & MOLISE

Loreto Aprutino
Le Magnolie — 16

BASILICATA

Bernalda
Relais Masseria Cardillo — 26

Chiaromonte
Costa Casale — 27

Trivigno
La Foresteria di San Leo — 31

CALABRIA

Morano Calabro
La Locanda del Parco — 39

Nocera Terinese
Vota — 41

Pianopoli
Le Carolee — 42

Torre Di Ruggiero
I Basiliani — 44

CAMPANIA

Ceraso
La Petrosa — 55

Fisciano
Barone Antonio Negri — 58

Furore
Sant'Alfonso — 59

Ischia (Isola D')
Il Vitigno — 62

Melizzano
Mesogheo — 64

Paestum
Seliano — 68

Perdifumo
La Mimosa — 69

Ruviano
Le Olive di Nedda — 71

Vico Equense
La Ginestra — 73

EMILIA-ROMAGNA

Carpineti
Le Scuderie — 84

Castel D'Aiano
La Fenice — 85

LOCAL PRODUCE BREAKS

Castenaso
Il Loghetto — 87

Monghidoro
La Cartiera dei Benandanti — 96

Santarcangelo di Romagna
Locanda Antiche Macine — 103

Verucchio
Le Case Rosse — 107

FRIULI VENEZIA GIULIA

Dolegna Del Collio
Venica e Venica - Casa Vino e Vacanze — 113

Vivaro
Gelindo dei Magredi — 119

LAZIO

Canino
Cerrosughero — 126

LIGURIA

Castelnuovo Magra
La Valle — 150

Imperia
Relais San Damian — 153

Levanto
Villanova — 155

Santa Margherita Ligure
Roberto Gnocchi — 158

LOMBARDIA

Bascapé
Tenuta Camillo — 167

San Benedetto Po
Corte Medaglie d'Oro — 184

Valdidentro
Raethia — 192

MARCHE

Montefortino
Antico Mulino — 204

Urbino
Ca' Andreana — 221

PIEMONTE

Alba
Villa la Meridiana-Cascina Reine — 228

Barolo
La Terrazza sul Bosco — 231

Boves
La Bisalta Locanda del Re — 232

Canale
Villa Cornarea — 234

Canelli
La Casa in Collina — 235

Carmagnola
Margherita — 239

Cassine
Il Buonvicino — 240

Cellarengo
Cascina Papa Mora — 243
Cureggio La Capuccina — 247

Diano D'Alba
La Briccola — 248

La Morra
La Cascina del Monastero — 252

Novello
Il Noccioleto — 261

LOCAL PRODUCE BREAKS

Sinio
Le Arcate — 267

Trezzo Tinella
Antico Borgo del Riondino — 270
Casa Branzele — 271

PUGLIA

Alessano
Masseria Macurano — 285

Andria
Biomasseria Lama di Luna — 286

Avetrana
Masseria Bosco — 288

Fasano
Masseria Narducci — 289

Noci
Le Casedde — 294

Poggiorsini
Masseria il Cardinale — 296

SARDEGNA

Aggius
Il Muto di Gallura — 305

SICILIA

Carlentini
Tenuta di Roccadia — 321

Piana degli Albanesi
Masseria Rossella — 328

Randazzo
L'Antica Vigna — 330

Siracusa
La Perciata — 337

Trapani
Baglio Fontanasalsa — 338

TOSCANA

Campiglia D'Orcia
Casa Ranieri — 351

Capalbio
Ghiaccio Bosco — 352

Corsignano
Fattoria di Corsignano — 362

Manciano
Galeazzi — 381
Poggio Tortollo — 383

Marciano della Chiana
Il Querciolo — 384

Massa Marittima
Podere Riparbella — 385

Montalcino
Il Poderuccio — 387

Montieri
La Meridiana-Locanda in Maremma — 397

Pergine Valdarno
Fattoria di Montelucci — 402

Pontremoli
Costa d'Orsola — 405

Radda in Chianti
Castelvecchi — 406
Podere Terreno — 407

Radicondoli
Fattoria Solaio — 409

San Casciano in Val di Pesa
Salvadonica — 410

San Gimignano
Il Casale del Cotone — 411
Fattoria Poggio Alloro — 412
Podere Villuzza — 413

San Quirico D'Orcia
Il Rigo — 419

LOCAL PRODUCE BREAKS

Sarteano
Le Anfore — 421

Suvereto
Bulichella — 428

Vada
Villa Graziani — 430

TRENTINO ALTO ADIGE

Dro
Maso Lizzone — 457

Giovo
Maso Pomarolli — 459

Lagundo
Plonerhof — 460

Merano
Sittnerhof — 461

UMBRIA

Assisi
Malvarina — 486

Calvi Dell'Umbria
Santa Brigida — 490

Cannara
La Fattoria del Gelso — 492

Gubbio
Le Cinciallegre — 498

Monte Castello di Vibio
Fattoria di Vibio — 501

Montecchio
Poggio della Volara — 502

Montefalco
Camiano Piccolo — 503

Norcia
Casale nel Parco dei Monti Sibillini — 504

Orvieto
Borgo San Faustino — 505

Perugia
San Felicissimo — 507

Pietralunga
La Cerqua e la Balucca — 509

Spello
Le Due Torri — 511

Titignano
Fattoria di Titignano — 517

Todi
Casale delle Lucrezie — 518

VALLE D'AOSTA

Sarre
L'Arc en Ciel — 530

Verrayes
La Vrille — 532

VENETO

Caerano Di San Marco
Col delle Rane — 541

Longare
Le Vescovane — 549

Ponte Di Piave
Cà de Pizzol — 555
Rechsteiner — 556

San Martino Buon Albergo
Musella — 558

Vittorio Veneto
Alice-Relais nelle Vigne — 569

INDEX OF HOTELS AND B&B'S

ABRUZZO & MOLISE
Alba Adriatica
La Pergola —————— 14
Celano
Le Gole —————————— 15
Mosciano Sant'Angelo
Casale delle Arti ————— 17
Pescasseroli
Villa la Ruota ——————— 18
Termoli
Residenza Sveva —————— 19

BASILICATA
Barile
La Locanda del Palazzo —— 25
Matera
Locanda di San Martino —— 28
Sassi Hotel ———————— 29
Terranova Di Pollino
Picchio Nero ——————— 30

CALABRIA
Cirella
Ducale Villa Ruggeri ——— 37
Gerace
La Casa di Gianna ————— 38
Morano Calabro
Villa San Domenico ——— 40

CAMPANIA
Agropoli
La Colombaia ——————— 51
Bacoli
Villa Oteri ————————— 52
Castellabate
La Mola ————————— 53
Castelnuovo Cilento
La Palazzina ——————— 54
Dragoni
Villa de Pertis ——————— 56
Dugenta
Torre Gaia Wine Resort —— 57
Giffoni Sei Casali
Palazzo Pennasilico ——— 60
Ischia (Isola D')
Casa Sofia ————————— 61

INDEX OF HOTELS AND B&B'S

Massa Lubrense
Piccolo Paradiso — 63

Napoli
B&B L'Alloggio dei Vassalli — 65
Belle Arti Resort — 66
Il Convento — 67

Pozzuoli
Villa Giulia — 70

Sant'Agata de' Goti
Mustilli — 72

EMILIA-ROMAGNA

Albinea
Garden Viganò — 81

Busseto
I Due Foscari — 83

Ferrara
B&B Corte dei Gioghi — 88
Locanda Corte Arcangeli — 90
Locanda della Luna — 91

Finale Emilia
Casa Magagnoli — 92

Misano Adriatico
Locanda i Girasoli — 95

Ostellato
Villa Belfiore — 97

Pavullo Nel Frignano
Vandelli — 98

Portico Di Romagna
Al Vecchio Convento — 99

Reggio Nell'Emilia
Del Vescovado — 100

Reggiolo
Villa Montanarini — 101

Santarcangelo di Romagna
Il Villino — 104

Torriana
Il Povero Diavolo — 106

FRIULI VENEZIA GIULIA

Medea
Kogoj — 114

Muggia
Taverna Famiglia Cigui — 115

Santa Maria la Longa
Villa di Tissano — 116

Sauris
Schneider — 117

Tarvisio
Edelhof — 118

LAZIO

Bagnoregio
Romantica Pucci — 125

Casperia
La Torretta — 127

Civita Castellana
Relais Falisco — 128

Montefiascone
Urbano V — 130

Picinisco
Villa il Noce — 132

Rieti
Park Hotel Villa Potenziani — 133

Roma
Anne & Mary — 134
A Casa di Serena — 135
58 Le Real de Luxe — 136

INDEX OF HOTELS AND B&B'S

San Donato Val di Comino
Villa Grancassa — 137

Sermoneta
Principe Serrone — 138

Tarquinia
Pegaso Palace Hotel — 139

Tuscania
Locanda di Mirandolina — 140

Velletri
Da Benito al Bosco — 141

Veroli
Antico Palazzo Filonardi — 142

LIGURIA

Camogli
La Camogliese — 149

Cenova
Negro — 151

Finale Ligure
Rosita — 152

Levanto
Stella Maris — 154

Monterosso al Mare
Locanda il Maestrale — 156

Portovenere
Locanda Lorena — 157

LOMBARDIA

Argegno
Locanda Sant'Anna — 165

Ballabio
Sporting Club — 166

Bergamo
La Valletta Relais — 168

Briosco
LeAR — 169

Calolziocorte
Locanda del Mel — 170

Cantello
Madonnina — 171

Carnago
Villa Bregana — 172

Cervesina
Il Castello di San Gaudenzio — 173

Cologne
Cappuccini — 174

Gambara
Gambara — 176

Ganna
Villa Cesarina — 177

Gardone Riviera
Bellevue — 178

Gravedona
La Villa — 179

Iseo
Relais Mirabella — 180

Montorfano
Santandrea Golf Hotel — 181

Pozzolengo
Antica Locanda del Contrabbandiere — 182

San Felice del Benaco
Bella Hotel e Leisure — 185

San Giovanni in Croce
Locanda Ca' Rossa — 186

Sesto Calende
Locanda del Sole — 187

INDEX OF HOTELS AND B&B'S

Sirmione
Bolero — 188
Ideal — 189

Tremezzo
Villa Marie — 190

Tremosine
Villa Selene — 191

Valmadrera
Villa Giulia-Al Terrazzo — 193

MARCHE

Castelraimodo
Il Giardino degli Ulivi — 199

Fabriano
Villa Marchese del Grillo — 201

Macerata
Le Case — 202

Montecosaro
La Luma — 203

Montelparo
La Ginestra — 205

Pesaro
Locanda di Villa Torraccia — 206

San Benedetto del Tronto
Locanda di Porta Antica — 207

San Costanzo
Locanda la Breccia — 208

San Lorenzo In Campo
Giardino — 209

San Severino Marche
Locanda Salimbeni — 210

Senigallia
Antica Armonia — 211
L'Arca di Noè — 212
Bel Sit — 213
Locanda Strada della Marina — 214

Serrungarina
Casa Oliva — 215
Villa Federici — 216

Sirolo
Locanda Ristorante Rocco — 217
Monteconero — 218

Treia
Il Casolare dei Segreti — 219

PIEMONTE

Alagna Valsesia
Casa Prati — 227

Barolo
Ca' San Ponzio — 230

Bra
L'Ombra della Collina — 233

Cannero Riviera
Il Cortile — 236

Cannobio
Del Lago — 237
Pironi — 238

Castellinaldo
Il Borgo — 241

Cavour
Locanda la Posta — 242

Cisterna D'Asti
Garibaldi — 244

Cocconato
Locanda Martelletti — 245

Corneliano D'Alba
Antico Casale Mattei — 246

INDEX OF HOTELS AND B&B'S

Dronero
Cavallo Bianco — 249

Govone
Il Molino — 250

La Morra
Bricco dei Cogni — 251
Corte Gondina — 253
Villa Carita — 254

Mombello Monferrato
Ca' Dubini — 256

Moncalvo
Locanda del Melograno — 257

Monforte D'Alba
Le Case della Saracca — 258
Il Grillo Parlante — 259

Novello
B&B Abbazia il Roseto — 260

Orta San Giulio
La Contrada dei Monti — 262

Penango
Relais il Borgo — 263

Roddi
Cascina Toetto — 264

San Damiano d'Asti
Casa Buffetto — 265

San Giorgio Canavese
Foresteria del Castello — 266

Tigliole
Vittoria — 268

Tortona
Casa Cuniolo — 269

Usseaux
Lago del Laux — 272

Verbania
Aquadolce — 274

Verduno
Real Castello — 275

Vezza D'Alba
Di Vin Roero — 276

PUGLIA

Andria
Tenuta Cocevola — 287

Galatina
Palazzo Baldi — 290

Gravina in Puglia
Madonna della Stella — 291

Locorotondo
Sotto le Cummerse — 292

Maglie
Corte dei Francesi — 293

Ostuni
Novecento — 295

Taviano
A Casa tu Martinu — 297

Trani
San Paolo al Convento — 298

Uggiano La Chiesa
Masseria Gattamora — 299

SARDEGNA

Bosa
Sa Pischedda — 306

Calasetta
Bellavista — 307

Quartu Sant'Elena
Su Meriagu — 308

INDEX OF HOTELS AND B&B'S

San Pietro (Isola Di) - Carloforte
Hieracon — 309

Santu Lussurgiu
Antica Dimora del Gruccione — 310

SICILIA

Avola
Masseria sul Mare — 319

Caltagirone
Villa Tasca — 320

Catania
La Vecchia Palma — 322

Eolie (isole) Filicudi
La Canna — 323

Modica
Palazzo Failla — 324

Nicosia
Baglio San Pietro — 325

Noto
Masseria degli Ulivi — 326

Pettineo
Casa Migliaca — 327

Ragusa
Il Barocco — 329

Sciacca
Villa Palocla — 332

Scopello
Tranchina — 333

Siracusa
Dolce Casa — 334
Giuggiulena — 335
Gutkowski — 336

TOSCANA

Arezzo
Casa Volpi — 346
I Portici — 347

Barberino Val D'Elsa
La Torre di Ponzano — 348

Bibbiena
Relais il Fienile — 349

Borgo San Lorenzo
Casa Palmira — 350

Castellina In Chianti
Fattoria Tregole — 353
Salivolpi — 354
Villa Cristina — 355

Castiglion Fiorentino
Casa Portagioia — 356

Certaldo
Osteria del Vicario — 357

Chiusi
La Casa Toscana — 359

Civitella in Val di Chiana
L'Antico Borgo — 360

Corsignano
Casa Lucia — 361

Firenze
Antica Dimora Firenze — 363
Locanda di Firenze — 364
Residenza Apostoli — 365
Residenza Giulia — 366
Residenza Hannah e Johanna — 367
Residenza Johanna — 368
Tourist House Ghiberti — 369
Villa la Sosta — 370
Villino il Magnifico — 371

Fivizzano
Il Giardinetto — 372

INDEX OF HOTELS AND B&B'S

Gaiole In Chianti
Borgolecchi — 373

Lucca
La Cappella — 375
Alla Corte degli Angeli — 376
Alla Dimora Lucense — 377
La Romea — 378
Villa Alessandra — 379
Villa Romantica — 380

Manciano
Le Pisanelle — 382

Montaione
Vecchio Mulino — 386

Montecarlo
Antica Casa dei Rassicurati — 388
Antica Dimora Patrizia — 389
La Nina — 390

Montecatini Terme
Petit Château — 391
Villa le Magnolie — 392

Monteriggioni
Borgo Gallinaio — 394

Monteroni d'Arbia
Casa Bolsinina — 395

Montevarchi
Relais la Ramugina-Fattoria di Rendola — 396

Montieri
Rifugio Prategiano — 398

Montopoli in Val d'Arno
Quattro Gigli — 399

Pelago
Locanda Tinti — 401

Poggio Murella
Il Cantuccio — 403

Pontremoli
Cà del Moro — 404

San Giovanni D'Asso
La Locanda del Castello — 415
La Locanda di Montisi — 416

San Miniato
Villa Sonnino — 417

San Quirico D'Orcia
La Locanda del Loggiato — 418

Sansepolcro
Relais Palazzo di Luglio — 420

Saturnia
Villa Clodia — 422

Siena
Antica Residenza Cicogna — 423

Sorano
Della Fortezza — 424

Sovana
Pesna — 425

Subbiano
La Corte dell'Oca — 426
Relais Torre Santa Flora — 427

Tavernelle Val di Pesa
Antica Pieve — 429

Vagliagli
Casali dell'Aiola — 431

Villafranca In Lunigiana
Gavarini — 432

Vinci
Tassinaia — 433

Volterra
Villa Rioddi — 434

INDEX OF HOTELS AND B&B'S

TRENTINO ALTO ADIGE

Aldino
Krone — 441

Alta Badia
Alpenrose — 442
Ciasa Montanara — 443
La Ciasota — 444
Tamarindo — 445

Appiano Sulla Strada Del Vino
Ansitz Tschindlhof — 446
Bad Turmbach — 447
Schloss Aichberg — 448

Campo Di Trens
Bircher — 449

Canazei
Stella Alpina — 450
Al Viel — 451

Carano
Maso El Giata — 452

Chiusa
Ansitz Fonteklaus — 453
Unterwirt — 454

Cimego
Aurora — 455

Dimaro
Kaiserkrone — 456

Fiera di Primiero
Chalet Piereni — 458

Mules
Stafler — 462

Novacella
Ponte-Brückenwirt — 463

Pergine Valsugana
Castel Pergine — 464

Pozza Di Fassa
Antico Bagno — 465

Racines
Sonklarhof — 466

Renon
Bemelmans Post — 467

Riva del Garda
Villa Miravalle — 468

San Pellegrino (Passo Di)
Rifugio Fuciade — 469

Santa Cristina Valgardena
Geier — 470

Selva Di Valgardena
Villa Pra Ronch — 471

Spiazzo
Mezzosoldo — 472

Valfloriana
Fior di Bosco — 473

Vandoies
Tilia — 474

Vigo Di Fassa
Millefiori — 475
Olympic — 476

Villandro
Ansitz Zum Steinbock — 477

Vipiteno
Kranebitt — 478

UMBRIA

Bettona
Il Poggio degli Olivi — 487
Torre Burchio — 488

Bevagna
Poggio dei Pettirossi — 489

INDEX OF HOTELS AND B&B'S

Campello Sul Clitunno
Le Casaline — 491

Castiglione Del Lago
Locanda Poggioleone — 493

Corciano
Locanda Solomeo — 494

Ficulle
La Casella — 495

Foligno
Villa Roncalli — 496

Gubbio
Locanda del Gallo — 499

Magione
Bella Magione — 500

Panicale
Villa Lemura — 506

Piegaro
Ca' de Principi — 508

Spello
LaBastiglia — 510

Spoleto
Palazzo Dragoni — 513
San Sebastiano in Spoleto — 514

Stroncone
La Porta del Tempo — 515

Terni
Locanda di Colle dell'Oro — 516

Todi
San Lorenzo Tre — 519

Trevi
Trevi — 520

Vallo Di Nera
La Locanda di Cacio Re — 521

VALLE D'AOSTA

Champoluc
Le Vieux Rascard — 527

Cogne
La Barme — 528

Saint Pierre
La Meridiana Du Cadran Solaire — 529

Valsavarenche
L'Hostellerie du Paradis — 531

VENETO

Albaredo D'Adige
Locanda Arcimboldo — 539

Belluno
Nogherazza — 540

Carrè
Locanda La Corte dei Galli — 542

Castenuovo Del Garda
La Meridiana — 543

Cavaso Del Tomba
Locanda alla Posta — 544

Dolo
Villa Goetzen — 545

Follina
Dei Chiostri — 547
Villa Guarda — 548

Mestre
Ca' Nova — 550

Mira
Riviera dei Dogi — 551

Mirano
Park Hotel Villa Giustinian — 552

INDEX OF HOTELS AND B&B'S

Villa Patriarca — 553

Pieve di Soligo
Da Lino — 554

Quarto d'Altino
Villa Odino — 557

San Polo Di Piave
La Locanda Gambrinus — 559

Sappada
Cristina — 560
Haus Michaela — 561

Torri Di Quartesolo
Locanda le Guizze — 563

Treviso
Il Cascinale — 564

Trissino
Cà Masieri — 565

Valeggio Sul Mincio
Faccioli — 566

Venezia
Casa Rezzonico — 567
Locanda Gaffaro — 568

INDEX OF COUNTRY GUESTHOUSES

ABRUZZO & MOLISE

Agnone
Selvaggi — 13

Loreto Aprutino
Le Magnolie — 16

BASILICATA

Bernalda
Relais Masseria Cardillo — 26

Chiaromonte
Costa Casale — 27

Trivigno
La Foresteria di San Leo — 31

CALABRIA

Morano Calabro
La Locanda del Parco — 39

Nocera Terinese
Vota — 41

Pianopoli
Le Carolee — 42

Rossano Stazione
Trapesimi — 43

Torre Di Ruggiero
I Basiliani — 44

CAMPANIA

Ceraso
La Petrosa — 55

Fisciano
Barone Antonio Negri — 58

Furore
Sant'Alfonso — 59

Ischia (Isola D')
Il Vitigno — 62

Melizzano
Mesogheo — 64

Paestum
Seliano — 68

Perdifumo
La Mimosa — 69

Ruviano
Le Olive di Nedda — 71

Vico Equense
La Ginestra — 73

INDEX OF COUNTRY GUESTHOUSES

EMILIA-ROMAGNA

Besenzone
Le Colombaie — 82

Carpineti
Le Scuderie — 84

Castel D'Aiano
La Fenice — 85

Castelfranco Emilia
Villa Gaidello — 86

Castenaso
Il Loghetto — 87

Ferrara
Alla Cedrara — 89

Gazzola
Croara Vecchia — 93

Malalbergo
Il Cucco — 94

Monghidoro
La Cartiera dei Benandanti — 96

Salsomaggiore Terme
Antica Torre — 102

Santarcangelo di Romagna
Locanda Antiche Macine — 103

Terenzo
Selva Smeralda — 105

Verucchio
Le Case Rosse — 107

FRIULI VENEZIA GIULIA

Dolegna Del Collio
Venica e Venica - Casa Vino e Vacanze — 113

Vivaro
Gelindo dei Magredi — 119

LAZIO

Canino
Cerrosughero — 126

Grotte di Castro
Castello di Santa Cristina — 129

Orte
La Locanda della Chiocciola — 131

LIGURIA

Castelnuovo Magra
La Valle — 150

Imperia
Relais San Damian — 153

Levanto
Villanova — 155

Santa Margherita Ligure
Roberto Gnocchi — 158

LOMBARDIA

Bascapé
Tenuta Camillo — 167

Drizzona
L'Airone — 175

Salò
Fattoria il Bagnolo — 183

San Benedetto Po
Corte Medaglie d'Oro — 184

Valdidentro
Raethia — 192

MARCHE

Fabriano
Gocce di Camarzano — 200

Montefortino
Antico Mulino — 204

INDEX OF COUNTRY GUESTHOUSES

Urbania
Mulino della Ricavata — 220

Urbino
Ca' Andreana — 221

PIEMONTE

Alba
Villa la Meridiana-Cascina Reine — 228
Antignano d'Asti Locanda del Vallone — 229

Barolo
La Terrazza sul Bosco — 231

Boves
La Bisalta Locanda del Re — 232

Canale
Villa Cornarea — 234

Canelli
La Casa in Collina — 235

Carmagnola
Margherita — 239

Cassine
Il Buonvicino — 240

Cellarengo
Cascina Papa Mora — 243

Cureggio
La Capuccina — 247

Diano D'Alba
La Briccola — 248

La Morra
La Cascina del Monastero — 252

Magliano Alfieri
Cascina San Bernardo — 255

Novello
Il Nocciloeto — 261

Sinio
Le Arcate — 267

Trezzo Tinella
Antico Borgo del Riondino — 270
Casa Branzele — 271

Verbania
Il Monterosso — 273

PUGLIA

Alessano
Masseria Macurano — 285

Andria
Biomasseria Lama di Luna — 286

Avetrana
Masseria Bosco — 288

Fasano
Masseria Narducci — 289

Noci
Le Casedde — 294

Poggiorsini
Masseria il Cardinale — 296

SARDEGNA

Aggius
Il Muto di Gallura — 305

Stintino
Depalmas Pietro — 311

SICILIA

Carlentini
Tenuta di Roccadia — 321

Piana degli Albanesi
Masseria Rossella — 328

Randazzo
L'Antica Vigna — 330

INDEX OF COUNTRY GUESTHOUSES

San Michele Di Ganzaria
Gigliotto — 331

Siracusa
La Perciata — 337

Trapani
Baglio Fontanasalsa — 338

Ventimiglia di Sicilia
Crapa Licca — 339

TOSCANA

Arcidosso
Rondinelli — 345

Campiglia D'Orcia
Casa Ranieri — 351

Capalbio
Ghiaccio Bosco — 352

Chiusdino
Il Mulino delle Pile — 358

Corsignano
Fattoria di Corsignano — 362

Grosseto
Poggio degli Ulivi — 374

Manciano
Galeazzi — 381
Poggio Tortollo — 383

Marciano della Chiana
Il Querciolo — 384

Massa Marittima
Podere Riparbella — 385

Montalcino
Il Poderuccio — 387

Montemerano
Le Fontanelle — 393

Montieri
La Meridiana-Locanda in Maremma — 397

Palazzuolo Sul Senio
Le Panare — 400

Pergine Valdarno
Fattoria di Montelucci — 402

Pontremoli
Costa d'Orsola — 405

Radda in Chianti
Castelvecchi — 406
Podere Terreno — 407

Radicondoli
Fattoria Solaio — 409

San Casciano in Val di Pesa
Salvadonica — 410

San Gimignano
Il Casale del Cotone — 411
Fattoria Poggio Alloro — 412
Podere Villuzza — 413
Il Rosolaccio — 414

San Quirico D'Orcia
Il Rigo — 419

Sarteano
Le Anfore — 421

Suvereto
Bulichella — 428

Vada
Villa Graziani — 430

TRENTINO ALTO ADIGE

Dro
Maso Lizzone — 457

INDEX OF COUNTRY GUESTHOUSES

Giovo
Maso Pomarolli — 459

Lagundo
Plonerhof — 460

Merano
Sittnerhof — 461

UMBRIA

Assisi
Il Giardino dei Ciliegi — 485
Malvarina — 486

Calvi Dell'Umbria
Santa Brigida — 490

Cannara
La Fattoria del Gelso — 492

Gubbio
Castello di Petroia — 497
Le Cinciallegre — 498

Monte Castello di Vibio
Fattoria di Vibio — 501

Montecchio
Poggio della Volara — 502

Montefalco
Camiano Piccolo — 503

Norcia
Casale nel Parco dei Monti Sibillini — 504

Orvieto
Borgo San Faustino — 505

Perugia
San Felicissimo — 507

Pietralunga
La Cerqua e la Balucca — 509

Spello
Le Due Torri — 511

Spoleto
Convento di Agghielli — 512

Titignano
Fattoria di Titignano — 517

Todi
Casale delle Lucrezie — 518

VALLE D'AOSTA

Sarre
L'Arc en Ciel — 530

Verrayes
La Vrille — 532

VENETO

Caerano Di San Marco
Col delle Rane — 541

Fara Vicentino
Le Colline dell'Uva — 546

Longare
Le Vescovane — 549

Ponte Di Piave
Cà de Pizzol — 555
Rechsteiner — 556

San Martino Buon Albergo
Musella — 558

Susegana
Maso di Villa — 562

Vittorio Veneto
Alice-Relais nelle Vigne — 569

ESTABLISHMENTS WITH DINING FACILITIES

ABRUZZO & MOLISE

AGNONE (IS)
SELVAGGI — 13

CELANO (AQ)
LE GOLE — 15

LORETO APRUTINO (PE)
LE MAGNOLIE — 16

MOSCIANO SANT'ANGELO (TE)
CASALE DELLE ARTI — 17

BASILICATA

BARILE (PZ)
LA LOCANDA DEL PALAZZO — 25

BERNALDA (MT)
RELAIS MASSERIA CARDILLO — 26

CHIAROMONTE (PZ)
COSTA CASALE — 27

TERRANOVA DI POLLINO (PZ)
PICCHIO NERO — 30

TRIVIGNO (PZ)
LA FORESTERIA DI SAN LEO — 31

CALABRIA

CIRELLA (CS)
DUCALE VILLA RUGGERI — 37

GERACE (RC)
LA CASA DI GIANNA — 38

MORANO CALABRO (CS)
LA LOCANDA DEL PARCO — 39
VILLA SAN DOMENICO — 40

NOCERA TERINESE (CZ)
VOTA — 41

PIANOPOLI (CZ)
LE CAROLEE — 42

ROSSANO STAZIONE (CS)
TRAPESIMI — 43

TORRE DI RUGGIERO (CZ)
I BASILIANI — 44

CAMPANIA

AGROPOLI (SA)
LA COLOMBAIA — 51

BACOLI (NA)
VILLA OTERI — 52

ESTABLISHMENTS WITH DINING FACILITIES

CASTELLABATE (SA)
LA MOLA — 53

CASTELNUOVO CILENTO (SA)
LA PALAZZINA — 54

CERASO (SA)
LA PETROSA — 55

DRAGONI (CE)
VILLA DE PERTIS — 56

DUGENTA (BN)
TORRE GAIA WINE RESORT — 57

FISCIANO (SA)
BARONE ANTONIO NEGRI — 58

FURORE (SA)
SANT'ALFONSO — 59

ISCHIA (ISOLA D') (NA)
IL VITIGNO — 62

MASSA LUBRENSE (NA)
PICCOLO PARADISO — 63

MELIZZANO (BN)
MESOGHEO — 64

PAESTUM (SA)
SELIANO — 68

PERDIFUMO (SA)
LA MIMOSA — 69

POZZUOLI (NA)
VILLA GIULIA — 70

RUVIANO (CE)
LE OLIVE DI NEDDA — 71

SANT'AGATA DE' GOTI (BN)
MUSTILLI — 72

VICO EQUENSE (NA)
LA GINESTRA — 73

EMILIA-ROMAGNA

BUSSETO (PR)
I DUE FOSCARI — 83

CARPINETI (RE)
LE SCUDERIE — 84

CASTEL D'AIANO (BO)
LA FENICE — 85

CASTELFRANCO EMILIA (MO)
VILLA GAIDELLO — 86

CASTENASO (BO)
IL LOGHETTO — 87

FERRARA (FE)
LOCANDA CORTE ARCANGELI — 90

MALABERGO (BO)
IL CUCCO — 94

MISANO ADRIATICO (RN)
LOCANDA I GIRASOLI — 95

MONGHIDORO (BO)
LA CARTIERA DEI BENANDANTI — 96

OSTELLATO (FE)
VILLA BELFIORE — 97

PAVULLO NEL FRIGNANO (MO)
VANDELLI — 98

PORTICO DI ROMAGNA (FC)
AL VECCHIO CONVENTO — 99

REGGIOLO (RE)
VILLA MONTANARINI — 101

SALSOMAGGIORE (PR)
ANTICA TORRE — 102

SANTARCANGELO DI ROMAGNA (RN)
LOCANDA ANTICHE MACINE — 103

ESTABLISHMENTS WITH DINING FACILITIES

TERENZO (PR)
SELVA SMERALDA — 105

TORRIANA (RN)
IL POVERO DIAVOLO — 106

FRIULI VENEZIA GIULIA

MUGGIA (TS)
TAVERNA FAMIGLIA CIGUI — 115

SANTA MARIA LA LONGA (UD)
VILLA DI TISSANO — 116

SAURIS (UD)
SCHNEIDER — 117

TARVISIO (UD)
EDELHOF — 118

VIVARO (PN)
GELINDO DEI MAGREDI — 119

LAZIO

BAGNOREGIO (VT)
ROMANTICA PUCCI — 125

CANINO (VT)
CERROSUGHERO — 126

CIVITA CASTELLANA (VT)
RELAIS FALISCO — 128

ORTE (VT)
LA LOCANDA DELLA CHIOCCIOLA — 131

RIETI (RI)
PARK HOTEL VILLA POTENZIANI — 133

SAN DONATO VAL DI COMINO (FR)
VILLA GRANCASSA — 137

TARQUINIA (VT)
PEGASO PALACE HOTEL — 139

TUSCANIA (VT)
LOCANDA DI MIRANDOLINA — 140

VELLETRI (RM)
DA BENITO AL BOSCO — 141

VEROLI (FR)
ANTICO PALAZZO FILONARDI — 142

LIGURIA

CASTELNUOVO MAGRA (SP)
LA VALLE — 150

CENOVA (IM)
NEGRO — 151

FINALE LIGURE (SV)
ROSITA — 152

LEVANTO (SP)
STELLA MARIS — 154

PORTOVENERE (SP)
LOCANDA LORENA — 157

SANTA MARGHERITA LIGURE (GE)
ROBERTO GNOCCHI — 158

LOMBARDIA

ARGEGNO (CO)
LOCANDA SANT'ANNA — 165

BALLABIO (LC)
SPORTING CLUB — 166

BASCAPÉ (PV)
TENUTA CAMILLO — 167

BRIOSCO (MI)
LEAR — 169

CANTELLO (VA)
MADONNINA — 171

ESTABLISHMENTS WITH DINING FACILITIES

CARNAGO (VA)
VILLA BREGANA — 172

CERVESINA (PV)
IL CASTELLO DI SAN GAUDENZIO — 173

COLOGNE (BS)
CAPPUCCINI — 174

DRIZZONA (CR)
L'AIRONE — 175

GANNA (VA)
VILLA CESARINA — 177

GARDONE RIVIERA (BS)
BELLEVUE — 178

GRAVEDONA (CO)
LA VILLA — 179

ISEO (BS)
RELAIS MIRABELLA — 180

MONTORFANO (CO)
SANTANDREA GOLF HOTEL — 181

POZZOLENGO (BS)
ANTICA LOCANDA DEL CONTRABBANDIERE — 182

SALO' (BS)
FATTORIA IL BAGNOLO — 183

SAN FELICE DEL BENACO (BS)
BELLA HOTEL E LEISURE — 185

SAN GIOVANNI IN CROCE (CR)
LOCANDA CA' ROSSA — 186

SESTO CALENDE (VA)
LOCANDA DEL SOLE — 187

SIRMIONE (BS)
IDEAL — 189

VALDIDENTRO (SO)
RAETHIA — 192

VALMADRERA (LC)
VILLA GIULIA-AL TERRAZZO — 193

MARCHE

CASTELRAIMONDO (MC)
IL GIARDINO DEGLI ULIVI — 199

FABRIANO (AN)
VILLA MARCHESE DEL GRILLO — 201

MACERATA (MC)
LE CASE — 202

MONTECOSARO (MC)
LA LUMA — 203

MONTEFORTINO (AP)
ANTICO MULINO — 204

MONTELPARO (AP)
LA GINESTRA — 205

SAN LORENZO IN CAMPO (PU)
GIARDINO — 209

SAN SEVERINO MARCHE (MC)
LOCANDA SALIMBENI — 210

SENIGALLIA (AN)
ANTICA ARMONIA — 211
L'ARCA DI NOÈ — 212
BEL SIT — 213
LOCANDA STRADA DELLA MARINA — 214

SERRUNGARINA (PU)
CASA OLIVA — 215
VILLA FEDERICI — 216

SIROLO (AN)
LOCANDA RISTORANTE ROCCO — 217
MONTECONERO — 218

TREIA (MC)
IL CASOLARE DEI SEGRETI — 219

ESTABLISHMENTS WITH DINING FACILITIES

URBANIA (PU)
MULINO DELLA RICAVATA — 220

URBINO (PU)
CA' ANDREANA — 221

PIEMONTE

BOVES (CN)
LA BISALTA LOCANDA DEL RE — 232

CANNERO RIVIERA (VB)
IL CORTILE — 236

CANNOBIO (VB)
DEL LAGO — 237

CARMAGNOLA (TO)
MARGHERITA — 239

CASSINE (AL)
IL BUONVICINO — 240

CAVOUR (TO)
LOCANDA LA POSTA — 242

CELLARENGO (AT)
CASCINA PAPA MORA — 243

CISTERNA D'ASTI (AT)
GARIBALDI — 244

COCCONATO (AT)
LOCANDA MARTELLETTI — 245

CUREGGIO (NO)
LA CAPUCCINA — 247

DIANO D'ALBA (CN)
LA BRICCOLA — 248

DRONERO (CN)
CAVALLO BIANCO — 249

NOVELLO (CN)
IL NOCCIOLETO — 261

PENANGO (AT)
RELAIS IL BORGO — 263

SINIO (CN)
LE ARCATE — 267

TIGLIOLE (AT)
VITTORIA — 268

TREZZO TINELLA (CN)
ANTICO BORGO DEL RIONDINO — 270

USSEAUX (TO)
LAGO DEL LAUX — 272

VERBANIA (VB)
IL MONTEROSSO — 273

VERDUNO (CN)
REAL CASTELLO — 275

VEZZA D'ALBA (CN)
DI VIN ROERO — 276

PUGLIA

ALESSANO (LE)
MASSERIA MACURANO — 285

ANDRIA (BA)
TENUTA COCEVOLA — 287

AVETRANA (TA)
MASSERIA BOSCO — 288

FASANO (BR)
MASSERIA NARDUCCI — 289

GRAVINA IN PUGLIA (BA)
MADONNA DELLA STELLA — 291

NOCI (BA)
LE CASEDDE — 294

OSTUNI (BR)
NOVECENTO — 295

POGGIORSINI (BA)
MASSERIA IL CARDINALE — 296

TAVIANO (LE)
A CASA TU MARTINU — 297

ESTABLISHMENTS WITH DINING FACILITIES

TRANI (BA)
SAN PAOLO AL CONVENTO — 298

UGGIANO LA CHIESA (LE)
MASSERIA GATTAMORA — 299

SARDEGNA

AGGIUS (SS)
IL MUTO DI GALLURA — 305

BOSA (NU)
SA PISCHEDDA — 306

CALASETTA (CA)
BELLAVISTA — 307

QUARTU SANT'ELENA (CA)
SU MERIAGU — 308

SAN PIETRO (ISOLA DI) - CARLOFORTE (CA)
HIERACON — 309

SANTU LUSSURGIU (OR)
ANTICA DIMORA DEL GRUCCIONE — 310

STINTINO (SS)
DEPALMAS PIETRO — 311

SICILIA

AVOLA (SR)
MASSERIA SUL MARE — 319

CALTAGIRONE (CT)
VILLA TASCA — 320

CARLENTINI (SR)
TENUTA DI ROCCADIA — 321

EOLIE (Isole) Filicudi (ME)
LA CANNA — 323

MODICA (RG)
PALAZZO FAILLA — 324

NICOSIA (EN)
BAGLIO SAN PIETRO — 325

NOTO (SR)
MASSERIA DEGLI ULIVI — 326

PETTINEO (ME)
CASA MIGLIACA — 327

PIANA DEGLI ALBANESI (PA)
MASSERIA ROSSELLA — 328

RAGUSA (RG)
IL BAROCCO — 329

RANDAZZO (CT)
L'ANTICA VIGNA — 330

SAN MICHELE DI GANZARIA (CT)
GIGLIOTTO — 331

SCIACCA (AG)
VILLA PALOCLA — 332

SCOPELLO (TP)
TRANCHINA — 333

SIRACUSA (SR)
LA PERCIATA — 337

TRAPANI (TP)
BAGLIO FONTANASALSA — 338

VENTIMIGLIA DI SICILIA (PA)
CRAPA LICCA — 339

TOSCANA

ARCIDOSSO (GR)
RONDINELLI — 345

AREZZO (AR)
CASA VOLPI — 346

CAMPIGLIA D'ORCIA (SI)
CASA RANIERI — 351

ESTABLISHMENTS WITH DINING FACILITIES

CERTALDO (FI)
OSTERIA DEL VICARIO — 357

CHIUSDINO (SI)
IL MULINO DELLE PILE — 358

CORSIGNANO (SI)
FATTORIA DI CORSIGNANO — 362

FIVIZZANO (MS)
IL GIARDINETTO — 372

MANCIANO (LU)
LE PISANELLE — 382

MASSA MARITTIMA (GR)
PODERE RIPARBELLA — 385

MONTECARLO (LU)
ANTICA DIMORA PATRIZIA — 389
LA NINA — 390

MONTEMERANO (GR)
LE FONTANELLE — 393

MONTERIGGIONI (SI)
BORGO GALLINAIO — 394

MONTERONI D''ARBIA (SI)
CASA BOLSININA — 395

MONTEVARCHI (AR)
RELAIS LA RAMUGINA-FATTORIA DI RENDOLA — 396

MONTIERI (SP)
LA MERIDIANA-LOCANDA IN MAREMMA — 397

MONTIERI (GR)
RIFUGIO PRATEGIANO — 398

MONTOPOLI IN VAL D'ARNO (PI)
QUATTRO GIGLI — 399

PALAZZUOLO SUL SENIO (FI)
LE PANARE — 400

PERGINE VALDARNO (AR)
FATTORIA DI MONTELUCCI — 402

PONTREMOLI (MS)
CÀ DEL MORO — 404
COSTA D'ORSOLA — 405

RADDA IN CHIANTI (SI)
CASTELVECCHI — 406
PODERE TERRENO — 407

RADICONDOLI (SI)
FATTORIA SOLAIO — 409

SAN GIMIGNANO (SI)
IL CASALE DEL COTONE — 411
FATTORIA POGGIO ALLORO — 412
IL ROSOLACCIO — 414

SAN GIOVANNI D'ASSO (SI)
LA LOCANDA DEL CASTELLO — 415
LA LOCANDA DI MONTISI — 416

SAN MINIATO (PI)
VILLA SONNINO — 417

SAN QUIRICO D'ORCIA (SI)
IL RIGO — 419

SANSEPOLCRO (AR)
RELAIS PALAZZO DI LUGLIO — 420

SARTEANO (SI)
LE ANFORE — 421

SUBBIANO (AR)
LA CORTE DELL'OCA — 426
RELAIS TORRE SANTA FLORA — 427

SUVERETO (LI)
BULICHELLA — 428

TAVARNELLE VAL DI PESA (FI)
ANTICA PIEVE — 429

VADA (LI)
VILLA GRAZIANI — 430

ESTABLISHMENTS WITH DINING FACILITIES

VILLAFRANCA IN LUNIGIANA (MS)
GAVARINI — 432

TRENTINO ALTO ADIGE

ALDINO (BZ)
KRONE — 441

APPIANO SULLA STRADA DEL VINO (BZ)
ANSITZ TSCHINDLHOF — 446
BAD TURMBACH — 447

CAMPO DI TRENS (BZ)
BIRCHER — 449

CHIUSA (BZ)
ANSITZ FONTEKLAUS — 453
UNTERWIRT — 454

CIMEGO (TN)
AURORA — 455

FIERA DI PRIMIERO (TN)
CHALET PIERENI — 458

GIOVO (TN)
MASO POMAROLLI — 459

MULES (BZ)
STAFLER — 462

NOVACELLA (BZ)
PONTE-BRÜCKENWIRT — 463

PERGINE VALSUGANA (TN)
CASTEL PERGINE — 464

POZZA DI FASSA (TN)
ANTICO BAGNO — 465

RACINES (BZ)
SONKLARHOF — 466

RENON (BZ)
BEMELMANS POST — 467

RIVA DEL GARDA (TN)
VILLA MIRAVALLE — 468

SAN PELLEGRINO (PASSO DI) (TN)
RIFUGIO FUCIADE — 469

SPIAZZO (TN)
MEZZOSOLDO — 472

VALFLORIANA (TN)
FIOR DI BOSCO — 473

VANDOIES (BZ)
TILIA — 474

VIGO DI FASSA (TN)
MILLEFIORI — 475
OLYMPIC — 476

VILLANDRO (BZ)
ANSITZ ZUM STEINBOCK — 477

VIPITENO (BZ)
KRANEBITT — 478

UMBRIA

ASSISI (PG)
IL GIARDINO DEI CILIEGI — 485
MALVARINA — 486

BETTONA (PG)
IL POGGIO DEGLI OLIVI — 487
TORRE BURCHIO — 488

BEVAGNA (PG)
POGGIO DEI PETTIROSSI — 489

CALVI DELL'UMBRIA (TR)
SANTA BRIGIDA — 490

CAMPELLO SUL CLITUNNO (PG)
LE CASALINE — 491

ESTABLISHMENTS WITH DINING FACILITIES

CANNARA (PG)
LA FATTORIA DEL GELSO — 492

CASTIGLIONE DEL LAGO (PG)
LOCANDA POGGIOLEONE — 493

CORCIANO (PG)
LOCANDA SOLOMEO — 494

FICULLE (TR)
LA CASELLA — 495

FOLIGNO (PG)
VILLA RONCALLI — 496

GUBBIO (PG)
CASTELLO DI PETROIA — 497
LE CINCIALLEGRE — 498
LOCANDA DEL GALLO — 499

MONTE CASTELLO DI VIBIO (PG)
FATTORIA DI VIBIO — 501

MONTECCHIO (TR)
POGGIO DELLA VOLARA — 502

MONTEFALCO (PG)
CAMIANO PICCOLO — 503

NORCIA (PG)
CASALE NEL PARCO DEI MONTI SIBILLINI — 504

ORVIETO (TR)
BORGO SAN FAUSTINO — 505

PIETRALUNGA (PG)
LA CERQUA E LA BALUCCA — 509

SPELLO (PG)
LABASTIGLIA — 510
LE DUE TORRI — 511

SPOLETO (PG)
CONVENTO DI AGGHIELLI — 512
SAN SEBASTIANO IN SPOLETO — 514

TITIGNANO (TN)
FATTORIA DI TITIGNANO — 517

TODI (PG)
CASALE DELLE LUCREZIE — 518

VALLO DI NERA (PG)
LA LOCANDA DI CACIO RE — 521

VALLE D'AOSTA

COGNE (AO)
LA BARME — 528

SAINT PIERRE (AO)
LA MERIDIANA DU CADRAN SOLAIRE — 529

SARRE (AO)
L'ARC EN CIEL — 530

VALSAVARENCHE (AO)
L'HOSTELLERIE DU PARADIS — 531

VERRAYES (AO)
LA VRILLE — 532

VENETO

ALBAREDO D'ADIGE (VR)
LOCANDA ARCIMBOLDO — 539

BELLUNO (BL)
NOGHERAZZA — 540

CASTELNUOVO DEL GARDA (VR)
LA MERIDIANA — 543

CAVASO DEL TOMBA (TV)
LOCANDA ALLA POSTA — 544

DOLO (VE)
VILLA GOETZEN — 545

FARA VICENTINO (VI)
LE COLLINE DELL'UVA — 546

ESTABLISHMENTS WITH DINING FACILITIES

LONGARE (VI)
LE VESCOVANE — 549

PIEVE DI SOLIGO (TV)
DA LINO — 554

PONTE DI PIAVE (TV)
CÀ DE PIZZOL — 555
RECHSTEINER — 556

SAN POLO DI PIAVE (TV)
LA LOCANDA GAMBRINUS — 559

SAPPADA (BL)
CRISTINA — 560
HAUS MICHAELA — 561

TORRI DI QUARTESOLO (VI)
LOCANDA LE GUIZZE — 563

TREVISO (TV)
IL CASCINALE — 564

TRISSINO (VI)
CÀ MASIERI — 565

PHOTO CREDITS

Manufacture Française des Pneumatiques Michelin
Société en commandite par actions au capital de 304 000 000 EUR
Place des Carmes-Déchaux, 63 Clermont-Ferrand (France) - R.C.S. Clermont-Fd B 855 200 507
© Michelin, Propriétaires-Editeurs - Dépôt légal Février 2007

No part of this publication may be reproduced in any form without the prior permission of the publisher.

Printed in Italy 01-2007/3.1

Typesetting: Maury imprimeur, Malesherbes
Printing and Binding: La Tipografica Varese, Varese

Layout: Studio Maogani
Layout adaptation: Studio Bib

Cover layout: Laurent Muller
Cover-Layout adaptation, illustrations and colours: Christelle Le Déan/Domestiestudio

Photos of country guesthouses, hotels and the regions
Project manager – Production photos Alain LEPRINCE
SARL Leprince & Pourrias agence
25 alllée de la Chardonnière
91280 St Pierre du Perray
Tél/Fax 01 64 85 08 36
We would like to thank the guesthouses and hotels who granted us their authorisation to use their photo free of charge.

Cover: G. Bouchet/PHOTONONSTOP
    Graphic project, editor and regional introduction layout: Rubber Band
    Photographs of culinary specialities: Rubber Band
    Data collection: Rubber Band
    C. so Quintino Sella, 102 - 10132 Torino - Tél. (39) 011.813.26.46

Published in 2007

YOUR OPINION MATTERS!

To help us constantly improve this guide, please fill in this questionnaire and return to:

Michelin "Hotels & Country Guesthouses in Italy 2007",
Michelin Travel Publications,
Hannay House, 39 Clarendon Road, Watford, WD17 1JA, UK

› 1. You are a:

Man .... ❏   Woman .... ❏

< 25 years old .... ❏   25-34 years old .... ❏

35-50 years old............. ❏   > 50 years............. ❏

Student .... ❏

Farmer, Worker in primary industry .... ❏

Technical/Administrative worker .... ❏

Service worker, Craftsman,
Owner of small business .... ❏

Retired .... ❏

Manual worker .... ❏

Manager/executive, Professional .... ❏

Unemployed .... ❏

› 2. How often do you use the Internet to look for information on hotels and restaurants?

Never .... ❏

Occasionally (once a month) .... ❏

Regularly (once a week) .... ❏

Very frequently (more than once a week) .... ❏

› 3. Have you ever bought other Michelin guides?

Yes .... ❏   No .... ❏

› 4. If yes, which one(s)?

The Michelin Guide Italia .... ❏

Other Michelin Guides (please specify titles) ... ❏
....

The Green Guide (please specify titles) .... ❏
....

Other (please specify titles) .... ❏
....

› 5. If you buy the Michelin Guide Italia, how often do you buy it?

Every year .... ❏

Every 2 years .... ❏

Every 3 years .... ❏

Every 4 years or more .... ❏

› 6. How do you rate the different elements of this guide?

1. Very Good   2. Good   3. Average   4. Poor   5. Very Poor

	1	2	3	4	5
Selection of establishments	❏	❏	❏	❏	❏
Number of establishments	❏	❏	❏	❏	❏
Hotel/country guesthouse mix	❏	❏	❏	❏	❏
Geographical spread of establishments	❏	❏	❏	❏	❏
Prices of rooms	❏	❏	❏	❏	❏
Practical information (prices, activities)	❏	❏	❏	❏	❏
Photos	❏	❏	❏	❏	❏
Description of the establishlment	❏	❏	❏	❏	❏
General presentation	❏	❏	❏	❏	❏
Distribution of establishments by region	❏	❏	❏	❏	❏
Information on food and wine	❏	❏	❏	❏	❏
Restaurant Selection	❏	❏	❏	❏	❏
Themed indexes	❏	❏	❏	❏	❏
Cover	❏	❏	❏	❏	❏
Price	❏	❏	❏	❏	❏

› 7. Please rate the guide out of 20   / 20

YOUR OPINION MATTERS!

> 8. Did you buy this guide:

   For holidays? .... ☐

   For a weekend/short break? .... ☐

   For business purposes? .... ☐

   As a gift? .... ☐

> 9. Which aspects could we improve?

   ....
   ....
   ....
   ....
   ....

> 10. Was there an establishment you particularly liked or a choice you didn't agree with? Perhaps you have a favourite address of your own that you would like to tell us about? Please send us your remarks and suggestions.